TOWARDS A POLITICS
OF COMMUNION

TOWARDS A POLITICS OF COMMUNION

CATHOLIC SOCIAL TEACHING IN DARK TIMES

Anna Rowlands

LONDON • NEW YORK • OXFORD • NEW DELHI • SYDNEY

T&T CLARK
Bloomsbury Publishing Plc
50 Bedford Square, London, WC1B 3DP, UK
1385 Broadway, New York, NY 10018, USA
29 Earlsfort Terrace, Dublin 2, Ireland

BLOOMSBURY, T&T CLARK and the T&T Clark logo are trademarks of Bloomsbury Publishing Plc

First published in Great Britain 2021

Copyright © Anna Rowlands, 2021

Anna Rowlands has asserted her right under the Copyright, Designs and Patents Act, 1988, to be identified as Author of this work.

For legal purposes the Acknowledgements on pp. xiv–xvi constitute an extension of this copyright page.

Cover image: Hagia Irene (Hagia Eirene) Eastern Orthodox church in the outer courtyard of Topkapi Palace in Istanbul. Tony Roddam / Alamy Stock Photo

All rights reserved. No part of this publication may be reproduced or transmitted in any form or by any means, electronic or mechanical, including photocopying, recording, or any information storage or retrieval system, without prior permission in writing from the publishers.

Bloomsbury Publishing Plc does not have any control over, or responsibility for, any third-party websites referred to or in this book. All internet addresses given in this book were correct at the time of going to press. The author and publisher regret any inconvenience caused if addresses have changed or sites have ceased to exist, but can accept no responsibility for any such changes.

A catalogue record for this book is available from the British Library.

Library of Congress Cataloging-in-Publication Data
Names: Rowlands, Anna, author.
Title: Towards a politics of communion: Catholic social teaching in dark times / Anna Rowlands.
Description: London; New York: T&T Clark, 2022. | Includes bibliographical references and index. | Identifiers: LCCN 2021027894 (print) | LCCN 2021027895 (ebook) | ISBN 9780567242730 (pb) | ISBN 9780567219084 (hb) | ISBN 9780567212337 (epub) | ISBN 9780567003539 (epdf)
Subjects: LCSH: Christian sociology–Catholic Church. | Catholic Church–Doctrines.
Classification: LCC BX1753 .R69 2022 (print) | LCC BX1753 (ebook) | DDC 261.8–dc23
LC record available at https://lccn.loc.gov/2021027894
LC ebook record available at https://lccn.loc.gov/2021027895

ISBN: HB: 978-0-5672-1908-4
PB: 978-0-5672-4273-0
ePDF: 978-0-5670-0353-9
ePUB: 978-0-5672-1233-7

Typeset by Deanta Global Publishing Services, Chennai, India

To find out more about our authors and books visit www.bloomsbury.com and sign up for our newsletters.

No one is an island all alone. We are bound to each other even if we do not know it. The landscape binds us, flesh and blood bind us, work and speech bind us. However, we are not always conscious of these bonds. When solidarity is born, this consciousness is awakened, and then speech and word appear, and at that point something that was hidden becomes manifest. All our bonds become visible.
Józef Tischner, *Spirit of Solidarity*

A man's good or evil actions, although not ordained to the good or evil of another individual, are nevertheless ordained to the good or evil of another, i.e. the community.
Thomas Aquinas ST I-II, 21.3 ad 1

In its social meaning liberation of every kind belongs to time; salvation is for eternity, and for that reason always anticipates time.
Henri de Lubac, *Brief Catechesis*

CONTENTS

Preface	viii
Foreword	xi
Acknowledgements	xiv
Introduction	**1**
1 The emergence of modern Catholic social teaching	15
2 Human dignity: Philosophical and theological trajectories	47
3 Human dignity and (forced) migration	73
4 Human dignity and the question of social and structural sin	93
5 The common good: The long tradition in context	111
6 The common good: Patristic and medieval context	125
7 The common good: The encyclical tradition	151
8 The body politic: Political community in the social encyclicals	177
9 Subsidiarity: A principle of participation and social governance	215
10 Solidarity: A developing theory	239
11 The universal destination of goods: Towards an integral ecology	269
Conclusion: Towards a politics of communion: Between time and eternity	293
Appendix 1	303
Index	306

PREFACE

At the height of the first wave of the Covid-19 pandemic, and faced with his own relative isolation within the walls of the Vatican, Pope Francis initiated a series of talks aimed at making some sense of the virus and its social and theological dynamics. Each talk, presented as part of what would have been his busy Wednesday public audience, unpacked the main themes of CST in accessible form. These talks became a primer both in the social teaching of the Church and as helpful catechetical background to the second of his social encyclicals, *Fratelli tutti*, which he was to launch two months later. In the first of these addresses the Pope outlined what he describes as the key social principles developed by the Church over centuries. He lists these as 'the principle of the dignity of the person, the principle of the common good, the principle of the preferential option for the poor, the principle of the universal destination of goods, the principle of the solidarity, of subsidiarity, the principle of the care for our common home'. He continues: 'These principles help . . . those responsible for society, to foster growth and also, as in the case of the pandemic, the healing of the personal and social fabric. All of these principles express in different ways the virtues of faith, hope and love'.

The resulting talks expounded a vision for a more truly human life, less atomized and isolated, less objectified and unequal. He proposed a vision of a common origin, common home and common destination for all humanity. Using the language of viruses and antibodies, he suggested that a profound sickness attends our social bodies: indifference, objectification and the commodification of the human person. From social media to the trade in persons, we are increasingly the product to be consumed. He contrasts this with the gaze of God, which begins with the assumption that we are created as gift, for purposes that unfold over time, and have a capacity to share and return the love we are created in and for. We are as gripped by the age-old desire for possession and mastery, and even more than our predecessors we are addicted to the idea of unlimited material growth. A revolution that begins with the capacity to stop and contemplate the world in new ways

Preface

is his dream. Moving from a logic of mere use to one of contemplation of value is woven into each of the principles of the Church's social teaching: dignity of the person; the possession of material goods so that they meet the needs of all and bring value to the community, the protection of the earth as a common home; the willingness to suffer with others for the sake of solidarity; the search for new solutions that value the participation and contribution of each person in their own redemption, to build creative new social solutions with, and not simply for, others.

One way to think about the developing tradition of CST is, in this way, as a developing canon of principles which seek to give expression to both the account of human–divine social relations found in the Gospels and the tradition of reflection on the theological virtues. These sources are brought into dialogue with our embodied human experiences of living lives in time. These principles offer guides for the discernment of the challenges and opportunities of each moment and age; the teaching develops in interactions with those realities. For others, the nature of CST is better understood as a historically evolving encounter between the Church and its social, political and economic contexts – and most particularly an encounter between the Church and modernity. The Church is not simply the purveyor of a treasure chest of principles but rather a dynamic subject of history, working out its own identity, calling, subjectivity in interaction with the shifting contours of work, exchange, political power, and social identities in modern and now late modern societies. CST tells us as much about the Church's own striving and seeking, its position in relation to the many forms of power in the world, as it does about the modern state, industrial and post-industrial economies, and the prevailing ideologies of the age.

This book, published in the 130th anniversary year of the promulgation of the first papal social encyclical *Rerum novarum*, attempts both to explore the development of the principles that Pope Francis names in his Covid-19 catechesis and to offer some sense of the dynamic interaction of the Church, shaped by, shaper of and thoroughly situated within, a modern and late modern age. The tradition that began self-consciously with the publication by Pope Leo XIII of *Rerum novarum* in 1891, and which has its roots in the very origins of Christian communities, remains a dynamic, changing yet recognizably coherent body of social thought. Indeed, it's teachings, and their development, have become a cornerstone of this most global and publicly notable of papacies. In a moment when we have returned to

Preface

the restless language of 'we the people', this book aims to explore what a tradition shaped by the vision of being a people, a city, a community shaped by the Gospel, for the sake of the world, might offer – and receive in return – as gift and challenge.

Anna Roper Rowlands
Feast of the Epiphany, 2021

FOREWORD

I was waiting for this book, everyone needs it, and now we have it. I was delighted to read it.

Part of my itinerary as a Jesuit priest has included confronting many pressing social concerns: the murderous disregard for human rights in 1980s El Salvador, for example; the plight of millions in Africa due to the twinned viruses of HIV/AIDS and the resulting stigma; and, most recently, the manifold vulnerabilities of displaced, fleeing and trafficked persons. Each engagement intensified my appreciation of touchstones of Catholic social teaching (CST).

These experiences were a constant reminder that CST is primarily concerned not with dos and don'ts but with bringing the Good News into the public sphere and directing practical responses to real problems posed by current events, in the light of the Gospel and Catholic tradition.

Other episodes of my lifetime mission have involved a broader swath of typical CST concerns. As the Social Justice Secretary of the Society of Jesus (1992–2002), I observed the myriad involvements of members of our Order and its collaborators in serving faith, promoting justice and exercising the 'preferential option for the poor'. Eight years later, I joined the Pontifical Council for Justice and Peace, founded by St Paul VI in 1967, which promoted CST culminating in the useful *Compendium*. Through these assignments, I have been privileged to participate in the continued application, elaboration and development of CST, this multicolour beacon for following the teaching of Christ in our 'public' lives with others in economy, polity, society, ecology, etc.

In her new book Anna Rowlands very successfully parses the essential and interconnected principles of CST and deepens our understanding and appreciation – without which, empowerment might go awry. Not with a definitive 'final word' interpretation, an aim she disavows; rather, by providing numerous points of entry into contemporary CST, allowing us to pursue our own paths and, crucially, participate in its further development.

Professor Rowlands' programme is clearly signalled by the two halves of the title.

Foreword

The second portion, 'Catholic Social Teaching in Dark Times', echoes the dark times of the 1930s and 1940s when Pope Pius XII wrote – perhaps discretely but certainly bravely and incessantly – against the deepening horrors of those times. Rowlands carries her historical account through to the manifold analysis that Pope Francis makes of today's threats to human survival.

Rowlands may surprise readers with her account of Pius, who tends to be either forgotten or reviled these days. But our fair-minded guide shows that in spite of never writing a social encyclical during his nearly twenty years as pope, Pius XII was a central hinge figure in the emergence of late-twentieth-century CST. He moved CST towards a personalist account of the rights and duties attaching to the dignified human person. This dignity stems from multiple sources – from all human beings created in God's image, from our possession of reason and conscience, from our irreducibly communal nature and from everyone's capacity to be moral agents. Rights discourse, therefore, does not emerge from a social contract between autonomous individuals, but rather from the ontological status of human person and community.

The first half of the title, 'Towards a Politics of Communion', points unabashedly at the solution. We must reject politics that no longer serves the common good. Socially and environmentally, 'we are all in the same boat' (*Fratelli tutti*, 30). Rowlands' answer to the 'dark times' lies in CST. She argues that its enduring principles – most notably human dignity, the common good, solidarity, subsidiarity, the universal destination of goods, and integral ecology – offer a road map for building a more fraternal world. Or, in our author's phrasing, a 'politics of communion'.

For Rowlands, the essence of CST lies in its nature as a public philosophy centred in living a dignified life in community. Yet CST is not simply one of many philosophies. Its uniqueness lies precisely in its transcendental claims.

At its core, CST is centred on people as 'beings-in-relation'. Indeed, it sees relationality as defining fundamentally what it means to be a human being. This is the true meaning of 'communion' in a culture of encounter and closeness, as Francis elaborates in his encyclical *Fratelli tutti* – a culture that looks for humans to be bonded together in common purpose in our common home rather than isolated in individualism and market ideology, which are leading to our destruction. An overwhelming focus on 'liberty' and 'equality' tends to push 'fraternity' to the side. This is why, as Rowlands shows, *Fratelli tutti* wholeheartedly rejects the ideology of individualism, which leads to inequality, exclusion and a throwaway culture.

Readers might wish to focus on the chapters that recount the evolution and explain the meaning of this or that tenet of CST. One that interests me especially is *solidarity*. This goes all the way back to *Rerum novarum* (1891), which is replete with solidaristic themes including covenant and cooperation, civic friendship, associationalism and a just distribution of goods. Later CST focused more on the unequal relationships between countries, chiefly the global north and global south. For his part, St John Paul II often wrote that solidarity requires us to recognize the other as not merely a competing bearer of rights but an image of the living God united with all in a common paternity, which Pope Benedict XVI then details in terms of fraternity, drawing out ideas of reciprocity, gift and gratuity.

To this growing heritage of *solidarity* our current Holy Father adds, first, the option for the poor and a condemnation of inequality (in *Evangelii gaudium*); then sustainable development and intergenerational concern (*Laudato si'*); and most recently an emphasis on encounter and service (*Fratelli tutti*), because we are all related to all and responsible for all. We're all in the same boat, including migrants, towards whom the only justifiable moral attitude is welcome and solidarity.

We all owe a debt of gratitude to Anna Rowlands for this magnificent work. It offers essential insights into CST in critical dialogue with modernity. It explores the roots of recent CST not only in biblical and patristic sources but also through the lens of modern papacies, with special attention to fruitful intellectual developments in the nineteenth and twentieth centuries. And crucially, it presents the thought of Pope Francis in direct continuity with this tradition. In doing so, it gives a fresh insight into *Fratelli tutti* and helps point towards a 'politics of communion' that can serve as an antidote to 'dark times'.

In short, this book is indispensable for Catholics interested in a hope-filled evaluation of their own tradition and for all people seeking a more fraternal world.

Card. Michael Czerny S.J.
Under-Secretary
Migrants & Refugees Section
Dicastery for Promoting Integral Human Development
San Calisto, Rome, July 2021

ACKNOWLEDGEMENTS

A series of extraordinary events – global, national and local – provided the stimulus for me to rediscover the roots of a tradition of Catholic social teaching thought/action I first encountered through the Young Christian Worker movement as a teenager in the 1980s and 1990s Irish Catholic diaspora of the North West of England. This tradition remained a background influence during my years of studying social and political theory at university in Cambridge, only to come back full circle in the years following the financial crash of 2007. For me, the events of our early new millennium rang out a call for a return to thinking about virtue (the good), community, place, solidarity and the common good as the basis for social renewal. Meanwhile, my increasing exposure to another social reality – the politics of forced migration – provoked in me a desire to return to CST as a resource capable of helping us to think about both the most local and most global of the realities now facing us.

The increasingly evident fracturing of a particular model of economic, social and political life sent me back with force to my intellectual roots. Yet, that tradition had not stood still in the intervening years: I was returning to a tradition entering a fascinating new phase of renewal and contestation.

Even prior to the evident focus upon social teaching which would be a hallmark of Pope Francis' papacy, the opportunities for CST to become a serious public resource again seemed clear to me. And yet, the tradition was also clearly fraught with its own inner and outer tensions. As with any tradition of social thought, there is a constant renewing labour involved in its development. CST is not a tradition of dry principles in want of a ready context of downward application but rather a complex intersecting theory and practice – an agonistic praxis – aiming to bring some illumination to the shifting patterns of our lives. Its task is as much negative as it is positive: in its properly theological form it seeks to expose the pretentions to authority, legitimacy and truth that distort our social, political and economic life. It assists the common search for the good by naming our tendency to both yearn for that good and misrecognize it – and to fix such (mis)recognitions into social structures. On the other hand, the task of CST is more than mere critique. It is one of profound social midwifery: to inspire the birth of new forms of solidarity, love and justice, including and especially from places and relationships that might seem impossibly difficult. It is a tradition that believes in transformation and

Acknowledgements

conservation: it is committed to learning through historical consciousness, to the preservation of social memory, and to discerning together across generations the abiding social goods we discover as life-giving over time.

Given that the tradition itself bears the same risks of speaking, acting and discerning goods in history that are born by all social actors, it remains a fragile tradition with its own gaps and lacunae. These matters must be addressed constructively and with energy by those most passionate about its history and its future, not only by its critics, although both have a role! This book is an attempt to contribute towards this task of communal articulation and development.

Writing is often seen as a solitary affair. Conversations with the following colleagues and friends over more than a decade have helped shape this book and make the experience more convivial than solitary: Andrew Mein (who first suggested I write this book); Neil Thorogood who prepared some lovely drawings that have had to find a different outlet but for which I am grateful; Maurice Glasman, Jonathan Cox and Carina Crawford Rolt (from whom I learnt much in community organizing); Jon Wilson (for many stimulating conversations); my colleagues at the Centre for Catholic Social Thought and Practice); Sr Marg Beirne (for a joyous week of conversation in Sydney); Dan Finn, Frankie Ward, Sarah Teather and all at the Jesuit Refugee Service (for hospitality, friendship and collaboration); Frank Turner SJ and Jim Sweeney CP (for early conversations when my interests in CST were still developing); Kristin Heyer and Ellen Van Stichel (wonderful colleagues reshaping the teaching and research of CST); my 'refugee hosts' colleagues Elena Fiddian-Qasmiyeh, Yousif M. Qasmiyeh, Fraser Murray, Lyndsey Stonebridge and Aydan Greatrick; Susan O'Brien, Matt Guest, Beth Phillips, Amy Daughton, Susie Snyder, Susy Brouard, Flo O'Taylor, Helen Dawes, Andrew Grinnell, Pat Jones, Maria Exall and Charlotte Bray (colleagues and doctoral researchers who have widened my thinking); Michael Czerny SJ, Augusto Zampini, Enda Murphy, Tony Currer and Michelle Hough (for Roman hospitality, conversation, friendship and collaboration); the group of parliamentarians (cross party and cross House) I have had the privilege to work in conversation with over the last few years. My colleagues in the Department of Theology and Religion at Durham University, and the Centre for Catholic Studies especially, including Paul Murray (who deserves great thanks for years of supportive chivvying and conversation), Rik Van Niewenhove, my Head of Department Chris Insole, and above all, Karen Kilby. She has been an invaluable academic dialogue partner with whom to test and refine ideas, a peer mentor who has provided helpful practical ideas and encouragement for writing, and an enormous personal support as a friend. For friendship,

Acknowledgements

generous intellectual conversation and comments on drafts, Julian Coman, Gary Wade, Andy Walton, Theo Hawksley, Anna Blackman, Charlotte Bray and Nicky Burbach have assisted with reading or research at various stages. Kate Sotejeff-Wilson assisted brilliantly in proofing and editing. Meghan Clark and Christy Zenner have been a source of wonderful trans-Atlantic conversations. Rachel Rose, Ferdia and Anita Gallagher, Claire and David Bodanis offered generous hospitality whilst I was writing. Above all, for the love, support and most lovely companionship necessary to get this over the finishing line, Tom Sidaway; and to Tomos and Elisabeth for youthful encouragement: *have you finished the book yet*?! For the gift of the roots that fostered this interest, and a love of learning, to my parents Shelagh and Ged Roper. Our deepest debts are the hardest to express.

During the early stages of writing this book two close friends and academic dialogue partners, Emile and Amanda Perreau-Saussine, died. Both influenced the early stages of this book and were endlessly encouraging of this project. Their memory is to me a blessing and their deaths still a grief.

In the history of the Church, and in my own life, it has often been women religious who were the most luminous guides to the lived reality of the Catholic social tradition. The book is dedicated to Sr Pat Robb CJ. I worked with her in immigration detention facilities in the UK, watched her befriend, house and advocate for refugees and challenge unjust power. She represented the persistent widow, the virtuous and difficult woman who faithfully believes in a truth beyond mere power and witnesses to it until justice is rendered. She stands for a generation of women, written out of the magisterial pages of the tradition, but who have led and inspired social renewal.

Chapter 3 is a revised and extended version of a chapter that first appeared in 'Pope Francis: A Voice for Mercy, Justice, Love, and Care for the Earth' (Orbis Books, 2019). It is reproduced in amended form here with kind permission of Orbis Books and the editors Barbara Wall and Massimo Faggioli.

A Secular Age by Charles Taylor, Cambridge, Mass.: The Belknap Press of Harvard University Press, Copyright © 2007 by Charles Taylor. Used by permission. All rights reserved.

Brief Catechesis on Nature and Grace, Henri de Lubac, Ignatius Press, 1984.

Hope in a Democratic Age, Alan Mittleman, Oxford: OUP, 2009. By kind permission of Oxford University Press.

The End of Work, John Hughes, John Wiley & Sons: 2007. By kind permission of John Wiley & Sons.

The Spirit of Solidarity, Jozef Tischner, Harper & Row, 1984. By kind permission of Harper & Row.

INTRODUCTION

Illuminating dark times

In 1968 Hannah Arendt wrote a short book on an eclectic range of twentieth-century figures. In homage to Berthold Brecht's poem 'To Posterity', Arendt titled the book *Men in Dark Times*.[1] Her reference to the darkness of the times was not, as might be assumed, a gloomy claim that the twentieth century was the worst of all times but rather an attempt to write about the 'flickering light' of lives that throw the darkness into relief and therefore guide a generation towards some kind of real hope. She wrote defiantly: 'we have a right to expect some illumination'.[2]

Arendt's focus on a seemingly disconnected array of individuals was not intended to form a litany of secular saints or to suggest a latent school of individuals who could form the basis for an alternative philosophy or movement that would save us all. The book is not about solutions. Her figures do not commit to the same ideas, institutions or identities but rather the pattern of their lives simply illuminates the difficulty and possibility of living in the first half of the twentieth century. Arendt's concern is to dig deeply into questions of temporality: what does it mean to be creatures of time, to live well in time? The book took twelve years to write, and Arendt expresses her intention that it be read as an exploration of how persons 'lived their lives, moved in the world, how they were affected by historical time'.[3]

Arendt's book was nonetheless part of her wider project to explore the grounds of a life that is truly public. She writes, it is 'the function of the public realm to throw light on the affairs of men by providing a space of appearances in which they can show in deed and word, for better and worse,

---

[1] Hannah Arendt, *Men in Dark Times* (New York: Harcourt Brace, 1970). Despite the title, the book includes a range of men and women, including Rosa Luxembourg and Isak (Karen) Dinesen.
[2] Ibid., preface, ix.
[3] Ibid., preface, vii.

who they are and what they can do'. She continues, 'darkness has come when this light is extinguished by "credibility gaps" and "invisible government", by speech that does not disclose what is but sweeps it under the carpet, by exhortations, moral and otherwise, that, under the pretext of upholding old truths, degrade all truth to meaningless triviality'.[4] Each of the people to whom Arendt dedicates a chapter is understood as a public figure, not because they held office or achieved rank (although many did) but because the manner in which they lived their lives as writers, philosophers or religious figures illuminated truth, contributed to creating a space in which they and others might appear to each other as dignified subjects and agents of history, thus sustaining what is truly and properly public.

The third chapter of *Men in Dark Times* is, perhaps a little surprisingly given Arendt's well-known critique of Christian political thought, dedicated to Pope John XXIII. Its title – 'Angelo Giuseppe Roncalli: A Christian on St Peter's Chair from 1958 to 1963' – derives from a Roman chambermaid who, as John XXIII lay dying, exclaimed to Arendt that somehow, in defiance of all (grittily low) expectations of the Church, a *true* Christian had briefly occupied the seat of St Peter. How? Of course, the comically combined pessimism and optimism of this comment delighted Arendt. Roncalli emerges from Arendt's pen as a figure whose capacity for public illumination was rooted in a profound and difficult interiority. Whilst Arendt writes little about Roncalli's formal role in developing the Church's social teaching, Arendt was, I think, right to sense an echo of her own concerns in Roncalli's reflection on the historical and material dimensions of being in the world.

In ways often misunderstood even by Arendt herself, this being in the world is also the heartbeat of the (developing) tradition of modern Catholic social teaching (CST). It is a tradition that aims to reflect on the material circumstances of being human in historical time. Arendt would construct her own account of truth differently to the papal social tradition – CST insists on the transcendent origin and destiny of the human person as the most important frame for all meaning and Arendt does not – but we can learn from her outsider perspective on the tradition.

CST is not a form of pure unchanging theory, a simple repetition through history applied downwards, but rather a circling round the very materiality of the truth as it comes to us in the span of each age and might be

---

[4]Ibid., preface, viii.

understood as the basis for action in a lifetime. It is also an intergenerational act of meaning-making, interpretation of the time that is passed – accepting that history is not always for everyone. The past is a witness, knowledge, confession, wisdom to another generation, who bear their own task of interpreting the truth of their own historical lives. As Arendt suggests, forms of theory and action – be they artistic, political, philosophical, humanitarian – that illuminate the conditions of any age and open us to recognizing truth become, *precisely by virtue of their illumination*, public. It is the relationship to the pursuit of truth that makes CST a public thing and to be judged adequate in the light of its contribution to this task. Every area of human life offers a contribution to this task: art, music, politics, literature, journalism, acts of justice and acts of care enable a public realm to come into being in the space between us. We need this public space between us to know, to breathe, to act, to create, to sustain. Such quality of thought and practice enables the 'appearance' of things and persons, and thus in turn the recognition of spaces and places that might be considered the basis of a life capable of holding things and persons in common. This is the path towards the kind of social love that the Church can speak of as communion. The goal of the Church's social teaching, as of great art, is not merely a form of cohabitation but a more profound form of mutual living and social gift exchange.

We do not help ourselves understand the kind of thing CST is if we begin our intellectual or political journey determined to bifurcate the world into avenues of private beliefs and public reasons – the former considered to belong to the realm of inwardness and personal motivation and the latter to outwardness and common appearance. Although Arendt and the authors of the CST tradition disagree about whether love can be considered a public and political thing (for Arendt, no; for CST, yes), Arendt can help us think creatively and critically, beyond the tired, blunt, narrow modern binaries that separate the supposedly personal and private and the supposedly public and political.

Arendt understood that the distinction between what is public and what is not public is not primarily spatial, territorial or institutional (although each of these matters) nor is it crudely concerned with what can be considered secular versus religious. Rather, the public is action, practice and thought that enable persons to appear, to themselves *and* to one another, and so constitute the basis of a dignified life together. CST, as Arendt claims of Roncalli's own life, is a properly public thing in this sense. It can be considered, echoing Arendt's *Men in Dark Times*, a contribution to the illumination of an age – an illumination we have a right to expect. The reference to dark times in the title of this volume is, therefore, less a fundamental pessimism about our own volatile moment and more an homage to Arendt's provocation: that what matters more than easy denunciation is that we demand illumination in the darkness and are prepared to risk trying living so that we become part of such illumination. The language of appearance and illumination is, of course, only one kind of language we might use to explore the character of the body of modern CST; I should note again clearly that I am borrowing this language from a social philosopher who writes outside of that tradition.

What, then, divides CST from the social theory of Arendt? What makes CST distinct as a social theory is not specific views on the economy or the common good but rather the specific account of transcendence – of the relation of Creator to creature and natural material world – that grounds it. This is not to say that other forms of secular social theory do not make transcendent claims. They do. Not all are honest and upfront about the kind of transcendence they trade in. In effect, all social theories have some version of a set of ideas about immanence and transcendence. The question is this: What *kind* of account of transcendence and immanence is best suited to grounding an account of our human ways of living in, and seeking to conserve and transform, a common world? Arendt had answered this by insisting on an immanent frame of reference for her account. Christian transcendence in social theory from St Augustine onwards, she argued, had led to a lessening of the emphasis on civic citizenship and this was to be feared. If anything is transcendent in her account it is simply the fact of birth or natality, that which transcends the limits of the moment is the possibility of the new which exists in the material fact of birth, a new departure, a new beginning. Transcendence in CST, which is the beginning and end of its social theory or story, is rooted in the fact of a divine Creator who is the original birth-giver and the ultimate redeemer of all that lives in time. Revelation in the form of the Scriptures, reason as we come to know it in our own nature, contemplation as it gives access to a mystical way of knowing and the witness of the whole material world are our guides to discerning the truths of this grounding transcendence. It is not a truth with social application or consequence but rather a truth that can only be known in and through the sociality of our creaturely life, but which will be fully known in a form of sociality beyond it. It is already therefore, in its very nature, radically social in every way. Part of the task that CST sets itself therefore is to explore and express this truth and to open to scrutiny the many dominant mythic structures or storylines embedded in our economic, political, cultural and societal perceptions of human social living.

In this sense, CST can be seen in continuity with a scriptural register of both 'positive and 'negative' Christian social thought evident in the writings of the Hebrew prophets and St Paul. A Christian social doctrine offers a series of positive affirmations of who we are called to be as people and societies, but it is also as much about challenging claims to authority, legitimacy and truth that appear to erode human dignity, justice and the common good. The negative political task reveals to us the things we make de facto religions of in our cultures and tests the grounds of such beliefs and practices against a Christian vision of justice, neighbour love and human flourishing. The 'negative' task of a Catholic social doctrine and its 'positive' task of living into a future with hope are not separate stages in a process but mutually constitutive activities.

CST begins its story of social action with divine action. The first 'social' action is a divine act of creation ex nihilo, and therefore the first human social action is conceived as receptive, relational and desirous in response to the gift of life itself. In this light, human social life at its core is thought about as covenantal rather than contractual or merely transactional. The 'end' of the story of human social life also lies in an account of promise and covenant – in a peace and justice granted as gift, as healing and as something we cannot fully effect as a simple human will to power. All basic Christian doctrines – creation, sin, incarnation, resurrection, the Trinity, eschatology and the communion of the saints – are social concepts.

Whilst making strong claims for the practical nature of justice, for the distribution of goods and for the role of the political community that flow from this covenantal account of the relation between God, humanity and the common created goods of the earth, it is also important to note that CST's origin and end are ultimately contemplative and mystical. They are rooted in a truth and a relation that is revealed as, and in, gift and encounter with what and who is other than ourselves and can only partly be known. The Catholic social tradition implies a certain way of gazing at the world, of coming to know it and make it one's own and of handling the question of what can and cannot be known. Contemplation is not what happens when we run out of answers but rather the very ground that births and sustains a vision of knowing and of social action and transformation.

Towards a Politics of Communion

Abundance and limit as social themes

Dignitatis humanae, the Second Vatican Council's document on religious freedom, notes that CST is 'born of the encounter of the Gospel message and of its demands (summarised in the supreme commandment of love of God and neighbour in justice) with the problems emanating from the life of society'.[5] The basic storyline of the tradition is this: we are persons in communities, inhabitants of deep stories and creatures oriented towards interdependence and cooperation. We seek to associate, organize, create, care and be cared for and struggle to overcome all that isolates, fragments and destroys. We are oriented towards our welfare and when faced with harm, we are wounded in our deepest selves, for it offends against this basic sense of the good we seek and are promised. We seek this good in our relations with God, with neighbour, and in and from the landscapes and environments that host us. All of this is fragile. We are also fallen beings who misrecognize the good, actively refuse it, disengage in fear, fall into forms of passivity and act as agents of direct individual and structural violence and harm. The fundamental theo-dramatic construct of CST lies in a vision of social communion, gifted to us, fractured by us and continually in a process of restoration in which we are active, graced, fragile, failing and resilient participants in time.

All of us encounter structures that limit, constrict and harm: we interact continually with the accrued and endlessly inventive history of 'structural sin'. As a result, we are continually called to make new social beginnings in the middle of things and in anticipation of the ends of things. The social forms we create through institutions of government, social and economic exchange, leisure and culture are further external dimensions of this anthropology. They can be ordered to our good, make use of, draw on and can increase the created goods of our common world but are susceptible to the same processes of misrecognition and refusal that mark our individual journeys. The social analysis of the Church's teaching draws most fundamentally from this anthropology and its scriptural and doctrinal roots, yet it comes to share much with other secular forms of social thought and action too.

In a little-commented upon address to British parliamentarians in Westminster Hall, London, in September 2010, Pope Benedict XVI

---

[5]*Dignitatis humanae*, §72.

Introduction

suggests that we view CST as embodying and exhorting a form of reciprocal solidarity between faith and reason.[6] He suggests that the seismic crises of the early twenty-first century enable us to see once again the need for a less self-sufficient and more mutually engaged and interdependent model, in which reason and faith constantly encounter one another. Reason, when rightly ordered, participates in the purification of religion. However, reason without the accompanying insights of faith can also be open to corruption. Disordered loves produce disordered 'common sense' which we can falsely deduce as legitimate expressions of *either* faith or reason. The histories of slavery, racism, sexism and so forth teach us this; what appears 'natural' to us may well be a form of misrecognition. The encounter of reason and faith enables us to learn to better recognize and know what is true and what is good.

CST is also a form of virtue theory. In his recent Covid-19 catechesis Pope Francis tied his reflections on dignity, care for creation and the common good to the great virtues of hope, faith and love. Pope Benedict XVI devoted his social teaching to trying to reflect on caritas or love as a theological social virtue. The CST tradition views earthly justice as necessary, but not on its own sufficient, and more likely to be realized if it is open to the theological virtues of hope, faith and love that hold open the space, and motivate the desire for justice, especially in adversity. Love and justice are mutually implicating categories. The pathway to love must take in justice, love must witness to justice where it is absent, and strive to make it a reality. Nonetheless, love requires more than formal justice; it is a language of self-giving, care, self-completion, of forgiveness, which requires a social vocabulary.

CST is grounded in reflection on the paradox of abundance and limit as markers of human life: our natality is gift and possibility, but we live within mortal limits, ecological limits and strive for ideals we cannot fully or completely secure. We cannot abolish – although we can limit – evil; we cannot save ourselves; we cannot raise the dead; and we cannot remove all suffering from human life. To borrow a phrase from outside the tradition, we constructively and without ceasing 'fail towards' certain goals in time.[7]

---

[6]The text can be viewed here: http://www.vatican.va/content/benedict-xvi/en/speeches/2010/september/documents/hf_ben-xvi_spe_20100917_societa-civile.html (accessed 6 January 2021).
[7]Gillian Rose, *Love's Work* (London: Virago, 1995).

Towards a Politics of Communion

Living ethically as time-gifted, time-bound and historically accompanied creatures, with all the possibility and within the limit of human life, is a key theme for the Church's social tradition.

Towards a politics of communion?

Whilst Hannah Arendt welcomed John XXIII's public witness, she was notoriously sceptical of the kind of contemplative-active Christian social and political theory I have just sketched the outlines of. She argued repeatedly that invoking the language of faith, transcendence and eternity as the basis for social theory drained politics of its urgency and potency and constantly risked retreat into something primarily private and introspective, into something less than a full response to the demands of love and justice made in living a fully public and civic life, one that imagines that all we have is the historical moment. In *The Human Condition* Arendt argues that what masquerades as a Christian politics – the medieval idea of the common good – in fact falls short, for in her view it 'recognises only that private individuals have interests in common'; it imagines a world of private interests and common duties that private persons must attend to, but it stops short of recognizing 'that curiously hybrid realm where private interests assume public significance that we call "society"'.[8] The Christian idea of the common good may sound thoroughly political and public, but Arendt believed risked doing little to overcome 'the gulf between the sheltered life of the household' (which Arendt sees as the central moral and spiritual focus of Christian social doctrine) 'and the merciless exposure of the *polis*'.[9]

In the same passage in which Arendt criticizes as pallid the Christian politics of the common good, she notes the profound ethical association between the idea of forming households and the language of *companionship*. Arendt is surely right to draw out this insight, for the language of home, of conviviality and reciprocal exchange, is woven through Christian social visions of both heaven and earth. For Augustine, this is the life that endures when all else passes away. However, Arendt notes this distinctive social imaginary not to praise it but to highlight

---

[8] Hannah Arendt, *The Human Condition* (Chicago: University of Chicago Press, 1958), p. 35.
[9] Ibid.

its limitations. She argues that, historically speaking, Christian culture created an analogical imagination in which businesses (companies), traders' guilds and fraternities were modelled on the language of the household, being com-panions (*com-panis*), 'men who have one bread and one wine'. She suggests that this language of *com-panis* limits the political imagination to a mere extension of the life of private individuals. Public life must be more and different to this. Whilst I will dispute that this is where companionship language takes us, Arendt is quite right and indeed more astute than many commentators when she rightly spots that communion language is indisputably at the heart of a Christian vision of the common good.[10]

This book is a partial reply to Arendt's claims, and as such a defence of the notion that Christian social and political thought – here in the specific historical form of CST – can and does illuminate, and can in fact be a truly *public* and *social* form of life on Arendt's helpful terms and on its own terms.[11] In these pages I propose an account of the common good that could ground a strenuously plural, open-ended public and social life, in which Arendt's aims are 'failed towards': that we come to appear to each other, to speak and be heard, to care and to regenerate our lives together, as seekers of a common life worth living.

I remain committed to exploring the more theologically resonant, although not unproblematic, language of communion, invoking the imagination of those who might have or share, in conviviality and out of necessity, 'one bread and one wine'. Communion is a language of being-in-relation. It suggests that the exchanges of relationality are *the* basic and most fundamental context for human being. It does not deny categories of justice, duty and obligation, nor refuse the reality of fracture, domination and failure, but grounds all of these things in something wider. It also prevents us from collapsing theology, religion and faith into nothing more than the ethical and yet insisting it is *always* thoroughly ethical. Communion language is a form of doctrinal thinking that, as Joseph

---

[10]Ibid., pp. 53–4 – worth reading for a further exposition on the 'worldlessness' of Christianity. Arendt was clear that it did not matter how 'worldly' Christianity attempted to be, ultimately it is unworldly and therefore more truly private than it is ever meaningfully 'public'.

[11]This defence is of the *possibility* of CST contributing in this way. Arendt is quite right to criticize the historical failures of CST through the early and mid-twentieth century with regard to fascism and some forms of national corporatism. This is a theme we return to in the following two chapters.

Towards a Politics of Communion

Ratzinger noted, gives dignity to multiplicity as to unity or, as Pope Francis expressed it in *Fratelli tutti*, expresses the tensive love that moves us beyond ourselves into a truly social reality. The Spanish version of Pope Francis' text makes much clearer that this tensive love is born of a struggle, interior and exterior. Communion invokes helpfully material imagery and language – a fact that Arendt notices. The one bread and one wine which expresses and enacts the ritual of communion is taken from the stuff of the earth. It assumes creation as blessing and its provisions to meet the widest possible of our needs – a single creation, plural in form, is destined to meet the needs of, and for the enjoyment of, all, without privilege or exception. This notion is expressed in what the CST tradition, echoing the patristic and medieval theologians, names the universal destination of goods. It is as much an expression of a logic of communion as of distribution: the two ideas are bound together.

However, I aim to take seriously the double challenge that Arendt sets out. I contend that her challenge to avoid a pallid individualism-plus-duty social ethic is a good one for any system of social theory or theology and that the language of love in politics does of course bring dangers. It is powerful and often misused. It can be deeply unstable language and become a language of power, abuse and domination or suppression of its own. In service of that careful task, I ought to make clear that I do not intend to invoke the language of 'the politics of communion' in order to make exclusive sets of claims for those admitted to Eucharistic participation in a Catholic ecclesial context. Nor do I wish to imply a refusal of religious pluralism, nor to indulge in a Christian triumphalism. Rather, I utilize the language of my tradition in literal and analogical form, and in a spirit of dialogue and encounter, to outline both a Christian social anthropology as the core of CST and an approach to the 'social' questions shaped by the reality of pluralism and difference. This language has the virtue for me of not being primarily a language of trade (the good as negotiated shared self-interests), consensus and cognition (the good as seminar room disputation process), or contract (a negotiated, enforceable, transactional exchange of value) – although it precludes none of these things as elements of the good.

An equal and rather different danger is implied in Arendt's fear of smallness and limit: that the phrase 'the politics of communion' sounds like a laughably or even dangerously naïve overreach. Communion of peoples in the realm of politics is not what an age of rising ethno-nationalism, intractable refugeedom, pandemic, economic instability, surveillance

Introduction

capitalism and climate change look like. Nonetheless, the horizon towards which politics must be oriented on a Christian account is surely the life of communion. This task is not the work of politics alone, but it is its horizon. In the end, the language of communion belongs in the realm of the political because it can help open up a space in which to speak of both intimacy and public-ness, can relate bodily humans to their material created context and can continue to figure transcendence, gift and exchange as part of our public conversation. It is difficult to see a change of mindset on the major issues that face us without such a language. Despite the epic failures of our history and our times, and the dangers of its co-option for violent and oppressive purposes, this language continues to offer possibilities to shatter the atomism of the lives we have come to live.

Purpose and limits of this book

This book does not aim to offer a definitive or even comprehensive account of CST but rather attempts to enable a wide variety of readers to navigate their way into and through selected parts of the Catholic social tradition. It hopes to enable many pathways in, rather than a single definitive route through. Many other introductions work on the assumption that readers already 'think Catholic'. I have tried not to make that assumption and to take seriously the claim made by the post-Vatican II authors of the CST tradition that they wish to produce a body of work addressed to 'all people of goodwill', engaged with wider streams of thought and public conversation. As such this book offers an orientation to the tradition, a detailed account of some of its core principles and an account of how these principles relate to, or illuminate, some of the key social challenges today. As its British author, I am writing in a largely European context. Whilst I am a theologian and a Catholic, the text raises self-critical questions about the strengths and weaknesses, insights and lacunae of the Catholic social tradition.

Many of the concepts that this book examines may look a little worn around the edges: worn from overuse and under-definition, from banal repetition, from a collapse into a kind of sentimentality or from a cynical mocking. Talk of human dignity, the common good and solidarity can often feel rather like that. Yet such ideas can also seem worn in a different way: because despite their presence in our cultures over the last half a century at least, they seem to have failed us. We have talked of dignity, the common

Towards a Politics of Communion

good and solidarity but we have not secured the vision. Nearly eighty years after the Holocaust, in a century of vast inequality and newly animated forms of social division and facing the prospect of new very serious bioethical, environmental and political challenges, and in a Church struggling to come to terms with its own legacy of domination and abuse, what can the old and sometimes worn offer us now? This question both haunts and animates this text in equal measure.

Structure of this book

This book has perhaps had an unconventional start. In order to approach the question of what CST is, outside of the frame of a narrow liberal imagination, I have attempted to frame its uniqueness in dialogue with the work of Hannah Arendt. Sometimes critical friends prove the best dialogue partners. The first chapter of the book, which follows this introduction, seeks to extend this beginning and to explore some of the key features and character of the evolving tradition. Our entry shall be via three letters written during the mid-twentieth century, and we shall move from here to consider why the Church addresses what it calls newly 'the social question' and how its own social claims might be thought about. The introduction proceeds to offer some further historical and methodological context. Chapters 2, 3 and 4 focus on the development of human dignity as a concept. Throughout the book I attempt to offer a detailed account of the historical and theological development of the principles of CST but in illuminating dialogue with the wider flows of secular social thought of which it is a part – in other words, I comment on and engage with a range of non-CST sources. Consideration of each principle of CST also includes an engagement with a key thematic area of CST that draws heavily on that principle. Thus, in Chapters 3 and 4 I examine human dignity in terms of themes of social sin and human migration. Chapters 5, 6 and 7 focus on the development of the idea of the common good. Chapter 8 offers a reflection on the themes of democracy and political community. In Chapters 9 and 10 I explore the twin principles of solidarity and (the often misunderstood) subsidiarity, and finally in Chapter 11 I give an overview of the developing focus on the theme of integral ecology, including the universal destination of goods and a theology of work. The book concludes with a reflection on the use of the parable of the Good Samaritan.

Introduction

Definition of terms

In his book *Field Hospital* William Cavanaugh alludes to the Monty Python sketch 'How to Do It', in which the endlessly cheerful Python crew enact various scenarios ridiculing the idea that really difficult things might be simply explained and/or instantly achieved – how to . . . split the atom, irrigate the Sahara, reconcile the Russians and Chinese, cure all known diseases. Patronizing and generalized responses are given. How to play the flute? 'Well, you blow in one end and move your fingers up and down.'[12] Cavanaugh draws on the sketch to note the similar dilemmas facing popes and bishops producing CST documents. Here is a world problem: here is how to fix it. Readers of papal encyclicals are often caught between a desire to do exactly this and relieve our anxiety of action by explaining simply what can be done and a suspicion of simplistic generalizations. In truth, a social encyclical is not a 'how to' guide, although they do wish to inspire action; they are not generationally comprehensive documents. Rather, the task of the papal social tradition is to shape a social imagination: to foster the questions about value, virtues and capacities that lie at the heart of the difficult issues we face. Its exact method for achieving this task varies between papacies. Its most consistent, although not uniformly adopted, approach has been some version of a see, judge, act method. A reading of the signs of the times is produced in dialogue with the training in ways of seeing and knowing provided by the biblical and philosophical tradition and through the use of human reason. This structured reflection on embodied realities, of being in the world, in turn inspires a new form of practice, a renewed action focused upon the telos of the good.

In formal terms, 'Catholic social teaching' is generally taken to be a phrase that refers to a range of papal social encyclicals dating from 1891 onwards, beginning with *Rerum novarum*, and addressing a range of social and economic themes. It is generally differentiated from a wider corpus of Catholic moral teaching according to its form, focus and methodology. Papal apostolic exhortations, the constitutions of Vatican Councils and teaching documents emerging from episcopal synods and national bishops' conferences also add to this body of work. In 2004 the Vatican added a synthesizing summary document, the *Compendium of the Social Doctrine*

---

[12]To view the sketch (to be recommended!), see https://www.youtube.com/watch?v=J_r yjjeNc5k

of the Church. Some authors also use the phrase 'Catholic social thought' to refer to a wider, more porous and inclusive body of formal and informal writings. The informal writings included within this category include the works of individual theologians, laypersons, individual priests and religious and faith-based social agencies and movements. I maintain this broad definitional focus on thought throughout the book. The task of discussing the plethora of rich and varied Catholic social practice, often referred to as social Catholicism, falls largely outside the remit of this book although where possible Catholic social practice is foregrounded as a necessary part of any discussion of the composition and reception of the canon of CST. No binary between the thought and practice is imagined here. For a list of the key documents that are generally agreed to compose the CST tradition, see Appendix 1.

CHAPTER 1
THE EMERGENCE OF MODERN CATHOLIC SOCIAL TEACHING

Three letters: Catholic social teaching as political theology

Within the space of eighteen days in the spring of 1937 Pope Pius XI issued three letters to a world in turmoil. The first letter, issued on 10 March, was written in secret and smuggled from Rome into the heart of Nazi Germany. *Mit brennender sorge* (With burning concern) was to be read from the pulpit of every German Catholic Church on Palm Sunday 1937. The letter reversed the earlier attempt – which many had warned was ill conceived – to form a treaty with Hitler in the hope of protecting the rights of the German Catholic Church to self-determination. Explaining his change of stance, Pius denounced the appeal to false forms of order, the dark impersonal destiny that appeared to lie at the heart of National Socialism and the exaltation or divinizing of race, the people or the state 'above a standard value'.[1] Pius, alarmed at the denial of the personal dimensions to justice and dignity in Germany, wrote: 'Our God is the Personal God, supernatural, omnipotent, infinitely perfect, one in the Trinity of Persons, tri-personal in the unity of divine essence.'[2]

Divini redemptoris, issued just a week later, was intended for a rather different audience and one that the Catholic Church had perhaps been more consistent in criticizing. Written as a condemnation of atheistic communism, the text outlines the objection of the Church to Bolshevism's suppression of individual natural rights. Rejecting both liberal individualism and atheistic communism, Pius called for a Christian civic humanism as the root to a social order able to respect individual self-determination brought about 'by means of an organic union with society and by mutual collaboration'.[3]

---

[1]*Mit brennender sorge*, §8.
[2]Ibid., §9.
[3]Two caveats should be noted: first, as modern historian James Chappel argues in *Catholic Modern: The Challenge of Totalitarianism and the Remaking of the Church* (Cambridge,

Towards a Politics of Communion

The final letter issued on 28 March, *Nos es muy conocida*, was addressed to the bishops, priests and laity of Mexico. Following the deaths of around 5,000 priests and Catholic laity and the exile of many more, Pius wrote to the Catholics of Mexico to set out his condemnation of their persecution and to outline a set of principles that could be drawn upon to inspire legitimate resistance. He argued that Catholics had a right and a duty to take their inspiration from the imitation of Jesus Christ, to be inspired by the call to a life of prayer, sacrifice and love. Such an imitation and pattern of life would naturally produce a form of social renewal, a form of Christian citizenship focused on the needs of the poorest and resistance to all injustice including injustice that refuses the right to religious expression and education.

During the course of the mid and late 1930s Pius had written on a dizzying range of social challenges: nativism in Germany and France, anti-Semitism in Europe and North America, economic injustice, migration and religious persecution. Yet, what connects these three letters is not only a common set of social issues besetting the 1930s (with some alarming contemporary resonance) but also the papal attempt to address the presence of, what were considered to be, rival pseudo-theological ideas present in the secular or even self-avowedly atheistic, public sphere. Each of the letters from the spring of 1937 attempts to name these 'secular' political theologies and their weaknesses, and to set out a contrasting Christian story of human nature and social order.

Pius was clear that the draw to Nazism and Bolshevism was not merely economic or social but also, in an important sense, 'theological'. *Mit brennender sorge* did not name or denounce Hitler personally, but it did make clear that Nazism sought to replace God with man and to deify a particular leader, race and nation. In each of the letters of 1937 Pius outlines the theological failures of political movements that he views as more than a mere economic or social settlement. He viewed both Nazism and Bolshevism as determined to erase the personal, Trinitarian God of Christianity and to propose to its people a 'false messianism' and 'deceptive mysticism'. These

---

MA: Harvard Press, 2018), often the Church divided on social terms according to who was perceived as the greater enemy rather than according to a full and positive embrace of a particular political position. He notes it is perhaps more accurate to view social Catholics of the twentieth century as anti-fascist or anti-communist. Second, whilst the Church was open to its condemnation of communism, there was support for forms of Christian Socialism including individuals attempting to express such commitments in concrete political projects, for example in the Viennese Christian Socialism of Engelbert Dolfuss.

supposedly secular movements were viewed as rival, inadequate theologies, drawn to the mystical and messianic as much as any theology. They produced and traded in their own idols, putting to use their own ultimate meanings and versions of classic narratives of sin, purity, sacrifice and redemption. Whilst he criticized German fascism and Russian Bolshevism concretely for the denial of material justice to their members, Pius believed that it was incumbent upon the Church to also demonstrate that they perpetrated their injustice in theologically resonant language. The political messianism of totalitarianism was for the modern papacy but one form of such modern pseudo-theology – all the more disguised for its refusal of overt religion and displacement of the Church from its public realm.

This opening chapter begins with Pius' three letters not because they are definitive or oft-cited texts (they are not) but rather because they illustrate something important and not always well understood about the core of the post-1891 Catholic social tradition. In the first instance, I have used them here to illustrate the fact that CST in its modern form is as much a tarrying with the *ideas* that constitute modernity as with its concrete *practices*. In the second instance, the letters illustrate that CST is both uniquely modern in its form – it gradually comes to accept the separation of Church from state and the de facto independence of social, political and economic questions from direct church competency – and it also functions as a social philosophy that never fully baptizes a liberal philosophy or settlement. It remains locked in a complex dialogue – and often a drama of recognition and misrecognition – with liberal modernity.

The documents issued by popes and bishops' conferences do not view any of the major thought traditions of the last three hundred years as *fully* compatible with the revealed truth of the Gospel concerning human nature and the transcendent purpose of the social order. Neither does the church hierarchy view such thought traditions, despite their claims, as *fully* 'secular': that is to say, devoid of religious or implicitly 'theological' claims. The modern state, so the authors of CST imply, still trades in its own secular version of notions of sin and salvation, manifesting fairly readily identifiable eschatological beliefs. In this light, the political theological questions posed by the popes to a secular audience might be simplified and articulated in the following ways: Who or what do you think will save you, and what do you want to be saved from and for? What are your sources of authority and legitimacy and who, or what, grounds or guarantees them? What kind of freedom results and for whom? Who is your 'Other' and what work do they (are they made to) perform in your social vision?

Thus, none of the major ideologies that have formed the post-Reformation world are seen as neutral ideologies for Christians. Nonetheless, the kind of speech act that formal CST represents is bound up with the conditions, thought forms and societal settlements of the modern industrial era: it represents a deeply material form of thought that emerges from a particular crucible of history and indelibly bears those historical marks. It does not simply peer downwards into its own historical moment from a space of material protection or abstraction.

Thus, CST is not properly 'political' *on its own terms* because it seeks to draw a direct line between the Scriptures and public policy as a rival to the tough vocation of the politician to work out the common good. It cannot offer society a shortcut to a theologically infused set of political answers, cutting out the uncertain and risky business of political judgement, negotiation, sacrifice and decision-making. Nor does it have to offer revealed knowledge of which political system works best. Nor can it claim a higher right to political knowledge or power.

The Church, as articulated in its social teaching, is political because the Church sees in the Scriptures a call to proclaim a social vision of the human person within a human and divine community, to live this out in its own life and to proclaim it to the world as a way of living. This social vision proposes basic things about the human person fully alive (the message Christ bears to the world): human interdependence, co-creativity, vulnerability to others, singular value and dignity and completion through others is core to this. Equally, the Scriptures are seen to contain a necessarily negative political theology: a call to unveil and critique forms of power which make of themselves rival deities, forms of domination, and in the process distort the image of God in creation and deny the person fully alive.

The Church is political in its negative form (as critique) insofar as the political is given to lapsing into its own forms of deadly politicization that threaten a vision of social living that the Church is called to stand for. This is especially clearly the case when politics erroneously makes the political the supreme and dominating reality and loyalty, rather than a form of service to the common good and relative to other goods. The Church, as we have noted, is rightly attentive to the ways that the political tends to be 'theological' in its own way: through the co-option of religious language and symbol as tools of power or through its own value system of ultimate claims that ought to be duly socially scrutinized. Whilst we may talk rightly of the separation of Church from state, it is simply evident that we cannot divide the political from the theological in any final or absolute way. The political remains part of how we make and find theological meaning, for truth is suffused throughout the material order; the political has always been drawn to propose fundamental visions of human society. And political systems continue to deploy religion for ends that are political; the draw to religious and theological symbol, ritual and language is rightly to be engaged and scrutinized in the light of the Gospel.

In its constructive form this 'negative' political task can still be one of dialogue – it seeks a reflective engagement with the leading thought proponents and movements of its time, an invitation to any political movement or system to think what it is claiming and doing. It is an invitation to thoughtfulness about the grounds, limits, incompleteness and possible misrecognitions latent in any system of political action – a constructive engagement with the fallibility, imperfection and limit of any human system that aims after goods. A clear example of this spirit of critical dialogue in operation is found in *Fratelli tutti*. Pope Francis invites liberalism to consider the moral performance of its ideological commitment to the ideals of liberty, equality and fraternity.[4] He notes that liberalism finds it easier to deal in the first two of these ideals and tends to neglect fraternity, which seems in the end the necessary grounds for achieving the other two ambitions. His call is partly for liberalism to understand itself reflectively and evaluate itself against its own ideals.

In its more severe form, this 'negative' task can be a simple prophetic calling out. Whilst *Fratelli tutti* is reflective and nuanced in its engagement with liberalism as a political philosophy, it is outright in its opposition to individualism. It denounces the products of this individualism: a throwaway culture, an objectification and commodification of the human person, and indifference to suffering and inequality. *Fratelli tutti* is not against liberalism, but it is, in unapologetic terms, against individualism.

None of this exists separately from the equally 'political' character of the Church as an ecclesial polity or community, visible in the ways it chooses to structure its own life of community, enacted through worship, propounded through teaching, structured in governance and decision-making and extended in the forms of care it enacts or fails to enact. This is the fragile political work of the Church, in which it too is accountable for the ways that it conceives of, and uses, truth and story. For this reason, the sexual abuse

---

[4] See §103-105 of *Fratelli tutti*. There has been consistent feminist critique of the use of the language of fraternity by both Pope Benedict and Pope Francis.

Towards a Politics of Communion

crisis that has gripped the Church and its cover-up, and the role of women and the laity in governance, are necessarily and properly political questions for the Church.

The Church is thus political in all these ways, which are not always easily captured, represented or adequately critiqued in other forms of liberal social and political theory.[5]

The social question and the Church as a society

In *Rerum novarum* Leo XIII adopted a phrase that would come to frame the popes' new interventions into modernity, the Church addressed 'the social question'. *Rerum novarum* defined its task as commentary on the fundamental shape of the social order and the new patterns of economy, statehood and social value that were shaping a newly industrialized, bureaucratized and increasingly centralized social order. The development of a theological language for discussing defined 'social questions' might be viewed in two ways: one secular and one theological.

Through the upheavals of the eighteenth and nineteenth centuries, the idea of 'society' took shape as something beyond and between the state and Church, and distinct from previous conceptions of spiritual and temporal power. Ideas that had previously found their home in a single, intrinsic (if constantly disputed) cosmic order in which spiritual and temporal powers shared a division of labour within a single whole, shifted into new forms. In this process questions of identity and action were self-consciously 'social' questions.

The Church's adoption of the new language of the social question had a number of dimensions. The first concerns the shifting relationship between the state, market and civil society. Letters and encyclicals issued between

---

[5]In the wake of the Second World War the papacy came to accept that the Church can operate in a liberal democratic era and indeed praised some of liberal democracy's achievements. This is not best thought of as a paradigm shift caused by the war alone but a movement a century in the making. Nonetheless, through each social encyclical following *Rerum novarum* the popes make clear that they do not baptize the (multiform) philosophies of liberalism underpinning contemporary democratic practice. They remain critical of the tendency of some forms of liberalism to embrace pantheism. Such liberalism is marked by an absence of attention to history and time and an over-identification of man with God. They are also critical of forms of liberal rationalism that deny the personal experience of faith as well as the possibility of a transcendent or eternal reason.

Vatican I and Vatican II tend to lament the growth of industrial, technocratic and transactional forms of social organization. They saw in this shift an inexorable drive towards centralization. They feared the suppression of local, diffuse, plural and more organic forms of social cooperation.[6] In the eyes of the popes, these tendencies were not the preserve of only one expression of modernity. They occurred, to varying degrees, in liberal democratic as well as totalitarian states and lay at the heart of modern capitalism. The shrinking space for rich civic association and the suppression of a space for the development of localized forms of social virtue become constant themes in mid and late twentieth-century encyclicals. Whilst society had become a new reality to be engaged, the space between market, state and person seemed in fact somewhat less 'social', less rich, increasingly denuded and at a cost.

The second discernible and recurrent social theme engaged by the popes concerns the changing nature of the state itself. Following the Reformations of the sixteenth and seventeenth centuries both Catholic and Protestant traditions had increasingly ceded powers to monarchs and national governments, and both traditions had consequently produced (in different forms) new ways of conceiving of the power, purpose, legitimacy and limits of human government, viewed theologically. Whilst CST is often referenced primarily for its economic teaching, much of the tradition is taken up with themes of social and political governance and virtue under the conditions of modernity. The social conditions of statehood therefore become a critical encyclical theme.

The third social theme concerns the constantly shifting relation of labour to capital and the dignity of work. CST teaches the absolute priority of human labour over capital, as well as the basic social creativity core to the experience of human work or labour. It discerns in capitalism a constant tendency to reverse this priority and to exploit and oppress the productive capacity of the human person. Communism in turn denies the true personalism at the heart of work. The popes conceive of the social question as inherently connected to the shifting relation of labour to capital and of the meaning of human productivity. In turn, to address questions of labour, work and value is also to address the realm of creation: land, property and

---

[6]See *Rerum novarum* §50–4 and *Quadragesimo anno* §78–80. This same theme re-emerges in John Paul II's social teaching, in *Caritas in veritate* and in Pope Francis' critique of the technocratic paradigm and his proposal of a polyhedral social ethic in *Evangelii gaudium*.

the distribution of material goods. In more recent papacies these sets of connections have become a more explicitly ecological ethic, but their roots spread wider than a (necessary) contemporary environmentalism and connect across the whole ecosystem of CST.

There remains a further explicitly theological use of the language of the social stimulated by the Church's dialogue with late nineteenth-century modernity. The Church of this period was wrestling with the implications of residing in a liberal political system that did not easily accept the Church's claim to be a public body. In the patristic language of a *societas perfecta*, the Church found its call to be a perfected society, a language that did not posit the Church as a simple power rival to the liberal secular polity.[7] In the Augustinian formulation, the social realm, including the Church as a society, had a more enduring status than the political. Yet the political remains a crucial reality for the forging of the common good in a fractured world. According to the patristic formulation, the body of the Church was itself a society, a social body and an expert in social questions. The Church had a message to share, a commentary to offer on social questions, which included but also exceeded the political and which existed as an expertise in ways legitimately autonomous from the secular political and non-rivalrous.

Such a self-conception enabled the Church to argue for its own free action in the world, expressed in institutional form – potentially harmonious in its wider social expression, but where necessary legitimately existing as a form of counter-cultural resistance. Re-adopting the language of the Church as a *societas perfecta* in modern form also enabled the Church to imagine itself as the larger body that contained the necessary and legitimate activity of the body politic rather than the other way round, without reinventing the throne-altar rivalries of previous centuries. Ideally a state would see this necessary co-belonging, but should it not, the Church could still, within the economy of salvation, claim this theo-political rationality as the basis for its own actions. This definition comes to its fullest fruition, via gradual development, in the Second Vatican Council's treatment of religious freedom as a social question in *Dignitatis humanae* (1965).

Such a struggle for a new political theology of society was not limited to Catholic polities alone. In early twentieth-century Anglicanism, John

---

[7]For a more extended discussion of this, see Emile Perreau-Saussine, *Catholicism and Democracy: An Essay in the History of Political Thought* (Princeton, NJ: Princeton Press, 2012), pp. 91–5.

Neville Figgis, as part of the Anglican Pluralist movement, articulated the same dilemma and struggle to find a theological language in which to speak of the Church in the modern world.[8] Figgis noted that liberal legal entities struggled to recognize the character of the Church as a distinct social group in ways that cohered with the Church's own self-understanding, as the law tended to recognize individuals but not social groups as true actors. For Figgis the Church thus remained an indigestible entity, unable to accept a prescription of itself as a body of private belief but also unable to clearly account for itself as a social actor in the terms offered by liberalism.[9]

During this same period from the 1840s onwards, largely through the work of religious orders and lay social Catholicism, the Church devoted considerable energy to developing the structures of an alternative Catholic civil society. It did so, not as an outright rival to the state, for it was retreating gradually from such a view. Rather it sought a full expression of a Catholic social world – within a social world in which it found itself often not totally at home – through the foundation of hospitals, universities, schools, welfare services and new intellectual publications. These were tangible signs of not only the fullness of its own life, but also its dislocation in important ways from its own secular contexts. These civic initiatives were each conceived of as means to ensure the formation in faith in a world seen as increasingly hostile to faith, as well as enactments of Christian service within a world consecrated to Christ. This Catholic civic world was not simply a counter-cultural rejection of, or separation from, modernity: it created deeply social expressions of a shifting Catholicism in complex dialogue with its context.

1891: New departures

Pius XI was the first pope to suggest that his predecessor, Leo XIII, had begun a formal, ongoing tradition of official social teaching. Whilst in no sense overlooking or repudiating the pre-1891 tradition of Catholic

---

[8]John Neville Figgis, *Churches in the Modern State* (London: Longmans, Green & Co Press, 1913). For a consideration of Anglican Pluralism in its context, see Matthew Grimley, *Citizenship, Community and the Church of England: Liberal Anglican Theories of the State Between the Wars* (Oxford: OUP, 2004).
[9]We will return to this line of thought, as it has influenced contemporary debates in Catholic political theology, when we explore the work of William Cavanaugh, influenced by Figgis, in Chapter 9 on the principle of subsidiarity.

moral and political thought, Pius assumed that Leo XIII's social encyclical *Rerum novarum* (1891) had begun a distinctive, new and worthy tradition for the Church in the modern age. Whilst Michael Schuck has argued that the tradition of formal modern papal social teaching begins in the age of revolutions, as early as 1740 under the papacy of Benedict XIV, Pius and each of his papal successors have viewed 1891 as the genesis of an official tradition to which they have (variously) given the name 'Catholic social teaching' or 'Catholic social doctrine'.[10] Each later papal social letter refers back to an anniversary of an earlier landmark post-1891 papal letter, revisiting and updating its themes. In his initial definition, Pius XI defines this body of teaching to include the work of popes, bishops, lay theologians and Catholic 'statesmen'. Later definitions offered by commentators (rather than the popes themselves) have tended to differentiate the documents produced by popes and bishops' conferences from work by lay theologians and public figures, referring to the former as Catholic social teaching or doctrine and the latter as Catholic social thought.[11]

Leo XIII's *Rerum novarum* makes a novel contribution to an earlier tradition of Catholic commentary on modernity in several ways. First, *Rerum novarum* offers both a critique of modernity focused explicitly on economic relations and a set of constructive solutions that include, but extend beyond, the merely economic. Second, it utilizes rights-based language as part of a Catholic social theory but places modern rights discourse within the framework of a Catholic account of liberty or freedom. Third, *Rerum novarum* proposes that deep social analysis requires a religious framework but that these insights can be expressed in the language of reason and be grasped by all.

The explicit theme of *Rerum novarum* is 'the condition of work' and the relation of labour to capital in the context of industrialization and capitalism. Lay Catholics, clergy and bishops – including notably French factory owner Léon Harmel, René de la Tour du Pin (both involved in worker pilgrimages to Rome), Bishop Wilhelm von Ketteler of Mainz and Cardinal Manning in London (both involved in industrial disputes) – had

---

[10] Michael Schuck, 'Early Modern Catholic Social Thought, 1740-1890', in *Modern Catholic Social Teaching: Commentaries and Interpretations*, Second Edition (Washington D.C.: Georgetown Press, 2018), pp. 103–29.

[11] Such as the more recent US-influenced attempt to define Catholic social teaching as the formal teaching of Popes and bishops' conferences and Catholic social thought as the wider work of lay and clerical theologians and Catholic social practitioners and commentators.

been offering a critique of capitalism in France, Germany and UK since the turn of the nineteenth century. In addition to involvement in industrial disputes, von Ketteler delivered six sermons in which he laid out the basis of a Catholic critique of absolute rights to private property and proposed a model of legitimate state social intervention. *Rerum novarum* builds on these insights and produces a model of economic life that defends, above all, the priority of labour over capital, a right to private property as part of, and subject to, broader criteria of the just use and distribution of created goods. These goods are to meet the needs of all. The encyclical teaches the necessity of a just wage for human development and flourishing as much as mere survival, the right and need of workers to organize in guilds and unions, and the duty of the state to foster just distribution in all areas of social and economic life.

Rights to private property are defended by Leo XIII as the basis of a more just and harmonious social order. Upholding the rights of all to meaningful ownership is seen as part of the solution to the social problem. Rights to ownership stem from the rational nature of the human person (compared to other creatures) and their desire to plan for stable futures. They stem from the right to dominion over the earth within limits set according to just distribution of goods based on both need and effort, from the manner in which labour provides us with a relationship to land and its goods – what we steward materially takes on the imprint of our personality. From the needs of the family (which exists prior to claims of state and market) for security and stability. This teaching renders earlier Christian teaching on the communal dimensions of property less clear (and is picked up again by Popes John Paul II and Francis), but it does also provide an account of the role of the modern state in ensuring attention to just distribution of goods, with a priority for the poorest.

Rerum novarum establishes the need for a just wage (adapted from earlier scholastic teaching on just prices) to ensure basic sustenance and a basic level of meaningful social participation in education and leisure. Interestingly, the encyclical resists formalizing the Catholic lay movements' draw towards corporatism in economic affairs (this has to wait until Pius XI's *Quadragesimo anno* forty years later) and instead emphasizes unionization and workers' associations as the basis for necessary mutual assistance. The state may regulate such groups when they constitute a threat to the public benefit but should avoid suppression of workers' associations at all costs.

Rerum novarum reads as curiously both progressive and conservative in equal measure. The conservatism of the document lies in its fixed view of the social order: class roles are seemingly divinely ordained yet class harmony, dignity of work and justice in distribution as well as a right to ownership are key to a modern economic ethic. New forms of social mediation are necessary to foster distributive justice in wages, conditions, social ownership of the means of production and the wider goods of creation. Both the state and new civic bodies are required to foster such a model. A strong vein of paternalism runs through the core of the document. Women are viewed solely in relation to reproduction and household labour and rarely as agents in their own right. A more positively framed – although equally open to debate – paternalism structures discussion of just wages for male breadwinners and household heads. The fundamental model of the social order proposed by *Rerum novarum* is the household or family unit, headed by a male labourer and provider. This is the first society that all other forms of society in economy and polity serve. Paternalism and neo-scholastic renderings of justice are thus hard-wired into the political anthropology of *Rerum novarum* and therefore of early CST.

The text is suffused with the broader anthropological themes that troubled the Church in modernity. Given that the first draft was prepared for Leo XIII by the Jesuit Matteo Liberatore, this should not surprise us. Liberatore, an editor of the Catholic journal *La civiltà cattolica* and the main intellectual influence behind the text, had worked extensively on neo-Thomistic accounts of liberty, and he brought this work to bear on the drafts of *Rerum novarum*.

The document ought not to be read as simply concerned with economic relations. Rather, it sets out an ambitious and complex – although incomplete – account of Catholic concerns about the tendency of modernity towards the atomization of social life (the private, meaning-seeking person as the core of the social order), the mechanization of social life (the movement away from a form of guild cooperative associationalism, the disassociation of product and producer) and the privatization of social life (the removal of religion to a private realm of inner belief and motivation). Each is viewed as dynamics antithetical to a Catholic view of social order, and in rational terms, is judged to lead to the diminishment of justice and the public good. The text thus circles around questions of the construction of the moral self, of the nature of labour, of a constructive social view of political community and of the necessity of the religious as a public reality. Contra Arendt, *Rerum novarum* suggests that we cannot be properly public without religion, without proper transcendence.

The document can be argued to adopt rights language but only as part of an account of the person always within communities of mutual moral obligation and gift exchange. *Rerum novarum* refutes the idea of mere contract or transaction as the basis of social justice, including just wages, and insists on notions of covenant and an objective measure of just exchange that protect the essential needs of the person set in a fabric of social relations. Rights language is viewed increasingly through the lens of the developing mid-century tradition of philosophical personalism and particularly the work of Emmanuel Mournier and Jacques Maritain. Whilst critiques of the adoption of personalist rights language rose during the mid-century – Simone Weil wrote robustly to reject personalism as a properly theological thought form – its influence lasted through the second half of the twentieth century, and in fact gave Catholic rights language a grounding in an anthropology of rights that differed in important ways from the standard rights talk of the Enlightenment and Protestant traditions.

For all these reasons, *Rerum novarum* becomes the initial basis of what can credibly be called a new and distinctive tradition of CST.

With hindsight, the view that *Rerum novarum* adopts such social relations is arguably too static, too a-historical. Despite its focus on themes of justice, there is little sense of a fundamentally egalitarian social order and much emphasis still on paternalist and hierarchical ordering, especially in its treatment of class and gender. It is also important to note that autocratic regimes and movements of the political right were as likely to see a legitimation of their own programmes in this letter as those of the reformist Left. The Falangists of Spain (1936–75), the Salazar regime in Portugal (1932–68) and the Austrian Dollfuss regime (1932–34) saw themselves as pursuing the kind of conservative social ethics, combined with a syndicalist and corporatist economy they thought was hinted at in *Rerum novarum* and its successor document *Quadragesimo anno*. On the one hand the document leads to a genuine flourishing of initiatives amongst workers, and in establishing grassroots movements, and on the other, a strong strand of paternalist conservative politics which drew directly on these documents (admittedly selectively); in some instances these regimes were openly nationalistic and fascistic in character. Although Charles Maurras' Action Française was denounced by the Church in 1926, the ties between the Church and the regimes in Spain and Portugal continued well into the mid-century period, and the history of these regimes bore a clear relationship to the Church's social teachings.

Towards a Politics of Communion

A plural tradition

The publication of *Rerum novarum* has been read over the last century optimistically either as the re-energizing of a centuries-long Catholic political tradition or, in more ambivalent terms, as a sign of the humbling of the Church in social and political matters. Was the emergence of the encyclical tradition as much an outcome of a Church now stripped of its overreaching and inappropriate power and prestige, and thus in some measure a child of the loss of the temporal power of the Church?

The emerging social encyclical tradition can perhaps be read as the spirited rebirth of a necessarily humbled form of political Catholicism. What is less often noted is that the nineteenth-century Catholic Church, out of which *Rerum novarum* emerged, found the emerging settlement with temporal power, in *both* its nascent liberal *and* more absolutist forms, often less than comfortable. Thus, from the mid-nineteenth century into the start of the twentieth, in document after document the Church attempted to articulate not only a vision of social order and a form of social critique fit for a modern industrial age but also an account of her own nature, calling, and liberty under new conditions: conditions the Church found challenging in ways we do not capture fully when we talk only about the birth of the new or the loss of the old.

With this in mind, we might be wise to resist the temptation to tell the story of the birth of modern social and political Catholicism as a simple paradigm shift in 1891. Modern CST is a tradition of post-Reformation and post-Revolutionary Catholic thought which emerges through the slow dying of a dominant (but never singular) model of political Catholicism and the gradual, painful, incomplete but also sometimes deeply creative shift to a different kind of settlement, again never singular. This journey remains necessarily incomplete and certainly imperfect.

CST is a tradition marked by deep continuity and constant internal contestation, as well as by an ongoing complex relationship between social theory and social practice. When Pius XI wrote his three letters in the spring of 1937, he drew on the ideas of those who drafted the documents for him, including his successor Pius XII whose emphasis would prove different to his own. Pius' letters offered correction and comment on the development of independent Catholic social movements that were drawing on the teachings and principles articulated in *Rerum novarum* and *Quadragesimo anno* (1931). He condemned the nativism of the French monarchist movement Action Française, and whilst praising Catholic Action in Mexico

Pius reminds Catholics involved in such new movements of the limits of the social action the Church might undertake in the name of CST.[12]

The world of CST in its formal papal guise exists within a wider porous, plural and contested terrain of modern Catholic social ideas, not exhausted by attention to the formal teaching tradition itself. It is a space not only populated by the work and witness of the individual popes and national bishops' conferences who have produced its formal documents but also shaped profoundly by the pluralism and personalism of Jacques Maritain and Emmanuel Mounier's, the radical solidarity and Catholic anarchism of Dorothy Day and Daniel Berrigan, the political mysticism of Charles Péguy and Simone Weil, and more recently the alternative economic models of the Italian Economy of Communion and Civil Economy schools, and the alternative ecological communities of contemporary religious. This is to name but a handful of the best-known examples from the last century. Some of these sources have been more integrated into the bloodstream of formal CST than others. Popes have disagreed with each other on emphasis, and lay movements have drawn from, influenced and sometimes moved beyond the development of official teaching. Both individual popes and leading lay and clerical theological proponents of CST have leaned closer to liberalism or further away, towards more Romantic and integralist accounts of social teaching, towards more Augustinian or more Thomistic sources. This is the internal dialogue and 'political' form of the tradition itself.

Today, the 'social question' remains just as lively, contested and contestable and indeed it appears at the very heart of disputes within the Church as well as a traceable source within a new generation of social and political movements. CST is being put to use both by neo-populist movements and regimes and by those resisting such politics. Nowhere more than the

---

[12] Action Française was a pro-monarchy, counter-revolutionary throne and altar, political movement in France, founded in 1899, and led to prominence in the early twentieth century by Charles Maurras. Maurras was agnostic but supported the re-establishment of Catholicism as the official religion of France – largely based on a view of Catholicism as a utility for social cohesion. AF attracted significant Catholic support and membership, although it was condemned by the papacy in 1926 and its newspaper placed on the list of banned texts for Catholics. Catholic Action, popular in countries that had experienced significant anti-clericalism, was a more diffuse set of movements without a single political agenda and based loosely around a concept of Catholic social action. From the late nineteenth century, and connected with *Rerum novarum*, it provided a way for lay Catholics to seek to form movements and influence society. Movements such as the Young Christian Workers, Cursillo and Young Christian Student groups existed under this banner.

Towards a Politics of Communion

United States currently demonstrates the politicization of Catholicism and the continued plural construction of the tradition. And yet, its territorial centres of gravity are also shifting. A Latin American papacy and a more African and Asian focus are likely to produce a continued shift towards a more globalist social teaching. There is no sign that social Catholicism will become any less contested, plural or alive in the decades ahead.

Natural law and the vocation to be human

Having offered some historical-theological context, in the second half of this introductory chapter I move to address a series of major thematic and methodological areas that act as necessary grounding for our transition into a consideration of the main principles of CST.

Pope Francis outlined in his Covid-19 catechesis, offered in place of his public audience addresses in the summer of 2020, that the Church has to offer the world the Gospels, a tradition of reflection on the theological virtues, and its accrued body of social teaching. The latter, CST, attempts to draw the Scriptures into dialogue with the ethical theological tradition and the signs of the times. That the tradition would draw from the Scriptures may seem obvious, although there is plenty of controversy about its way of doing so! However, the CST tradition has also depended heavily – and equally controversially – on the tradition of natural law thinking.

The coherence of *Rerum novarum* as a document depended in large part on its formulation of natural law theory. Natural law theory has its origins in the philosophy and literature of the classical world and became central to Catholic theological methods through the work of medieval scholastics. Leo XIII's renewed engagement with Catholic universities and seminaries, as well as his development of CST, was predicated on deploying this scholastic method as part of a renewal of Catholic mission in the modern world. Leo assumes the insights of previous natural law teachers and also proposes new applications of such theory to an industrial age. Whilst its application shifts across a full century-plus of social teaching, natural law theory remains a fundamental intellectual building block for CST.

CST draws largely from Thomist and nineteenth-century neo-scholastic traditions of natural law thinking. Aquinas taught that natural law was best understood as the rational creature's participation in the eternal law. This formula has the benefit of brevity and a tight logic but needs a little unpacking.

Law, in this context, is not understood as simply a command, dictate or coercive measure intended to restrain. It does not carry connotations of law and governance as primarily a punishment for sin. Rather, law is conceived as a structure of virtue that leads a thing towards its fulfilment and true ends. This is not language devoid of notions of discipline, of course. Nor is it devoid of a history of interpretation and use that ties it to controversy and implication in troubling historical practices, but it is important to note that its self-conception is not automatically coercive.

Aquinas explained law analogically through a fourfold typology of law as eternal, divine, natural and positive. The eternal law is the fullness of God's governing law that creates, sustains, orders and redeems the universe; this law is known in this life through its revelation in the life of Christ, the movement of the Holy Spirit in history and through the Scriptures, but it will be only fully known at the end of time. These various theological sources listed here constitute the divine law. In turn, Aquinas argued, the human being is created by the Father as a rational creature capable of apprehending universal truths about the created order and about human nature itself. Reason is itself an attribute of God, and God's governing law is seen as the act of reason, and therefore crucially not just an act of the will, that might be beyond human scrutiny. Human creatures are also capable of exercising reason and participating in the (divine) process of reaching their own fulfilment and perfection. We exercise this capacity, guided by a longing for the eternal law, the presence of divine law in Scripture and the possibility of discerning basic precepts of a natural law from the rational observation of the natural and social world, and thus formulating the final kind of law: human or positive law. This form of law acts as the law that forms and sustains political communities. For these reasons Aquinas defines any form of law as 'an ordinance of reason for the common good, promulgated by him who has care of the community'.

Aquinas discerns the presence of a concept of natural law in Romans 2:15. Here Paul notes that the Gentiles without knowledge of the Gospel show the law to be 'written on their hearts' and as a result their 'consciences bear witness'. Aquinas offers basic precepts of the natural law which he believed to be available as knowledge to all those who exercise reason. These truths are generic truths that express a universal and objective order of creation towards which we incline for our well-being. He argued that we incline most fundamentally towards the good rather than towards evil, that we seek self-preservation, marriage, family life and procreation, that we seek meaning and ultimately the divine.[13] Figures from the second scholastic period in the sixteenth and seventeenth centuries, notably Francisco di Vitoria (1483–1546), also developed the Roman law tradition of reflection on a further kind of law: the law of nations or *jus gentium*, integrating this into a Catholic moral teaching.[14] The *jus gentium* is envisaged as a form of universal human law deduced from the natural law and acting beyond, within and prior to the laws of individual political communities; these laws concerned fundamental accounts of human dignity that must be protected across international boundaries and within the laws of individual nations. This forms the basis for some traditions of thinking about international law.

Natural law theory is predicated on the idea that ethics should, and can, have a descriptive coherence and must correspond to what we find to be practically reasonable. It proposes that reason plays a key role for religious and non-religious believers in forming the basis for peaceable living in pluralistic society. Nonetheless, natural law theorists propose that reason does not operate in a zone of separation from faith for those who profess Christian belief. Faith, revealed through the Scriptures and Christian life, extends and deepens the truths we can reason from the created order and enables us to receive and engage the mysteries that any reasoned view of life reveals and confronts us with as difficulty or as blessing. This is not a dualistic, relativistic or binary theory. At its best, natural law theory tries to avoid the idea of two realms – nature and grace, public and private – in which one subjugates the (unruly) other. In place of an inherent conflict or master–slave relation of subjugation between faith and reason, nature and grace, natural law theories propose the (not always easy) anticipation, completion and refining of one by the other, a participation of one in the other and the situatedness of nature within an order of grace. The closest to a public theology rendering of this view in recent CST comes in Benedict XVI's address to British politicians in his Westminster Hall address on 17 September 2010.[15] Thus, the logic of scholastic natural law theory, read

---

[13]Contemporary new natural law theorist John Finnis has codified these primary goods as a natural orientation towards life, knowledge, play, friendship, practical reasonableness, religion and aesthetic experience. See John Finnis, *Natural Law and Natural Rights*, Second Edition (Oxford: OUP, 2011).

[14]See Francisco di Vitoria, *De Indis* [On the American Indians] and *De potestate ciuili* [On Civil Power] both reproduced in *Vitoria: Political Writings*, Eds., Anthony Padgen and Jeremy Lawrance (Cambridge: CUP, 1991).

[15]Benedict XVI Westminster Hall Address. See http://w2.vatican.va/content/benedict-xvi/en/speeches/2010/september/documents/hf_ben-xvi_spe_20100917_societa-civile.html

on its own terms, is social, participatory and ultimately inseparable from an account of the supernatural. It is not an account of nature separate from an account of grace, nor should it constitute a form of naturalism that derives an eternal 'ought' from a current 'is'. Nonetheless, as critics rightly observe, these are constant temptations for those developing ideas about natural law.

CST draws from the natural law tradition and in so doing also develops and extends the tradition. It does this by extending the use of natural law ideas into the realms of modern economics and politics and by attempting a late twentieth-century integration of scriptural and philosophical reflection in service of social questions. In this context it is worth emphasizing that CST, in its deployment of natural law, both *imports* a political theology already embedded in the structure of natural law theory – a set of claims about the nature of divine governance and human governance of the world we outlined previously – and *proposes* a further broad set of rational principles about the nature and form of political life suited to the common good. It is also true that periods of particular political instability have driven new phases of development in natural law thinking, from Vitoria to Grotius to contemporary natural law thinkers. *Rerum novarum* continues within this tradition and trajectory.

Leo XIII had already set out his views on human government in his text *Immortale dei* (1885). *Rerum novarum* continues to extend these views on the state as a natural form of order ordained for pursuit of the good. He saw the state as a natural form of order, although follows in the earlier scholastic tradition of not prescribing a single form of government as 'Christian'. His view of political society remained hierarchical, organic and paternalist. Leo used natural law theory to defend the idea of a natural inequality and an organic, hierarchical and harmonious social order. Leo taught both a neo-Thomist ethic of just distribution of goods and a static view of the social order. He applied natural law thinking to what he viewed as new economic conditions and uses natural law reasoning for his defence of just or living wages, call for workers' associations, defence of justly distributed private property, advocacy of rest, leisure, family and worship time.

A gradual shift towards papal integration of modern rights language into the heart of natural law reasoning begins with Pius XI and Pius XII's assertion of inherent rights to bodily integrity (in the face of Nazi policies), property ownership (in the face of communism) and self-determination

---

(accessed March 2019).

(in the face of various forms of mid-century totalitarianism). However, a fuller integration of rights and natural law thinking only occurs during the papacies of John XXIII and Paul VI.[16] Vatican II preserved the basic Catholic understanding of the social and political order. First, it reaffirmed the dignity of the human person, who is the bearer of certain rights and responsibilities. This is a vision of mutual obligation. Second, Vatican II reaffirmed the teaching of the early social encyclicals, that the civic order requires a healthy – plural – range of small and medium-scale organizations. These are vehicles to foster virtue through convivial association, skill and gift exchange and mutual assistance. Third, the council affirmed that the common good is the end of all social life. The council stressed social interdependence as the most fundamental social reality and the necessary context for any moral discussion of rights. Nonetheless, it dispensed with the hierarchical and static view of inequality as hard-wired into the social order that had marked earlier natural law social teaching under Leo XIII and Pius XI. Whilst *Gaudium et spes* notably adopted a more explicitly Christocentric understanding of both Church and society, it is perhaps *Pacem in terris* which offers the most profound shift after *Rerum novarum* in the way that natural law is used within formal social teaching.

Pacem in terris offered a post-war Catholic political theory, developing on the foundations of, and arguably moving beyond, the work of Pius XII. The document begins by reiterating the basic framework of a Catholic view of social order, but it innovates in its treatment of democracy, human rights and natural law. The most significant change in the deployment of natural law theory in *Pacem in terris* concerns the framing of individual rights. Where previous Catholic teaching had emphasized duties over rights, and rights subordinate to a system of social obligation, *Pacem in terris* extends teaching on the primacy of individual rights. *Pacem in terris* should not, however, be read as removing rights from a system of mutual obligation or from an embeddedness in social context. *Pacem in terris* advances a Catholic communitarian theory of rights rooted in the idea of moral order; it integrated understanding of rights and obligations in the context of solidarity, common good and universal destination of goods. *Pacem in*

---

[16]See Stephen Pope, 'Natural Law', in *Modern Catholic Social Teaching: Commentaries and Interpretations*, Second Edition, ed. Kenneth Himes et al. (Washington D.C.: Georgetown Press, 2018).

terris also innovated in making human rights the point of universal testing amongst plural cultural models.

A further development in the articulation of a natural law theory occurs in Paul VI's social encyclical *Populurum progressio* and his Apostolic Letter *Octogesimo adveniens*. Paul VI proposes the language of 'integral human development'. *The Compendium of the Social Doctrine of the Church* was produced by the Vatican's Pontifical Council for Justice and Peace during the pontificate of John Paul II and bears the hallmark of his papacy and his view of social teaching. For John Paul II the heart of CST lay on the one hand in the theological anthropology of the Church and on the other hand in the social processes of the judging, acting historical agent: the lay Catholic in the world. The active historical agent 'represents the heart and soul of Catholic social thought', and the documents of the popes act as 'milestones' on the path of social thought.[17] John Paul II's turn towards both phenomenology and Christology can be seen in the renewed emphasis on the human person as 'the subject, foundational and goal' of social life.[18] The task of the Church's social teaching is to critique and oppose all in the social order that refuses the 'active and responsible' subjectivity of the human person and to insist that society must be directed 'towards the human person'.[19] Insisting on the subjectivity of the human person as the central both meditative and political focus of social teaching, the *Compendium* notes that the Church itself is 'not outside or over or above' but exists exclusively in and for persons in communion. This is CST's understanding of the situated sociality of the Church itself. The *Compendium* situates its account of natural law in an account of freedom. Human freedom is a freedom to will the good, for the human person to remain under the control of his or her own decisions. The purpose of this freedom is to seek the Creator. This freedom is 'situated' in several senses. Freedom is meaningful in relation to an everyday life that is full of both limitation and possibility; it is meaningful in the context of the constant need to form and execute judgements; and it is meaningful in the context of the constraints that come with exercising freedom in the context of

---

[17] *The Compendium of the Social Doctrine of the Church*, Pontifical Council for Justice and Peace, §104, p. 54.

[18] Ibid., §106, p. 55. This phrase is a direct quotation from Pius XII's Christmas message broadcast in 1944.

[19] Ibid., §106, p. 55.

unjust social conditions. The proper exercise of freedom is intelligible in relation to particular social, political, economic, ecological, cultural and juridical conditions – the absence of which threatens freedom. Such a conception of freedom, the *Compendium* argues, implies something akin to a natural law as a guide to conscience and judgement and as the basis for building social communion across radical forms of difference. It proposes natural law as a unitive and integrating framework that, without obliterating plurality, bonds rights to duties and peoples to each other. The *Compendium* summarizes the purpose or goal of the natural law as providing a fundamental orientation towards the Creator and towards a necessary recognition of equality with other creatures. Finally, the *Compendium* follows the wider theological emphasis of John Paul II's Christology and his (at times difficult) engagement with theologies of liberation in noting that human freedom whilst given as gift and situated in relations of divine and human interdependence needs to be liberated from the reality of sin and death. The full experience of human freedom – the person freed for communion in the depths of the self, with others – is dependent on accepting the liberation that Christ brings. The new communion in Christ through his death and Resurrection makes possible the fullness of fragile human freedom.

The last three popes have largely assumed the natural law foundations of their predecessors as a given, adopting the more historically and culturally dynamic understandings of the Second Vatican Council, but have focused more explicitly on a return to Scripture and to doctrinal themes of love and mercy. Through the papacies of John Paul II, Benedict XVI and Francis we have witnessed a move from an earlier theological focus on the doctrine of creation to Christology and eschatology. As we shall see in the discussion of just war theory in the next section, such a shift has material consequences for the content of the Church's social teaching as well as its methodology. Significant questions remain about the use of natural law thinking in contemporary CST. Some critics express a concern that all forms of natural law thinking are inherently problematic, tending towards a naturalistic fallacy (formalizing the practices of any given era as universal moral givens – a kind of false empiricism that can take a number of different forms). Other critics note the tendency of natural law thinkers to elevate the rational as a supreme form of human motivation which is belied by observations of complex human behaviour and motivation; for others the problem lies in the historical use of the idea in the context of debates about race, empire, sexuality and gender.

War, peace and non-violence

Questions of war and peace occupy a central place in the Catholic moral tradition, and a considerable volume of commentary in the encyclical tradition is taken up with an ongoing reflection on questions of war, peace, violence and the trade in arms. However, Catholic moral reflection on war and peace, both within the encyclical tradition and within the longer tradition of moral theology, has largely developed piecemeal in response to the historically contingent experience of war and conflict. Therefore, although a formal body of teaching does exist on questions of war and peace, upon more careful scrutiny it is less complete and less systematic than often assumed. It is also, when read carefully, much less clearly a source for justification of war than the notion of a just war theory might be taken to imply. The central hermeneutic of a just war CST is to push for a more exacting social practice of peacebuilding. In turn, this push to peacebuilding varies in its optimism about achieving peace in this life as a more fragmentary ethic or one of total social transformation. As Theodora Hawksley points out, what also remains in motion in the tradition is the very definition of what we consider war and peace each to be.[20]

The major twentieth-century historical contexts for the development of official CST on war and peace are, fairly obviously, provided by two world wars including the development of a global nuclear capacity, the Cold War and its attendant arms race. Its more recent context, however, is what Pope Francis calls a 'third world war fought piecemeal'. What he appears to be viewing under this title is a new generation of civil wars, so-called wars on terror, and the non-state conflicts that bring death and displacement to many – including cross-border drug wars.

It is often assumed that the social encyclicals propose just war theory as official church teaching and that just war theory defines the contribution of CST to questions of war and peace. In fact, neither supposition is true. Twentieth-century CST continues to explore both just war and pacifism as two legitimate options to guide Christian responses to conflict. Yet, neither

---

[20]Theodora Hawksley, *Peacebuilding and Catholic Social Teaching* (Notre Dame, IN: Notre Dame University Press, 2020). On these themes, see also Matthew Shadle, *The Origins of War: A Catholic Perspective* (Washington D.C.: Georgetown Press, 2011); Robert Schreiter, R. Scott Appleby and Gerard R. Powers (Eds), *Peacebuilding: Catholic Theology, Ethics and Praxis* (Maryknoll, NY: Orbis Books, 2010); and Lisa Sowle Cahill, *Love Your Enemies: Discipleship, Pacifism, and Just War Theory* (Minneapolis: Fortress Press, 1994).

stance is adopted as a formal, singular teaching; and neither exhausts or contains all that the official social tradition has to say on conflict and its avoidance and resolution. Whilst the modern social teaching tradition sees social conflict and some level of force (in the light of sin) as an inevitable part of social life, it does not see violence or war as inevitable. Both the use of human reason and a cooperation with divine grace make it possible for human societies to avoid or minimize war and social violence, and the central hermeneutic is one of struggle for peace. Given this is a theological account of the struggle for peace, this is not a saccharine view of peace but one that takes seriously the draw to violence and its spiritual harm. In this sense, the stable core of the teaching on war concerns the cessation, avoidance or overcoming of violence through the pursuit of a just peace as the true end of both persons and societies.

CST draws heavily on earlier church teaching on just war theory, developed during the fourth and fifth centuries, and thirteenth- and seventeenth-century high periods of Christian theo-political reflection, respectively. As the fourth- and fifth-century Church became more closely tied to the state, so two new forms of Christian reflection took shape.

In the first instance, the work of Ambrose and Augustine provided the basis for a new account of the legitimate actions of a Christian government in self-defence of the body politic. However, this work only makes theological sense if it is seen in the context of its concern with the wider exercise of responsibility for combatting evil and the pursuit of the common good through the life of virtue. Margaret Atkins notes that it can be misleading to see Augustine as an enthusiastic developer of a just war theory. Whilst Augustine's canon has become a key source for reflection on just war theory, Atkins suggests it might be fairer to view him as largely an inheritor of a classical just war line of thought, adapted from Roman jurisprudence. Theologically speaking, it is clear that Augustine is a thinker of peace. His central theological emphasis is on an ontology of peace, which defines the activity of God and the destiny of the human person in the heavenly city. Caritas is his central ethic, and peace our destiny and desire. All moral action and theological reasoning must be intelligible in the light of these truths. Nonetheless, Augustine's view of fallen and sinful humanity leaves him in no doubt about the conflictual nature of human life in this realm and its consequences for how Christians see their social existence. His theological account of the history of conflict interprets war as an outcome of the disorder of desire. It is the false loves, loves turned away from their true source, that drive conflict. Above all the idolatrous love for power and vainglory drives violence and conflict.

For Augustine, it is not the fact that war might lead to death that should trouble the Christian – mortality is not the main crisis for a person who has lived their life well – but rather the scale of disordered desires, manifest in cycles of violence. For this reason, Augustine is able to think of war as both the manifestation of the depths of human sinfulness and something that might be necessary in a fallen world to defend virtue and the right ordering of a community, and thus to restrain or admonish evil. In this second context, war could be an act of courageous justice-seeking and neighbour love. Augustine proposed that political order was a condition for all forms of civil and ecclesial life to flourish and that Christians needed to take seriously matters of formal political order. In this context the defence of order could be seen as a form of neighbour love, where love demands protection of the vulnerable and of the common good in all its dimensions. Augustine views the use of force as a consequence of sin and not an original divine intent for the world. It becomes a feature of the necessity of life in a fallen world. Nonetheless, the true goal of social life remains to reach towards a form of peace that is not merely the absence of war but the tranquillity of just social relations. This is the life that the Christian community is called to live. Pursuing this life in the life of the household, ecclesia and civil community requires a graced willingness to preserve and pursue peace, a peace which is real and of immense value but is only an analogy of the peace of the Kingdom. The *City of God* does not offer a blueprint for either the conduct of wars or a wholesale Christian transformation of the civil order. It does attempt to offer a vision of rightly ordered desires: the desire for the life to come can order our desires in and for this world now. For these reasons, it seems most sensible to say that for Augustine, whilst war might be considered on occasion just, love, peace and the right ordering of desires remain his central moral categories. Given these are his central concerns, he offers no more than a rudimentary and unsystematic just war account scattered through his writings, shaped in response to his immediate context and times.

In the second instance, this same historical period saw the foundation of religious orders and Christian communities offering a space for the development of a second strand of distinctly and radically non-violent Christian witness. These communities have remained of significance, not only for their own radical practice but also because in a millennium of development, these same religious orders allied with universities to later provide the context for the next major wave of Christian just war thinking.

The medieval and early modern period saw two important waves of Christian just war thinking centred around the moral theology of Thomas

Aquinas. Developing earlier classical and patristic thought on just war, Aquinas argued that for a war to be considered just the following conditions must exist: there must be a just case (repelling an attack, righting a wrong, the punishment of an evil); there must be a legitimate authority to execute the action of war (an authority capable of defending and securing the common good); and there must be right intention towards the establishment of peace.

Whilst Aquinas provides a basis rooted in claims to natural rights for the pursuit of a just war, in the *Summa* his framing question for handling questions of war is phrased in the negative: Can it can ever be just to pursue war? He pursues a line of Christian thinking that admits war but sees it as justified in the most limited of circumstances. For Aquinas war is a constantly fraught moral question requiring the careful exercise of creative and rational human judgment, not merely generic rules. Aquinas places significant emphasis on the role of reason in the order of virtue for securing the good. Whilst continuing to appeal to a form of neighbour love that secures true peace beyond simply the absence of violence, his categories are more oriented towards the idea of a natural reason that harmonizes the teaching of Christ with what can be known based on sound reason. Both Augustine and Aquinas frame the debate about just war in terms of the needs of the body politic, justice and the rule of law. Both thinkers – in rather differing ways – emphasize an ethics of love necessary for the completion of the search for a peace which lies beyond the cessation of violence but whose condition remains justice.

The later neo-scholastics of the Salamanca School augmented Aquinas' account. Francisco di Vitoria (1492–1546) repeated the formula of a just war as *jus ad bellum* (the conditions pertaining to declaring a just war): legitimate authority, just cause and intention focused on the defence of the common good and establishment of peace. Vitoria noted that there ought to be a reasonable prospect of success. Condemning expansionist wars, he emphasized the importance of diplomacy at all points and its primacy in the pursuit of justice and peace. He also outlined the conditions for *jus in bello* (conditions for conduct during a war): non-combatant immunity, proportionality between the harm caused in war and the good to be achieved. Vitoria also built upon the Roman and medieval tradition of reflection on the *jus gentium* (law of nations) helping to create a tradition of Christian jurisprudence on international law and justice, including questions of war and peacebuilding. The *jus gentium* functions in Catholic moral thought as a form of law that seeks to interpret the general precepts of the natural law and to guide or provide a customary law framework for the positive law conclusions arrived at by individual political communities or nations and for the conduct-guiding relations between nations. It is deduced by reason based on what is judged to be universal in human nature and necessary as universal conditions to be protected or enacted for the pursuit of justice.

In their treatment of themes of war and peace the papal social encyclicals have tended to favour the scholastic framework offered by Aquinas and the Salamanca School, framing just war discussion primarily in terms of natural justice and the pursuit of peace and the common good. Arguably, they have also inherited a degree of confidence in the possibilities for Christian action for widespread social transformation. Nonetheless, the journey through CST on war and peace needs to be seen as of a piece with the wider philosophical and political anthropology of the modern CST tradition. We might usefully note three phases in the development of thinking on war and peace in the encyclicals. These in turn correlate to three phases of development in wider CST reflection on the nature of political order. The papacies from Leo XIII to Pius XII produce documents which emphasize a largely hierarchical view of social order and territorial-communal notions of the common good. They tend to emphasize the necessity of state self-defence but prohibit wars of aggression, expansion or vengeance. Each pope teaches arms control and encourages forms of disarmament, and emphasizes that war is a matter of last resort. As late as the end of the Second World War the papacy remained silent on the use of carpet bombing and did not recognize conscientious objection – other than the long present idea that an entire people might oppose a war declared by a legitimate government and by so doing render it unjust.

The papacies of John XXIII and Paul VI bring a greater focus on the responsibilities borne by states to pursue diplomacy, disarmament and conflict resolution via international means and offer less focus on states' rights to unlimited sovereignty. Both popes focus on the necessary cooperation and inevitable interdependence between states, the pursuit of a regional and global common good, and the role, responsibility and benefits of international-level organizations in facilitating and promoting peace. Conscious objection is recognized as a legitimate possibility, and the developing reflection on nuclear capacity renews a language of pacifism in the modern tradition. Lisa Sowle Cahill refers to the 'relative pacifism' of *Pacem in terris* and later papal documents.[21] The objection to the use of

---

[21] Cahill, *Love Your Enemies*, see pp. 205–13.

nuclear weapons is based not on an absolute teaching that one must not kill but on questions of moral proportion in the case of killing in self-defence and a question of what builds or frustrates harmony and trust amongst nation states in the international order. The focus of moral reasoning in such documents is less on the hard teachings of Jesus and more on considerations of justice, reason and the common good in continuity with the longer neo-scholastic tradition. For this reason, there is some confusion over the teaching on deterrence in CST. As Theodora Hawksley also notes, there is a subtle shift in the very way that war itself appears to be defined – less a theological analysis of the disordered desires that drive violence and more a Kantian-influenced notion of war as a conflict of interests.[22]

What also shifts in this mid-century period is the ecclesiology that roots social teaching. This more globalist conception of the common good, faith in international governance and cooperative social vision is situated within the wider context of the deployment of more egalitarian and kinship-oriented ecclesiological language during the Second Vatican Council (1962–5). A return to a language of kinship or neighbour relations is not quite a return to Augustine's own framing of these issues, however. As Matthew Shadle notes, it is difficult to separate teaching on war and peace in CST from the assumption popes have made about the nature of political order.[23] Shadle argues that John XXIII worked on the basis of three assumptions that expressed both a neo-scholastic and a liberal framework: states are rational actors; fear, partiality and ignorance are key causes of war; and international institutions are the solution to these weaknesses. This framework comes to dominate the papal interventions on war and peace in the second half of the twentieth century, arguably holding until the papacy of Benedict XVI. Benedict XVI's papacy witnesses a shift to a more Augustinian theory of political order, reintroducing an Augustinian ethic of caritas as the framework for all social analysis. However, Benedict wrote little directly on re-evaluating just war doctrine in his social encyclicals, and so whilst the wider narrative takes an (contemporary) Augustinian turn the implications for just war doctrine and non-violence remain (tantalizingly) unclear.

---

[22]I am grateful for Theodora Hawksley's insights on this question during the delivery of an unpublished paper on themes of war and peace in *Fratelli tutti* for a seminar I organized in February 2021.
[23]See Shadle, *The Origins of War*, pp. 95–159.

The papacy of Francis has been suggestive of a further and clearer shift. Francis has emphasized the localization of peace, aid and development agendas, and the renewed role of civil actors alongside national and international bodies; he has spoken less often of the possibilities of world government and has hinted at increased integration of teaching on just war and non-violence Christian witness. Such shifts in Francis' teaching have their own social context: crises in notions of state sovereignty, the impact of late capitalism and forms of neo-colonialism on claims to state sovereignty, the failures and limitations of international-level bodies and the paradox created by increased capacity for both destruction and restraint in use of violence by states, the increased role of non-state actors in violence and conflict. His theological framework is less obviously neo-scholastic or Augustinian, but its themes are decidedly eschatological, refocusing on the Kingdom and the hard sayings of Jesus.

In *Fratelli tutti* Francis returns to the methodological fault-line in CST on war and peace Lisa Cahill noted some decades ago. As we have seen, whilst the early church tradition offers an account of violence in all its forms as a violation of charity and deals with themes of violence in the context of an account of Christian caritas, CST tends towards a natural law tradition focused on rational conditions for the pursuit of peace and justice. Therefore, whilst the 1960s mark the beginning of a return to a language of Christian pacifism, methodologically and theologically speaking, the papal and bishops' conference documents speak newly of modern pacifism within a methodological framework that remains scholastic and neo-scholastic and bears only traces of early church forms of reasoning. The teaching on pacifism between John XIII and Francis relates to questions of moral law based on rules and the deduction of conditions that might be met or not in a given case. Second, despite a common implicit scholastic framing, whilst documents after *Pacem in terris* offer both pacifism and just war theory as possible legitimate stances, it is not clear how these two traditions are integrated in practice as a single strand of moral thinking in CST. The integrating theology is missing. Thus, there remains a lack of clarity about both how older traditions of Christian teaching on non-violence and newer modern traditions relate, and how the dual contemporary traditions of pacifist and just war doctrine integrate. *Fratelli tutti* begins – but does not complete – a process of attempting the kind of integration Cahill calls for.

Fratelli tutti offers a self-reflexive evaluation of the Christian basis for an appeal to a just war theory. The encyclical does not reject or repudiate just war theory, but it places it at greater distance from the centre of its analysis of violence and peace, and it requires Christians to reflect on both the moral draw towards legitimating war at all in the contemporary era and the moral performance of just war theory itself as a means to limit violence. A combination of the conditions of modern warfare and the availability of mechanisms for negotiation of conflicts – if the will exists to pursue them to their limits – means there can be little reason to justify a war in present circumstances. Francis also expresses a studied scepticism that just war theory actively helps in the avoidance or negotiation of conflict. Francis writes:

> Every war leaves our world worse than it was before. War is a failure of politics and of humanity, a shameful capitulation, a stinging defeat before the forces of evil. Let us not remain mired in theoretical discussions, but touch the wounded flesh of the victims. Let us look once more at all those civilians whose killing was considered 'collateral damage'. Let us ask the victims themselves. Let us think of the refugees and displaced, those who suffered the effects of atomic radiation or chemical attacks, the mothers who lost their children and the boys and girls maimed or deprived of their childhood. Let us hear the true stories of these victims of violence, look at reality through their eyes, and listen with an open heart to the stories they tell. In this way, we will be able to grasp the abyss of evil at the heart of war. Nor will it trouble us to be deemed naive for choosing peace.[24]

In this sense, Francis returns the CST tradition to a more theo-centric account of the disordered desires that surround conflict, and as Matthew Shadle argues, to a view of war and peace that integrates a preferential option for the poor. In a sense, and helpfully so, the whole of *Fratelli tutti* is taken up with the meta theme of social violence and social peace in our age: the economy, inequality, digital communications and the fragility of democratic cultures are all viewed through these lenses. What remains less clear is the extent to which a more adequate just war theory is to be actively pursued by Catholic thinkers at all, as well as the development of humanitarian thought around the Right to Protect. Missing from the encyclical is a testimony to the work of Christian peacebuilders – often women – and what might be learnt from their experience.

---

[24]*Fratelli tutti*, §261.

That the modern tradition has reintegrated a pacifist emphasis is the result not only of a mid to late century papal reflection on the advent of nuclear wars but also of the presence and influence of grassroots Catholic organizations committed to peacebuilding and non-violence. Catholic peace movements were gathering momentum and publishing significant reflections on themes of war, peace and non-violence from the 1920s and 1930s onwards. American Catholic anarchist, pacifist and devotee of Catholic social action and teaching Dorothy Day (1897–1980) became a critical figurehead in the development of these movements. An account of the development of the Worker Movement and of Pax Christi is beyond the scope of this text, but it is important to note the differences in theological emphasis that have marked the development of twentieth-century peace movements and parallel papal social teaching. Todd Whitmore argues that the peace movements make more use of direct appeals to Scripture and teachings of Jesus, tend to focus in their writings on building up the theological resourcing and formation of committed Christians, and focus their moral and theological reasoning on the person in civil community in the light of the Gospel rather than on the role of government alone. Different substantial conclusions are reached about war and the route to peace by drawing on a different balance of sources, particularly by giving priority to the hard sayings of Jesus.

It is therefore possible to say in summary that the modern encyclical tradition tends towards a just war position without adopting this as its formal or settled teaching. As Whitmore argues, whilst it is not a standard of taught doctrine just war theory has 'achieved the force of history by the accrual of writing and teaching over time'.[25] Nonetheless, since the 1960s, the Church has combined a plural set of teachings on relative nuclear pacifism, possible conscientious objection and just war theory. Its methodological framework remains largely natural law-based. This settlement on questions of war and peace looks fraught with certain ambiguities and continues to leave untapped a wider reservoir of theological reasoning from the early church tradition that focused on the notion of a distinctive Christian witness from territorially based Christian communities that could be used to generate a renewal of Christian thought on violence and conflict in the late modern world.

---

[25]Todd D. Whitmore, 'The Reception of Catholic Approaches to Peace and War in the United States' in *Modern Catholic Social Teachings: Commentaries and Interpretations* (Washington D.C.: Georgetown Press, 2018), p. 581.

Towards a Politics of Communion

Change and development in CST

CST works on the basis of an appeal to hermeneutics of both continuity and change. Whilst commentators debate the internal consistency of teaching on capitalism, welfare and democracy, more significant methodological questions apply to the evident change of teaching on religious freedom, human rights, pacifism and capital punishment or the death penalty. There remains considerable debate amongst scholars about the extent to which such shifts represent changes in teaching or a consistent ethic of teaching on law and justice which when applied to changing historical circumstances implies a new stance on a particular issue. Francis' teaching on the death penalty is a case in point. In August 2018 Francis amended the catechism – the formal document that summarizes Catholic belief and doctrine – to note that support for the death penalty was 'inadmissible' on the basis that it cannot now be considered consistent with Catholic teaching on justice and dignity. Previously the catechism had taught that the death penalty was perhaps possible in the most extreme of cases but placed such caveats around it that it viewed capital punishment as almost inadmissible in practice. John Paul II's document *Evangelium vitae* had moved significantly towards a statement of total inadmissibility. The reasoning offered by Francis for the new statement is threefold and relates to two main factors: the changing context of criminal justice as well as the teaching of the New Testament and early Church on justice tempered with mercy. Francis argues that the teaching of the catechism needs to reflect the deepening contemporary awareness of the dignity of the person, an increasing sensitivity to the limits of the role of the state in acting in cruel and irreversible ways in matters of justice, and the increased possibility for securing public order through detention that lessens any moral argument for killing as part of a system of criminal justice. The actions of the state must be framed and limited – from a Christian point of view – by the call to repentance, mercy and communion. Holding open the horizon of forgiveness within a system of public order trumps any desire for vengeance in the order of virtue.

The question of change and development is a complex and nuanced one and admits of few generic answers but rather careful historical tracing. In this light, in the course of charting the historical and theological development of the core principles of CST, in each following chapter I attend to questions of change and development.

CHAPTER 2
HUMAN DIGNITY
PHILOSOPHICAL AND THEOLOGICAL TRAJECTORIES

On the morning of Christmas Day 1944 Pius XII issued the latest in his series of Christmas messages addressed to the world at war. It is here, especially in the messages of Christmas Day 1942 and 1944, that he first deploys the language of human dignity as a category of defining importance for official Catholic social teaching (CST). Of course, the idea of human dignity can be seen as a crucial hinge for earlier Catholic social reflection, and it had become an emerging watchword for lay Catholic intellectuals and political activists on the political Left and Right in the 1930s. Its more systematic articulation as a principle and norm of the Church's emerging modern social doctrine begins in earnest and, not without coincidence, in response to the rise of the ideologies of fascism and communism, and the devastation of war.

Pius' message, read from the balcony of St Peter's on Christmas morning 1944, included this notable section:

> The holy story of Christmas proclaims [the] inviolable dignity of man with a vigor and authority that cannot be gainsaid – an authority and vigor that infinitely transcends that which all possible declarations of the rights of man could achieve. Christmas, the great feast in which heaven stoops down to earth with ineffable grace and benevolence, is also the day on which Christianity and mankind, before the Crib, contemplating the 'goodness and kindness of God our Saviour' become more deeply conscious of the intimate unity that God has established between them. The Birth of the Saviour of the World, of the Restorer of human dignity in all its fullness is the moment characterised by the alliance of all men of goodwill. There to the poor world, torn by discord, divided by selfishness, poisoned by hate, love will be restored, and it will be allowed to march forward in cordial

harmony, towards the common goal, to find at last the cure for its wounds in the peace of Christ.[1]

Pius XII connects the doctrine of the Incarnation to the notion of human dignity; he argues for the important role that a theological account of dignity can play as a discourse prior to claims for the rights of man; and he indicates the teleological structure of human dignity, which pulls us through history towards the peace of Christ. Here are three of the essential theological hallmarks of a Catholic theological interpretation of dignity.

In his Christmas message two years earlier, Pius had structured his text around a Catholic vision for 'The Internal Order of States and People'. Here he sought to address the grounds for 'integral peace', laying out what he believed to be the theological resources available for assisting in the moral, social and political reconstruction of post-war Europe. Eschewing the understandable desire for lamentation about the perilous state of things, Pius called instead for a determined focus on a plan for social regeneration according to his 'Five Points for the Ordering of Society'. Human dignity emerges as the central social-theological axis in this vision of regeneration. Using the analogy of stones laid to create a pathway, Pius identifies five facets of a political culture that builds the dignity of its people and thus enables deep and sustained social renewal: a formal espousal or recognition of dignity, a movement beyond liberal individualism towards a commitment to the defence of society as an intrinsic social unity, action to guarantee the dignity of labour, a restoration of judicial order and recognition of a Christian conception of the purpose of the state. He proposes that upholding dignity requires opposition to treating humanity through anonymous group identities: 'the herding of men as if they were a mass without a soul' – the recognition of personal rights to maintain and develop one's bodily, spiritual and moral life, a right to worship and to carry out religious acts of charity, to marry (or not) and to maintain family life, a right to work and a right to the use of material goods.[2] Pius is critical of impersonal mass responses – social 'herding' – which fails to see the particularity of the individual person and the intrinsic cohesion of the whole. As Christians we are called to follow

---

[1] Pius XII, 'Christmas Message, 1944', in *The Major Addresses of Pope Pius XII, Volume 1: Selected Addresses and Christmas Messages*, ed. Vincent Arthur Yzermans (St Paul: The North Central Publishing Company, 1961), p. 88.
[2] Pius XII, 'Christmas Message, 1942', in *The Major Addresses of Pope Pius XII*, Vol. 1, p. 60.

Christ in seeing the multitude and having pity upon them; however, Pius emphasizes that truly seeing the multitude requires a capacity to see and hear the unique unrepeatable person, an absolute in himself or herself. Elsewhere he sees this intrinsic unity-in-plurality in providential terms.

Any reader schooled in the Catholic social movements of the 1920s and 1930s will know that these ideas were not in themselves new to Catholic thought, although they were perhaps being put to a new or revised purpose. Pius emphasizes themes that would have been familiar to his hearers: the paternalist idea of an inherent organic social unity and the dignity of labour and family life. Nonetheless, Pius' messages represent something of a watershed moment in Catholic reflection on the modern social order. In the spring and summer of 1937 Pius' predecessor had issued two significant statements, *Mit brennender sorge* and *Divini redemptoris*. Both texts experimented with the language of dignity (and rights) as a foundational category for CST. Both proposed dignity-rights language as basis for rejection of the metaphysics of communism and fascism.

This use of language to critique both communism and fascism found its mirror or parallel in the equally experimental deployment of the language of dignity by European Catholic intellectuals on both the political and economic Left and Right in the 1920s and 1930s. Appeals to the language of dignity were as likely to be made by advocates of the social order focused on the Catholic family, private property and the corporatist state as much as those who were experimenting with the development of ideas of political federalism, organized labour and human rights. The appeal to dignity and rights as two categories to be thought together undergirded both kinds of Catholic political project.

Pius' Christmas messages are the moment when these innovations in mid-century Catholic social thought become more clearly the basis for a major strand of twentieth-century papal thinking. It is in the foment of the Second World War, rather than with the much-poured over texts of the Second Vatican Council of the 1960s, that Catholic thinking on dignity as a key social principle for political modernity comes to take its place centre stage. This is why I have begun this chapter with the less well-known radio messages of Pius XII.

Foundations: Secular and religious

Whilst we can be relatively clear that human dignity arose as a concept central to the Church's formal social teaching in the mid-twentieth century, there is much greater debate about the origins of the secular use of dignity as a key social and juridical concept. Scholars continue to argue over whether human dignity first became a driving cultural idea in the Middle Ages, the revolutions of the eighteenth and nineteenth centuries, as part of the anti-slavery movement, during the interwar years or as a post-war, post-Holocaust movement. Each theory has its proponents and detractors. It is not my task to settle such an argument here. What we can note, echoing Samuel Moyn's insights, is that the mid-twentieth century is a key moment when secular and religious movements simultaneously – and sometimes in dialogue – develop theories of dignity for political institutional use.[3]

Moyn argues for a direct line of influence from Catholic social thought to new constitutional and legal forms. He claims, for example, that the publication of *Divini redemptoris* offered fresh language to resolve theo-political dilemmas facing the Catholic drafters of the Irish Constitution of 1937, who eventually proposed the adoption of dignity as a conceptual part of the document's preamble. The 1945 UN Charter and 1948 Universal Declaration of Human Rights both adopted the language of human dignity as a conceptual cornerstone. Moyn argues that Pius XII's Christmas messages were key, enabling texts in this regard. In post-war Germany, influenced by both Catholic social thought and Kantian philosophy, the Grundgesetz or Basic Law gave the idea further liberal democratic constitutional form. Equally striking is Moyn's insight that the appeal of the idea of dignity lay partly in the world of political emotions; that the destruction of civil society and its institutions during the war had produced a kind of political and civic trauma that the concept of dignity, articulated by Catholic thinkers amongst others, spoke to.[4]

Jacques Maritain famously quipped that the great achievement of the Universal Declaration of Human Rights was to secure agreement on the use of dignity as a foundational value, but that such consensus held only for as long as nobody asked 'why'? Political philosopher Johannes Morsink summarizes three main (equally contested) answers to this question within Western thought.[5] The first answer is predicated on a directly religious

---

[3]Samuel Moyn, *Christian Human Rights* (Philadelphia: University of Pennsylvania, 2015). See chapters 1 and 2.
[4]Ibid.
[5]See Johannes Morsink, 'The Philosophy of the Universal Declaration', *Human Rights Quarterly* 6:3 (1984), pp. 309–34, and *The Universal Declaration of Human Rights: Origins, Drafting and Intent* (Philadelphia: University of Pennsylvania Press, 1999).

Philosophical and Theological Trajectories

justification: human dignity stems from the revealed teaching that we are made in the divine image. The second theoretical base is rooted in a more implicit religious account, drawn from either traditions that emphasize natural law or traditions that teach forms of deism: dignity stems from human beings' possession of reason, self-determination and conscience. This account works on the basis of analogical thinking about the relation of the person to a divine Creator and a universal capacity for rationality and self-reflexivity. A third foundational claim is evident in more materialist and Marxist accounts, which place the material basis of dignity, variously, in the inner freedom of the person, in the capacity of all persons to be moral agents and in the nature of the person as an end in themselves. It is interesting to note that societies adopting atheistic communism tend to make least use of the language of dignity. CST belongs most obviously to the first of these traditions of thinking dignity, although it affirms elements of the other two schools of thought.

Mette Lebech offers an alternative typology for differentiating traditions of thought on human dignity.[6] She suggests that there are four main schools of thought, relating to four main historical periods and four founding thinkers. She identifies Cicero with a classical approach to the question, focused on nature. This she calls the *cosmo-centric* approach. Thomas Aquinas is offered as the figurehead of the medieval approach, which he describes as *Christo-centric* and rooted in dignity defined in relation to Jesus Christ and relativity to a Trinitarian God. Kant represents modernity, producing an alternative *logo-centric* approach that prioritizes reason as the grounds for dignity. Her least obvious and perhaps most contentious choice is that of Mary Wollstencraft, author of *A Vindication of the Rights of Woman*, as representative of a nascent post-modern shift towards dignity understood as social acceptability and predicated upon ideas of social integration and participation. This she labels a *polis-centric* conception of dignity.

Lebech suggests that fragments of the classical, medieval and modern understandings of dignity are all present and traceable within the secular documents of the 1940s. The texts remain open to – without giving foundational authority to – the invocation of reason, nature or relativity to God as the basis of dignity in public discourse. Thus, following Lebech, it

---

[6]Mette Lebech, *On the Problem of Human Dignity: A Hermeneutical and Phenomenological Investigation* (Würzburg: Köningshausen & Neumann Press, 2009).

seems reasonable to say that the political reconstruction of the 1940s whilst embodying a secularized concept of dignity, in fact relied either implicitly or explicitly (depending on the context and the specific document under consideration) on a form of relatively open-textured secularism. This secularism was open-textured and porous insofar as its proponents and texts remained open to the possibility that individuals or social groups might reasonably hold to broadly teleological, including religious, concepts of both the person and the social order. This was a moment-in-thought that arguably has not entirely endured.

Theological anthropology as the hinterland to the principle of dignity in CST

Distinguishing between talking about the *principle* and the *idea* of dignity is crucial, Lebech argues. To talk about the *principle* of dignity is to note the sheer importance we wish to ascribe to the idea: it is something of pre-eminence or first importance, relating to the status we wish to give to this idea. To talk about the *idea* of dignity is to talk about a concept that has a history – and a complex and ambiguous one at that. We will reflect on dignity as a *principle* and dignity as an *idea with a history* in the following sections.

Any understanding of the principle of dignity as it appears in the encyclicals requires first an appreciation of the deeper ideas about personhood that underlie the texts of the CST tradition, a set of ideas that is often assumed as background rather than spelled out in systematic detail in the more pastorally oriented texts themselves. Whilst the idea of persona or personhood is traceable to Greek drama and Roman jurisprudence, St Augustine is arguably the first thinker to bequeath to theology a more developed use of the idea. As Joseph Ratzinger (later Pope Benedict XVI) notes in his extended essay on human personhood, early Christian readers of the Bible realized that to read these texts was to understand that events progress through dialogue between personae.[7] Ratzinger says that when we look carefully at Scripture, we realize that God speaks in the plural and speaks with Godself, thus we cannot

---

[7]Joseph Ratzinger, 'Retrieving the Tradition Concerning the Notion of Person in Theology', translated by Michael Waldstein, *Communio: International Catholic Review* 17 (Fall, 1990), pp. 439–54.

Philosophical and Theological Trajectories

interpret the Bible unless we have some kind of concept of persons. This concept begins with a God who speaks and human beings who are addressed and who are in turn drawn into responding to God and addressing each other and the whole of creation. Therefore, from the outset the person must be understood as a relation; and that being-as-relation draws the human person into forms of communion with God and with other creatures. She 'enters into unity with the one to whom [s]he is related'.[8] This leads Ratzinger to conclude that the best way to understand the heart of the concept of human personhood is to grasp that the person is an event of relativity. Whilst the human person is not a unity in multiplicity in the way we understand God to be, nonetheless the movement of relationality forms the basic and most fundamental context for human being.

Ratzinger's reflections centre on Christology: if the idea of the Father as Creator leads naturally to the idea of an 'I' and 'Thou' or 'you', then it is the persons of Christ and the Spirit that draw us as human persons more fully into our nature as part of a corporate body, creating a sense of being also a 'we'. Christ comes to renew in us our call to recognize ourselves as persons: the Incarnation performs a distinctly pedagogical function. However, to grasp what Christ has to teach requires us to remember that Christ is not a creature of exception (a crude superhero figure) but rather the fulfilment of what God intends for the human person, the new and the final Adam set amongst us, set before us. In this sense Christ opens up a space – the space of his own body – in and through which it is possible for us to gather in a new way as persons on the way to life in the Father.

This is a vision of the peace of Christ that Pius XII spoke of in his 1944 Christmas address with which we started this chapter. At the end of his reflections on personhood, Ratzinger makes one of the most striking and overlooked claims of his political theology: this Christian concept of God refuses the idea of monarchia or rule as pure singularity. Whilst antiquity 'considered multiplicity the corruption of unity', '[t]he Christian concept of God has as a matter of principle given dignity to multiplicity as to unity'.[9] To grasp personhood as simultaneously – and most fully – a movement of I, thou and we is to move as unique and singular human beings caught up in a movement of relationship – and falling away from relationship – within the plural but unified life of Father, Son and Spirit.

---

[8] Ratzinger, 'Retrieving the Tradition Concerning the Notion of Person in Theology', p. 445.
[9] Ibid., p. 453.

Towards a Politics of Communion

This is a helpful place to begin a consideration of the underlying theory of the person that CST rests upon because what Ratzinger articulates very clearly is a distinctively relational approach to the theory of human nature as *imago dei* based on a reading of Genesis. Other schools of thought focus on structural factors of human nature such as intellect or free will, and on biological factors or functional approaches such as the self-determining dominion of the human person in defining human uniqueness and personhood. To be clear: it is not that CST denies or deprioritizes these facets of being human, far from it, as we will see in a moment. Rather, these human characteristics are placed within the framework of a scriptural account of the drama of human relationality and the paradox of Creator–creature relationship in difference.

Drawing on Boethius' definition of the person as an individual substance in a rational nature, Catholic accounts of personhood emphasize free will, intellect, self-determination and the fundamentally social nature of the person. For this reason, we can affirm that CST draws from an approach to being human that sees the person as unique, unrepeatable, rational and free willing. Whilst CST considers an account of the rational free agent core to its understanding of dignity, the texts of the tradition also note dangers in placing too great an emphasis on function, structure, capacity or capabilities alone. Reason, self-determination and intellect become means through which we are invited to receive and enact the good, which is freely offered and communicated by God in creation. This is the life of being-in-relation to others that Ratzinger speaks of. According to this account positive freedom – the freedom to act to shape our lives – exists for the sake of human excellence: this excellence is understood as the fulfilling of our nature and a partaking in the life of paschal mystery and of communion.

We should note that this teaching is not driving towards a narrow moralistic idea of 'being good' but rather a more expansive vision of how we pursue the excellence for which we are made, an excellence which embraces – rather than takes flight from – the paths of finitude, failure and fragility. Thus, the notion of human excellence (as it pertains to talk of dignity) present in the texts of the CST tradition reflects the positive traits of sociality, reason, self-reflexivity, vulnerability, precarity and solidarity. Reason plays a crucial role in attaining such excellence by enabling us to recognize and name dignity for what it is, but reason alone will not ensure the protection of dignity in the world.

Nor does a description of the operation of reason capture the fullness of dignity as we apprehend it in the everyday world of the ordinary or the sublime. In shifting from a more general discussion of personhood to a consideration of human dignity, Lebech helps us to see a further, correlated point: whilst we rightly and necessarily look for rational and formal categories to finesse our account of dignity, we have to look elsewhere for the *content* of the idea of *being* dignified – to the world of affective relations, to our human experience of love, loss and friendship and the things we learn about ourselves as humans in these contexts.

James Hanvey expresses differently some of these same insights; he argues that three headings help us make sense of the distinctively Catholic hinterland to claims about dignity.[10] First, as much as we might begin feel the need to trace an account of dignity from the beginning of the scriptural story (Genesis), we must also begin our account of the nature of dignity with an appeal to the 'end' of the story: soteriology or a theory of salvation. Believing that we live within an unfolding economy of salvation shifts the way we see dignity: it is seen as simultaneously something we *possess* and something we *become*. Dignity is something we can seriously debase in ourselves or for others, but it is not something that we can fundamentally lose or become completely alienated from, for whilst dignity is something we can be said to possess it is not something that we ourselves found or guarantee. Rather, dignity is based on a gift given and is something capable of endless renewal through the same divine initiative. Thus, for Hanvey, explaining Catholic teaching on dignity requires an understanding of the 'social' doctrinal narratives of sin and salvation.

For Hanvey it follows from this foundation that dignity can never be thought of in solely individualistic terms. Developing on Hanvey's account we might say that dignity is both something we become and also something we are called to help others realize, including something we might be required to hold *in trust* for others through specific practices of care. *Entrustment* is a repeated theme in the formal tradition of CST and in the work of Catholic social theologians.

If this sounds a perplexing claim then it might be helpful to draw to mind the example of those who care for others in the context of a degenerative illness such as dementia or perhaps a less obvious example: the importance we tend to place on the dignified burial of the dead, especially in contexts where dignity in dying has been most obviously violated. Two examples

---

[10]James Hanvey, 'Dignity, Person, Imago Trinitatis', in *Understanding Human Dignity*, ed. Christopher McCrudden (Oxford: OUP, 2013).

bring this truth home. Fr Daniel Groody, an American Catholic priest and academic, works with activists on the US/Mexico border who are inspired by the work of mercy that commands Christians to bury the dead. The sole purpose of one of the groups he works with is to enter the desert in order to locate the bodies of migrants who have died en route to the US border and to reunite them with their families for a decent burial. The purpose of the group is to enact one of the Christian works of mercy: to bury the dead.[11] Social scientist Elena Fiddian-Qasmiyeh and poet and Palestinian writer Yousif M. Qasmiyeh write of the significance of family visits to cemeteries in Palestinian refugee camp settlements in Lebanon.[12] They write of the ritual importance of visiting the graves of ancestors in a refugee camp and note that such visits become ways to connect the living with the dead, as well as ways to dignify the still living to each other as they honour the idea of place, homeland, heritage, memory and communal identity. They are ways of practising into being a dignity denied to both the living and dead; in ritual and acts of care for the dead the fabric of dignity is rewoven. All three examples – the dementia sufferer, the migrant returned in death to their families and the graves of the displaced as animating points of dignity denied and re-founded – express dignity held in trust and underline the idea that acts that bear dignity are often complex covenantal acts of reciprocal gift exchange. Such acts are not simply performed on behalf of others but rather are ways that the carer or actor rediscovers or is returned to their own dignity through honouring that of another. These particular examples are also helpful insofar as they highlight the grounds for Lebech's insight that dignity is a persistently motivating, affective driver of human action: the repetition of the idea itself becomes a motivation for moral action.

Such examples also illustrate Hanvey's second 'theological' claim for dignity read through the Catholic tradition: dignity is understood as a *task*, as a striving for virtue and therefore as *an active social principle*. For dignity to be an active social principle requires individuals, groups and institutions who are willing to embody and espouse dignity as a structural practice and value. It needs to become both the ritual habit of a particular community

---

[11] See Daniel Groody, 'Crossing the Line: A Spiritual View of the US-Mexico Border', accessible at https://www.theway.org.uk/back/432Groody.pdf (accessed 1 February 2021).
[12] See Elena Fiddian-Qasmiyeh and Yousif M. Qasmiyeh, 'Refugee Solidarity in Death and Dying', accessible at http://refugeehistory.org/blog/2017/6/30/refugee-refugee-solidarity-in-death-and-dying (accessed 1 February 2021).

and part of its conscious memory. Theologically speaking, the Church ought to be such a community par excellence.

Finally, Hanvey claims that Catholic teaching rests on the belief that to talk about dignity is necessarily to confront *mystery*. This is the kind of claim that might well lead secular proponents of dignity to throw their hands up and exclaim the uselessness of religious accounts. However, such a claim is far from a philosophical or political dead end.

The claim that dignity is rooted in mystery calls our attention to several important and rich philosophical paradoxes thrown up in debates about dignity. As David Walsh argues, when we think about human dignity, we are being invited to contemplate a reality that we know and can speak about because it is constitutive of our own embodied experience, yet we are also being invited to reflect on something that, because we inhabit it and did not found it, we cannot fully know. To say that the person is made in the image of God is to say that the person is grounded in a reality that he or she both *is* and is *not*. It is also to say that the dignified human person is made in the likeness of something that has no likeness. In this light Walsh argues: 'It is a concept that says what we cannot fully say.' Likeness and difference relate to each other in an important way in a theological account of dignity. Such insights are socially and theologically significant, although they are the least well developed in the field of official social doctrine, tending as it does to steer away from negative or apophatic political theological themes.

Dignity in the encyclicals

As we noted earlier, whilst a key focus of *Rerum novarum* was the dignity of labour and the dignity of the worker, in fact the development of human dignity as a systematic first principle of the Church's social teaching emerges with greatest intensity during the period 1937 to 1965, beginning with Pius XI's 1937 *Mit brennender sorge* and *Divini redemptoris* and ending with the Second Vatican Council's document on religious freedom, *Dignitatis humanae*. The high point of the exegesis of dignity as first principle comes in the Christmas messages of the 1940s, *Pacem in terris*, *Gaudium et spes* and *Dignitatis humanae*.

In *Rerum novarum* and *Quadragesimo anno* dignity tends to be referred to as it pertains to the excellence of the human person in relation to the performance of particular roles or institutions: work, marriage and leadership through governance and so forth. It exists as a *corporate principle* of social life. These social roles are more than mere functions; they become part of the performance of personhood and the formation and expression of character: of individual character, and by extension over time, the character of groups or institutions. Dignity refers in some way to the status of the person and the excellence that attends them in their being *and* as their personhood relates to the performance of their social roles. Most of the references to dignity in the early social encyclicals relate, therefore, to the erosion of dignity in the context of capitalist industrial cultures and practices. The presence of this corporate emphasis on respect in relation to the status, being and role of the person in social context is an important and continuous strand of the Catholic social tradition. Nonetheless, the shift that occurs through the teachings of Pius XII is twofold. In the first instance, Pius moves CST towards deepening a personalist account of the inalienable rights and duties conferred upon the dignified human person. In the second instance, he continues to strengthen a corporatist account of dignity in its political as well as economic dimensions. The experience of fascism and war seems to bring this latent Catholic social insight into clearer relief.

The fruits of these mid-century developments are seen visibly in the developments of Vatican II. *Pacem in terris* issued in April 1963 by Pope John XXIII deploys the term 'human dignity' with much greater frequency than earlier encyclicals and in doing so gives the term some further flesh. *Pacem in terris* defines personhood in terms of the use of reason and exercise of free will and self-determination. This understanding is rooted in Catholic doctrine but viewed as available to all people through exercise of reason.

Pacem in terris also invokes a direct appeal to the role of a wider Christian revelation, which 'incomparably increase[s]' our valuing of dignity. This intensification in appreciation for dignity is Christological in character: for in Christ there is victory over death and a way to eternal life, and through grace we become God's kin. In this dual context – natural law and Christology – the document engages the newly emerging secularized use of the idea of dignity. Three paragraphs are devoted to noting general although not unconditional approval of the Universal Declaration of Human Rights: 'the document should be considered a step in the right direction', that is, towards 'the establishment of a juridical and political ordering of the world community'.[13] Its underlying philosophy is described as rooted

---

[13]*Pacem in terris*, §144.

in a recognition of personal dignity and the freedom of the person to seek the truth, to follow moral principles, to enact the duties of justice and to strive to lead a truly and fully human life. John XXIII seems to accept that there is room within the UN document for those who recognize morality as intrinsic and society as oriented towards the search for truth.

Pacem in terris is also of interest for its emphasis on dignity as the genesis of both rights and responsibilities. John XXIII emphasizes that being endowed with reason means that we can be held responsible for our actions. Because we have reason, we bear duties or responsibilities. Pope John's document therefore portrays a unique vision – Pauline and fraternal in emphasis – on the social body built up towards a unity-in-plurality through each person acknowledging, seeking to give expression to and living out his or her own rights and duties towards others. This is a profoundly social, interactive vision of dignity and responsibility. It does not presuppose homogeneity as a fact or a goal, nor propose easy agreement on moral norms, but it does propose a vision of personhood in which the struggle for truth and for opportunities to be formed in traditions of truth-seeking is of paramount importance. This is how he sees that truth will be sought and embodied in social life. This is not best understood as a riskily individualistic or relativistic stance but rather an exploration of personalist and Thomistic ideas in a now evidently pluralist social context. However, we should not miss the fact that in contrast to earlier social encyclicals, *Pacem in terris* continues Pius XII's journey towards the expression of a properly Catholic but far less hierarchical and paternalist view of dignity: the journey away from the organic fixity of *Rerum novarum* continues. *Pacem in terris* also continues the development of themes of dignity, racism and war begun in the letters of 1937 and the wartime messages. John XXIII talks of the 'natural dignity' of the person, which presupposes the equality of all and opposition to racial discrimination. The document also uses claims to dignity as the basis for calls for disarmament.

Of particular significance, given our earlier discussion of corporate and personalist accounts of dignity, is the continued presence in *Pacem in terris* of corporate ideas of 'dignity as office': once again the two traditions come to sit alongside one another. The encyclical still relies on the idea of the dignity of state officials derived from the sovereign authority of God, and its author also reminds us of the dignity of states (when viewed as meaningful political communities) and the danger of offending against the honour and dignity of a nation.

Towards a Politics of Communion

The promulgation of the Constitution on the Church in the World, *Gaudium et spes*, in December 1965 inaugurated perhaps the most extensive use in CST of dignity as a foundational social theory. The entirety of the first chapter of this major conciliar document is devoted to an exposition of human dignity. Mirroring the treatment of the topic in the later summary *Compendium*, the text begins with reference to Scripture. Drawing from Genesis and the Psalms, the Council argues that Scripture reveals a vision of personhood rooted in our capacity for knowing and loving God, created as stewards of a creation made to display the glory of the Creator (Ps 8:5-7). The root 'reason' for dignity discerned from Scripture is the call to communion planted in the human soul; human creatures alone are invited into this form of relation with the Creator. The human person is created in and for interpersonal communion, with liberty inclined towards the good but mysteriously also towards falling away into evil. Later in the document the Council Fathers note that this truth and the example of Christ's new law mean that forgiveness is a necessary social practice for the maintenance of dignity. We are called to reflect on the highest possibilities of the human vocation, as well as comprehension of the depths of human misery. Reflecting this paradox of human experience, the document opens with a striking reflection on the dual temptations to render personhood in either overly exalted or too despairing terms, both accounts bearing the falsehood of over optimism and unwarranted pessimism.

Drawing on classical theological themes the text teaches the unity of man, the unity of body and soul, the materiality of the human person and the consequent importance for Christian reflection and action of the bodily life. Intellect is presented as a sharing in the light of the divine mind, seeking its perfection in wisdom. Natural law (the guiding light of reason in us) is viewed as a guide not only to upholding dignity but '[to] obey natural law is to obey the very dignity of man'.[14] Freedom is central to this account of dignity, for dignity is something we achieve in free acts oriented towards the good; this is a crucial part of the dynamic process within history of restoration of the tarnished divine image. The Council Fathers are also quite concrete and specific in naming the conditions which 'insult human dignity' including subhuman living conditions, arbitrary detention, deportation,

---

[14]*Gaudium et spes*, §16.

slavery, prostitution, selling of women and children, poor working conditions and use of the human person as a tool for profit. Inequality is referenced as a threat to dignity – a theme Benedict XVI develops in *Caritas in veritate*.[15] *Gaudium et spes* also discusses the need for attention to the material conditions that produce a consciousness of dignity and insists that the protection of dignity requires institutions that take seriously an explicit orientation towards dignity. The document is thus marked, once again, by both personalist and corporate renderings of dignity.

Dignitatis humanae, the Second Vatican Council's Declaration on Religious Freedom also issued in December 1965, repeats the themes of preceding documents, placing emphasis on the dual pathways to knowledge of dignity: reason and revelation. The council proposes that the right to religious freedom has its foundation in the dignity of person – where the person is understood as oriented towards both the exercise of reason and an inclination to search for the divine. These orientations are constitutive of the human vocation. The Council Fathers repeat the intimate connection between notions of dignity, rights and duties, noting that 'being endowed with reason and free will' we are 'therefore privileged to bear personal responsibility'.[16]

This language should not be conflated too quickly with the duty and obedience language that we might associate with legal and political traditions that emerge from the divine right of kings tradition, which teaches: I am dignified because I am capable of duties. In formal CST the emphasis tends to fall the other way around: I have responsibilities because I am a dignified being, and the shape of these responsibilities, as Karl Rahner expresses it, is self-forgetting in love of neighbour. We have an inescapable responsibility for ourselves, which is simultaneously a loving responsibility towards neighbour. Finally, the text teaches that the meaningful development of human freedom requires the aid of education, communication, dialogue and mutual assistance: if we are truth-seeking and mutually interdependent beings, we require the institutional and communal means to pursue that nature without frustration and with aid.

The documents that followed from 1967 to the present have repeated these earlier teaching developments on dignity. Whilst there is little deep conceptual novelty, the later encyclicals are marked by an attempt to find

---

[15]*Caritas in veritate*, §32.
[16]*Dignitatis humanae*, §2.

fresh ways to present dignity in a compelling way. In *Populorum progressio* Paul VI offers the language of integral human development as the central key to exploring dignity. In *Sollicitudo rei socialis* John Paul II explains that attending seriously to dignity requires practices of solidarity, a commitment to the option for the poor and attention to structures of sin, ideas we will unpack in later chapters.

One of the most significant resources for the study of CST produced during the papacy of John Paul II was the *Compendium of the Social Doctrine of the Church*. This document develops the theological material presented in the first chapter of *Gaudium et spes* and represents perhaps the most systematic single summary of social teaching on dignity. However, whilst the *Compendium* offers a more systematic summary of social teaching as formal doctrine, it tends not to demonstrate any historical consciousness of the development of the teaching itself nor engage self-reflexively with the use of CST over time within the practical realm of social Catholicism. Thus, its uses are limited.

The *Compendium* repeats the relational definition of personhood made *imago dei* found in *Gaudium et spes*, neatly presenting distinctively human capacities for self-knowledge, self-possession and self-giving as the threefold heart of the matter. Personhood is again presented as most fundamentally a matter of orientation towards relations of communion rather than sameness or discursive agreement. In this light we are reminded that the language of covenant and communion, as well as sin and salvation, is basic to a Catholic social imaginary of dignity. Themes of plurality are also emphasized: the dynamic of difference and reciprocity is an image of God. The *Compendium* makes clear that this applies in the case of sexual difference but is a wider social truth not limited to sexual difference. This text also develops further scriptural reasoning for arguments positing the inviolability of dignity. The command to neighbour love in both Leviticus and Matthew is used as a justification for teachings on both the inviolability of dignity and the idea that dignity is best thought of as something entrusted. Finally, the *Compendium* bears the hallmarks of a trend or turn in John Paul II's papacy towards a marginally less anthropocentric ethic of dignity and care. The text notes that teaching on dignity, relationality and communion implies a care entrusted in relation to all creatures/creation. Insofar as there is any conceptual novelty in the handling of dignity it lies, perhaps, here.

Benedict XVI does not make especially novel use of teaching on dignity per se in his social teaching; however, his encyclicals do mark a shift towards greater awareness of the way that biomedical and technological change impact theories of dignity and personhood in potentially very significant

Philosophical and Theological Trajectories

ways yet to be theorized by CST. He argues dignity can no longer be thought of as merely a social question but must also be conceived as a wider anthropological one, in which what it means to be human is perceived – or acted upon – as malleable. In this context he warns against materialistic and mechanistic approaches that can attend these developments. He also notes the importance of negotiating, and where possible agreeing upon, fundamental narratives of the human good as the basis for the development of just social structures which support dignity.

The early stages of Francis' papacy have seen a return to more frequent use of the language of human dignity. He has used the language of dignity often in his response to the situation of refugees and migrants and also in the context of a creation-wide ethic of care. In *Laudato si'* Francis emphasizes the dignity of the human species as a whole and the dignity of the person as it relates to the environment (which can also be conceived of as dignified). He also connects the dignity of humans to the suffering of animals. Thus, Francis intensifies John Paul II's turn towards a less anthropocentric account of dignity. For the age of the Anthropocene he proposes a dialogical, dramatic and mystical relation between creation and human creatures. Manifesting his liberationist influences, Francis has also focused much more on the connection between the idea of dignity and the manner in which we practise or perform social teaching: he has emphasized the need for proximity to those who suffer, for a culture of direct encounter between – increasingly estranged – human persons as the basis for dignity and social transformation, although it remains unclear how such *pastoral* proximity might lead to a greater *theological* proximity as a hallmark of CST itself. Francis also focuses on foregrounding the dignified human person as a contemplating being in search of transcendence. The practice of contemplation becomes core to his notion of right relation. In *Fratelli tutti* he describes at some length the politics of *indignity*. These relate to a wider analysis of a culture which sees some human life is disposable (he singles out migrants, the disabled, the unborn and the elderly in various of his addresses and in this document); and he implies that upholding dignity involves a constant struggle.

Evaluating the encyclicals

A number of things are worth noting about the emergence of the idea of human dignity in these various papal texts. The first is that the founding texts of the modern social encyclical tradition tended to focus slightly more on economic than on political concerns. However, the wartime period in the 1930s and 1940s witnessed intensification in thinking about freedom and justice in the context of the social and political order, states and democratic systems. It is also the period during which the Catholic Church begins to think constructively (rather than merely negatively) about Catholic theories of constitutionally liberal states. It is out of the crucible of this theo-political reflection that human dignity emerges as a key, sustained category of Catholic social reflection.

The second thing we might notice is that this turn towards the political enables CST to recognize and more clearly articulate a dual focus in its teaching on dignity. The earlier encyclicals – *Rerum novarum* and *Quadragesimo anno* – imply and repeat the well-established idea that we should respect the dignity of specific human roles, groups and tasks, and the dignity and stature of human nature as such. These insights relate primarily to the nature of work, craft and family and the corporate nature of being human. In placing emphasis on these elements of social life the encyclicals convey a dignity that relates to rank, title, task – the dignity of office, of institution or of labour itself. What happens anew from the 1940s is that CST develops a more consciously personalist account of human dignity. It is the paradox of the acknowledgement of the modern state as well as the seeming failure of liberal democratic states in the face of rival forms of totalitarianism and war that seem – at least in part – to impel this move. David Kirchhoffer argues that we can discern a theological shift in the documents of the Second Vatican Council from a primarily supernatural account of the dignity of man in relation to divine origin to arguments for the dignity of man revealed in the natural, social order. He argues that this should not be seen as supplanting the supernatural for the natural, but rather as a greater focus on the supernatural and natural grounds of dignity that can be perceived through use of reason and can be shared as the basis for a secular civic order.

Whilst this is clearly a genuine dimension of the conciliar teaching on dignity, we should also note that the exposition of the idea of dignity during the period 1937 to 1965 is clearly rooted in scriptural reflection. Pius' own appeal to dignity in his Christmas messages begins with Revelation and is codified in simultaneously biblical and doctrinal terms: social dignity is interpreted in the light of Incarnation and the narrative of Bethlehem and Nazareth, leading to Jerusalem. *Gaudium et spes* repeats this movement. The turn towards a more detailed account of the natural grounds for dignity should not be interpreted as a turn away from the sources of Revelation.

A further striking feature of the teaching on dignity developed during this high period is the invocation of dignity and rights as mutually intersecting categories, from Pius XII's message onwards. It is sometimes suggested that CST prefers the language of dignity to rights, even that we might read dignity and rights as discourses existing in fundamental tension. Whilst this chapter will not explore this knotty debate in detail, it is worth noting that rights language tends to sit alongside dignity language throughout the encyclicals. This is true in *Rerum novarum* and especially so in the development of dignity language between 1937 and 1965. In this initial framing of the principle of dignity in 1942/4, personal rights, construed as positive freedoms to corporal, spiritual and moral life, religious education, the performance of works of mercy and integrity of family life, are foregrounded as a necessary path to dignity. The language of dignity and rights is concerned with a world of mutual obligations, positive liberties and gift exchange. It is a receptive and performative language.

A consistent critique of Enlightenment traditions of thinking about rights is framed more obviously in terms of a challenge to the core account of liberty or human freedom that underlies certain claims to 'the rights of man'. Whilst this critique of liberty shifts subtly over time, it is perhaps most accurate to suggest that the critique is anthropological – that is to say, concerned with the fundamental stories which the Enlightenment tells about autonomous personhood. Rights discourse in CST does not emerge from theorizing a social contract but rather from what we can know about the ontological status of the person. Rights are not created through social recognition, as a fabrication of the body politic (the artistry of politics as Thomas Hobbes would have it), but rather are recognized socially through law and contract as part of a pre-political truth or order of nature that can be discerned independently of the foundation of the state and must be honoured by the state. This is not to deny the possibility or function of a social contract but is to challenge the idea that this is the foundation or artifice upon which rights rest. It is perhaps fairest to say that the encyclicals propose a distinctively and simultaneously communitarian and personalist theological reading of the relation of rights to dignity.

In summary, we have seen that CST places emphasis on corporate and personalist aspects of dignity, on the intrinsic moral basis for teaching on dignity and the inherently social nature – a sociality extending to all creaturely life – of any claim to dignity. The texts expound a supernatural theological foundation for teaching on dignity, but precisely because of the nature of this theological foundation – the kinds of claims it makes about reason and faith, nature and grace – the tradition teaches that God's providential ordering of creation means that dignity can be recognized, upheld and striven for by those of other religious and non-religious world views. This does not mean, however, that Catholic perspectives on dignity might not be used to critique and challenge other secular or religious accounts of dignity, even if such detailed engagement has been a much weaker element of the tradition to date.

Some problems with the idea of human dignity

Whilst social encyclicals, papal addresses and letters offer a powerful articulation of dignity as a foundational social principle, and the second half of the twentieth century witnessed significant investment in the idea of dignity as a grounding for secular law, the idea of dignity remains strongly contested in both secular and theological debate.

Critiques of the notion of dignity range widely. Dignity, some argue, can be presented in unhelpful ways as an absolute limit in arguments about ethics. Others claim it is often used as a conservative principle deployed to prevent radical change. Conversely, it is criticized as an idea that lacks a single core meaning and whose vagueness leads either to a social idea with no real bite or to an idea which ends up being filled up and co-opted by a range of (potentially troubling) ideological positions. Examples from the mid-twentieth century are given as evidence for this final claim. The appeal to dignity made by authoritarian regimes in Austria, Portugal and Vichy France tended to stress the social importance of corporate groups and deployed the idea to lay emphasis on the social obligations of the individual to the social whole. In doing so such regimes sacrificed the personalist dimension to dignity. These examples are used to demonstrate that simply deploying the language of dignity in public discourse guarantees little and moreover requires much critical enquiry.

Questions are also raised about the extent to which dignity can function as a universal, trans-contextual principle. In the first instance this concern relates to differences in cultural norms and fundamental world views. Critics suggest that, paralleling Maritain's insight into the development of the Universal Declaration of Human Rights, common agreement is either impossible or would be weak and unstable. However, the point might also be made in a more historical-juridical form. Dignity can be demonstrated to be an idea that functions quite differently across legal and political traditions; thus, talking in the abstract and metaphysical sense often misses the significance of negotiating dignity in concrete historical and societal terms.

In his compelling work on the moral foundations of UK human rights law, Benedict Douglas notes a contrast between concepts of legal personhood at work in political systems that view being human primarily in terms of duties and systems that view personhood in terms of freedom for self-determination.[17] In political systems founded on the idea of the person as capable of bearing duties, and deriving from a philosophy and theology of the divine right of kings, the idea of dignity has tended to be less present in formal legal reasoning. However, in political systems founded after the revolutions of the eighteenth and nineteenth centuries and grounded in appeals to positive law, dignity has re-emerged as a normative pre-political foundation for the lawful actions of individuals and the state. For this reason, appeals to dignity ground the work of the European Court of Human Rights but not the work of UK courts interpreting the Human Rights Act: the UK legal system has thus far not thought in these terms. In cases as diverse as the so-called right to die or those of migrants seeking rights to entry, to family reunification or to remain in their country of residence, such differences in views of legal personhood make a material difference. Ultimately, as Douglas argues, they betray an 'unrecognized conflict' between different conceptions of what it means to be human.

Finally, living in the age of the Anthropocene, others are more concerned to note the largely anthropocentric use of the idea of dignity in Western discourse. Whilst Francis has begun to talk about the dignity of creation as a whole, this is not yet a fully developed theme.

Talk about dignity may not be going away anytime soon, but engaging with the idea of dignity requires proper attention to a range of historical as well as metaphysical particularities. One reason why paying attention to critiques of dignity matters is that dignity functions as both a coherently reasoned first principle for public debate and an idea that has been put to very particular and powerful historical use. There is a danger of being seduced by the world of social encyclicals into abstract high theory and forgetting the power of social movements and charismatic individuals

---

[17]Benedict Douglas, 'Too Attentive to Our Duty: The Fundamental Conflict Underlying Human Rights Protection in the UK', *Legal Studies* 38 (2018), pp. 360–78.

who are able through the power of repetition in a particular moment to use language as a potent force to shape history. We have noted already that the 1930s and 1940s provided a particularly resonant context for the development of the principle of human dignity. Samuel Moyn showed that Pius XII's Christmas messages became powerful utterances that influenced the post-war history of European institutional reconstruction and impelled new forms of constitutional and political structure. Popular level journals such as French twentieth-century philosopher Emmanuel Mounier's *Esprit* carried these ideas into popular debate. This period also saw the development of quite different – even conflicting – political uses of the term. On the one hand the idea of dignity provided the basis for Christian democratic legal constitutions and movements in interwar Ireland and post-war Germany, emphasizing the dignity of the person as the fundamental basis of democratic legal structures and state action. On the other hand, the idea of dignity was also used as the basis for corporatist-influenced constitutions in Portugal (1933) and Austria (1934) and was deployed by the Vichy regime, with very different outcomes. In each of these cases we can trace a set of direct Christian and Catholic social-theological influences.

Addressing the relationship between the idea and its material social and political history helps us to notice one of the features of CST: its lack of formal historical self-reflexivity. CST tends not to reflect on the relationship between its own development as a form of high – if largely pastoral – theory and the historical experiments that it both gives rise to and implicitly draws from. This history of the interconnection between social Catholicism and CST is left largely unthought by the Church. Strangely – although for different reasons – the same pattern tends to be traced in writing on the Catholic social tradition by historians of ideas, social historians and theologians. We tend to treat, by and large, *either* social Catholicism *or* Catholic social theory. Nonetheless, to those who wish to analyse the coherence of the idea itself such historical consciousness is important. Whilst it is not the task of this book to offer a full account of this complex social history, it is important to at least note the complex interaction between the papal documents and political action. This helps us to grapple with the complex and ambiguous history of appeals made to the idea of human dignity as a Catholic social norm.

In partial service of this wider task, as we find dignity invoked both across the texts of the Catholic tradition and in secular legal and political usage it can be helpful to ask: to what and to whom does dignity attach? As David Kirchhoffer asks, 'what do the proponents of a particular position mean when they appeal to human dignity. What is it about human individuals that these proponents hold to be most worthy of respect? What is their "scale of values"? In so doing, one can uncover the values and goods that a particular position believes are at stake in a particular ethical issue'.[18] Scholars of Catholic social thought have yet to attend to this in any detail, although Karl Rahner's work on dignity from the 1950s and Anglican-Catholic theologian John Milbank's more recent critique draw us in this direction.

Milbank has contributed to this discussion on key questions about the secular tendencies to frame dignity in a form of liberal individualism that is fundamentally tied to modern capitalism. He proposes that a deep theological account of dignity – a re-sacralization of the concept – is needed as a resistance to both authoritarian appropriations of dignity and those made in the name of a market-driven liberalism. His answer to Kirchhoffer's question would be to point to the over-dominance of a Lockean tradition that proposes: 'I am dignified because I own myself.' Milbank argues that such a liberal account of dignity (of course, there are other liberal accounts available) ensures the protection of the economic interests of one class against another and by implication fails to foster the necessary links with solidarity and the common good that CST demands. He proposes that the secularization of the concept, which weaves together a plurality of traditions, leads us to experience a fundamentally unstable alliance between dignity and rights, an instability hidden under the veneer of a secular, pluralist consensus. Milbank argues that only an account grounded in a Catholic Christian narrative of personhood as relationality can challenge a secular politics of dignity that tends – by its very anthropology, the structure of its politics and institutions – to work in favour of those with capital. Whilst Kirchhoffer defends the possibility of liberal pluralism as a hospitable environment for CST, drawing on the same teaching Milbank largely denies this possibility.

Nonetheless, it is striking to me that it remains more valuable to ask 'what does each account of dignity – secular or religious – imply ought to be protected, transcended, overcome or resisted?' than to ask merely

---

[18]David Kirchhoffer, 'The Roman Catholic Church on the Secularization of the Concept of Human Dignity', *Louvain Studies* 39 (2015–16), pp. 240–60, p. 259. See also David G. Kirchhoffer, *Human Dignity in Contemporary Ethics* (Amherst: Teneo Press, 2013).

'can religious ideas be used in a secular age'? Questions about protection, transcendence and resistance operate as categories in *both* religious *and* secular contexts. Both contexts share an appeal to at least *implicitly* theological ideas. A deeper historical perspective can enable us to map the gradual migration of the idea of dignity from a social sphere where human persons were thought of in terms of both individual personal consciousness and overlapping and contested social roles – a realm of corporate identities, responsibilities and roles – to a space in which we seem to understand transcendence and identity in terms of the self-willing, choosing agent who is self-defined, interior and self-giving. Mette Lebech marks something close to this movement in her four typologies of dignity that we explored earlier: from classical to post-modern. What is at stake in debates about dignity is, thus, perhaps less an antagonism of religious-versus-secular perspectives and more competing accounts of personhood and transcendence in secular and religious guise.

The necessity and difficulty of talking about dignity

In his critical defence of the idea of dignity Michael Rosen argues that the question we should ask is not primarily 'should we accept or reject the idea of dignity' but rather 'why is the idea of dignity so deeply morally entrenched'?[19] As James Hanvey argues, 'it is part of our own search for the meaning of who we are and the sort of societies we are called to create'; the idea of dignity is both our 'terminus a quo and our terminus ad quem', our point of origin or the limit from which we set out and our goal, the limit towards which we reach. As resolutely secular thinkers Kateb and Rosen argue, dignity is a concept that acts as an important placeholder, an idea that remains something of a philosophical mystery but which can help us keep focused on both the idea of corporate human stature and the idea of individual status: the moral significance of being human and human beings.

It is the concrete conditions of daily life that beg the question of dignity and the dialogical texts of the tradition that posit a foundational but incomplete answer. The answer is incomplete for two main reasons: because history itself is incomplete and because the history of dignity requires us to

---

[19]Michael Rosen, 'Dignity: The Case Against', in *Understanding Human Dignity*, ed. Christopher McCrudden (Oxford: OUP, 2013), p. 153.

take possession of ourselves for the sake of an end for which we are made but which lies beyond the self; to recognize that the pursuit of this end will require losing ourselves in the divine mystery and in the complexities and ambiguities of neighbour love. The urgency of the question and the value of the idea emerge from our concrete reflections on the complexities and contradictions of our participation in, exclusion from and resistance to the many forms of human isolation, affliction and degradation. Christianity is a religion of the Cross; it does not refuse the question of affliction but places it at the centre of its concern. As Karl Rahner argues, the 'sign of a genuine humanism is a man nailed to a Cross', and we might add, risen again for the sake of all. To posit dignity as principle and practice, it is necessary to continually ask the question of affliction: to inquire as to its presence, meaning and its overcoming. To refuse to ask questions about suffering and affliction is to deny dignity. It is worth noting that those who wish to close down the human dignity conversation – to render the very talk of dignity (and even affliction) superfluous – have often been those regimes most dedicated to the erasure of the very characteristics of self-determination and positive freedom (to be exercised as solidarity with others) that lie at the core of CST's teaching on dignity. Primo Levi's account of the deliberate manufacture of the degradation of Auschwitz prisoners paraded for visiting groups of German youth who were instructed that the subhuman appearance of the incarcerated men confirmed their animal status is a powerful example of such a process of thought in action. To ask the dignity question is to do something that is implicitly necessary to our nature and to the excellence for which we are made.

This is the value of the continued use of dignity, despite its metaphysical and political ambiguities. It continues to be a way to beg the question of suffering and injustice as a loss of the goods and excellences we seek; a placeholder that forces the difficulty of definition and the openness of constructive response to become a beginning-in-the-middle rather than an end of the ecclesial or civic conversation. The incompleteness, breadth and mystery invoked by any genuine consideration of the idea of dignity does not necessarily see us collapse back into passivity or resort to authoritarian social norms. Rather, as human rights thinker Conor Gearty argues, these features of dignity can impel us into the space of political love: deliberative, plural spaces through which we can wrestle with our commitments and responsibilities towards taking up the task of human relating. These need to be spaces in which we can talk of the affective side of human relations, the relations of love, loss and friendship which enable us to give content to the idea of dignity. Such a notion of dignity is intrinsic *and* performative. This helps us to see the integral connections between the idea of human dignity and the idea of the common good.

The common good will be the next major principle to which we will turn in our evolving story of CST, but before that, in the next two chapters I explore two different facets of the teaching of human dignity in the CST tradition. In Chapter 3, I explore the long CST tradition of reflection on the theme of human migration and its connections to the principle of human dignity. In Chapter 4, I consider the distinctive and incomplete teaching on social and structural sin as it connects to themes of human dignity and indignity.

CHAPTER 3
HUMAN DIGNITY AND
(FORCED) MIGRATION

Before its demolition in 2016, in the sheltered entrance to the Eritrean church in the 'Jungle' migrant camp in Calais stood a striking picture of Christ. The large painting by a young Eritrean refugee and former camp resident depicts Christ knocking on the door of the soul. It is a peaceful, bucolic image, framed by rolling green hills and (fittingly) the sea. Inside the building, constructed from timber and sheets of thick grey plastic, another image drawn from the book of Revelation is reproduced. It is an image of war, a depiction of the cosmic battle between good and evil recounted in Revelation 12. The war that breaks out in heaven draws the Archangel into combat. The forces of evil are overcome through the power of God and the authority of his Messiah, and the devil is cast down to earth. With foreboding it is foretold that earth and sea shall be disturbed by the one who brings conflict in his wake. The Christian response to this victory of good over evil is rejoicing in the victory won for the peaceable Kingdom and a prayer made through the saints for the endurance, wisdom and faith needed to negotiate the conflicts that blight the earth before the final judgement. In the image painted for the little Calais church, the Archangel Michael holds a sword in his right hand and in his left hand the scales of justice.

When asked why the book of Revelation had been such an important source for the paintings in the makeshift 'Jungle' church, the refugee pastor explained to me that these were the scriptural texts that had spoken most powerfully to the church community's experience of being migrants in Calais.[1] This religious art represented an act of careful communal theological reflection and interpretation.

---

[1] This conversation, and visit to St Michael's Church, occurred during a visit I made to the Calais camp in 2015 with a joint British–French delegation of parliamentarians and Catholic social action agencies, hosted by Caritas France (Secours Catholique) who had a permanent

The use of the narrative from Revelation and the creation of religious artefacts representing the experience of migration situate the church community in Calais within a long, enduring tradition of Christian reflection on the experience of human migration. The texts of 1 Peter represent the early Church reflecting on its own experience of migration and turning this experience into reflection on the very nature of the Christian life itself: a call to recognize Christian selfhood as defined by the experience of pilgrim stranger-hood, the condition of being *parakoi*.

As Marcella Althaus Reid argues, the Scriptures provide a profound resource for forced migrants not only because they offer transcendent accounts of human meaning that foster hope and resilience, as well as ethical norms for the treatment of those on the move, but also because they narrate experiences of terror, affliction and torture, representing and describing what can – and often cannot – be said in the face of such devastating experience.[2] From the prophetic narratives of Jeremiah and Ezekiel formed in the context of expulsion and displacement, via the alluring account of Ruth who is often portrayed as the ideal immigrant, to the complex and disturbing purity narratives of Ezra Nehemiah, the Scriptures offer – in a significant literary mix of poetry and prose – a complex, multifaceted response to the reality of migration. Nonetheless, whilst the Scriptures are utterly suffused with the themes, experiences and memories of migration, no single 'ethic' of migration can be drawn from their pages. Migration in the Scriptures remains an experience to be narrated, tarried with, interpreted and reinterpreted in light of both God's promises to His people and the struggle to make sense of the varying human experience of migration in any particular era.

Any, even cursory, reading of Scripture and Christian history offers a sober reminder of the complex connections between faith and migration and suggest that we should seek to avoid constructing a simplistic, heroic or demonic, account of the relation between Christian faith and migration. Religious belief can act as a cause of forced migration as much as it can be a reason for persecution, death or exile; and whilst it can also be a

---

base inside the camp, until its demolition. A full report can be found here https://www.abc.net.au/religion/fierce-and-fragile-life-report-from-the-calais-jungle/10097220 (last accessed 6 January 2021).

[2]Marcella Althaus Reid, '*Veníamos de Ostras Tierras*: A Reflection on Diasporas, Liberation Theology and Scotland', in *God in Society*, ed. William Storrar (Edinburgh: St Andrew Press, 2003).

likely source of vital assistance, resilience and protection for those on the move, it can also compound various vulnerabilities faced by migrants. The history of Christian politics includes both the development of sanctuary provision and the establishment and policing of ghettos. Most recently, it has included the revival and morphing of white Christian supremacist politics in North America and Europe, with migrants chosen as a particular focus for expulsion and social hatred. It has also included difficult realities for Christians in parts of the Middle East, whose forced migration brings with it a historical shift in Christian presence and the dispersal of ancient communities.

All this is important context for understanding both the genesis of Catholic social engagement with migration and the evolving context addressed by the framework of principles it comes to propose. Whilst, as we have noted, we tend to date the origins of modern Catholic social teaching to 1891, in fact migration has been a significant theme for the Church's wider social reflection since at least the 1850s. The migrations out of Europe to the Americas during the mid and late nineteenth century resulted in the need to make provision for the religious and pastoral needs of Catholic migrants. This led to the formation of religious orders, perhaps most notably in the field of ongoing migrant care the Scalabrinians, whose mission was to ensure practical care and religious instruction for those on the move. The next major impetus for a development in CST on migration came with the internal and external displacement of Europeans following the Second World War. In 1952 Pius XII promulgated his apostolic constitution on forced migration, *Exsul familia*. The title comes from the reference in the first line of the document to the exilic journey of the Holy Family with the child Jesus. An indication of the significance of this document can be found in the archives of religious orders, whose publications indicate that they, above all, acted quickly to translate the document into the grassroots language of the communities in which they lived and worked. In this vein the Daughters of Charity produced a striking statement in a 1955 edition of their monthly Paris-based publication *The Echo*, presenting a clear engagement with Pius XII's wartime addresses we discussed earlier and bearing the influence of Jacques Maritain's personalism and the newly promulgated teaching of *Exsul familia*:

> Respect for the human person is much spoken of today. People talk of it constantly. The Declaration of the Rights of Man have been drawn up at Geneva at the United Nations Associations, and it is

most amusing to see certain signatures such as that of Russia, who sign for the respect due to the human person (!), side by side with those of certain Western nations. There is a certain tragic humour in this, but definitely respect for the human person is much spoken of in the world nowadays. Do we truly show respect of the human person in our institutions and in our manner of treating those who come to us?.... Try to understand the stranger, the immigrant who does not belong to your land, who is not one of 'my own people'. Try to understand him, not only in his speech and manner ... but also try to understand him equally in the working of his mind. Understand the very depth of his character and do not be too quick to say, as we sometimes do 'Look at such a family. If I was in their place, I would not follow their example. I would act differently and know how to get along much better.' You ought to say instead on the contrary: 'If I was in their place – but I am in my own home instead – am I sure that, driven out of my home, I should do.' WE must take into consideration where the immigrant has come from, his loneliness, his difficulties in making friends, and his despondency.... There must be no mass treatment or no treatment of all on the same level, if there is to be respect for the human person. Each must be allowed his personality.[3]

Acting as a text that would shape official CST on migration for half a century until the papacy of John Paul II, *Exsul familia* complemented the pastoral emphasis of earlier teaching by offering the beginnings of a more systematic and biblical framework for reflection on migration. Drawing on the theological trope of the Holy Family as both the models and protectors for all displaced persons, Pius devotes much of the heart of the document to an outline of the practical history of Christian ministry amongst migrants. Emphasizing the initiatives of the institutional Church that have aimed to increase the security and dignity of migrants, Pius argues for the reception and integration of migrants within stable political communities and strongly against their encampment. The document argues for provision of culturally and linguistically appropriate pastoral and spiritual care and for an awareness of ways to mitigate the dreadful choices that face the destitute. *Exsul familia* was shaped by a European context in which, seven

---

[3] I am grateful to Dr Susan O'Brien for a copy of this text from the archives of the Daughters of Charity.

years after the end of the war, refugee camps for the displaced remained in Europe. Those displaced by the war and without a way to return to their country of origin – Armenians, Poles, Latvians, Estonians, survivors from concentration camps, Greeks, Russians, Ukrainians, Czechoslovaks, Yugoslavians – were held in camps in Germany, Austria and Italy until as late as 1959.

The next major migration document issued by the Vatican took another fifty-two years to arrive. Issued by Cardinal Hamao and Archbishop Marchetto, president and secretary of the Vatican's Pontifical Council for the Pastoral Care of Migrants and Itinerant Peoples in May 2004, *Egra migrantes caritas Christi* repeats many of the earlier themes but updates the Church's social teaching to reflect the changing nature of migration flows. The increasingly global and South–South, as well as more politically (and religiously) contested South–North and East–West, migrations that shaped the turn of the second millennium lead the document's authors to note that any theological discussion of migration must be properly global and take account of ecumenical and interfaith perspectives. Addressing the question of the causes of migration in a more systematic and structural way than previous documents *Egra migrates caritas Christi* calls for the intensification of a search for a new economic order that better represents the universal destination of goods and therefore reduces the need for survival migration. This is a key moment in a developing line of CST on migration, which would be picked up with new emphasis in Pope Francis' social teaching on migration fifteen years later. It is worth pausing to note its significance.

Whilst the Church has made a particular priority for refugees who lack the most basic provision of state protection, it has addressed questions of migration in economic as well as political dimensions. It refuses a binary between the economic and political whilst still distinguishing between different kinds of moral and political claims for membership. Questions of economic migration can never be separated from political considerations, and claims for political membership relate to a wider set of economic questions – insofar as 'economic' is understood in its widest sense as connected to questions of access to, exchange and distribution of, goods. Political questions of refugee flows are therefore not disconnected from fundamental questions about the wider communication of material, as well as moral, goods. For this reason, human dignity and the universal destination of goods are repeatedly foregrounded as the two foundational principles for guiding a Catholic social response to the ethics of migration.

Towards a Politics of Communion

The universal destination of goods (discussed in Chapter 11) concerns the access to and use of the material or created goods of the earth: to use Thomas Aquinas' language, it concerns their 'communication' in the community of persons, especially to those with particular needs. Justice takes in this full dimension of the communication of goods. CST teaches that the created goods of the earth are intended to meet the needs of all, are sufficient for this task with good stewardship and should be justly accessible and distributed in this light. Created goods exist to be communicated, shared, used, enjoyed and to flow and move through the human community. To do so they require care, management and distribution with a mind to individual need and common benefit (these two are not seen to be in tension but as dual considerations). Thomas Aquinas argues that we possess a two-fold 'competence' in relation to material things. First, a competence to care for goods and distribute them justly. Second, a responsibility to use and manage created goods for common benefit and to alleviate or meet need. Aquinas emphasizes that this does not mean all must be held in common with no individual ownership, but rather all forms of use and ownership must be attentive to the responsibility to ensure common benefit and the welfare of all. Deciding how this use and management, care and distribution happens is not legislated for in natural law but is a rational process to be managed through political negotiation and decision-making. Thus, access to goods, the exchange and communication of goods, relies on a healthy political process. Once again, we see that a separation of the economic from the political in pure terms is not possible; these are necessarily interdependent, interwoven processes to secure the good. And we can note that the politico-economic migration of goods through a community, itself a good, is core to how we think about the flow of human migration.

When Aquinas uses this language of communication, implying flow and movement of material goods, he is drawing on, and adding to, the moral and social teaching of the early church fathers on material goods. He quotes Sts Basil, Augustine and Ambrose, balancing and mediating their teaching on private property and the common benefit to be derived from created goods. CST draws on, indeed directly quotes elements of this teaching, to insist that where the foundations of the social order do not respect this principle, political and economic instability ensues. A failure to ensure the universal destination of goods, especially with a priority to those with particular need, is a factor that drives forced migration – economic and political – and also forms a context for the reception or failed reception of migrant claims for membership and protection. This failure also has a history; it exists as a structural reality that shapes moral agency and requires more than a presentist analysis. It is also clear from the encyclicals, with increasing emphasis from the Second Vatican Council social documents onwards, that the scale on which we consider the pattern of the destination of goods is global. De facto in a globalized era, the community through which goods flow is global, with little respect for political borders, although still affected by the dynamics of sovereignty.

Interestingly, *Erga migrantes caritas Christi* also notes the important internal social dimensions of migration for the Church as a social body. The document repeats earlier teaching on the need for appropriate pastoral and missiological provision for migrants but also names internal challenges for the order of the Church itself as it negotiates the relations of different Catholic cultures brought together in new forms of interaction and division in local and national church contexts. The pluralism question relates to the life of the Church as a migrant body as much as to the secular *polis*.

Erga migrantes caritas Christi also delivers a much more explicitly eschatological and teleological framework for social reflection on migration. Faith is said to discover or encounter itself through its engagement with a social 'other' in a special way in migration. Faith becomes itself in both the prophetic act of denunciation of the forms of evil that manifest in survival and forced migratory experience – deportations, dispersals, exploitation and criminalization – and the revelation of exile as our condition and salvation as our yearning. The authors of the document argue that any reflection on the meaning of migration from a Christian point of view must take as its end point (and work back from) the ultimate purpose of human relations: the call to universal communion.

Given the natural law flavour of much of the official CST tradition, it is interesting to note that reflection on migration from the 1950s onwards begins with a distinctive (although arguably not unproblematic) biblical theology. *Erga migrantes caritas Christi* begins with themes of Exodus and Covenant, reminding the Church that we continue to live out of the exilic memory. The prophetic tradition is drawn upon to offer a model of social critique as well as a vision of hospitality and care for the stranger and the oppressed, and to remind us that God chooses the displaced to be difficult messengers of a mysterious truth. We might note in passing that CST does tend towards some proof texting in this regard – for example, nothing is said about the difficulty of interpreting what the divine message might *be* in these contexts, or about contrasting biblical texts which appear to suggest we should embrace borders and boundaries between self and other and thus dissolve our relations with foreigners and strangers.⁴ Understanding the difficulty and mystery of the divine self-communication through the stranger is the territory that CST hints towards but has yet to more fully explore.

The doctrinal focus of *Erga migrantes caritas Christi* starts with the idea of the Incarnation as a concrete migration of God through human history. It notes that the earthly ministry of Christ is dominated by the exilic motif.⁵ This exilic motif embraces the role of Jesus as the Incarnate Word, as itinerant preacher and as migrant who transgresses the logic of death and thus transforms the boundaries of human suffering. There are also strong soteriological themes drawn from both the book of Revelation and a particularly strong emphasis on the Pentecost narrative. Ethical import is drawn from the Pentecostal character of the Church as an ever more vast and varied intercultural society, held in a relationship of fraternity, communication and difference. The pluralism of Pentecost – a community of difference in communication – becomes, by analogy, a model for all forms of human community.⁶

There is a notable widening of social and theological analysis of migration in the encyclicals issued by John Paul II and Benedict XVI. Both refuse to treat migration as an issue separate from discussion of nuclear weapons, food security, ecological change and increases in global inequality. Consequently, they exhort the world to closer analysis of and better responses to the deep roots of displacement – including proposing the need for new systems of international governance.⁷ John Paul II judged that the impact of globalized migrations was to intensify patterns of socialization and argued for greater

---

⁴For a developed biblical theology of migration, written by an Anglican theologian, see Susanna Snyder, *Asylum Seeking, Migration and the Church* (Aldershot: Ashgate Press, 2012).
⁵See discussion of the biblical context and figure of Christ as refugee in *Erga migrantes caritas Christi*, (Vatican City: Pontifical Council for Pastoral Care of Migrants and Itinerant Peoples, 2004).
⁶See Catholic Bishops Conference of England and Wales document, *The Dispossessed: A Brief Guide to the Catholic Church's Teaching on Migrants*, 2004.
⁷In *Sollicitudo rei socialis*, John Paul II reads forced migration in the context of a logic of death which refuses to engage deeper moral reflection on social changes which could lead to a 'more human life' and true human development. He notes the continual failures to seek a peaceful international order and suggests that the isolationism of modern states mitigates against solutions to systemic issues which lie at the root of migration concerns. See §23–5. In Benedict XVI's *Caritas in veritate*, migration figures in the sociological context of all that challenges authentic human development and the opportunities for cooperation and solidarity which exist within the universal human family. See ibid., §62.

Human Dignity and (Forced) Migration

attention to be paid to the moral corollary of such increased socialization: practices of human solidarity. Interdependence is a fact but solidarity is the moral perspective we use to interpret the meaning and possibility for virtue implicit in this fact. Solidarity is not, then, simply a duty to respect rights in the face of globalized movements of people but calls for a deeper form of social creativity, in which our communities are re-fashioned as socialization gives way to concrete forms of solidarity. Benedict XVI focused particularly on the duty to create well-ordered systems to manage migration flows. He argues in light of his reconsideration of the principle of subsidiarity that the appropriate level for moral engagement with this issue is now between states at an international level:

> We can say that we are facing a problem of epoch-making proportions that requires bold, forward-looking policies of international cooperation if it is to be handled effectively. Such policies should set out from close collaboration between migrants' countries of origin and their countries of destination; it should be accompanied by adequate international norms able to coordinate different legislative systems with a view to safeguarding the needs and rights of individual migrants and their families, and at the same time, those of the host countries.[8]

Natural law principles and migration

As might be expected given the historical importance of Catholic natural law thinking for developing international jurisprudence on questions of borders, sovereignty and membership, the post-1891 documents develop a distinctive set of natural law principles aimed at informing questions of law and politics in the context of migration. In some ways, the teaching on migration has been far more specific and concrete than on many other social questions.

The Church begins by proposing the right not to be displaced or emigrate – a 'right to remain'.[9] This principle is less an Enlightenment natural right and more an expression of a Thomist Catholic political anthropology. If the human

---

[8] *Caritas in veritate*, §62.
[9] See *Erga migrantes caritas Christi*, §21, summarizing *Gaudium et spes* §65.

person is by nature a social and political creature, oriented to negotiating their own good as part of a common good, then achieving basic human flourishing implies the need for membership of a functioning political, economic and ecological community. Thus the 'right to remain' stems from an emphasis on the social, political, economic and cultural (including religious) protection due to the person who belongs to a covenantal community. On a Thomist model of government this implies a governmental responsibility to protect citizens and de facto members from harm.

However, given the frequent failures of political community, a second principle is that where there is conflict, persecution, violence, hunger or an inability to subsist or thrive, the individual has natural and absolute rights to migrate and a natural right to seek sanctuary and membership within an alternative 'safe' political community.[10] This principle honours the agency of migrants in seeking their good as a matter of natural law.

CST proposes a transcendent humanism, which recognizes that the well-being of the person is tied to the good of both the local and national bounded community but as an expression of a meaningful global citizenship, or universal belonging to a human family without borders. Thus, CST is neither straightforwardly a pro- or no-border ideology. Where borders provide for stable community, the fostering of culture and a stable practice of hospitality they may well serve the common good. However, they exist always in relation to an ethical norm and transcendent reality that forms a prior law: that of human universal belonging and siblinghood.

The task of government, then, is to evaluate claims for membership based on a balance of local and universal duties to the common goods, including based on a consideration of the universal destination of goods. This implies a duty to think through issues of integration and the universal distribution of goods, such that cultures are enabled to engage dialogically and labour markets act to support the basic needs of migrant and settled populations in a non-exploitative manner. As Pope Francis makes clear, if dialogue and exchange of goods and values are key parts of a humane approach to migration, then access to decent work is a key facet of how we engage in social dialogue.[11] The right to migrate implies, then, a third

---

[10] See Vatican II, *Gaudium et spes*, §65.
[11] This same emphasis on contribution and belonging emerged from interviews and fieldwork I conducted with the refugee community at the Jesuit Refugee Service UK, findings published as For Our Welfare and Not for Our Harm (https://www.jrsuk.net/for-our-welfare-and-not-for-

principle: a moral requirement placed upon existing political communities, especially the most materially privileged, to receive migrants and hear and assess with justice their claim for admission, transit or membership.

This teaching is nuanced by a fourth principle: the (imperfect) right of a sovereign political community to regulate borders and control migration. In CST borders are conceived as a relative good and recognized as legitimate only insofar as they protect the common good of the established community and are porous and humane, enabling the established community to enact its duty or obligation to offer hospitality and recognize its part in a common good that lies both within and beyond itself. Political communities are invited to include within the exercise of sovereignty the establishment and oversight of just measures for those who arrive seeking sanctuary and for effective global governance, to minimize and accommodate forced migration flows. Contra forms of politico-economic discourse which imply that the duty of hospitality weakens sovereignty, sovereignty and hospitality emerge in CST as mutually implicating. Legitimate sovereignty in CST is exercised always with reference to three prior principles: the universal destination of all goods, recognition of prior and inalienable moral unity of humankind, and the requirement to regulate borders according to basic conditions of social justice.[12]

Finally, recognition of the social and political nature of the person implies a need for migrant integration as full and dignified members of a community and therefore a shared responsibility (of migrants, civil society and the state) to enable the meaningful social, economic, civic, political participation of migrants in the 'host' community.[13] To fail to do so offends against the requirements of contributive and social justice, the universal destination of goods and the basic teaching on dignity as an active principle. The model for sociality is one of participation, communication and mutual enrichment within a shared social space. This vision does not capitulate to a model of integration rooted in the assimilationist logic of market and state but rather takes as its form the Pentecostal ecclesiology noted earlier: a logic

---

our-harm/) and acted as the basis for a second report on CST and asylum policy: https://www.jrsuk.net/wp-content/uploads/2021/04/Being-Human-in-the-Asylum-System_JRS-UK_April-2021.pdf (last accessed 21 April 2021).

[12] See Benedict XVI's *Caritas in veritate*, 2009, §62.

[13] See John Paul II, *Message for the Day of Migrants and Refugees*, 2001, §3. See also, on the question of just legislation to enable integration and participation in host communities, John Paul II, *Laborem exercens*, 1981, §23.

of encounter, participation and communion, seeking to foster a genuine human plurality within a harmonious whole.

Pope Francis and migration

Pope Francis' papacy has coincided with an intensification in patterns of global migration. This is represented in both a rise in the numbers of internally and externally displaced persons and an increased politicization of the issue of migration. Francis has chosen to make both the practical questions attendant upon forced migration and the new ideological and political focus on migration more generally, central to his papacy, producing an unprecedented volume of teaching on the subject through homilies, addresses and public statements. In tune with a pontificate that has made gesture such a central part of its teaching, Francis has made physical journeys to the heart of the geopolitical sites that most represent Europe's struggle with migration questions – in particular, to the shores where migrants arrive by sea and to in-country holding facilities.

In choosing to make repeated pastoral visits to centres of reception and detention, Francis seems deeply aware that migrants seeking entry to Europe find that many of the fundamental challenges to dignity in the migration process occur now in the spaces between states – both at sea and in the spaces of encampment and transit that we have created within nation states, where normal law is often suspended and where the border appears suddenly in the midst of ordinary interactions to secure rights to remain, lodge, work and receive education and health care. As Kristin Heyer argues, Francis understands that the theological-political dynamics of contemporary migration questions are about more than border fortifications and entry criteria.[14] In *Fratelli tutti* Francis addresses the ideological barriers to ethical migration, naming isolationism and populism as ideologies that have increased cultural hostility and fuelled public policies that have proved deadly to migrants in transit.

The experiences described by contemporary migrants indicate that the failures of nation states to provide well-ordered and just processes for

---

[14] See Kristin Heyer, 'Walls on the Land and in the Heart', Berkley Forum Blog, accessible at https://berkleycenter.georgetown.edu/responses/walls-on-the-land-and-in-the-heart-fratelli-tutti-and-migration (accessed 5 April 2021).

reception, handling and later integration do not simply impact the dignity of individual migrants but also create a pervasive culture which affects the overall possibility of a just outcome. This insight and experience are echoed in Francis' analysis of social sin and its structural manifestation as a barrier to hospitable and just cultures. Justice and hospitality emerge as co-dependent, interrelated realities rather than simply separate categories. Partly for this reason, Francis has refocused the Church's migration teaching on contexts of local humanitarianism and civil action, rebalancing the heavy emphasis on global political actors in Benedict XVI's social teaching and positioning the Church as itself a critical local actor. Francis has turned the focus of moral agency back to the local, emphasizing the local as the embodied context in which the universal finds its expression.

Francis' best-known address on migration, prior to his more extensive treatment in *Fratelli tutti*, was made during a homily on the island of Lampedusa in 2013. Here he placed the wider political dynamics that shape the migration experience in the context of Christian narratives of creation, fall and redemption.[15] Francis begins with a reflection on the first two questions which God asks humanity in the Scripture: Adam, where are you? Cain where is your brother?[16] Francis interprets these passages as stories of human disorientation, of the first signs of a tendency in humankind to lose our place within creation, to lose our orientation as creatures towards a Creator. Thus, to Fall is to be disorientated, to lose our bearings. It is striking that Francis juxtaposes an account of the risk of the disorientation of the 'settled' in relation to the orientation of the displaced. In order to identify what might be going wrong in a failure to respond adequately to the challenge of the displaced, we must first see our own disorientation. Francis roots this disorientation not only in a classic account of the Fall but also in the particular conditions of late modernity. In various different addresses and homilies, Francis roots indifference to migrants in a culture of individualism, which he thinks breeds a sense of anxiety and cynicism, in a capitalist market culture which reduces people to narrow economic value and in a culture obsessed with what he calls well-being. He argues that our own transient cultural ways – what he later, echoing Simone Weil, calls an

---

[15]Text of Pope Francis' homily: http://w2.vatican.va/content/francesco/en/homilies/2013/documents/papa-francesco_20130708_omelia-lampedusa.html (last accessed 22 April 2015).
[16]The narrative of Cain and Abel is a trope to which Francis has returned on numerous occasions, most recently in his treatment of integral ecology in *Laudato si'*.

uprootedness in culture – breed indifference towards truly transient people. Thus globalization, which creates ironically the cultural transience of the settled, produces too, as its by-product, the globalization of indifference. In turn, the by-product of the culture of indifference is that we ourselves become anonymous – we seem unable to understand ourselves as named, particular and responsible in relation to named, particular and responsible others. 'The globalization of indifference makes us all "unnamed" . . . without names and without faces.'[17]

Francis emphasizes that this dynamic of anonymity is the opposite of the Creator–creature relationship. The relation of Creator to creature involves a mutual cycle of naming, including a clear command that we are named and related beings, called to account for other named beings. This approach to the ethics of migration deals less with the external borders of the nation state (although it has clear implications for thinking about borders) and more with the prior internalized borders of the human will as the 'matter' at the heart of theological ethics. These two sets of borders – one geopolitical and one interior to the human self – are read as inherently related to each other. This is why, for Francis, a theological-political account is necessary to make sense of the deepest dynamics of the migration question and experience. A solely external political analysis fails to grasp the relation of the soul and the city that drives the politics of indifference.

In *Laudato si'*, Francis connects the failure of law to respond to the pressing challenges brought by increased forced migration to a deep failure in civil society. Indifference to migrant suffering suggests not just the failure of government, or the individual, but – of central concern to CST – 'the loss of that sense of responsibility for our fellow men and women upon which all civil society is founded'.[18] This logic is expanded in *Fratelli tutti*. What we have lost is a social commitment to the idea of fraternity – to seeing all people as a single human family, and the earth as our common home and a fully common and social ethic that embodies this. In both documents he emphasizes the contemplative and mystical roots of this teaching and thus the pathway back into a more adequate fraternity. On the one hand, contemplation is the capacity to sit with the beauty and the relatedness of all things in creation and in Christ; on the other it is – in this light – a willingness to look reality in the face, to

---

[17] See link to Lampedusa sermon in note 15.
[18] *Laudato si'*, §25.

be unafraid to sit with the suffering of others and oneself. This kind of attention to reality – to the graced nature of the world and to the weight of suffering and negation – is extremely demanding, and it is not aided by a culture of 'well-being' that seeks to avoid being weighed down by suffering with others.

Using something close to Augustine's description of the two cities – earthly and heavenly – Francis offers a strongly eschatological dimension to the idea of social contemplation. Contemplating the life of the New Jerusalem – a community for which we are destined but which is also present in the historical here and now through the pilgrim community of the faithful – allows us to see the life of the earthly city differently. Contemplating a perfected community, of which we are members in time and for eternity, enables a vision of value and truth that breaks into the pervasive culture of indifference. The 'fruits' of this contemplation are a spirit of dialogue and encounter. This dialogue and encounter are the basis for a new creativity: new forms of service, justice and love that the Spirit can inspire. Through openness to this, including when such engagement is interfaith, the Christian encounters Jesus Christ. This is the flesh on the bones of Francis' call to see 'fraternal communion' as the end goal of the ethics of migration and the vision behind his notion of social friendship developed in *Fratelli tutti*.

Francis' teaching offers a more overtly place-based vision of migrant response that his two predecessors, emphasizing the constantly interconnected relationship of the local and the global, the particular and the universal, mediated through the action of the embodied moral agent, committed to the process of becoming a neighbour, whether migrant or 'host'. *Fratelli tutti* and Pope Francis' interview-based book produced during Covid-19, *Let Us Dream*, provide an important insight into Francis' wider metaphysics, within which he situates the migration question. Francis notes the productive and necessarily tensive relationship between the poles of the global and the local, the universal and the particular, the part and the whole. Drawing from his unfinished doctoral work on the German priest-philosopher Romano Guardini, Francis explains that here he found the language to contrast two movements of conflict: one oppositional, one relational.[19] The oppositional mode of conflict he names as contradiction. Contradictions (*Widersprüche*)

---

[19]Pope Francis, *Let Us Dream: The Path to a Better Future*, ed. Austen Ivereigh (London: Simon & Schuster, 2020), pp. 79–81. A more detailed account of Guardini's influence over Francis'

manifest as two opposite positions, one of which is a negation of the other and which therefore requires choice. This is the case in the opposition between good and evil, right and wrong. These are not positions to be mediated or dialectically engaged, for one has substance, the other does not. There is no productivity in the tension. By contrast, contrapositions (*Gegensätze*) are productive tensions between two 'living polarities'. The relation of the global to local, horizon to limit, part to whole are given as examples. These are not either/or choices or inherent oppositions, but difficult, productive relations to be laboured at by the time-bound, time-gifted creature. Lazy, manipulative, mediocre thinking reduces contrapositions to contradictions – hence much of the political malaise of our own times. Rather, the difficult labour that must be engaged (and not evaded) is to listen, discern and wait upon the tension in the hope of a common discernment, across differences, of the goods that must be retained in each. In this situation the paradox is one of both limitation (the limit of another, who rightly make a call on me) and excess or abundance (the possibility of an overflow of love, meaning, grace, reciprocity). Rather than imagining a Hegelian dialectical synthesis, the suggestion is that the tensive relationship becomes one of overflow, like a dam bursting, as the tension becomes fruitful. This is about more than cognitive resolution or mutual accommodation.

Francis uses this kind of thinking about tensive relations and productive conflicts that can be mediated by social dialogue to open up new ways of thinking about the supposedly oppositional relation of the migrant as a figure of the global and universal to the local. The question is not the austere 'how many is too many/enough' or 'who takes precedence'? This is the either/or, the mediocre shift from contraposition to contradiction. It is misrecognition in action. The question is one of a mutual, challenging becoming, in which difficult reality gives way to something new. The Spanish translation of *Fratelli tutti* makes much clearer than the English that the path towards a politics of communion is one of tensive struggle, in which goods need to be wrested from the difficult sites of history. What makes the difference is the contemplative gaze which precedes the engagement with difficulty: the choice to receive the world as graced, gifted, covenanted, shattered and redeemed. It is the social imagination and the openness to a transcendence beyond the willing self, which enables a community of difference to know

---

thought can be found in Chapter 3 of Massimo Borghesi, *The Mind of Pope Francis: Jorge Mario Bergoglio's Intellectual Journey* (Collegeville: Liturgical Press, 2017).

the difference between contradiction and contrapositional realities, and to remain patient with the task of labouring at each. Inherent in Francis' account of migration is, therefore, a kind of political mysticism.

In the fourth chapter of *Fratelli tutti* Francis argues for both concrete practices of welcome, protection, promotion and integration, and a wider disposition of reciprocity, gift exchange and gratuitous openness to others. This openness is fed by rootedness (this is the tensive relation of the local and the universal): open cultures provide for rootedness; uprootedness by contrast produces closed and narrow cultures. This openness fosters, and is fostered by, social dialogue. Two facets of Francis' teaching on social dialogue are worth noting. Francis proposes that cultures are by themselves both of value and, taken in isolation, incomplete. They express truths but do not complete the truth and of course may also badly lose their way and stand in need of renewal from within and without. Encounters between cultures through migration are part of how we experience and develop a fuller knowledge of truth, and part of the cycle of necessary renewal for cultures that manifest a tendency to fallenness. However, Francis does not have an abstract or solely personalist or individualist account of how this social dialogue takes place. He roots the possibility of social dialogue in access to work, land and lodging, and sees it expressing itself in something like a synodical process. These are the ways that we come to have a social stake, to form the basic bonds that move us towards a constructive common project. These are the material conditions and contexts for social dialogue within a living community, open to both its past and its future, and able to get to grips with the reality of its present.

Francis also updates the Church's social analysis of contemporary migration trends and integrates the principles of CST into this picture. He proposes that the key causes of contemporary displacement are armed conflict and social violence, poverty, economic crisis and exploitation, ecological change and climate vulnerability, political instability and corruption. He proposes that the current practice of border closing can itself constitute a form of cooperation with moral evil when shown to lead to intensification of the criminal exploitation of forced migrants and a cycle of death. He repeats that the only possible ethical response to migration flows is solidarity.

In *Fratelli tutti*, fraternity and social friendship are seen as the core practices that enable the re-founding of civil society as well as the founding of a better politics, acting as the antidote to indifference and individualism which the document identifies as the core viruses which cripple the social body. In a range of speeches and addresses, Francis argues that fraternity can take on structural forms through coordinated national, regional and local action, including an expansion of humanitarian corridors and visas, and community sponsorship. Francis also updates and expands the natural law principles outlined by his predecessors. He does this in two ways. Following the motif of his pontificate he presents the principles in more accessible and concrete form. He simplifies the natural law teaching described earlier into 'four verbs': to welcome, to protect, to promote and to integrate.[20] 'Conjugating these four verbs is a duty', writes Francis; to do so is 'a duty of justice, civility and solidarity'. He defines welcome as the provision of safe and legal programmes of reception, providing personal safety for arriving migrants and access to services. Protecting implies availability of relevant and accurate information, defending basic rights independent of legal status and a special duty of care for child migrants. Promoting is defined as ensuring the conditions for migrants to develop according to their own needs and capacities and those of native citizens. Francis places greater emphasis than his predecessors on the duty of state and civil society to promote mutual integral development of migrants and citizens and to facilitate new forms of sustainable hospitality. Supporting integration implies providing opportunities for intercultural encounter and active citizenship.

To understand what Francis means here requires us to recall what solidarity stands for in CST. It doesn't mean a weak universal benevolence but rather a structural orientation towards ensuring the dignity and development of the human person. In the same spirit Francis criticizes what he sees as reductionist views of human personhood that dominate debates about migration: persons are reduced to economic, legal and political aspects. Such reductionism offends against the principle of human dignity and is most visible in debates about legal and illegal migrants and when deciding national priorities for legal immigration pathways. Francis repeats both the paternal and fraternal corporate themes of earlier CST, emphasizing the particular threat to the family posed by current migration patterns shaped through inadequate or hostile policies. The separation of families, the increased risk of exploitation arising from the closure of borders, the failure of dignified reception processes and the inherent trauma of forced migration are all noted as threats to the dignity of the family.

---

[20] *Fratelli tutti*, §129.

Human Dignity and (Forced) Migration

The moral framework through which Francis views migration continues to be that of the natural mobility of humankind and (without fundamental contradiction) a natural search for rootedness, and a common life through which the human person comes to self-knowledge and fulfilment. We are built for both settled rooted lives and a life that exceeds this in cultural exploration and exchange, as well as love and service, and which comes to be dependent upon such exchange and service when uprootedness tears the soul from its setting. Francis continues to teach that even when migrant journeys are brought about by loss, disaster and evil God finds ways to wrestle blessing. God's commands to love of neighbour require an openness to cooperate with that process of wrestling blessing from loss, beauty for ashes.

Further challenges

Whilst Pope Francis' teaching on migration has received unprecedented attention both within and beyond the Church, significant ethical debates about how to respond to migration as a key sign of the times remain. Such debates include questions about the ways in which capitalist market systems interact with migration flows, concerns about how migrant communities can best be assisted to access rights and dignity, foster resilience, participation, justice and possibilities for moral agency and self-determination in community. CST needs to develop a framework of thinking about migrants as not merely a threat, burden or dependent suffering victims but as interdependent moral agents with citizens, all seeking particular kinds of goods. These goods are both material and moral, and claims to them need to be negotiated in community. Equally, questions of the moral purpose of borders, the principle of free movement, relations of labour to capital in markets where migrant labour is either used extensively or denied entirely and the moral function of citizenship within nation states all remain to be addressed more fully. Francis has moved CST closer to thinking about social conflict and conflicting claims than his predecessors, but this is not yet a fully developed theme.

Paralleling Francis' own attention to the local, development policy makers have also turned towards embracing local forms of humanitarianism (the localization agenda) and become more interested in partnerships between state and faith-based organizations to deliver effective relief and development at a local level. This creates a new interest in, and possibility for, engaging the distinctive Catholic tradition of teaching and practical provision for accompaniment and advocacy on migration matters.

Forced migrant communities whose political capital seems low remain overlooked and therefore draw little interest or resourcing, most obviously the largest forced migrant population of internally displaced persons in the global South. Both liberal and authoritarian states are currently moving towards increased use of detention and destitution as formal techniques for deterrence through the creation of so-called hostile environments. Questions of forced migration are not merely reducible to the political and economic, to the realm of the natural. They relate also to the relation of natural and supernatural, to questions of meaning and transcendence as they are found within the frame of the immanent. Liberal systems have not dealt well with the questions of culture, religion, identity and meaning that attend contemporary migration flows – beyond narrow questions of rights. These are sometimes presented as pre-political questions, but they are increasingly politicized and require urgent cogent responses and frameworks for public engagement. Given its emphasis on the co-belonging of the religious and social dimensions of everyday life, CST ought to be well placed to respond, engage and challenge a myopic form of liberalism that struggles with the transcendent, religious, theological and spiritual.

CHAPTER 4
HUMAN DIGNITY AND THE QUESTION OF SOCIAL AND STRUCTURAL SIN

An important and distinctive debate in late twentieth-century Catholic social thought concerned the meaning and usefulness of the newly minted terms 'social sin' and 'structural sin' as ways to describe processes of contemporary dehumanization and as a threat to human dignity and justice. This is distinct theo-political language adopted by Catholic social teaching as core to its social analysis, rooting the tradition in a fundamental account of sin and salvation as historical social forces. In the context of the rising theological and political prominence of liberation theologies in the late 1970s and early 1980s, this debate became a contested and difficult one internally for the Catholic Church. Whilst these concepts are now core to the canon of social teaching, they remain only partly clarified, with an important – if often unacknowledged – legacy for the Church today.

The rise to prominence of ideas of social and structural sin happened in the context of the development of Latin American liberation theologies. In documents published as a result of their gatherings in Medellín and Puebla (1968 and 1979) and most recently in Aparecida (2007), the Conference of Latin American bishops (CELAM) argued that sin resided in the social and cultural systems, structures, institutions and practices of a society, and that such structural manifestations of sin have an impact on the moral subjectivity and agency of all members of a social body. Social and structural sin takes the form of active injustice, lack and 'disvalue' and becomes hard-wired into the practices of a society.[1] This disvalue comes to be felt as an everyday social force acting upon and within the life of

---

[1] Kenneth Himes defines social sin as 'the disvalue . . . embedded in a pattern of social organisation and cultural understanding'. See Kenneth Himes, 'Social Sin and the Role of the Individual', in *Annual of the Society of Christian Ethics*, Vol. 6, 1986, pp. 183–218. See also Daniel Finn, 'What Is a Sinful Social Structure?', *Theological Studies* 77:1 (2016); Neil Ormerod, *Creation, Grace and Redemption* (Maryknoll: Orbis Books, 2007), pp. 47–66.

an individual and restricting the space for free action and for necessary humanizing experiences of love and justice. Crucially, such a force operates without an obviously blameworthy or traceable single human actor. This sin becomes the sin of a whole society and especially difficult for those with various forms of privilege to grasp and accept. The dispossessed – as the primary material victims of this sin – become the 'experts-by-experience' in matters of structural sin and thus its primary teachers.

The Latin American bishops and leading advocates of theologies of liberation argued that social sin, present at every level of a material culture, was a crucial block not only to earthly justice but also to the communication of the promise of salvation. Thus, social and structural sin was seen to have a multi-layered theological significance. Whilst the CELAM bishops did not use such language, what their documents articulated was a communitarian theology of sin and salvation as it pertained to questions of dignity.

To grasp why these ideas emerged as they did, becoming a matter of considerable debate and contestation amongst scholars and authors in late twentieth-century CST, it is important to attend to the kind of theological landscape out of which this debate emerged. The turn towards the historical and material had been a key feature of the work of European theologians and thinkers of social Catholicism writing in the mid-twentieth century. The move away from a neo-scholastic tradition of theological manuals that summarized Church doctrine as a series of principles for Christian living and towards a more textual, historical and narrative approach led to new articulations of social Catholicism. Whilst the nouvelle théologie of Henri de Lubac sought to emphasize the role of the Church as a social community embodying the relational and structural practices of an alternative social polity, fellow French thinker Emmanuel Mounier sought to articulate something close to – what would become three decades later in the work of liberation theologians – an account of social sin.

In his critique of modern industrial society Mounier wrote of a necessary distinction between *actes de violence* and *états de violence*.[2] Mounier argued that capitalist industrial systems could be seen to create states of violence in which whole societies lived with – and gave tacit support to – a continually enacted state of violence mediated through market forces. Mounier wrote of a pervasive 'established disorder' that the Church and social Catholicism should resist. Mounier's work, itself influenced by the

---

[2]Emmanuel Mounier, *L'egagement de la foi* (Paris: Parole Silence, 2005).

Human Dignity: Social and Structural Sin

poetic social mysticism of Charles Péguy, influenced the work of a range of Catholic social activists, including, through Peter Maurin, Dorothy Day and the nascent Catholic Worker Movement.[3]

The turn towards the language of structural sin in theologies of liberation was not, then, entirely novel but rather had its precursors in mid-century nouvelle théologie and personalist movements. Nonetheless, the reception of such mid-century European thought into the canon of official CST proved limited, and it would be the landmark texts emerging from Latin America that would both develop this language in new directions and, crucially, press the structural point home and onto the agenda of the authors of the official CST tradition.

The second feature of the theological landscape worthy of note concerns responses to developments within the canon of CST itself. With the mid-century theological turn towards the historical and material came the decline of the more abstract, static and organic view of the social order that had dominated the early phase of neo-scholastic, pre-Vatican II CST. Pius XII had moved the papacy away from this earlier conception of social order and towards a participatory, less hierarchical and more socially dynamic reading of order. The unitive focus or telos of the social order remained, but a more negotiated and participatory ethic was foregrounded. Both *Lumen gentium* and *Gaudium et spes* sought to offer an alternative theological and ecclesiological world view in support of these shifts. Nonetheless, this move appeared to many at the CELAM gatherings to be incomplete. Whilst not disputing the final eschatological goal of reaching a unitary society, the path to such a reality felt to those speaking and writing out of a Latin American context to be a much more conflictual, oppositional and agitational reality than either the nouvelle or personalist theologians, or the papacy, seemed able or willing to grasp.[4] This is an insight that Pope Francis, shaped by theologies

---

[3] For material on the influence of Mounier, see François Duchêne, *Jean Monnet: The First Statesman of Independence* (New York: W.W. Norton and Company, 1994); Douglas Brinkley and Clifford Hackett, *Jean Monnet: The Path to European Unity* (London: Macmillan, 1991); John Hellman, *Emmanuel Mounier and the New Catholic Left 1930-1950* (Toronto: University of Toronto Press, 1981). For further context, see also Michael P. Fogarty, *Christian Democracy in Western Europe 1820-1953* (London: Routledge and Kegan Paul, 1957).

[4] It should be noted that the CELAM texts of Medellín, Puebla and Aparecida do not express only a theology of liberation, but as many commentators have noted in fact integrate at least three parallel social ecclesiologies. On Medellín, see William Cavanaugh, 'The Ecclesiologies of Medellín and the Lessons of the Base Ecclesial Communities', *Cross Currents* 44:1 (Spring 1994), pp. 67–84. On the legacy of all three CELAM conferences, see Alejandro Crosthwaite

of liberation, brought into his social teaching fifty years later. A dual dialogue emerges through the CELAM texts: on the one hand, a pastoral dialogue with the peoples and cultures of the Latin American context and, on the other, a formal ecclesial-theological dialogue with the bodies that produce the Church's official teaching and whose social-theological imagination seemed out of kilter with much happening beyond the European world of Rome.

Neil Ormerod argues that what the CELAM bishops and theologians of liberation proposed to Rome above all was a necessary *imaginative shift in moral focus*: from the viewpoint of the individual perpetrator of sin and the operations of conscience in personalist perspective to an account of sin as a social reality, embedded in social structures and mediated through social encounters, whose presence and impact can be rendered visible, intelligible and open to change through attention to the life experience (material, moral and spiritual) of the dispossessed.[5] Thus, an 'option for the poor' is not just about paternalistic assistance but in fact about how we can know the truth of our social reality and of God's action in history.

This shift in viewpoint – towards a structural analysis in general and the life experience of the dispossessed in particular – enabled CELAM not only to address the presence of social realities that had been insufficiently theorized by a Eurocentric mainstream CST but also to problematize the Church's own social standpoint. It enabled them to propose that viewed through the eyes of the poorest in Latin America, the Church's accruals of power, capital and embeddedness amongst elites meant that the Church itself was perceived to be, experienced to be, problematically part of the nexus of social power and privilege. This was to introduce a sharp reflexivity into the Church's own bloodstream: it too was a historical actor, placed and conditioned by its material, social and economic location. Such a reflexive awareness of the significance of the positional power of the Church as part of the material conditions of its own social teaching as it pertained to dignity had not been a strong hallmark of earlier CST. The idea that the Church existed somehow outside of stratifying systems of race, class and gender, modelling a reconciled unity, was taken as a given.

The post-1968 documents produced by CELAM turned the Church not only towards the historical in general terms as a site for reflection on

---

OP, 'Aparecida: Catholicism in Latin America and the Caribbean at the Crossroads', *Journal of Society for Christian Ethics* 28:2 (Fall, 2008), pp. 159–80.
[5]Ormerod, *Creation, Grace and Redemption*, pp. 50–6.

Human Dignity: Social and Structural Sin

human dignity but specifically towards the *cultural*. Indeed, the handling of questions of social sin in the documents of Puebla (1979) cannot be understood apart from attention to this cultural turn. Puebla treats culture as a theological-anthropological matter; the documents approach culture as a system of values and ideas, and as a form marked by dynamics of power and force. Culture is the product of a community of persons, and it comes to form a structural reality in the life of a people: a turn towards the structural in social teaching is necessarily a turn towards the cultural. Puebla develops this line of analysis with regard to the impact of culture on the operations of conscience. A Catholic theory of society ought to articulate the deep connections between the life of the collectivity manifest in its cultural forms and the collective dimensions to the operation of conscience. Taking seriously the statement that 'culture is a historical and social reality' necessitates a Catholic theological analysis of the history of ideas – in this analysis, the history of ideas has a *materiality* that must be traced through attention to both individual and collective bodies.

The Latin American challenge to the authors and practitioners of CST was, therefore, to see that the values embedded in the practices, structures and institutions of a society are made visible in the experiences of the poorest, and that correspondingly the transformation of such cultures would require a recognition of, and calling forth of, the agency of the poorest. Two emphases are important here. Puebla emphasized that theological analysis of the failures and exclusions of a culture must be matched by a constructive commitment to promoting the evangelizing of 'all the value orders'.[6] Transformation – both the conversion of individuals and the creation of just structures – requires a transformation of 'the cultures of peoples'. Equally, part of the force of Medellín, Puebla and Aparecida comes from their calls for a communitarian ethic that ought to run like a golden thread connecting the critical analysis of social forms and the constructive proposal of new forms of transforming social and pastoral action. In the generation of base ecclesial communities – small local church communities of prayer, reflection and social action, which could be lay-led – as the gestational centres of a new ecclesial and social way of life, the communitarian analytical method matched the ecclesial politics of transformation.

The documents of Aparecida (2007) explore globalization as the most significant form of cultural life in need of sustained contemporary

---

[6]CELAM, Puebla Final Document, §452.

critical attention and ethical transformation. The CELAM bishops note: '[g]lobalisation impacts more than any other dimension our culture and the way in which we become part of it and draw from it . . . [w]e are living through a change of epoch, the deeper level of which is cultural.'[7] Globalization, they suggest, whilst offering the possibility of a deeper cultural unity, in its current form represents an insidious erosion of the 'unity of perception'. Resistance to the current forms of globalization does not mean that people are 'frightened of diversity' but rather 'what shocks them is rather being unable to combine the totality of all these meanings of reality into an integrated understanding that enables them to exercise their freedom with discernment and responsibility. . . . What is lacking is rather the possibility of converging into a synthesis, which, encompassing the variety of meanings, can project it towards a common historic destiny'.[8] 'Pluriculturality' is not a problem per se but what we lack is a unitary framework in order to ensure that it is lived in solidarity, dignity and for the common good.[9] Such teaching obviously draws from the natural law assumption that the human person is by nature drawn to be a seeker of truth. What Aparecida adds to the development of a Latin American-derived theology of social sin is a maturing account of the relationship between social sin and social virtue, structures of sin and structures of virtue in their cultural dimensions.

Why, then, is there a history of contesting this language of social and structural sin? The response of the papacy and the Congregation for the Doctrine of the Faith to the initial writings of theologians of liberation and to the social teachings of the CELAM conferences was to insist on caution in use of the language of social and structural sin. This caution focused on the following concerns: that sin could be described as 'social' only in an analogical sense and not in literal terms; that the turn towards the structural risked tipping into a form of moral determinism that failed to give both free will and grace their due; and that correspondingly a Catholic account of personhood required that individuals be understood as freely choosing moral agents culpable for their actions. John Paul II reminded the Church that only individuals could be said to sin, and that no structure could be understood to have moral agency independent of individual moral action.

---

[7] CELAM, Aparecida Final Document, §43.
[8] Ibid., §43.
[9] Ibid., §42.

He notes that regardless of the presence of undoubtedly unjust structures, the individual human person remains free, responsible, obligated and open to the operation of grace and conversion in relation to basic moral norms. The overt issue at stake was not, then, whether or not social structures could be viewed as profoundly disordered and unjust – no one was disputing that – but rather whether the language of sin should be deployed descriptively and analytically in this context.

John Paul II dealt with these questions in four major documents. In *Reconciliatio et paenitentia* (1984) he repudiates the idea of social sin as a descriptor for anything other than a sin committed by an individual, which always has an antisocial dimension, but in laying out this case he does suggest a limited legitimate analogical use of the term.[10] Clarifying that an entity which lacks consciousness of its acts and a capacity for personal conversion cannot be thought of in terms of sin but can be thought of in terms of measures of justice, John Paul II reaches for the language of 'obstacles' and 'structures'. There are obstacles whose presence in the moral landscape comes to block a smooth pathway towards dignified living and the pursuit of the good. When writing in such a vein, John Paul would doubtless have imagined himself to be working within the spirit and letter of *Gaudium et spes* and the 1971 Synod of Bishops' document *Justice in the World*. Both texts speak of unjust structures and objective obstacles that create inducements to further individual sin.

The most detailed engagement with questions of social and structural sin occurs in 1995 in *Evangelium vitae*. Here John Paul II adopts the language of structural sin (but not social sin) to describe a pervasive moral climate of uncertainty.[11] He pursues the idea that in a given age values themselves can become 'eclipsed', seemingly unavailable to a community of moral reasoning. Naming a 'culture of death', he argues that such an ideology can become 'a veritable structure of sin', one that 'denies solidarity'.[12] We can speak in this context about 'a war of the powerful against the weak: a life which would require greater acceptance, love and care is considered useless'.[13] He notes,

---

[10]See Finn, 'What Is a Sinful Social Structure?' and 'What Can You Do? Understanding Sinful Social Structures', in *Commonweal* Magazine, https://www.commonwealmagazine.org/what-can-you-do, both on analogical use of the idea of social sin in John Paul II.
[11]*Evangelium vitae*, §11 and 12. Notably, John Paul II includes ecological harm in this summary of social/structural sin.
[12]Ibid., §12.
[13]Ibid.

'[a]ll this explains, at least in part, how the value of life can today undergo a kind of "eclipse", even though conscience does not cease to point to it as a sacred and inviolable value.'[14] In this, his most far-reaching statement on structural sin, the pope goes beyond previous critiques of the use of structural sin and notes that widespread social injustice and a culture of moral uncertainty can induce sin and 'mitigate the subjective responsibility of individuals'.[15] This is the closest the papacy has come to acknowledging a liberationist or personalist-communitarian account of structural sin and integrating it into the Catholic Church's formal teaching on justice and dignity.

However, later documents, including the *Compendium*, produced under the oversight of John Paul II, do not expand upon this sentiment and appear to retreat from a more expansive understanding of structural sin. The *Compendium* defines social sin in the following manner: 'every sin is personal under a certain aspect; under another, every sin is social insofar as and because it also has social consequences.'[16] Sin is defined here as social by virtue of its outcome: a personal sin is committed and becomes immediately social 'by virtue of human solidarity which is as mysterious and intangible as it is real and concrete, each individual's sin in some way affects others'.[17] The following paragraphs outline a further acceptable usage of the idea of social sin as a direct offence against a neighbour, a sin against justice due between persons. The social consequences of sin, so the *Compendium* continues, accrue, consolidate and develop structural form, thus becoming difficult to remove. The *Compendium* repeats the view that all such sin remains personal in origin, and thus the language continues to attach to the will expressed in an originating individual, traceable act.

In *Solicitudo rei socialis* John Paul II uses the language of structural sin in two different contexts: corrupted power in a Cold War world divided into

---

[14]Ibid., §11.
[15]Ibid., §12.
[16]*Compendium*, §117.
[17]*Evangelium vitae*, §117, quoting *Reconciliatio et paenitentia* §16, and with the following explanatory footnote: 'The text explains moreover that there is a *law of descent*, which is a kind of *communion of sin*, in which a soul that lowers itself through sin drags down with it the Church and, in some way, the entire world; to this law there corresponds a *law of ascent*, the profound and magnificent mystery of the *communion of saints*, thanks to which every soul that rises above itself also raises the world' (footnote 226 attached to §117).

power blocs; and as present in the drive towards a relentless profit motif in economic life. He writes,

> [i]t is not out of place to speak of 'structures of sin', which . . . are rooted in personal sin, and thus always linked to the concrete acts of individuals who produce these structures, consolidate them and make them difficult to remove. And thus, they grow stronger, spread and become the source of others sins, and so influence people's behaviour.[18]

Thus, by the end of John Paul II's papacy structural sin remains simply the multiplication or accrual of individual sinful acts into consolidated, calcified structures. He does acknowledge that these structures create incentives to further individual sin and, on occasion, possibly mitigate responsibility for wrongdoing. What is absent in the papal account is the more comprehensive, doctrinally grounded engagement with theological interpretation of culture, violence and loss and the deep turn towards a historical construal of freedom and its material history that mark the mid-century *ressourcement* and personalist writings, and parts of the emergent Latin American corpus. Also absent is the *locus theologicus* of the dispossessed that is the hallmark of the liberation theologians.

Whilst Daniel Daly argues that both Benedict XVI and Francis avoid using the language of social or structural sin entirely, neither repudiating nor repeating it, what Daly curiously overlooks is the move made by both popes to develop an account of structures of social virtue. In his 2007 address to the CELAM bishops at Aparecida, Benedict XVI noted: '[w]e inevitably speak of the problem of structures, especially those which create injustice. In truth, just structures are a condition without which a just order of society is not possible. But how do they arise? How do they function?'[19] Later in his address he excoriates both capitalism and Marxism for touting a false-doctrine that just structures could be established without need for prior individual morality and which, once established through a conscious will-to-power, would be self-perpetuating and automatic generators of the grounds

---

[18]*Sollicitudo rei socialis*, §36.
[19]See Benedict XVI's address to 2007 Aparecida meeting: http://www.vatican.va/content/benedict-xvi/en/speeches/2007/may/documents/hf_ben-xvi_spe_20070513_conference-aparecida.html (accessed 1 April 2021).

for their own communal legitimacy. Benedict argues for a foundationalist moral and religious account as the basis for enduring just and dignified social structures, and for a necessary ongoing process of uncovering and negotiating foundational moral motivations for a just common life. He writes: 'just structures will never be complete in a definitive way. . . . Just structures are, as I have said, an indispensible condition for a just society, but they neither arise nor function without a moral consensus in society on fundamental values, and on the need to live these values with the necessary sacrifices, even if this goes against personal interest.'[20] The CELAM bishops note in response to Benedict's words: '[t]here are no new structures unless there are new men and women to mobilise and bring about convergence in people's ideals and powerful moral and religious energies.'[21]

Francis, writing in *Laudato si'*, moves the discussion of sin and virtue in both a more contemplative-mystical direction and a more thoroughly materialist one. He writes of sin as a sickness manifest and visible in the natural world. He interprets sin as a consequence of an anthropology – a view of what it means to be human – that denies the truth that we are spirit, will and nature; a person is not only 'a freedom which he creates for himself'. Echoing classic Christian doctrines of sin Francis suggests that the myth of self-sovereignty and the refusal of the notion of creaturely limitation lie at the root of a fundamental personal and social malaise that poisons the earth, the social body and our own bodies – bodies, which he reminds us, are made up of the dust of the earth. The corrective framework which grounds human dignity and just structures lies in a logic of the 'sublime communion' of all things and a rejection of the temptation to adopt an extrinsic and instrumentalist relationship to the natural world, human and non-human others. Creation is 'the order of love . . . which calls us together into universal communion': communion – and thus dignity – is threatened by inequality, extinction, needless suffering and the disfigurement of the earth. For the first time Francis extends the use of the language of dignity to the earth itself, speaking of 'the intrinsic dignity of the world'. Where Benedict emphasizes foundational doctrines, Francis tends to emphasize a more general openness to transcendence and contemplation as the basis for entering into this process of communion over-against instrumentalization. Thus, Francis continues to move the debate about social sin beyond a

---

[20]Ibid.
[21]https://www.celam.org/aparecida/Ingles.pdf (accessed 1 April 2021).

question of mere human willing and the context of political-economic relations.

Fratelli tutti makes a further contribution to the integration of ideas of social and structural sin into CST by picking up the theme of cultures and ideologies that malform human beings' perceptions of the good. Nationalism, closed populism, racism and individualism are all singled out as examples of malformed social visions which come to condition ways of thinking about self, other and the social whole. These social visions are seen as social viruses which come to cause social harm and limit moral agency, warping our visions of universal relatedness and social interdependence. In essence this repeats and reinforces earlier teaching on social sin. However, in *Let Us Dream*, published several months after *Fratelli tutti*, Francis makes a cogent personal argument for the collective social discernment of the truth of the whole and resolution of conflict and difficulty.[22] In doing so, arguably Francis moves away from a narrow personalism of conscience. Moral agency is formed, in conscience, in the context of revealed teaching and the use of reason, but also through the processes of collective discernment – synodality. Addressing the vision of the Church at the Second Vatican Council, Francis makes a wide-ranging appeal for synodality as a vision for social as well as ecclesial judgement. Synodality helps resolve difficult issues and enables healthy social visions based on shared experience and reason to take shape, thus cutting through malformed social and ecclesial visions. He points out that a synodical approach allows unanticipated issues to emerge, and the purity of one's position is 'unmasked': this reveals the unacknowledged 'tares growing amongst the wheat', releasing thought from its own imprisonment.[23] This turn towards political ecclesiology is an interesting and suggestive one for the development of an account of social sin and social virtue.

We should also note the appearance of the theme of race in *Fratelli tutti*. A long-neglected theme in CST, *Fratelli tutti* offers the beginnings of an analysis. As C. Vanessa White argues, *Fratelli tutti* opens the door to talk about race but does not accomplish much more.[24] White argues that racism is viewed in *Fratelli tutti* as a virus, an attitude that is contagious, but that

---

[22]Francis, *Let Us Dream*, pp. 74–83.
[23]Ibid., p. 86.
[24]C. Vanessa White, 'Still Waiting for a Harder Look at the Sin of Racism', *America* Magazine, https://www.americamagazine.org/voices/c-vanessa-white (accessed 6 January 2021).

the document evades a properly structural analysis of race and the ways in which racism ruptures the body of Christ. She writes, as Bryan Massingdale has written over decades, about the refusal to note the systemic advantage that racism gives to Whiteness and the burden it lays upon Blackness.[25] CST has a Thomist and Augustinian language to talk about injustice in burden and benefit, and about the manifestation of privation in social forms. But it has failed to develop its own tradition adequately in the case of race.

Viewing racism as an original sin woven into the foundation of the US social body, Massingdale argues that the two main US bishops' conference documents on race remain profoundly inadequate. *Brother and Sisters to Us* (1979) and *Open Wide Our Hearts* (2018) – the latter written in response to the events in Charlottesville – attempt to engage CST with racism in the United States. Massingdale argues that both documents are profoundly inadequate for three main reasons. First, they speak in general and abstract terms about the social harms of racism, failing to deal with questions of moral agency and responsibility. They speak in passive terms about harms experienced but will not address the question of who and how? They avoid naming White privilege or fundamental anti-Blackness. Second, they write without engaging the authorship or collective social experience of Black communities. They are documents written *for* (at best) not *by* or *with* Black Catholics. As such they fail to draw on Black experience as a *locus theologicus* in the ways we noted earlier. Massingdale notes how much more writing there is on questions of race and from Black experience in other Christian traditions. CST is notable for its almost complete absence, despite an available CST methodology to at least begin the task. Third, both US documents lack practical engagement with questions of social action and change. The implication of Massingdale's argument is that both the social encyclical tradition and the CST produced by bishops' conferences fail to enact as substance and method the insight in the Church's own social teaching on social sin.

Whilst *Fratelli tutti* moves race onto the CST agenda, most of the work – theological and political – remains to be done. *Fratelli tutti* does develop previous teaching on social sin, noting the power of pervasive

---

[25]See Bryan N. Massingdale, *Racial Justice and the Catholic Church* (Maryknoll: Orbis Books, 2010). See also an interview with Massingdale, 'Worship of a False God', *Commonweal Magazine*, https://www.commonwealmagazine.org/worship-false-god (accessed 6 January 2021).

ideologies of self and society that form and malform consciences, and it does make connections between nationalist and populist agendas as well as radically individualistic ones and racism. Yet it has not yet extended its understanding of the historical accrual of sinful practices to take account of racism as accrued bodily privilege. To move both reflection on social sin and on racism forward necessitates not only a greater attention to the experience of Blackness but, as J. Cameron Karter and others have argued, a fundamental account of race as a theological category, including theological reflection on Whiteness as scripted into the social, political and ecclesial performance of Christianity.[26]

Conclusion

How, then, do we evaluate this emerging century of discussion about the structural and social dimensions of sin as a facet of concern for a properly theological account of human dignity? There is a traceable and distinctive developing CST tradition of discussion about the social and structural conditions of sin in late modernity. However, the development of this tradition appears to have been hampered by a level of discursive misrecognition in the back and forth between the theologians of liberation and the Vatican, and arguably both traditions remain incomplete. Ormerod rightly identifies in the theologies of liberation an attempt to shift towards a more thoroughly historical, material and dialectical account of dignity and sin, and a determined shift in standpoint, situating the experience of the most marginalized, dispossessed and victimized as the vantage point for narrating the social dimensions of sin and salvation. In doing so liberation theologians have drawn attention to an absent dialectical and phenomenological account of sin. The papacy and the Congregation of the Doctrine of the Faith continued to situate their own developing narratives of social and structural sin in the more general question of moral freedom and action. Thus, the two accounts begin in different places and come to articulate different dimensions of the same problem but without ever completing the task of producing a comprehensive, compelling Catholic narrative of the social and structural dimensions of sin.

---

[26] J. Kameron Carter, *Race: A Theological Account* (Oxford: OUP, 2008).

What, then, is missing from the CST tradition in its discussion of social sin? Arguably what is missing from both the liberationist and Vatican accounts, in different ways, is a properly theological – as opposed to primarily moral or ethical – account of sin. Classical accounts of original sin insist, although they do not use such language, that all sin is fundamentally both social and structural. Original sin is social in the sense that it is understood to function as a form of inherited alienation and guilt that operates in a pre-personal way, as the social context for all free-willing action. In other words, in the classical accounts, original sin forms a spatial-temporal *situation* that becomes the context of *being* for all morally autonomous action.

This catastrophic originating social narrative or myth functions to restrain theology in the face of the temptation to tell a moralistic story of sin as merely intrinsic personal, contingent action that gains subsequent extrinsic solidified social form. Yet it retains an important focus on moral autonomy. The fundamentally *social* doctrine of original sin functions to ensure that there can be no innocent or pure account of human action in history, and yet personal moral action in relation to a personal deity shapes time. The story of sin is always our own willed action for good or for bad and is always more than this action. Sin, inherited and experienced phenomenologically in the basic material structures of our lives, confronts us with this question of an intrinsic, common inheritance of the historical disordering of time and space, and the importance of our own struggle to act as free persons in time and space. As unique, relational, interdependent, contemplating and communicating beings, we are profoundly vulnerable to being shaped by this reality and yet also capable through the very same sociality of resisting this history and receiving and enacting the counter-logic available to us through the operation of grace. This is also, therefore, a narrative that invites us to wonder what grace – operative ontologically within the very structure of nature and throughout history – means as a force at work within the context of historical, material disorder.

In metaphysical terms the classic account of original sin insists that sin remains a contingent and not (ontologically speaking) a necessary feature of our moral lives. To argue for a historical situation, rooted in a pre-personal catastrophic disorder of human relations, need not imply an ontological account of sin but does insist on an ontology of grace. We are not united in a negative communion of dystopian determined futures, but we do experience a solidarity that is born of the fragility and precarity of action in a thoroughly material, historical and broken but also already graced-into-being world. The freedom to act for the good remains constitutive of personhood in classic accounts of original sin, but the inheritance of disordered relations forms the material conditions of the freedom we desire to express.

Thus, personal sin is always the decision of an inherently *social*, desiring self, and freedom expressed through being-in-the-world is always a properly historical and material matter, in both its fallen and graced dimensions. Thus, there is no fundamental separation of extrinsic and intrinsic between the givenness of a context in time in which one enacts freedom and the act itself. Karl Rahner writes: 'freedom inevitably appropriates the material in which it actualises itself as an intrinsic and constitutive element which is originally co-determined by freedom itself, and incorporates it into the finality of the existence which possesses itself in freedom.'[27] Such a situational but non-ontologizing account of sin, resolute in its insistence of a non-innocent beginning, often seems to be missing from the more consequentialist formulation of sin in the social encyclicals, including when they are addressing and defining social sin. Equally, the liberationist narrative, whilst certainly challenging this construal and positing a non-innocent account tends to focus on the social-structural temporal context and less on the fundamental theological dimensions articulated in earlier classical account of original sin. Both seem theologically incomplete.

The nouvelle and personalist theologians of the mid-century who were attempting to reconstruct a post-manual and more adequately textual and historical Catholicism arguably lacked sufficiently fine-grained attention to deep structural and political matters. Nonetheless, they sought to move Catholic theology in the direction of a properly material doctrinal account. This was also the space in which the mystical-political writer Simone Weil – whose work could have, but has not thus far, shaped the official CST tradition directly – articulated her own case for the social dimensions of sin. In a noteworthy piece and echoing Mounier's sentiments on states of violence, Weil writes on what she names the 'history of force'.[28] She argues that the path to love and justice must pass through a reckoning with the history of force, which conditions the possibility for moral action and the shaping of freedom. This continuous history of force sees the in-breaking

---

[27]Karl Rahner, *Grace in Freedom*, available online https://www.religion-online.org/book-chapter/section-8-true-freedom/ (accessed 1 April 2021).
[28]Simone Weil, 'The Iliad, or the Poem of Force', in *Simone Weil: An Anthology*, edited and introduced by Siân Miles (London: Penguin Books, 2005 edition).

of love and justice in the moments of reflection that create a pause in cycles of violence and acts of hospitality that stand as a proxy for justice owed and not yet rendered. These acts form a continuous history of their own; thus, we move between gravity and grace – each story cannot be told without the other. Weil sees this as a biblical witness, traceable through the Gospel. What is striking about her account is that the history of force is recognized as a constant shaping reality, a non-ontological historical condition that requires recognition by anyone who wishes to enact the love or justice spoken of and witnessed to by Christ. Her account also moves us beyond a standpoint that remains uncomfortably locked within a *locus theologicus* of individual perpetration.

A Catholic theology of sin in the service of an account of human dignity has no option but to resist a solely individualist metaphysics of sin, not only because the modern world and the recent failures of the Church itself challenge such a construct empirically speaking but because a thoroughgoing theology does too. The question remains: To what extent does recent CST achieve such a resistance and propose a sufficiently thorough alternative? John Paul II wanted to hold onto the question of personal responsibility, but arguably he only partially developed his account of responsibility. He failed to ask: How do we conceive of responsibility for what we know to be true of our material world but which we do not will? How do we think theologically about the calcified structures in our midst, about conditioned cultural forms of thinking and knowing, from which our individual and collective minds naturally shrink, and consequently, of which we are only partly aware? Why do we tend to fall silent in the face of a violent and abusive social reality – including within the Church itself – that begs for an account of failure that extends beyond individual wrongdoing? The cost of the theological failure to grapple with such questions is arguably (still) paid by the victims.

What remains missing from the canon of the social encyclical tradition is a thorough treatment of sin in its fullest social dimensions, theologically and metaphysically framed. This lack seems to correspond to a theological anthropology present in the encyclicals that often remains trapped within a more neo-scholastic treatment of the human person and human dignity. Missing is a more thoroughly theological account of the contemplative, desiring self. Also missing is a narration from the *locus theologicus* of the dispossessed, excluded and of victims or survivors. This is not merely a social location from which to perform better social analysis that can later be taken up into theology proper; rather the site of violence, loss and dispossession is already an intrinsic site of deep theological and anti-theological speech and action. To engage in such an analysis would require a return to classical accounts of sin in dialogue with the development of new methods to engage a wider whole-church practice of theological reflection. Whilst theologies of liberation offer us some important material towards this task, as William Cavanaugh has argued, their tendency to move away from a necessary theological investigation of ecclesial structures of authority, in favour of transformation through the establishment of radical ecclesial communities of love and justice, means that more work needs to be done to produce a genuinely whole social teaching.[29]

Finally, such a widened analysis in service of a fuller account of human dignity might also require a willingness to draw water from more plural theological wells. At the end of his brief consideration of structural sin in *Sollicitudo rei socialis*, John Paul II notes that we need such an analysis of sin and structures of sin to 'point out the true nature of evil'.[30] This task remains incomplete. However, we might wish to turn this point on its head and note that in drawing so heavily on a neo-Thomist canon CST has narrowed the wells it has been willing to draw theological water from. A return to – and reworking of – theological traditions of reflection on desire, privation and communion would offer us serious possibilities for future social teaching.

Above all, one issue is as yet unaddressed in any handling of discussions of structural sin or virtue or social teaching itself. What begs a development in this language is the continued revelations of clerical sexual abuse in the Catholic Church. To speak of human dignity held within the framework of doctrines of sin and salvation and not to address this issue in its social and structural dimensions seems incredible. The abuse crisis is manifestly an example of social sin turned inwards, and we live as yet with an absence of a fully adequate language to address this reality. Working towards an understanding of social and structural sin in the life of the Church might then become a renewing gift for its wider social teaching.

---

[29]Cavanaugh, 'The Ecclesiologies of Medellin and the Lessons of the Base Communities'.
[30]*Sollicitudo rei socialis*, §36.

CHAPTER 5
THE COMMON GOOD
THE LONG TRADITION IN CONTEXT

We can't decide any of the questions we argue about without implicitly relying on certain ethical ideas, certain ideas of justice, certain ideas of the common good. We can't be neutral on those questions even if we pretend to be. (Michael Sandel, *The Guardian*, 'Profile', 8 April 2012)

In 2015 the Spanish political party Podemos achieved a remarkable electoral feat. In the vanguard of early twenty-first-century European populist movements, over the course of just five years, Podemos moved from being a progressive grassroots political grouping with little money or profile to an electoral force that would go on to gain over 20 per cent of the Spanish vote. What fascinated me about Podemos' political philosophy was its overt appeal to the idea of the common good. Íñigo Errejón, a leading figure in Podemos, argued for a cautious re-embrace of the idea of the common good, venturing that politics is, above all else, about forging social unity through the formation of collective identities.[1] This process of identity formation happens as we struggle towards articulating visions of a genuinely common good. What we have lost, Errejón proposes, are the public spaces, the vibrant institutions and, within the realm of ideas, the understandings of public representation that are necessary conduits for channelling the inevitable conflicts we face in contesting these visions and moving towards plural democratic ends. On the one hand, Errejón fears that supposedly liberal moderns have reduced the notion of the common good to ideas of individual social choice and mobility. From this no truly collective identity and no fruitful politics can emerge. On the other hand, he is suggesting that we have suppressed both the *idea* of the common good and the *contexts, movements, spaces and places* that are necessary to turn

---

[1] Íñigo Errejón and Chantal Mouffe, *Podemos: In the Name of the People* (London: Lawrence and Wishart, 2016).

a powerful, if contested and often perplexing, idea into a contemporary reality.

Errejón is not an unalloyed fan of the long tradition of common good thinking. He warns us that the idea of the common good can be co-opted and presented as a theory of natural order that tends to shore up established power relations and to deny plurality, thus frustrating the truly difficult and ethically rewarding work of building a common life as an expression of proper freedom. The idea of the common good can, he fears, be used to foreclose rather than open up conversations about horizons of meaning by suggesting that goods can be arrived at, and locked down, in a fixed and final way. This produces a false pre-emptive 'unity' that excludes and suppresses, yet still in the name of the good. Errejón tells his reader that he prefers to think of the common good as playing the role of a horizon, an open-ended, contestable and necessary construct for any attempt to build 'a people'. The common good is a way of talking about a reality that we reach towards and which remains partly beyond us. It is, nonetheless, a kind of reality. For him, the common good is visible, known and comes into being in the struggle for common life and collective identities, expressed in the pursuit of justice in all its forms. His is an imminent-historical project of reconstituting a politics of the common good. It is rooted in a secular eschatological account of the now and not-yet of politics: politics as a radically incomplete process of struggle for a life that is both truly common and truly good, and cannot be foreclosed.

One of the reasons I am interested in Errejón's return to the concept of the common good – often rejected by the political Left over the last century as an inherently conservative notion – is that he presents a renewed vision of the common good as fundamentally 'agonistic' in nature.[2] Following Marx, the radical 'agonistic' tradition of the Left has tended to look with suspicion

---

[2] Chantal Mouffe, the co-author of *Podemos*, is well known for her distinction between agonistic and antagonistic thinking and action. Whilst antagonism implies a perpetual and necessary conflict, agonistic theorists tend to see disruption, challenge and struggle as a necessary part of the way that political action secures justice and that politics can also be settled – but it is, as Bonnie Honig notes, never a settlement without remainder. Agonism remains with this remainder. Many social or political theologies might also be seen as agonistic theories, although with a stronger rootedness in, first, the transcendent basis of this agonism and, second, the inherently theological character of the 'remainder' that needs still be to be addressed – which is to say, justice is never merely a political concern, and its remainder is always properly theological. American political theologian Vincent Lloyd addresses this theme.

on the idea of the common good. Both Marx and Nietzsche applied an ideological critique to theories of the common good, concerned that they tended to reinforce normative and practical-systemic forms of inherited power.[3] When viewing politics empirically or diagnostically Marxists have tended to argue that mainstream proponents of the common good fail to account for the political conditions – relations of power and production – under which notions of the common good themselves are produced, formulated and seek expression. Marxists have argued that common good theories tend to overlook the inherently conflictual and agonistic nature of political life as constituted in, and by, struggle, rushing too quickly towards the mediatory and (falsely) unitive. It is the moral and political performance, or track record, of common good theories in practice that the Left has wondered about.

This same concern about the moral performance of the common good in practice is directed at liberal invocations of the idea. Communitarian thinkers and some on the political Left suggest that liberal notions of the common good produce in practice a version of politics pared down to little more than procedures to secure, deliberate or broker private interests made public.[4] Communitarian philosopher Michael Sandel argues that the biggest 'common good' challenge we face is to find means to push back against the total life of markets, whilst Noam Chomsky laments that we have reduced the notion of the common good to an aggressive focus on maximizing private gain alone. For Chomsky, a dominant emphasis on market value in Western cultures actively suppresses the deep emotions of solidarity, mutual support and care, which are vital to our social well-being. Sandel singles out for particular criticism the idea that economic efficiency, 'defined as getting goods to those with the greatest willingness and ability to pay for them', defines what we commonly understand by the common good.

Nonetheless, both political and theological writers on dignity and the common good are re-emphasizing the necessity of collective struggle – not merely deliberation, mediation or aggregation. The Covid-19 pandemic has highlighted this re-emphasis. Social theorist Chantal Mouffe argues, in

---

[3] See Hans Sluga, *Politics and the Search for the Common Good* (Cambridge: CUP, 2014), on diagnostic versus normative politics (pp. 11–40) and on Marx as a diagnostic thinker of the political (pp. 95–6). Sluga's own theory of the common good will be analysed further.
[4] See Jane Mansbridge, 'The Common Good', in *The International Encyclopedia of Ethics, Vol II.*, ed. H. LaFollette (Oxford: Wiley-Blackwell, 2013).

ways interestingly parallel to contemporary Black theorists and theologians, that the 'good' of politics is found in contestation and the life of struggle in the midst of shifting historical manifestations of power. For the theologian, several concerns might remain with such accounts. First, that the conflict itself not be made the *basis* or *foundation* of the good; that dignity not be rooted in extrinsic ways in merely the action of struggle itself (although it may include that); and that the remainder in any struggle or settlement be seen as theological as much as political in character – the figuring of the 'not yet' of justice. An account of the common good that lacks an overt awareness of the operation of power in history and a commitment to struggle with others through forging collective identities fails. Such a model of struggle implies a pluralism, which is rendered ethical in so far as it is given expression as, and through, solidarity. The task of modern politics is to engage in this life of agonistic pluralism. Thus, Errejón's recent proposition that we face the erosion or erasure of spaces and ideas of the common good and require its reinvention is no simple historical repetition; it is a further moment in the migration of this complex and contested idea into the heart of a new, chaotically emerging politics.

Errejón and Mouffe belong to a generation of scholars who are turning back to the concept of the common good, but who are doing so in what German-American political philosopher Hans Sluga identifies as 'historical' and 'diagnostic' rather than normative and foundationalist terms.[5] Sluga distinguishes between 'normative' and 'diagnostic' accounts of the common good. For Sluga, the normative tradition, rooted in classical sources and revised historically, argues for an essential and fixed account of the nature of the political expressed in a set of either normative-naturalistic or normative-rationalistic claims. Drawing a line from Plato (rendered the father of utopian-normative thought) and Aristotle (father to a conservative-normative tradition of natural order) through Kant to John Rawls, Sluga argues that the normative tradition tends towards the production of general formulas, political norms and grand principles that propose trans-historical rational and natural values. He believes that they also promote a philosophical movement of ascent from the ground of political experience to the higher viewing plain of philosophical reason. This ascent is followed by a largely unaccounted for descent from the heights of new abstract

---

[5]Sluga, *Politics and the Search for the Common Good*.

knowledge to renewed practice. Sluga suspects that such accounts tend towards imagining the role of the philosopher in relation to politics as the expert who knows and helps lay the terms for political life.

By contrast, diagnostic accounts of the common good place the philosopher as participant in a public exercise of collective reasoning that occurs in the fray, or in the in-between of action, and in which they do not have sole or wholly sufficient expertise. Knowledge of the conditions of the political remains a collective task dependent on the discernment of a whole political community, in which the philosopher plays a small role alongside others. For Sluga, politics does not have a fixed, essential meaning and character but shifts and morphs historically in ways that pay little attention to normative constructs. The diagnostic task requires the collective observance and discernment or diagnosis of the shifting realities of political life, as lived in an age. Sluga writes: '[c]onsideration of the common good is thus part of the political practice, not something set above it, and for that reason partakes in the fallibility of everything political.'[6] He takes as exemplars of this form of common good thinking three twentieth-century figures: the controversial Catholic jurist Carl Schmitt, Hannah Arendt and Michel Foucault. Indeed, Hannah Arendt rejects the label of philosopher and claims the mantle of political theorists for precisely these reasons.

Sluga is, however, largely uninterested in the rise of more conservative and normative common good theories. His task is to convince us of the need to move to solely diagnostic-historical forms of thought. Nonetheless, attention to the full range of re-emerging conservative common good thinking is surely necessary.

The renewal of conservative common good thinking has derived its inspiration from figures such as the mid-century American conservative thinker Russell Kirk and, in a more contemporary setting, American writer Rod Dreher and British academics such as Roger Scruton and social commentator Phillip Blond. Conservative retrievals of the common good tend to focus more on themes of the intentional communities formed around modern social conservative and naturalized views of marriage and family, and sometimes also embracing a Romantic appeal to place. Nonetheless, this strand of conservative modern thought remains importantly liberal in one key respect: it tends to adopt a thoroughly liberal appeal to ideas

---

[6]Ibid., p. 20.

of limited government. These themes find their echoes in the academic writing of conservative Christian thinkers John Finnis and R. R. Reno.[7]

At the start of this new century the global revival of a distinctive form of right-wing populist politics drew overtly on common good ideas. In Eastern Europe, the appeal to ethno-nationalism and securitized borders – a populism notably different from Errejón's brand of Left populism – is often made in the name of the common good. So too are internal domestic political appeals to agendas of higher wages, 'meaningful' work and reduced domestic inequality. In Hungary, President Viktor Orbán has spoken of an outright tension between liberal social ideals of individual freedom and the common good. He argues for a family-oriented communitarianism that is also ethno-nationalist and describes Christianity as the 'only natural foundation' for such a politics.[8] He utilizes an account of 'Christian liberty' as a counterpoint to liberal individualism. The failure of liberal individualism to protect the person – social and interdependent in nature – requires a counter-political anthropology that sees the person as embedded in and protected by, and obligated to, the nation state. Such movements represent a return to a normative and substantive use of the idea of the common good, largely in reaction to social liberalism and different from other forms of conservative usage, certainly with less appeal to the idea of a limited state than might be true in recent American forms of conservative thought.[9]

What is striking from this brief illustrative list is, first, that despite rumours of its previous demise, an appeal to the common good is absent from no mainstream contemporary political form and that we are currently entering a phase when a sense of both a crisis in the functioning of the idea and its open contestation across movements and traditions is apparent. Second, forms of Christian social and political thought are present, implicitly and explicitly, right across this register, as part of this contestation. As we will go

---

[7]See John Finnis, *Human Rights and the Common Good: Collected Essays Volume III* (Oxford: OUP, 2011), especially the chapter on 'Limited Government'. See also R. R. Reno, https://www.firstthings.com/article/2018/11/common-good-conservatism (accessed March 2019).

[8]See Viktor Orbán's full 2015 speech – including his reply to Christian leaders who he believed were challenging the Christian grounds of his political programme: http://www.kormany.hu/en/the-prime-minister/the-prime-minister-s-speeches/the-next-years-will-be-about-hardworking-people.

[9]See, for commentary on Donald Trump's use of the common good, https://www.americamagazine.org/politics-society/2017/03/01/trump-cites-common-good-will-he-seek-common-ground (accessed March 2019).

on to explore, it is also clear that we need to diversify the intellectual models we have been using in recent years to account for the practical and political operation of this idea. Third, it is clear that whilst the idea of the common good is politically resurgent, no contemporary social or intellectual movement can claim singular ownership of the tradition or credit for its return.

It is equally clear, including in its secular manifestation, that there is much debate and disagreement about what the 'common good' means, its reference points and implications. Is religious belief its 'natural foundation', a ground and *telos* for reflection, or in fact a force that makes its achievement harder? Is capitalism part of the solution or antithetical to a truly common good? Do deliberative or aggregative models for the common good result in a kind of denial of what makes social or public life most truly social or public: a shared life together? Is some form of nationalism necessary, or inherently problematic, is it a value or disvalue for achieving the common good? Should we reject the idea of a singular conception of *the* common good and talk instead only about a plurality of *goods in common*? When we use this phrase, do we mean anything more than the sum total of other forms of public and personal goods: education, health care and a decent environment?

In wrestling with the contours of the common good and its contemporary usage, we need to contend with a darker history of the concept. We will not always agree on the exact boundaries of the darker side of the idea, and yet some attempt to grapple with its malformations must be made. We can posit that the long history of the use of the common good as an idea to justify repression, extermination and personal sacrifice in the name of the collectivity is endlessly renewed. The idea of the common good is no more immune, *a priori* – in *either* secular *or* religious guise – to integration into a set of exclusive ethno-nationalist claims that, as Pius XI noted, risk raising race, nation or politics beyond 'their standard value' and turning them into forms of death-dealing idolatry. The language of the common good is no less at risk of co-option into forms of authoritarian, corporatist and fascist politics or turned with overly assured fixity into a set of abstract social solutions than is the idea of human dignity, as we noted in the first and second chapters of this book.

Jane Mansbridge offers a typological response to such questions. She suggests that contemporary theories of the common good come in three main forms – aggregative, procedural and unitive.[10] She argues that

---

[10] Jane Mansbridge, 'Common Good', in *International Encyclopedia of Ethics* (Wiley Online Library, 2013).

aggregative theories, dating mainly from the eighteenth century onwards, focus on the good of everyone and the greatest good for the greatest number (the most justice, rationality, happiness, etc.), whilst procedural accounts focus on fairness of process and the conditions for adequate participation in decision-making and deliberation. Explicitly unitive theories focus on forging collective identities and experiences, often in the form of appeals to, either or both, God and nation.

Mansbridge identifies three dominant variations on the theme of unitive common good thinking. The first takes the form of a *functional* appeal to the idea of a greater whole to which one's good is tied. At one extreme, this kind of thinking is at work in authoritarian and totalitarian state claims on the individual, and at the other, on a more ordinary level in appeals to mundane collective action. Mansbridge's example of the latter is the substitution of players in a football match, resting on a sporting appeal to a greater whole to which one's own 'good' is tied and which might imply necessary sacrifice as part of its ethic. The second variation of unitive thought is found in overtly theological accounts of the common good that rest on (hierarchical, teleological and/or analogical) transcendent appeals to God as the source and summit of the good. The third variation on unitive appeals places emphasis on the value of things which are irreducibly social in everyday life, and which seem to exist and function beyond a mere convergence or aggregation of interest. Mansbridge offers Charles Taylor's example of the ways that a common language – he uses Québécois as his case in point – functions in building and expressing an 'us' as the basis of shared culture.

One of the most suggestive and helpful things about Mansbridge's brief typology is that she situates theological accounts of the common good alongside forms of ethno-nationalist and populist appeals to the idea. She posits a kind of intellectual kinship between these forms, noting that both make use of appeals to the unitive, albeit in different ways. This may, indeed, explain in part the simultaneous dialectic of rejection and co-option of the religious by fascism and totalitarianism in its various historical guises. It might also be suggested that what both kinds of unitive accounts have in common is the use of a politics of desire and an appeal to the affective and emotional as a form of political theologizing, albeit in very different forms. We will return to this point later.

Finally, Mansbridge's survey is interesting for its claim that the use of common good language in public discourse has remained relatively stable over the course of the last two hundred years. There are no great peaks and troughs, no simple replacement of common good language with self-interest language, although there is a move to develop more obviously aggregative liberal accounts of the good. And one might want to note – which she does not – the diminishing of a more overtly transcendent account of the common good, when used. Nonetheless, what we cannot claim based on Mansbridge's careful analysis is that there is either a deliberate suppression of common good language itself or any fundamental agreement in its contemporary deployment.

I think, therefore, that a modest consensus might be drawn around the claim that the common good is an intellectually and politically resilient idea with enduring appeal. It is an idea that migrates between, and takes root within, shifting political settlements. For reasons we must conjure with, this idea refuses to die, even when we render it problematic, out of keeping with the times, or useless. At the most minimal observational and sociological level we can observe that the idea of the common good operates in contemporary parlance as a kind of placeholder, a way that we can talk together about something difficult to put into words: forms of human longing and concrete social practices that express a desire for something beyond the private and instrumental and which require cooperative action to secure. It is also an idea open to malformation within and from a Christian point of view.

However, this book represents an attempt to offer a theological and not merely a sociological account of Catholic social and political ideas, and so in the course of the next two chapters I want to explore well-trodden and more tentative grounds for a strictly (but not narrowly) theological account of the common good.

In an essay on the nature of philosophy, twentieth-century Catholic philosopher Josef Pieper distinguishes between matters of 'common need', which relate to the everyday world of work and labour and which impel forms of protection of private and public goods, and the life of freedom which has an existence beyond supply and demand, distribution of goods and the world of production. He names this life 'beyond' the common good. Sustaining the common good – rather than simply responding to legitimate common need – requires a whole series of acts of being, gift-exchange and social relation that cannot be merely 'put to use', that do not exist 'in order that.' The common good depends not only on response to a world of need but on acts of gratuity, resistance, meaning-making and simple expressions of freedom that are not reducible to the logic of 'total work' and which, in Pieper's phrase, help us to 'pierce the dome', touching on the realm of transcendence. He suggests that philosophy itself exists in such a realm, vital to the common good but not understandable within the logic of 'common need' alone.

Therefore, taken in the round and according to Pieper's way of thinking, to think about acts as various as conceptualizing the conditions of being, giving blood, forging deep friendships, volunteering in a contagious virus clinic, forming movements to resist social violence or protect the environment, housing the displaced, forming deep attachments to place, disrupting the sale of arms, preserving a dying language: to talk about any of these things properly, even in a solely secular register, seems to send us in the direction of *some* kind of appeal to the language of the common good. These should not to be thought of as acts without a context but rather as acts that exist in a profound relationship of call and response to the deepest and most fundamental levels of our shared human situation. In other words, the language of the common good spills out from the sides of a too-narrow container of public life defined solely as shared self-interest, brokered goods and aggregated interests. It is a language of excess that speaks to what is in fact core to our sense of human purpose. It is, as Pieper says, neither a language of utility nor of supply and demand but of essential non-negotiable gratuity.

It is difficult to understand why Pieper would make this distinction between common need and common good, and place so much emphasis on the gratuitous fundamental nature of action for the common good, without offering some account of the theological vision that underpins his account. Pieper situates the common good within a wider Catholic metaphysics of the good.

To grasp what is at stake in constructing common good theory from these foundations, we will start with the concerns of contemporary common good doubters and work backwards. The fallacy of the idea of the common good is often explained with reference to the practical and ideological resistance of late modern societies to any singular or unitary vision of the good. We moderns simply disagree on what constitutes the good life and think it is importantly adult to tolerate such disagreements within certain ethical parameters. This is true with reference to both plural metaphysical systems and the plurality of practical decisions evident in everyday practices of decision-making and goal-seeking. Talk of *the* or *a* common good is argued to be both unrealistic and undesirable, and is feared to smack of the authoritarian and repressive on the one hand or the simply ineffectual and vacuous on the other. The doubters wait for a convincing theological response to this problem: Can theology provide the pragmatic and reconciling solutions to incommensurability and conflict, and can it act in support of tolerance and diverse goal-seeking?

What makes Pieper's brief – tantalizingly incomplete and sometimes frustrating – foray into writing on the common good so striking is not that he offers a brilliant solution to these secular challenges (he does not), but rather that he changes the terms on which theology might be seen as a contributor to this public conversation. He changes the terms of the question itself and defies expectations of what theology and the theologian might produce as a form of social value. Reading Pieper, one comes away with the idea that the task of theology is not to produce technical solutions to modern problems but the sharing in and articulation of the collective struggle to know and to act under modern conditions. He insists that the task of theology is 'to pierce the dome' – to access and speak of what is transcendent from within the framework of immanence – and in doing so to help reshape the possibility of what it means to inhabit and renew the world. His response is made almost exclusively in the register of the metaphysical. It is a deliberately useless response, bearing witness to a concept of the common good beyond utility.

What a theological metaphysics of the good offers to contemporary society is, then, twofold: first, it gives an account of the fundamental reasons why the language of the common good persists, even when we've written its death notice, even when we cannot guarantee that it can produce the necessary social solutions we crave and even when it can be co-opted by dark forces. Second, it offers us an account of the life of the social and political conditioned not solely by the life of necessity (the conditions of finitude) but related to and rooted in an argument for the value of a transcendent account of freedom, beauty and goodness for the possibility of making all things new. Neither of these contributions represents a set of solutions to complex late modern problems, but they do articulate something of the ethical disposition required to keep open the horizon of struggle towards a better version of a common life. As such a theological metaphysics of the good represents a historically conscious way of living into contemporary challenges. Such theology holds open the possibility – but not the guarantee – of movement beyond intractable conflict and difference partly in its account of the conditions of creativity and natality (as Arendt might say) itself.

In this sense, the theologian does not arrive into discussions about the common good and the nature of the political as the expert-hero of the hour

(Sluga's abstract philosopher-rescuer who has climbed the hill and dropped down pearls of wisdom), nor as the anti-foundationalist diagnostician-clinician (Sluga's located political theorist). Rather, the theologian emerges as the contemplator-actor who narrates a transcendent story of human longing and desire, a developing story received again and again from deep, empirical attention to texts and to lives lived, through time, and who is required to stake themselves in that story as accompanier. The theologian is implicated in the combined human task of discerning these longings and in struggling to explore through reason, and through a glass darkly, whether they correspond to worthy goods, whose character can be tested and found to render goodness for the benefit of each and of the whole. The theologian has at their disposal the texts of a revealed tradition and a body of normative Christian philosophical reasoning, both of which attempt to narrate the ever-present longing for the good and the struggle to discern and secure this good in history, and the blessed rage for order in the face of all that destroys the good. Above all they are called to attend to embodied human living, to attend to the body of Christ. Therefore, the theologian is never really operating without foundations or norms.

Nonetheless, such norms and foundations exist in the context of communities of action engaged in the empirical act of discernment and never merely within the realm of abstract logic. Hence Pope Francis' vision of discernment of the common good as a synodical process in *Let Us Dream*. The theologian cannot perform this full task of discernment alone. They perform a necessary, incomplete instantiation of a shared task. The mode of the theologian in this shared task is one of attention, disclosure and imitation. The double diagnostic task for the theologian is to disclose the operation of the good that seem to reveal itself in history and to attend to the conditions that threaten, suppress, distort and limit the possibility of the life of the good. The theologian, as metaphysician of the good, attends to both presence and lack as historical forces, and is diagnostic in both modes.

Whilst rejecting the binary of the normative-diagnostic in Sluga's account, I recognize the resonance for the theologian in Sluga's call, as quoted earlier and worth repeating here, to consider the common good 'part of the political practice, not something set above it' and for that reason a partaking 'in the fallibility of everything political'. It is precisely this space of fallibility in thought and action that the theologian shares in as thinker and actor. There is no space outside this reality. To think transcendence is not to think oneself into a space far away but to descend into an attention to the movement of Spirit and Word in the world, as a paradoxical sign of both all that is 'more' and the space of limit. In this sense the common good is closer to the life of the beautiful than the useful, although it is also useful.

A strict theological reasoning of the common good, therefore, tends to begin not with an account of the yearning for technical solutions that lessen the difficulty of living with this fallibility but rather with an account of origins and ends, to explore answers to questions of value and meaning. It is the value question that sustains us through difficulty into a future. In his *Summa Contra Gentiles* Thomas Aquinas writes: 'the supreme good, namely God, is the common good, since the good of all things depends on God.' As we shall see later in the next chapter, Aquinas' account of the good – which Pieper draws on heavily – is rooted in the idea of God as the *summum bonum* in two important senses. God is the common good in the sense that all created things working within time are dependent on the originating and sustaining life of the Creator and in the sense that a share in the eternal life of the Creator as a form of fully inaugurated communion is the promised destiny of the creature. The good is therefore not simply a concept but a foundational and sustaining reality – that which grounds the creature's possibility of being. The Trinity of Father, Son and Spirit is the reality which sustains all that is within time. The Trinity exists as the continued recreated promise of return, as a full and final consummation of the longed-for life of the good.

Starting with an account of God as the common good – where the nature of God is to be uncreated supreme goodness and supreme freedom, unconditioned and unlimited by all the forms of necessity to which human persons are subject – means starting with the idea of the good apart from, but not in denial of, immediate notions of utility, necessity and aggregation. It begins with an account of a supreme freedom and goodness for which human persons yearn, akin to or as a longing for home.

A theological account of the good, and the common good, thus begins with an account of being and of longing that exists as a relation within the self and between the self and its created and uncreated Other. Thus, the life of the common good is to be lived in pursuit of the dual commandment to love God and to love neighbour, through which we express and are returned to our deepest longings and inherent social value(s). In the most mundane forms of neighbour love, as well as in our most intimate desires, we find the threads of a connection that pulls us into something transcendent.

In this theological account we stand first and foremost in a relation of gift to what is not ourselves. For the Christian, the recreation and fulfilment of this life of longing and relation in history are found in the Incarnation and the life, death and Resurrection of Jesus Christ. The Spirit, given as gift to the world, is the weaver of community and sustains the relation of all created things in time before the final fulfilment. Spirit and Word present in the now and not-yet of history make possible the breaking through of love and justice, the new and creative, as rupture in the face of historical difficulty, fallibility, violence and loss. This diagnostic disclosure of renewal is as close to a solution to the problem of irreconcilable goods as a theological metaphysics gets. But we cannot be good diagnosticians or solution finders without a capacity to see and interpret these patterns of love and desire in their political and public guises. If we dismiss them, they will irrupt again and again in both legitimate and distorted form. This is the contribution that Pieper assumes when he tells his reader that the contribution that the Christian philosopher makes is to transcend the environment of supply and demand and step forth into 'the world'. To act humanly for something that exists beyond a mere want or even a need (good though those may be) speaks to an expression of a deep freedom that is a participation in something divine.

Pieper penned his words on the common good as a series of lectures given on the nature of philosophy in the midst of the post-war world of 1947. More contemporary theological accounts of the common good have often been seen as the preserve of CST and the associated practices of social Catholicism. These traditions and practices are not, however, external to either historical *or* current secular social debates. They remain ideas very much in play. Whilst it was possible for the historian of ideas Emile Perreau-Saussine to write in 2011 in *Catholicism and Democracy* that the social battle ground for Catholicism in relation to late modern culture had shifted definitively from the terrain of thinking about the common good in terms of the political and economic towards the moral realm of personhood and autonomy (he had in mind critical debates about same-sex marriage, gender and euthanasia), this argument must now surely shift again. We are back to contesting the common good and the grounds of the politics of membership as a theological, ecclesiological and political concern. Concerns about moral autonomy and personhood are now at the heart of debates about the common good. The shaky borders between debates about autonomy and identity and the wider politics of membership have been thoroughly transgressed, and we live with the intersections, the mixed-up-ness, of all of these questions.

Having staked myself on a broad metaphysical orientation towards the question of the common good, in what follows I begin to explore the theological and philosophical hinterland of the common good as it sets the frame for the emergence of the later social encyclical tradition.

CHAPTER 6
THE COMMON GOOD
PATRISTIC AND MEDIEVAL CONTEXT

A people is an assembled multitude of rational creatures bound together by their common agreement as to the objects of their love.

When US president Joe Biden gave his inauguration address in Washington on 20 January 2021, this is the extract from St Augustine's *City of God*, Book XIX, Chapter 24, that he chose to use. Whilst referencing of religion in its civic form is not an unusual feature of American political life, it was striking that President Biden chose to define the common good in this way. His speech nodded in the direction of Augustine's insight that what made a people so was not a claim to have achieved a perfect model of justice – this was the Ciceronian version Augustine was revising – but rather the ability to strive towards a set of common objects of love: objects judged worthy in the light of a genuine pursuit of truth. Biden's speech was a good reminder that the claim that the state exists for the sake of the common good, and that each political community is unavoidably confronted with the question of its common good (and its capacity to negotiate it through a healthy common life), is in no sense original to the traditions of modernity, secular or theological. Nor were the implications and meaning of this term any more agreed or homogenous then: Augustine wrote this passage in critical dialogue with Cicero, and others. If, then, in the previous chapter, we considered the presence of common good ideas within the contemporary political landscape, secular and religious, then the task of this chapter is to set the scene for the later social encyclical tradition of handling the common good by exploring its deeper historical roots in a time when an easy distinction between secular and religious is no less clear than perhaps it turns out to be today.

In his *Politics*, Aristotle argues:

> It is manifest therefore that a state is not merely the sharing of a locality for the purpose of preventing mutual injury and exchanging goods. These are necessary pre-conditions of a state's existence, yet

nevertheless, even if all these conditions are present, that does not therefore make a state, but a state is a partnership of families and of clans in living well, and its object is a full and independent life.[1]

Plato, Aristotle and Cicero all deployed concepts of a common good as the foundation and goal of the *polis* or *res publica*. Nonetheless, they differed in their accounts of how one should frame this commitment to the highest good. For Aristotle, the common good is a higher form of good than the private good because it bears a greater likeness to the divine. As dependent and relational creatures it is part of our very nature to desire, to need and to build right and good relations with our neighbours and fellow citizens. We are, for Aristotle, social and political creatures, and to live well, rather than just to live, we seek to express this nature in and through achieving the ends of the common good. Thus, for the Aristotelian, the particularity of our relationships in time, the given-ness of our interdependence with the people with whom we share a place and time, necessitates as a basic expression of living well, an account of, and a striving for, the common good.

Whilst Aristotle focused on the common good as the highest good of the particular small-scale political community, Cicero talks of the rootedness of the local and particular common good in recognition of a prior universal brotherhood of mankind.[2] Cicero implies that a capacity to recognize the universal dimensions to humanity and the common good is a critical condition for maintaining kindness, generosity, goodness and justice in the life of the particular person and the particular community. In other words, a trained *universal* disposition enables a depth of *particular* response, rooted in place. For Cicero, the denial of *either* particular local civic *or* wider intercultural duties erodes the common good: the two are dynamically inseparable. For Cicero, the *res publica* comes into being when an assemblage of people is able to recognize itself as a partnership sharing common interests, with a common welfare to be pursued, committed to living under the same laws and sharing in mutual obligations and benefitting from basic rights. As for Aristotle, the Ciceronian *res publica* comes into being as part of a longing for, and as the practical grounds to secure, the common good. Both of these classical emphases – the importance of a focus

---

[1] Aristotle, *Politics* (Cambridge: Harvard University Press, 1989), 1280a.
[2] Cicero, *On Duties*, translated by Walter Miller (Cambridge: Harvard University Press, 1989), III 28.

The Common Good: Patristic and Medieval Context

on the common good of a discrete human-scaled political community, and as part of this, a necessary focus on the universal common good – make their way in adapted form into the later theological tradition, with Christian theologians providing new ways to propose a mediated relationship between the particular and the universal.

A further interesting and often overlooked continuity between classical and contemporary sources is found in the classical emphasis on both material well-being and affective, soulful, non-material well-being – and indeed, the relation between the two – as part of the common good. As Jane Mansbridge notes, Cicero speaks of the common good as a matter of *salus*: health, well-being and soundness. This same notion of salvation as 'salus' becomes a key motif for Christian theology. Mansbridge helpfully reminds us that a lazy tendency to imagine that classical theories of the common good were about civics, modern liberal theories about material well-being and theological theories concerned with the soul doesn't really help us understand the more complex, contested and continuous history of common good thinking. Classical, liberal and Christian theological accounts all propose a relation between the soul, the city and what is considered sacred, in their own ways.[3]

Early Christian theologians took these classical strands of thought and, reading in the light of the Scriptures, developed their own reflections on the common good. Whilst the continuities are real and important, and Mansbridge is right to emphasize the ongoing multivalent use of the idea, there are certain distinctives that underpin a Christian theological account, and this is perhaps revealed with the greatest clarity in Augustine's wider corpus of writings, including, but not exhausted by, his fifth-century *City of God*. Here Augustine presents a view of true human fulfilment as profoundly social in nature and of eternal significance. The fulfilled life is a communal or social existence, here and in the world to come. As we noted, he adopts, but critically revises, Cicero's understanding of the *res publica* in time, as a people gathered according to a shared orientation to common objects of love. Nonetheless, he views this fulfilment, even in the *res publica*, as only truly rooted in the promise and reality of the heavenly city. In Christ, aided by the communion of saints, into whose life we are invited, we are drawn to desire this shared orientation towards true, sustainable and lasting loves. This notion is already suggestive of a conflictual, negotiated process of communal discernment. It is suggestive of

---

[3]Mansbridge, 'Common Good'.

a human, historical process of coming to understanding over time and a non-linear movement towards the good. It is suggestive of receiving into one's own life a good external to the self, which one can recognize as one's own desire. It draws us in to a form of cooperation rather than simply assertion. As such, this is a vision beyond self-sufficient individual consciences or an account of public virtue that can simply be announced rather than laboured at and negotiated out of the plurality of human seeking and striving. The communal, social life of the heavenly city, present imperfectly but concretely in time in the communities we live, is the true and final focus of our loving and desiring and our right orientation. But knowing it, understanding it, is the work of a lifetime, and we are without final certainty. Augustine's account is based on the promise of a final peace and justice, which we will know ultimately and can know, experience and achieve partly now. Despite the incompleteness of both our knowledge and our experience of this good, it is more than a simple horizon or heuristic device, as it is for Errejón: in a very real sense it already is *and* is to come in its fullness.

A very careful account of the radical value, and yet incompleteness, of our common life is core to Augustine's social vision. Augustine's account is built around the tension between a call to holiness and a necessary acceptance of misrecognition and failure. We are fallible creatures, set within the horizon of limit, and consequently given to misrecognizing as much as to striving for goods. In this light, we should collapse into neither over-optimism nor over-pessimism. We have no right to be radically pessimistic, because love, hope and justice do not depend on us. They are continually renewed in our midst. Our choice is a free one, impelled by grace, to cooperate with the movement of the good in time.

The value of, and incompleteness of, our striving for the common good is, for Augustine, inseparable from the idea that we are hard-wired to be seekers after truth. We are driven in our social striving by *epistemological* needs: to search for, identify and share what we believe to be true. Therefore, for Augustine all temporal social bodies long for, fall short of, but continue to desire to 'fail towards' (to use Gillian Rose's helpfully paradoxical phrase) the life of the heavenly city, as part of the pursuit of the life of truth itself. That Christianity should see public life in this way, as part of its own pathway to virtue, will bring some inevitable conflict in its wake. This is the epic theo-drama that the *City of God* narrates. Where the life of the earthly civitas prevents or diminishes that pathway to truth, to love and to justice, the Christian must enact and live by Christianity's own fundamental law, a law that if faithfully discerned can only renew the city and the soul over time.

However, as Augustine scholars make clear, to look only in the pages of Augustine's *City of God* for the distinctives of a Christian account of the common good is to miss the wider account of creation that underpins his view of social life. This is no mere detour, and matters for our purposes because it grounds what remains particular about a Christian view of the common good to the present day. Augustine's account of the social good is rooted in his view of the very origins of creation and particularly his foundational belief that God created the world out of nothing (*creation ex nihilo*). Meditating on the Genesis story, Augustine sets forth the following logic. God created the world out of nothing. This is to say: God did not create out of Himself (He is divine, we are not) or with pre-existing material. He created matter from nothing. All that we are, and all that we have, is a communication of the divine to the creaturely world, from nothing. Goodness itself is our origin, and we bear the communication of that goodness into our own being. That goodness is all that sustains the world. We share in that goodness, know it, participate in it, communicate it and are signs of it, but we are not goodness itself in an independent, self-sovereign way.

What the act of creation brings into existence from nothing is form, order and unity. As Carol Harrison notes in her exposition of Augustine, this means that all that is, is of God and that having been brought into being it will never again be, or count as, nothing. There is beauty in this truth. Furthermore, in so far as something communicates and participates in that constant reality of the form, order and unity of creation, it participates in and contributes to all that sustains life. Where something destroys or loses this form or order and unity, it is a diminishment of the good, a falling away back into the nothingness from which it came. It is a refusal of what is and what has substance. As Harrison notes, this is to think of absence and presence as we might think of the relation of darkness to light, silence to sound, lies to truth.[4]

In this way, evil comes to be seen as lack or absence of the good. Augustine wrote that evil was the privation of the good. This did not mean that he thought it insignificant, just that evil (*malum*) is a refusal of substance, a form of enacted non-being. Evil is of the greatest significance because it is a denial of what is, of being itself, and the invitation to participate in being. Nonetheless, in saying that evil is simply the lack or privation of the good and therefore a no-thing, a falling into formlessness, he did not mean that it

---

[4]Carol Harrison, *Augustine: Christian Truth and Fractured Society* (Oxford: Oxford University Press, 2000).

does not exist without a trace. Its narrative is all too apparent. As Harrison also notes, nothing that comes into existence as reality is allowed in God's providence to be mere non-existence, and its existence in time requires the active good for its redemption. In this way it is taken up into the providence of God in history. Crucially, it is the good – which has substance and lasting reality – that interprets the meaning of evil, evil cannot interpret itself. Part of the task of the good is to render order, form and unity where disorder, chaos and fragmentation threaten the purpose and life of the whole. Nonetheless, as we have noted, this work of mediating the good is not a creaturely task alone; it is, for Augustine, rendered possible by the constant operation of grace. Grace is a form of the common good, it sustains the common good until history is done. Grace is not compensation for sin but rather is built into the flow of relationship between God and humanity from the beginning. It is the sustaining possibility from the origin. As such, love (caritas) is the foundational social relation and its sustaining reality.

The idea that built into human nature and human community is a tendency to fall back into non-being, a chaos of the formless, is central to ongoing Christian accounts of the common good in several key ways. First, Augustine's version of creation from nothingness and in goodness posits temporality, the instability and fragility of our social natures and our capacity for failure, as simply the reality of our creaturely life, flowing from our creation *ex nihilo*. This nature is not itself a curse or punishment; it is the consequence of a relationship between a Creator who is being itself, unmade and immutable, and creatures who are made, fabricated with freedom of willing. Second, Augustine's account suggests that the most fundamental misrecognition or falling away from goodness is the denial that we are fundamentally social, relational and interdependent beings. It is the myth of self-sufficiency, self-sovereignty and total self-possession which is the first falling away into nothingness. Thing-ness, reality itself, is the (non-possessive) relationship of all things. We are all really related to all. Nothing is more real than this. Nothing is more insubstantial than its denial. All that is to be pursued as good, and all that is to be identified as lacking, all that is most beautiful and all that is most painful in our social life, is a pathway through this truth. This is why, drawing on the Augustinian tradition, we might say that the common good is held in the relationship between people.[5]

---

[5] I am grateful for a conversation with Sr Helen Alford OP, in which she used a version of this sentence to sum up her own understanding of the common good. She is not to be held

The Common Good: Patristic and Medieval Context

The account of Christian citizenship that emerges from Augustine's writings is unmistakeably shaped by his vision of the Scriptures and a developing Christian metaphysics drawn from those accounts. The first social action is God's, our receptivity to the gift of life is the beginning of a sustainable life open to the common good. It is a vision of the goods of the earth created as a simple gratuitous divine self-communication of love and intelligence diffused through the world. Within this vision, suffering must also be accounted for and confronted. There is a mystery to suffering as part of the life of the good and a necessary willingness to suffer with others with a greater truth, which is also justice. This is not suffering because it is beautiful or for its own sake, but because it emerges as the only broken path towards the attainment or restoration of goods desired, lost or betrayed. Suffering is ethical as part of the common struggle to be free from the grip of pain and sin. To do so is to cooperate with the work of our redemption, a redemption that flows into history as a permanent overflowing of renewing potential. Such a logic, combined with the biblical evidence of a God who reveals Godself to the most marginalized in history, implies a service to, journeying with and structural option for the poor as part of an account of Christian citizenship and the common good.

Therefore, stemming from, but not limited to Augustine, a core theme in early Christian social writings concerns the ways that our social nature leaves us, of necessity and for our good, dependent on wider social bodies. Yet, whilst of necessary value such bodies remain penultimate, fabricated, proximate and fallible ways to secure our lasting and longed-for final good. Nonetheless, our route towards the latter takes in the former, life is no mere waiting game. It is the participation in, and understanding of, what is most real. We cannot, therefore, merely withdraw or hold our Christian noses through the messier parts. To do so would be to use pseudo-religious reasons to justify falling a little into that no-thing-ness. It would be to avoid the demands and gifts of the journey of both love and understanding.

By way of a connection back to where we started this book, this, in the end, is what I think Hannah Arendt does not quite grasp or accept when she argues that Augustine was the last figure of the ancient world to truly know what it means to be a citizen *and* that he betrayed that vision in favour of a Christian world view. She believed that in its appeal to the otherworldly

---

accountable for my reading of Augustine, however!

as the ultimate frame of realization and meaning, Augustine helped lessen the drive towards proper citizenship. Augustine is certainly re-inscribing the common good within a Christian cosmology, in which creation from nothing and salvation into divine community is the 'beginning' and 'end' of any Christian account of the common good. But it is a point of debate – to which we will return at the close of this book – as to whether a transcendent Christian grounding of the common good makes more possible but also more complex, or simply less urgent and pressing (as Arendt would have us worry), the life of the citizen of the temporal res publica.

Wider patristic and medieval Christian treatments of the common good follow or echo Augustine in foregrounding a cosmic struggle between good and evil, as well as integrating Christian accounts of caritas, ethical suffering and the service of the poor as the grounds of a Christian citizenship. These metaphysical themes came to structure distinctively Christian approaches to the common good. A shift in thinking about the family and household is also a key feature of Christian theories of the common good. Whilst Aristotle believed the state to differ 'generically' from family and household, with the state prior to the household (the whole being prior to the part), both Augustine and Aquinas reverse this idea, presenting the family and household as prior to the claims of state, acting as the most fundamental basis of social order and the first context for social virtue. As Rowan Williams notes, with Augustine the Christian tradition reverses the view that the family functions as an essentially private realm without inherent political significance.[6] Christianity makes the household a foundational *societas*, a move that subtly but importantly changes its relation to the common good.[7] This move cannot be understood apart from the move the early Church makes to speak of itself as both *oikos* and *polis*, refusing an easy separation between the two notions and recognizing itself as both. Finally, whereas Aristotle's account of the common good is predicated on the idea of certain groups or classes of persons as social leaders, the Christian theological tradition in transition from patristic to medieval writings focuses increasingly on a Pauline vision of all persons in community imbued with diverse gifts and callings. This bequeaths to the common good tradition a clearer theological notion of a dignified body, or people, bound

---

[6] Rowan Williams, 'Politics and the Soul: A Reading of the *City of God*', *Milltown Studies* 19/20 (1987), pp. 55–72.
[7] Ibid.

to each other through participation in a communication of gifts, which builds the body of the church polity and the *res publica*.

Susan Holman focuses her analysis of patristic interpretations of the common good on St Basil the Great. Paralleling the earlier discussion, Holman argues for two faces of the common good in Basil's work: first, as a social norm relating to civic harmony and fostering actions that repair material injustices, and, second, as an ecclesial norm relating to doctrinal orthodoxy. We might note in addition that both invocations in Basil relate the common good to implied notions of right order and right relationship, and to forms of Christian practice that later became known as the corporeal and spiritual works of mercy. Holman draws attention to the importance of Matthew 25 for patristic writers. She argues that this text was used as the scriptural basis for a distinct Christian reflection on the common good: the command to feed the hungry and clothe the naked, visit the prisoner and welcome the stranger was understood as entirely literal common good practices. Such works of charity or caritas were very clearly related to an eschatological goal. Civic and social commitments to the poorest were part of both alleviating suffering and 'helping one another upwards' towards a common promise of salvation.[8] The stranger and the person in need, whose path crosses our own, is bound to us, and we to them in the most immediate bodily way and for the good of salvation. Eschatology was the basis for proclaiming this scandalous social relation and a model of just social exchange. So, we might say, seeking the temporal common good folds us into the eternal common good; receiving first the promise of the eternal makes it possible to sustain the difficult path of seeking the temporal. This is a double act of communication and reception of what is real: the life of the uncreated experienced as gift and longing by the creature, and the everyday world of necessity in which this promise manifests itself as a tangible, meaningful call and response.

Thus, at the heart of such patristic developments, what is offered to the Church is a new explicitly Christian *theological* grounding for the common good. Creation and eschatology now set a new frame for Christian politics. The Scriptures were taken up by Augustine and Basil, as for others, as resources for rethinking the category of community and the notion of a life lived in common. The teaching of the Pauline epistles and the Acts of the

---

[8]Susan Holman, 'Out of the Fitting Room: Rethinking Patristic Social Texts on "The Common Good"', in *Reading Patristic Texts on Social Ethics*, eds Johan Leemans, Brian Matz and Johan Verstraeten (Washington D.C.: Catholic University of America, 2011).

Apostles on gift, on reciprocity, on the status of the poor, on the harmony and plurality of the worshipping body provided a new focus for developing ideas about the common good. The migration of the classical constructs of the common good – themselves already plural – into the developing body of patristic thought both preserved and changed the dimensions of this idea for a Christian audience. The new hybrid space of the church-polity – 'a people' that existed neither simply an extension of household nor a shrunken polis, but being analogous to and a form of both – created a new space for thinking about the common good.

In the light of her survey Holman summarizes patristic views on the common good helpfully as follows:

> The 'common good' is a natural characterization of divinely ordered social harmony and interdependence. It is inseparable from mercy, philanthropic divestment, and almsgiving, which are distinct activities subordinate to rightly ordered justice in present and future life. Common-good justice is actualised in the present life by – but not limited to – mercy with regard to such tangible substances or relational experiences as the acquisition, use, distribution, or divestment of material property; and social and liturgical harmony. These manifestations best emerge rightly from the individual, voluntary expression of personal virtues, such as 'orthodox' Christian beliefs and 'proper' piety; to fleshly desires and material objects; and interdependence on God and others in the ordered community. For patristic authors, perfect attainment of the 'common good' is founded on, presupposes, and ultimately realized in an eschatological reality that subordinates material survival in this world to the rightly ordered, relational substance of the next.[9]

Thomas Aquinas and the medieval development of the idea of the common good

If the collapse of political authority following the fourth- and fifth-century fall of the Roman Empire formed a crucial stimulus for Augustine's reflections on the common good in his *City of God*, then we might argue that, conversely, an

---

[9] Holman, 'Out of the Fitting Room', pp. 122–3.

era of renewal and rediscovery fuelled Thomas Aquinas' writing on politics, virtue and the common good in the twelfth and thirteenth centuries. The active renewal of political authority, the development of new patterns of law and the rediscovery of the political and ethical thought of Aristotle provided a crucial stimulus for a new era of Christian social thought. Where Augustine had offered a fundamental account of creation and salvation to structure a Christian account of the common good, Aquinas built on this foundation to develop a Christian teleological account of the role and nature of law and justice in building up the common good. It was this medieval tradition (in its neo-Thomist form) that Pope Leo XIII revisited in the late 1890s as the basis of the development of a formal church social teaching and which continues to be a core methodological source for CST today.

Whilst Aquinas' writings on the common good can be found across a wide range of texts – from the commentaries on Aristotle's *Nichomachean Ethics* and Peter Lombard's *Sentences* to the letter to the King of Cyprus *De regimine principum* (*De regno*) – his most developed writings on the subject are found in the *Summa theologiae* and the *Summa contra gentiles*. Despite the central importance of Aquinas' writings on the common good to the later nineteenth and twentieth-century neo-Thomist Catholic social tradition, it may be surprising to learn that the common good emerges as neither a central nor a systematic idea in his thought. Much as the modern reader might wish it, the *Summa* does not offer a substantive account of the common good as a theo-political principle. Nor does it offer us a full development of the scattered common good themes we have just identified in patristic writings. What Aquinas does offer is a genuine and profound development on earlier Christian and classical philosophical writing in the form of a more focused, limited and particular account of the common good as the grounds for political authority and as rooted in a distinctive theological metaphysics of virtue. Aquinas' innovation is, as Jean Porter suggests, the extension of a Christian understanding of law and political authority such that each is seen to relate to a theological account of the common good. Aquinas also retrieves Aristotle for Christian social thought, thus building on Augustine's Neoplatonism *and* developing a contrasting analysis, in particular arguing for the 'good' of political life in itself, and greater grounds for possible Christian resistance to tyrannical rulers.[10]

---

[10] Jean Porter, 'The Common Good in Thomas Aquinas', in *In Search of the Common Good*, eds Dennis P. McCann and Patrick Miller (New York: T&T Clark, 2005), pp. 94–120; see also John Finnis, *Aquinas* (Oxford: Oxford University Press, 1998).

A Christian teleology of the political

In *De regno*, a text written as advice to a political ruler and probably the most accessible of his political writings, Aquinas suggests that to grasp what is at stake in thinking about the common good in any given moment, we begin not with the mess of our own circumstances but rather by focusing on the teleological question of the ultimate horizon of the human ends or goals that we believe to be our purpose and our truth. In *De regno* he proposes that in exploring the question of ends we might pay close attention to whether these ends are ultimately imminent or transcendent.[11] Aquinas notes that if human persons were destined only for an end or social purpose internal to the self, or relevant to an imminent realm alone, then the authoritative and coordinated care of the doctor, teacher and banker would be sufficient for us to live the good life. If the highest good of the person is to be found in seeking education, enjoying physical health and maximizing material goods, it follows that these are the goods that the virtuous ruler needs to be expert in and seek to protect on behalf of society as a whole. The common good could then be defined as the pursuit of the public grounds needed to secure individual health, knowledge and wealth maximization on a societal scale. However, Aquinas notes, this is not the vision of the good life presented in the Scriptures. Whilst health, knowledge and sufficient share of the goods of the earth is a baseline for human flourishing, the more fundamental task is to seek relations of love and justice, which includes a just relation of praise to the divine maker of all that is and with whom, alongside others, we seek a life of communion. What does political authority look like when it needs to protect our capacity to live together in peace, rendering mutual assistance, pursuing justice in a world of loss and in so doing learning to participate in something of the redeeming and restoring life of God?

Aquinas explains to his reader that the way we view political authority, its nature, task and limits, is tied to how we understand what it means to be human. The core question is one of anthropology: What do you understand

---

[11] Although of disputed authorship this letter is still read as part of Aquinas' canon. It is now generally thought that *De regno* was begun by Aquinas, although possibly completed by Tolommeo of Lucca (Bartolomeo Fiadoni). The text was possibly left incomplete by Aquinas because of the death of the addressee of the letter, Hugh II of Lusignan. It is a text strongly influenced by Aristotelian political themes and deals mainly with questions of political authority and tyranny. For further details, see R. W. Dyson's 'Introduction' to *Aquinas: Political Writings* (Cambridge: CUP, 2008 edition).

being human to be about? He answers this in part, drawing on Aristotle and Augustine, by noting that humans are both social and goal-seeking creatures. These are interconnected aspects of who we are, such that we seek our *telos* or goal in ways that are profoundly social: we possess a deep drive not just towards a flat 'being-with' others but a disposition of 'being-with' as a form of 'being-towards' a particular form of living. Our final goal, for which all social living now is a preparation and a participation, is to seek beatitude, or blissful union with God. This echoes the approach to Matthew 25 we noted in our discussion of Basil: we are interdependent not just for mere survival but bound together to help one another upwards towards salvation. For Aquinas sociality and goal-seeking co-inhere within our nature as a movement of, infused by and as expressions of, grace. Thomist scholar Servais Pinckaers explains what Aquinas means by beatitude in this context: a movement of the person beyond individualism towards God, along with others, in friendship.[12] This isn't – as it might sound – a form of naïve idealism that brackets out sin, failure and human weakness; it is in fact a reflection on how the *simultaneously* graced and sinful aspects of our nature enable us to grasp the full depth of our social nature. *Both* love *and* sin are profoundly and intrinsically – albeit radically differently – social realities. Once we begin to think in this way, we begin to think about our moral relationships and the common good within a framework of past, present and future relations.

To find these themes more properly developed requires us to move to Aquinas' *Summa*. Here this anthropology finds expression in Aquinas' rendering of political authority as both a response to created goodness and a form of restraint in the face of sin. The first discussion of the common good in the *Summa* occurs in the context of a discussion about the prelapsarian condition of humanity, the state of human nature as intended by God before the Fall. In his writing on politics Augustine had argued that political authority existed as a consequence of sin: had there been no sin, there would have been no need for coercive rule of one human over another. In a world where sin occurs, the restraining, organizing and peace building capacities of political authority become necessary. Aquinas, typically in sympathy with Augustine's theology, in this instance begs to differ. Instead, he roots

---

[12]Servais Pinckaers OP, *The Servais Pinckaers Reader: Renewing Thomistic Moral Theology*, eds John Berkman and Craig Steven Titus (Washington D.C.: Catholic University of America Press, 2012).

the political in created goodness, in the life of dialogue and negotiation of goods, as much as in the coercive power necessary to manage human failure.

Aquinas carefully distinguishes between forms of social organization that relate to human life in its intrinsic goodness and those that operate as a consequence of sinfulness. Political authority, he argues, operates according to *both* registers. On the one hand it is possible to imagine that even in a human community without sin it would be necessary to organize and negotiate for goods that are truly common. It is not the experience of sin in the social body alone that drives us to negotiate a common life. Deeply rooted within our nature is a desire to realize forms of the good necessary for human flourishing that can only be accomplished by seeking the good of all and of the whole: the fruits of goodness require and emerge from cooperation and shared fabrication or making. Seeking these goods requires forms of common action, mutuality and a capacity to conceive of, and communicate about, the life of the commonwealth. In other words, for Aquinas we are not simply coerced or compelled through fear and loss to seek the life of society and the common good. Rather, we are also driven to build the common good by the exercise of our rational and free wills. Through contemplation, in intelligence and in creativity, we seek what is common for the good of ourselves and of our neighbours. This remains a fragile process and subject to sin, failure and misrecognition, but it remains a fundamental part of a Christian view of the intelligence and intelligibility of the world, where goodness makes rational sense.

Such an understanding has consequences for the way we view political rule itself: to exercise this kind of political authority for the sake of the community is to seek to participate in a genuine good. The later modern CST tradition will draw on this Thomistic frame to argue that politics should be seen as the highest of vocations and indeed a form of public caritas, love. Anglican philosopher T. H. Green draws on Aquinas when he argues that a capacity to seek the good enables human creatures to be both the potential authors of law and subject to that law.

The flow of Aquinas' thought carries us from a discussion of the 'ends' or goals of political authority to a consideration of the nature of law. Aquinas offers this formula to help us think about how law might be oriented towards virtue: law is best understood as 'a norm of reason that is oriented towards the common good'. Jean Porter argues that this definition of law disrupts a simple line of association between law and virtue. Law alone does not make us good people, and law cannot know or prescribe what virtue is

The Common Good: Patristic and Medieval Context

in each case. Rather, law fosters virtue indirectly, by directing its ordinances towards the common good. A complex account of law as eternal (God's law, known fully only to God, enacted as grace in history), divine (set out in the Scriptures, as revelation), natural (known to humans through the use of reason and in tune with revelation) and human (the revisable positive law we create to run human affairs, which draws on the above) together helps the person to discern in concrete terms just, charitable and provisional-revisable ways to relate to many and diverse neighbours and goods.

Pursuing this indirect account of the relation of law, virtue and the common good enables Aquinas to set limits for the use of coercion in the name of law. Law is legitimate not simply because it is promulgated by a legislator or legislature with authority or power, but rather because it aims at the common good and can articulate objective criteria for justice. Law must be able to give account for itself in this way. It is reasoned ordinance, not simply will-to-power or command. Given that the power held by the ruler is defined by the search for the common good, Aquinas argues that certain kinds of laws can be judged therefore to be no law at all, becoming instead simple acts of promulgated injustice or public violence. He defines such unjust or tyrannical political acts as those which aim at the personal advantage of either the individual lawmaker or an oligarchic grouping, kill the innocent or political acts that fail to distribute burdens and social responsibilities in a fair and equitable manner. This is an interesting and helpful development of the idea of Christian resistance in public life, beyond the account the Early Church Fathers left us with. We will return to the method by which Aquinas calculates such distribution of burdens and benefits later.

Thomistic justice: Distributive and commutative

For Aquinas justice aims at right (*jus*), that is to say at what can be considered equitable and balanced in human affairs: to render to each particular person their due. Whilst Aquinas argues that charity (caritas) acts as the framework for all virtues, justice acts as the framework for the *moral* virtues. As such, justice paves the way for the order that makes peace possible; charity (caritas) makes peace a reality, but justice paves its way. It is therefore the virtue of justice that Aquinas primarily draws upon as the basis for his political and economic thought and the concrete grounds for discussion of the common good.

In the *Summa theologiae* Aquinas argues for two kinds of 'general' justice: natural and legal or positive. *Natural* justice refers to the kind of justice that people tend to recognize as just based on reason and experience of the world. This is justice that we naturally incline towards. That we should not murder or steal is thus viewed as a generally accepted natural inclination of the moral personality. This kind of justice is seen to provide general principles for guiding law and morality. *Legal* (positive) justice comes into being as a determination of the lawmaker acting on behalf of a political community. Thus, legal justice admits of significant variation: the speed limit for motorway driving in Germany differs from the speed limit in the UK, based on legitimate discernment in the context of two political communities. The relationship between natural justice and legal justice is complex, but we should be clear that natural justice does not dictate in pure terms the detail of legal justice: legal justice improvises on, and seeks to make meaningful, the inclinations of natural justice. This is a fallible, revisable process of acting, and learning, in time. Legal justice seeks to express natural justice in its orientation towards the common good, but it will inevitably be marked by some plurality.

Aquinas also follows Aristotle in distinguishing between the species, parts and forms of what he calls 'particular' justice. This leads him to distinguish *commutative* from *distributive* justice. Both kinds of justice are governed by the principle of equity, but each is characterized by a different kind of equitable or just relation: one interpersonal and one societal. The difference between the two types of justice is merely a difference in the *type* of what is due: something that I am due because of what already belongs or adheres to me (property or dignity), or a share of what belongs to the whole, a sharing in common goods or what Aquinas calls 'the common fund'. *Commutative* justice (the former) is concerned with just relations between individuals within a political community. *Distributive* justice (the latter) is concerned with just relations between the individual and the state as a whole. Although both particular forms of justice are concerned with generating relationships of proportionate equality in society, in each case equity (understood in Aristotelian fashion as the mean between more and less) is determined in a slightly different manner.

Thomist legal scholar John Finnis articulates the distinct character of commutative justice as follows:

> [a] loose, wide sense [of commutative justice] extends to rights and wrongs in any interaction (or dealing) {commutation} between individuals {singulari} or neighbours. A more precise sense extends only to the mutuality of making recompense, whether in 'exchange' for (as a

commutatio of) the loss A has (wrongly) imposed on B or in exchange for a good voluntarily transferred (but not simply donated) by B to A.[13]

Commutative justice is concerned to guard against the constant risk that we unjustly justify injury to one another in order to promote a greater good.[14] This is a key concern for Aquinas at various points in his writings on justice and the common good: whilst a free-willing individual might decide to undergo some kind of suffering for the sake of the common good – in contemporary terms, perhaps I am a whistle-blower or an anti-racism campaigner – I can never *compel* or justify the suffering of *another* for the sake of the whole. I might choose, when there is no other option, to take suffering upon myself for the good of others, but I cannot compel the suffering of another for a higher good. Likewise, justice itself requires that I attend to the kind of losses that might be imposed upon my neighbour in routine interactions or social exchange. Examples given for this kind of justice are often economic in nature: I must sell you the second-hand car for what it is really worth and not clock the mileage. But it might also apply to the unjust and humiliating treatment of a prisoner or a migrant without the protections of citizenship. The basic manner of treatment when we are stripped before the law is often what we remember most. We might say that where law becomes thinnest, or where the exercise of power renders a sense of cultural worthlessness, reflection on commutative justice becomes increasingly important in itself and to an overall sense of justice. This is a tradition Pope Francis has picked up in his writings and sermons: the politics of indifference, in which we are faceless and nameless before others, in which we are unmoved by the task of commutative relation, is part of a society that cannot in the end produce justice or dignity. He has also begun to think about the ways that digital communication relates to wider questions of justice.

Distributive justice concerns the proportionate distribution of benefits and burdens within a society. Society's benefits include the moral and material goods it has to distribute such as wealth and honour, and its burdens include such matters as taxes and general expenses of living, costly forms of labour and service, access to power in order to shape one's life in a dignified and worthwhile manner. Aquinas notes, '[W]e speak of injustice

---

[13]Finnis, *Aquinas*, p. 216.
[14]Thomas Aquinas, *Summa Theologiae*, Vol. 38, translated by Marcus Lefébure OP (Cambridge: Cambridge University Press, 2006), 2a 2ae 68 3.

with regards to inequity between one person and another, as for example when a person wants to have more [than another person has] of goods such as riches and honours and less of evils such as labour and losses.'[15]

The ways in which each society works out who deserves what will vary significantly according to conceptions of social value. Should wealth or birth, ethnicity, citizenship or virtue, act as the basis of social value? Augustine had written in his *City of God* that our common loves define us as a *res publica*. This sentiment is not simply future oriented and speculative – what would we like to honour and love – but an empirically revealing one. What does our current social structure tell us that we seem to love, and how do we feel about that on reflection? Are these worthy loves to carry into the future? Reflecting on this theme in his 2012 BBC Radio series on the common good, philosopher Michael Sandel suggests we ask: Does a footballer deserve to be paid more for his skill than a teacher or care worker; does a poorer 'unskilled' migrant have less right to enter a labour market than a wealthier 'highly skilled' migrant? The current coronavirus pandemic has seen the early twenty-first-century world confront the edges of this question anew: Who keeps the city running? Whose labour is indispensable? Who risks most for the common benefit?

Aquinas argues that inequity in exchanges between individuals and within a society force a breach in relationship. This separation occurs at two levels: between the person who takes advantage and the person who suffers loss, and between the person who seeks power over another and God. Such acts estrange the person from God, for God is goodness and pure relationship. For this reason, Aquinas argues, 'it is necessary to salvation to restore to a person what was taken away from him unjustly'.[16] Why is this so? Why would distributive injustice and salvation be connected? Both commutative and distributive injustice break relationship and isolate, and isolation from relationship with neighbour and God is impoverishing. Aquinas' understanding of justice is concerned with 'the transformation of the whole of creation so that it fully manifests the divine wisdom, beauty and goodness'.[17]

---

[15] Thomas Aquinas, *Summa Theologiae*, Vol. 37, translated by Thomas Gilby OP (Cambridge: Cambridge University Press, 2006), 2a 2ae 59 1.
[16] Aquinas, *Summa Theologiae*, Vol. 37, 2a 2ae 62.
[17] Matthew Lamb, 'Wisdom Eschatology in Augustine and Aquinas', in *Aquinas the Augustinian*, eds Michael Dauphinais, Barry David and Matthew Levering (Washington D.C.: Catholic

The virtue of charity

We noted that notions of almsgiving and concepts of mercy, drawn especially from Matthew 25, were integral to such patristic accounts of the common good. Whilst Aquinas does not always make formal connections between the language of the common good and works of mercy, he does relate justice to charity as the basis of a peaceable social order. The *Summa* subsumes discussion of the fourteen works of mercy under discussion of the virtue of justice, as a form of almsgiving. The works of mercy are both corporeal and spiritual. Corporeal works of mercy include feeding the hungry, giving drink to the thirsty, clothing the naked, welcoming the stranger, visiting the sick, giving ransom to the captive and burying the dead. Spiritual works of mercy – which are still conceived as part of the virtue of justice and as a form of giving alms – include admonishing the wrongdoer, educating the ignorant, counselling the doubtful, offering forgiveness for injuries, offering comfort to the afflicted, bearing wrongs patiently and praying for the living and the dead.[18] Scriptural warrant for these acts can be drawn not only from the obvious Matthew 25 but also from Hebrews 13 on solidarity with the stranger and the tortured 'as though you yourself were being tortured', Romans 12:13, and the powerful image of foot washing in John 13. Aquinas comments in his *Commentary on the Gospel of John*, '[w]e can say that by this action our Lord pointed out all the works of mercy. For one who gives bread to the hungry washes his feet, as does one who practices hospitality or gives food to one in need.'[19] Such acts are viewed as profound acts of friendship, and friendship builds the common good through social unity.[20] These acts might be considered a form of justice insofar as they return to the poor has been unjustly distributed, but in themselves they are debt-free acts of friendship.[21]

Aquinas outlines just two necessary conditions for almsgiving: that the giver has enough and can spare goods for another and that the recipient is in need. Aquinas sets no test of moral worth for the recipient, only a condition of need and capacity to give. There is an order of charity such

---

University of America Press, 2007), p. 259.
[18] Aquinas, *Summa Theologiae*, Vol. 34, translated by R. J. Batten (Cambridge: Cambridge University Press, 2006), 2a 2ae 32 2.
[19] Aquinas, *Commentary on the Gospel of John*, 13: lecture 3, §1779.
[20] Aquinas, *Summa Theologiae*, Vol. 34, 2a2ae 31 1.
[21] Aquinas, Summa *Theologiae*, Vol. 41, 2a2ae 114 2.

that we ought to give first to those in need who are closest to us, but at a level whereby need is met and surplus is maximized for giving to more distant neighbours, to whom we also owe duties guided by norms of justice and charity. These acts of giving alms, hospitality or care are central to a Thomist ethic of justice, and they are a crucial part of what protects peace and builds the common good.[22] Peace is achieved through acts of justice that facilitate social unity, but more significantly by acts of charity which in themselves mediate peace.[23]

The common good and private goods

Whilst Aquinas argues that private goods are the antithesis of the common good, it also makes sense for him to see no fundamental tension between what he views as true self-interest (framed in transcendent terms) and the common good. Aquinas views humanity's deepest desires as inherently common and relational. As the twentieth-century Thomist thinker Josef Pieper expresses it, the nature of the human person is that she lives in a world, where 'world' equates to a set of relations. For Pieper, channelling Aquinas, it is the Spirit who acts in the world as the power and capacity to relate both to other beings, human and non-human, and to relate to the totality of being. To say that something 'has being' is to say that it exists already in a field of relations, relations of necessity and of gift.[24] Thus Aquinas offers the grounds for a Christian philosophy of the common good, which argues not simply for natural order discernible by reason but for a theological grounding of all life, through the Spirit in the call to a dynamic, life-long deepening of relationships. It is the external–internal reality of such a Spirit at work that enables the person to 'venture all' in transcending borders and boundaries that limit relations of love and justice.[25] In this context, Aquinas sets no limit to the possible ethical demands of neighbour love. The CST document that perhaps gets closest to echoing this theme is *Fratelli tutti*, in its meditation on the Good Samaritan, arguing that Jesus turns the static question – who is my neighbour? – on its head. The theological question is

---

[22] Aquinas, *Summa Theologiae*, Vol. 35, 2a2ae 37 1.
[23] Aquinas, *Summa Theologiae*, Vol. 34, 2a2ae 29 3 ad 2.
[24] Josef Pieper, 'The Philosophical Act', in *Leisure: The Basis of Culture*, translated by Alexander Dru (San Francisco: Ignatius Press, 2009), pp. 114–16.
[25] Pieper talks about the life of Spirit enabling us as an expression of freedom to 'venture, and perhaps to venture all' in our relatedness to our 'world'. See *The Philosophical Act*, pp. 114–15.

a dynamic one: How, over a lifetime, do I continually grow in the ability to become a neighbour?

For Aquinas, there is then only the appearance of a tension between personal desires or private goods and common goods. The fundamental tension is between *disordered* self-interest and the common good. Frustratingly, for Aquinas this tension produced by disordered self-interest (sin and fallibility) is one that we are partly aware of but also partly blind to: this is the nature of sin, that we know our actions and motivations only partly. This partial blindness to what disorders the good makes living together and common discernment of what is truly good a critical part of upholding and discerning the good. Living as a 'people', in ecclesial and social terms, enables a wisdom, discernment and repentance necessary for growing in knowledge and virtue, through a glass darkly.

Writing before the modern era, Aquinas does not presuppose a particular ethnic and linguistic concept of nationhood as the grounding for being 'a people' who together discern the life of virtue. Rather, echoing and developing classical and patristic themes, he argues that being 'a people' involves an acceptance of being gathered (in difference) under one ordering and limiting set of laws and one government, so as to live well, rendering mutual assistance. We are called to assist each other according to the skills, capacities and resources we have as unique persons and as communities, and according to the acute needs of our neighbour. Thus, we give and receive based on an objective account of the Christian goodness towards which we are called and that calling is evidently into a life of plurality and communion.

Although Aquinas does not spend time, as contemporary thinkers might, exploring fundamental conflicts between the common good and private goods he does offer a clear account of the relationship between private or personal goods and the common good. We have established that, for Aquinas, the common good exists as a rationale for politics. As the person seeks their private good so the ruler seeks the common good; these are pursuits proper to each. Nonetheless, these terms work relationally and analogically; they are distinguishable but ultimately inseparable. Deploying a Thomist logic, and refusing a dualistic logic of private and common goods, we can say that the common good is how I talk about the social reality of all that is truly most personal. I am dependent on the life of the commons for the conditions necessary to pursue my deepest desires. In the act of working towards their fulfilment the common life is produced. As such, the common good is not the duty to be satisfied after I have secured my private interests but rather it is part of the grounds for all else. This is true in the sense that the person has basic needs for security, shelter and sustenance that require the security of membership of a political community. It is also true that securing my private good in a more expansive sense is dependent on forms of mutuality, the exercise of duties to and by others, and right relation with others.

As later authors have extrapolated, based on developing this Thomist logic, we can also say there are no truly private goods that are not also social in *some* form. Private property exists by virtue of circulating social norms about ownership within community; housing, work and trade all exist according to sets of social norms and sustained by common agreements or social consensus. The common good is therefore an affective public language that we use to help us think about forms of mutuality, gift exchange and right relation to near and distant neighbours and which functions as the very basis for what we might consider to *be* 'private'. It is of necessity a language of love and justice that runs through even our most private and intimate of concerns.

A second, corresponding emphasis for Aquinas is that the common good is composed of the good of each particular person. We are used to thinking that the common good requires me to pay attention to matters beyond myself, attending beyond self-absorption to the good of the whole. However, less well understood is that the common good is only truly common if I am able to pursue private goods and personal flourishing: my sporting, intellectual, musical or teaching skills, for example, or simply my search for truth. The common good is, therefore, not well presented as some additional set of collectivist duties laid on top of, or as a limitation to, meeting my private needs or rightful seeking of private goods. The common good is not to be reduced to an hour's volunteering on a Saturday afternoon.

Rather, echoing Pauline body language, Aquinas expresses a vision of flourishing rooted in seeking to exercise the particularity of personality and calling for the sake of, and within the context of, the building up of the whole community. Virtue is the singular category that holds together these diverse but related forms of the good. We will pursue many individual goods as an expression of our character in a lifetime. What matters are the truly *free* ends of this pursuit, right relation to self and other as we pursue such goods: that our appetites be directed freely towards what is truly good. Thus, the common good can be understood as *rightly ordered self-interest*; nonetheless, discerning and securing this involve the active struggle to form and maintain a common life with others.

Further questions remain about the conflict between goods. At a metaphysical level, Thomist common good theories face criticism for lacking sufficient attention to social malice and for a feared idealization of the human condition. Eleanore Stump notes a particular question which tends to arise for modern readers when deploying a Thomist account: Is Aquinas producing an inappropriately demanding moral system that requires individuals to routinely give more of themselves to others and to the social whole than they might wish, which consequently, despite its more abstract claims, produces a constant tension at an existential or phenomenological level between personal flourishing and the flourishing of the whole? How on earth do we actually live this life of constant relation and attention to the world? This seems a reasonable and important question to ask.[26]

Stump answers the question in the following way. The more demanding parts of giving to the common good are imagined by Aquinas to be matters of *volition*: acts of free will which cannot be demanded of the individual by the state or political community but which are given in freedom and, as Pieper argued, not simply *in order to* . . . However, in some limited circumstances and in response to this life of freedom, we find ourselves compelled to make a free choice within the life of community that brings risk of personal suffering or loss. We are not promised that pursuing the life of the common good will be a path away from all suffering. Stump suggests that Aquinas offers one example of such a case: giving moral reproof to a wrongdoer, issuing 'fraternal correction' or expressing 'social dissent'. Speaking out in the face of moral wrongdoing is a requirement of the common good for Aquinas, although he is careful to clarify that it must be done with great consideration being given to the timing and manner in which it is undertaken.

Stump offers us a contemporary reference point to extend and apply Aquinas' thinking. She explores the cases of the whistle-blower who calls time on the illegitimate practices of a business, the person who adopts a courageous stance in the face of an abusive political regime or perhaps the person who is pushed to take a stand for their religious beliefs. It is easy for all to see that the whistle-blower suffers for what she has enacted: such an act risks without guarantee a loss of status, wealth, friendships or health.

---

[26]Stump, *Aquinas* (London: Routledge, 2003), pp. 334–8. The material in these paragraphs is taken from a reading of chapters 2 and 10 of Stump's text, on goodness and justice as themes in Aquinas' work, pp. 61–91 and 309–38.

Towards a Politics of Communion

When someone gives with no promise of a balancing return, we might tend to assume that they would have been better off prioritizing their 'personal' or private good as a matter that could after all be determined separately from the 'common' good. Stump suggests that the choice is more simply one between two different kinds of suffering and limitation, and begs the question of the meaning and purpose of a human life as a whole. If the whistle-blower had not exposed malpractice she would *still* have suffered from a kind of difficulty and lack in response to reality and a world of relations, but she would have suffered *differently*. To understand that the whistle-blower suffers *either way* requires us to grasp the extent to which evil and wrongdoing creates a culture of suffering in which individual and structural manifestations of disordered goods incentivize forms of distorted relationship. We addressed this in our discussion of structural sin. The contrast is then not so much between a life lived quietly, going with the flow, and a life that brings suffering upon itself through foolhardy virtue, but rather between *different forms* of social difficulty or suffering. A corrupt politics, an abusive family or a business that incentivize unjust exchange is already a context in which flourishing is undermined, but we are often blinded to this. Deploying Aquinas, Stump asks: Is avoiding dissent destructive in its own way to one's flourishing, albeit in ways we tend not to think about? One might add, does it leave one adrift from both the pursuit of the truth and true relationship? For Aquinas, Stump notes, the question of justice is connected to the question of how an individual life may be used for the good of the whole community, according to the purposes of God.[27]

To rephrase and trespass a little beyond Stump's analysis, I think we can be led by Aquinas to say the following: the reality of evil, and the Christian belief that following the Resurrection, mortality cannot be thought of as the most fundamental crisis of human living, means that Christians might well be called upon to enact forms of social dissent and solidarity with victims of injustice that may bring suffering or difficulty in its wake. This is the case not because God desires us to suffer or because suffering in itself is any kind of good with inherent meaning or beauty – God does not and it does not – but because of *both* the pervasive social reality of evil *and* the possibility of transformative action brought about by (co-)operation with grace in seeking truth and goodness in the face of evil. The extent to which our lives

---

[27]Stump, *Aquinas*, p. 332.

are lived in quiet encounter with such evil necessitates – on occasion – a willingness to suffer for our own flourishing and that of others.

There are two crucial points to emphasize here: first, the suffering or difficulty in question, even when apparently altruistic, still *relates to* one's own well-being, and, second, a *willingness* to suffer should be distinguished carefully from a *desire* to suffer. No notion of the common good should demand or compel suffering as in itself a good. The idea of suffering for our own flourishing when set within Aquinas' understanding of justice and the common good is difficult, therefore, but not oxymoronic. Drawing on Aquinas, Stump thus concludes that Aquinas is reasonable, even when facing malice, in positing that 'the best or only way to pursue one's own wellbeing is by pursuing the good of all'. The good of all is pursued through the life of virtue, with pre-eminent attention being given to justice and charity as the framework for all social relations within the body politic.

Stump's case study does not, of course, give full answer to the critics who think this too demanding and/or too optimistic a system, nor does it handle all facets of the conflict of goods that arise in complex late modern societies. Arguably, that task is inherited, fundamentally incomplete, by our own generation. It is not yet a theme well developed in formal CST.

Conclusion

What we have in both the patristic and medieval traditions are the traces of a distinct, compelling, suggestive, yet incomplete Christian articulation of the common good. Its power lies in its fundamental account of the origin, purpose and end goal of human living, within a created order. As we shall see in later chapters, the modern CST tradition has made rather incomplete and often quite disintegrated use of the earlier tradition available to it. For these reasons, a reader new to this area should not be surprised to find both patristic and medieval accounts invoked incompletely and in divergent ways by popes and scholars alike.

What we might claim, based on these pre-modern sources, is that the common good is clearly seen as the core purpose for the existence of our total social world and within that the *res publica*. It is the origin of our very desire for the political, which sees the *res publica* come into being, and the goal it serves. Service of this goal requires a community living under a single body of law to share and use the material goods of the earth with justice, to honour the aspirations and longings, to search for meaning and truth as part of the life of the good itself, and to act to preserve the spaces which enable the communication and exchange of these material things, meanings and strivings. None of this is possible without basic just practices in access to all forms of goods, including power itself as a form of just relation. All matters of the good are in the end inescapably social matters and therefore beg wider reflection on the nature of freedom, autonomy, community and truth itself. For these reasons, eventually a Christian theological account of the common good becomes a reflection on caritas itself, lived within the limits and promise of time.

CHAPTER 7
THE COMMON GOOD
THE ENCYCLICAL TRADITION

The Canadian social philosopher Charles Taylor argues that the vital contribution made by Catholic social thought to modern ideas of the common good is found in two of its key emphases. First, in an age of individualism Catholic social thought insists on the irreducibly communal nature of meaningful human agency. Second, in an age that is so taken with negative definitions of freedom as primarily freedom *from* others and *for* self-determination, Catholic social thought proposes that all true freedom is ultimately a matter of freedom *for* relationship and *for* the good. Such a freedom requires freedom from want, from excessive coercion and force, from indignity, injustice and so forth, but its ultimate horizon is constructively and irreducibly relational and communal. In an age of pluralism, it supposes that the communal dimensions to our lives are plural and never simply singular or monolithic. Taylor proposes that a transcendent, theologically inflected concept and practice of the common good represents an indispensable language and practice of relationship in an age when we have tended over more than two centuries towards both an increasing moral and social atomism in the way we conceive of the good in public life and public policy, and an increasingly homogenous way of imagining that good.[1]

In building this case, Taylor has in his sights the assumption that seems to have guided much recent public policy discussion: that our common welfare is always reducible to the benefits enjoyed by individuals and can be managed in increasingly technocratic and managerial ways. Any public or common good on this account is in the end no more than the sum of its parts and is primarily a matter of calibrated systems and processes.

---

[1] See dialogue between Alasdair MacIntyre and Charles Taylor in the collected essays: John Horton and Susan Mendus (eds), *After MacIntyre: Critical Perspectives on the Work of Alasdair MacIntyre* (Cambridge: Polity Press, 1994). See also Charles Taylor, *Philosophical Arguments* (Cambridge: Harvard University Press, 1995), chapter 7.

Matters of the common good are important but largely impersonal in their public guise. Taylor explores the kinds of goods that do not fit easily within this register, including the goods of a shared language that endures over time (he gives the example of Québécois), and the goods associated with membership of different kinds and scales of community. His point is to name a sort of good that a political philosophy of liberal modernity and the operations of the nation state does not tend to name well: one that lies in the relationship between persons, that requires attention to the messy spaces of real embodied exchange and mutual recognition, and a shared understanding of the intrinsic value of such spaces and exchanges.[2] These goods are created out of, and held within, the relationship of persons, and they are dependent upon the factors that foster or break and fracture relationship. Many benefits come to the individual from participation in these goods, but they are not defined by individual benefit alone; each person is required to invest in and participate in this process, but individual action alone cannot guarantee the conditions that foster this good in action.

Such observations on the value of a transcendent account of the social good and the importance of a politics of recognition and relationship in an age of individualism provide a helpful context for the teaching on the common good presented in the modern social encyclicals. We noted the decline and fall of the Roman Empire as a critical stimulus for Augustine's political theology, and, with Aquinas, we noted the importance of the renewal of Aristotelian ideas of virtue and society and the development of a new generation of thinking about political authority, virtue and law. The paradoxical developments of increased global socialization, the sudden, unprecedented (perhaps brief) dominance of nation states as our pre-eminent category for political belonging, combined with increased social atomism and individualism, form the complex context for the modern encyclicals that renewed discussion of the common good.

Whilst the two earliest modern social encyclicals – *Rerum novarum* and *Quadragesimo anno* – presented the common good as a foundational principle of the Church's social teaching, curiously they offered no real explanation of what they assumed this term to mean. It is unclear whether Leo XIII and Pius XI simply assumed Catholic familiarity with the idea and its history or whether an articulate sense of how to communicate it in a modern age was only just developing in the hinterland of the new

---

[2]Ibid.

social encyclical tradition. It is striking that the first clear definition of the common good in the modern social encyclical tradition is made in the post-war papacy of John XXIII. Venturing a fresh definition, John XXIII's *Mater et magistra* (1961) defined the common good as follows: it 'embraces the sum total of those conditions of social living, whereby men are enabled more fully and more readily to achieve their own perfection'.[3] The only striking edit made to this definition by the Second Vatican Council was simply to add the reminder that the subjects of flourishing constituted individual persons and 'social groups', with social bodies recognized as vital organs for the pursuit of justice and charity (caritas).[4]

This definition clearly draws on the older Christian history of the term – the 'end' of the common good is our freedom to be drawn into the life of perfection, and it is primarily concerned with fostering the necessary social conditions that enable human flourishing and reaching towards the good – but John XXIII expresses it in a distinctively new formulation. It strikes the reader as a definition shaped to be heard in a secular age driven by the question of the individual. As we noted in earlier chapters, in this age the focus of the Church's social teaching is increasingly the dignity of the human person. Both these influences seem to shape this new definition.

Before moving to consider the context out of which this definition emerges, it is worth pausing to consider some of its notable features. Papal discussion of the common good in this post-war context focused on the proposition that the common good is most meaningfully understood as a way of talking about the common *conditions* of social life that enable the attainment of human flourishing (the good life) by all. In the first instance, this is a simple reminder that human beings are intrinsically social and interdependent creatures and cannot achieve their good alone. Whilst this definition is not followed by an exhaustive list outlining all the necessary conditions that enable persons to live well, the later encyclicals refer at various points to particular kinds of institutions, practices and processes which foster these social conditions (these include housing, education, decent wages, dignified work, health care, access to citizenship, criminal justice, employment and, in more recent documents, a healthy climatic system, as in *Laudato si'*). Interestingly, an appendix to earlier drafts of the *Gaudium et spes* document also note the importance of beauty, truth,

---

[3] *Mater et magistra*, §65.
[4] *Gaudium et spes*, §26.

love, liberty and justice as a necessary spiritual context for fostering the conditions for human development and the common good.[5] Later encyclicals, and the appendix draft for *Gaudium et spes*, also outline the fundamental connection between the just and equitable distribution of the goods of the earth and the conditions necessary for attaining the common good. We might also propose that we are drawn into reading the various principles of CST (solidarity, subsidiarity, participation, universal destination of goods, option for the poor) as further substantive reflection on the dynamic nature of the social conditions and practices necessary for attaining the temporal good.

Second, we might note that the language of the common good in conciliar and post-conciliar social documents – the sum total of conditions – sounds notably more modern, and even aggregative, than pre-modern definitions. This has worried some later commentators. Certainly, given that the focus of nineteenth-century utilitarian thought was precisely upon the aggregation of benefits to the individual as the basis of society, this language is striking. In one sense, it is a formulation that speaks the language of its context. But in another sense, it is precisely this world view that it seeks to contest. The sum of conditions is not, as the definition in the 2006 *Compendium of the Social Doctrine of the Church* is at pains to make clear, 'a simple sum'.[6] They are 'indivisible', stem from the 'dignity, unity and equality' of all persons and are only achievable for ourselves when we live *with* and *for* others. In our earlier discussion we noted that the notion of material well-being (*salus*) runs from classical, through patristic and medieval to contemporary common good thinking. The definition adopted by John XXIII and the council continues this line of thought, making clear that the conditions for well-being are the conditions necessary for full human development. These exceed the language of individual benefits and burdens and are profoundly and irreducibly transcendent, social, relational and thus related to wider questions of value. If we wish to use the language

---

[5]Several drafts of *Gaudium et spes* were produced before the final approved text. They contain further notes on, and more expanded definitions of, the common good. See *Acta Synodalia Sacrosancti Concilii Oecumenici Vaticani II,* vol. III, pt. 5 (Vatican City: Typis Polyglotis Vaticanis, 1975), pp. 151–2. See also commentary in V. Bradley Lewis, 'Catholic Social Teaching on the Common Good', in *Catholic Social Teaching: A Volume of Scholarly Essays,* eds Gerard V. Bradley and E. Christian Brugger (Cambridge: Cambridge University Press, 2019), pp. 235–66.

[6]*Compendium*, §164, see pp. 83–5.

of aggregation, then we must be clear that this is neither a simple addition sum nor solely individually aggregative. As civil economy thinkers have noted, if it is mathematical at all, it is closer to a multiplication sum than a simple majoritarian addition. If the conditions are zero for anyone, they are zero for the true common good of all.

Finally, following from the first two sets of observations, we should note that the end goal of such social processes is the production not merely of happiness or health but of the perfection or fulfilment in vocation of the person. Whilst the only definitions to make explicit reference to the fuller Thomist theological vision of beatitude as the end of the common good are in the 1992 revision of the *Catechism* and 2006 *Compendium*, the modern social encyclical definitions do conclude with a vision of the perfection of the human person.[7] This perfection is not an individual achievement but is inseparable from a cooperative social life and the operation of grace. These documents emphasize human persons as both the beneficiaries of these common social conditions and the historical subjects whose graced labour is the only guarantee of the existence and maintenance of these social conditions. This work to secure the common good is the work of both love and justice, both are essential and belong to community in different ways. This work remains inevitably unfinished and open-ended within history.

Mid-century renewal

To understand the context from which the new definition in *Mater et magistra* emerges requires us to explore both the hinterland to the encyclicals themselves and the developments in mid-century social thought with which we began our opening chapter. Much of what comes to fruition in the social thought of the council period arguably germinates quietly in the interwar years. This germination happens in the context of both the papacies of Pius XI and Pius XII and in the world of lay Catholicism – including movements such as the French and Italian Social Weeks, stimulated in part by *Rerum novarum* – and the developments in moral theology led by theologians of the major religious orders. As V. Bradley Lewis argues, a traceable line exists from Jesuit Luigi Taparelli's (1793–1862) 1840s natural law treatise,

---

[7]*Compendium* (2006), §170.

in which he proposes the common good be thought about in terms of rights and duties, aiding the individual to attain their happiness, which is only meaningful and possible through positive social cooperation, and the later emergence of this same language in the council's new definition.[8] This trajectory is, however, plural. Similar thinking emerges in the context of the French and Italian Social Weeks and in particular via the moral theology of Dominican theologians Marie-Benoît Schwalm OP and Joseph-Thomas Delos OP. Drawing from Thomist moral theology, the common good is viewed as concerned with the capacity to live a fully human life, and critical to this possibility is just forms of distribution of, and access to, material and moral goods. The goal of the common good is perfection in human living. This is achieved through every form of social cooperation and associational life from marriage and friendship, to business, education and political participation. Such associational life is protected and nurtured (but not replaced) by temporal government, whose task is to foster and regulate this complex map of associational life. It creates law that fosters peace, security and justice. It is a participation in the goods of order and form. In turn the ultimate framework for all of this activity is the divine or eternal order itself. This framing order limits and gives meaning to the temporal order. Temporal government exists always in a relation of service to the parts and the whole, and is in no sense ultimate. By the 1920s a range of such definitions were circulating.

Given the influence of Taparelli's thinking on the papacies of Leo XIII and both Pius XI and XII, and the flow of ideas from the Social Weeks into Roman curial thinking, it is unsurprising that the language of the moral manualists begins to trickle visibly into official papal social teaching. Pius XI's *Quadragesimo anno* notes at some length the importance of the distribution of wealth through 'various individuals' and 'classes of society' to 'the common good of all'. There is a right action by all members of society to ensure that 'the good of the whole community must be safeguarded'.[9] Pius notes '[b]y these principles of social justice one class is forbidden to exclude the other from a share in the profits'. He continues 'the distribution of created goods must be brought into conformity with the demands of the common good and social justice'.[10]

---

[8]Lewis, 'Catholic Social Teaching on the Common Good'.
[9]*Quadragesimo anno*, §57.
[10]Ibid., §57–8.

Divini redemptoris, published in 1937, echoes these themes, deploying a Thomist language of the relation of part to whole. Pius writes:

> But just as in the living organism it is impossible to provide for the good of the whole unless each single part and each individual member is given what it needs for the exercise of its proper functions, so it is impossible to care for the social organism and the good of society as a unit unless each single part and each individual member – that is to say, each individual man in the dignity of his human personality – is supplied with all that is necessary for the exercise of his social functions.[11]

What is notable about this paragraph is that Pius utilizes the language of both dignity and personalism to express his case for social justice and the common good. In the face of both an individualist liberalism and a collective socialism, Pius chose to emphasize the dignity of the relational, unique and unrepeatable human person. As we noted in earlier chapters of this book, the rise of the concept of human dignity and the interconnected growing influence of the philosophy of personalism shape profoundly the social teaching of the 1930s, and its legacy runs into the immediate post-war period in important ways.[12] Whilst, in arguing this, Samuel Moyn is primarily concerned to note the influence of such thinking beyond the bounds of the Church in law and society, in constitutional developments and developing human rights norms, it is clear that *ad intra*, within the life of the Church, this same thinking comes to subtly reshape thinking about the common good over the span of the twentieth century.

From its earliest inception, the rise of personalism as a framework for thinking about the common good and human dignity was not, however, without its critics. The mid-century philosopher Simone Weil wrote an impassioned critique of the growing influence of such thinking. She noted that personalism confused the grounds of what was sacred and dignified about the human person. Her target was the kind of personalism that rooted the claim to universal rights and the common good in the unique and unrepeatable characteristics of each individual person. Weil argued that personality is a dangerous line of thought because it is an opaque

---

[11]*Divini redemptoris*, §51.
[12]Moyn, *Christian Human Rights*.

idea unsuited to public speech and in her view, basing public morals on it is a dangerous pathway to tyranny. What endures and has value is not personality but what is most *impersonal* about the person. The impersonal is expressed as the capacity of the person to be caught up in something beyond themselves, which transcends the vicissitudes of personality and is universal and enduring. The human person is relieved of anxiety only by learning to move beyond the self, in attention, to the world and to God. This experience of being led beyond oneself, to something beyond one's own personality, returns the soul to itself. The next chapter will explore Weil's critique of personalism in more detail. Weil remained, however, an outsider voice and the growth of an association between developing common good thinking, the rise of human dignity as its core and personalism as its attendant philosophy, intensified both into the papacy of Pius XII and into the texts of John XXIII's *Mater et magistra* and *Pacem in terris*.

Between 1939 and 1945 Pius XII developed these themes. In *Summi pontificatus* he warns against viewing the material prosperity of society as the primary measure for success or for the attainment of the common good: '[t]hat good can neither be defined according to arbitrary ideas nor can it accept for its standard primarily the material prosperity of society, but rather it should be defined according to the harmonious development and the natural perfection of man.'[13] In his Christmas messages, Pius expanded on his vision of a comprehensive good served by the total political and economic activity of a society. In his 1942 broadcast he noted, '[a]ll of the political and economic activity of the state is directed to the permanent realization of the common good, which is to say of the external conditions that are necessary to all of the citizens for the development of their qualities and functions, of their material, intellectual, and religious life.' John XXIII repeats these same themes, noting that in the context of globalization and 'complex interdependence' the task is to organize a society such that maximum benefits accrue to citizens and minimum and fairly distributed burdens. But we should be clear (and we will return to this point shortly): whilst distributive justice is a crucial question faced by those pursuing the common good, the common good cannot be reduced solely to the distribution or aggregation of goods, benefits and burdens.

---

[13] *Summi pontificatus*, §59.

The Common Good: The Encyclical Tradition

The concept of the common good is carefully introduced by John XXIII in *Mater et magistra* in the context of his own interest in the idea of 'socialization' or complex interdependence. He views 'socialization' as a defining characteristic of the twentieth century. John XXIII brings to the concept of the common good an interest in particular time-bound circumstances that shape our action for the common good. For Pope John we are not interdependent in some abstract, generic fashion but in a thoroughly contingent and historical one. He uses the idea of 'socialization', therefore, to express the inherently relational and deeply historical character of the human person, whose interdependence and freedom are shaped in profound ways by the particular material cultures in which we live. Put more simply: technology, labour market relations, climate and conflict, tribe and ethnicity, amongst other factors, determine distinct generational patterns of interdependence, shaping our 'free' agency and the context in which conscience is formed. Socialization concerns the power of myth and story, as much as place, structures and institutional practices shape our social living and therefore the very way we think of the common good. Each concrete example of socialization in the encyclical confronts us with sharp challenges as to how we think concretely about what constitutes common bonds and how adequate these ways of thinking are to achieve a Christian vision of a worthy common life.

The common good is thus presented as the moral discourse that becomes necessary for making sense of our communicative and interdependent human nature, and as a constructive idea that can galvanize and motivate sustained action with others for justice and charity in a global age. *Gaudium et spes* builds on this account reminding the Church that speech about the common good is the primary language the Church has for talking about the economic, social and political dimensions of life in communion. Repeating Thomist themes, the common good is presented in the social documents of John XXIII's papacy as the highest purpose of the political community and therefore the rationale for the state. The political community – not narrowly co-terminus with the state alone – is the fundamental custodian of the common good; the state *serves* and partly constitutes rather than *founds* that political community. This emphasis is important. The mid-century social teachings seem at pains to point out that the political community exists to structure peace, security and justice, such that the person and the social group (a community within a network of communities) can seek their distinct goods. In the face of a (briefly) more powerful nation state – whether liberal, communist or authoritarian or fascist – they are at pains to uphold the value of the human person and smaller scales of community, and resist the colonizing of the person by the state. On the other hand, in the face of individualism, they wish to insist on the person as a social entity, with duties, obligations and needs that already beg the question of community. The appeal to the dignified person is an attempt to hold back the dam on both fronts. This is a theme we will develop in the next chapter.

Gaudium et spes proposes its own account of the social connections that form plural political community as an alternative – but not necessarily always diametrically opposed – account to that offered by social contract theory. The Council Fathers repeat that the flourishing of person and society is interdependent: they hinge on each other. Common social life is therefore the only way to develop all our human gifts and to rise to our destiny as persons. Not all forms of social life are identical in ethical form: family and political community constitute immediate, given social ties; other forms of social ties can be understood as elective and arising from free decision. Social life, in all its forms, in order to reach towards the common good must be 'founded on truth, built on justice, and animated by love: in freedom it should grow every day toward a more humane balance'.[14]

The key to inspiring and infusing this process of seeking the common good in society is the Holy Spirit, who breathes life into the common good. Whilst *Gaudium et spes* tantalizingly notes the pneumatological character of the common good, neither the Council Fathers nor subsequent encyclicals develop this insight more fully. The closest we find to such a development in parallel, non-official Catholic writing is found in the work of Josef Pieper, explored briefly in the next chapter. Addressing questions of soteriology, *Gaudium et spes* reminds the Church that the relational anthropology it proposes – where person and society thrive or/and struggle together – relates to the manner in which we are saved: we are saved by the refining process of being fashioned into a people. From the beginning of salvation history God covenants with 'His people'. And so again the idea of the common good is implicitly related back to a Pauline image of the Body and to a language of being the people of God.

Gaudium et spes contributes to the developing account of the common good a much-needed, but still limited, theological perspective. The Council Fathers invoke a range of Johannine and Pauline scriptural motifs: love, beatitude, kinship within a universal human family, neighbour love and

---

[14]*Gaudium et spes*, §26.

gift. Here we get hints – but frustratingly not the fuller development – of a Pauline Christological image of the body with its many parts and differential gifts and callings. *Gaudium et spes* offers the beginnings of a contemporary mystical, dynamic and fleshy image of plurality. These theological reference points are offered as the theological foundations of a political concept of the common good, but arguably they remain underdeveloped pastorally, politically and theologically.

This basic definition and theological framework for the common good proffered by John XXIII does not change markedly in later encyclicals. It is, however, supplemented by what might be seen as further helpful footnotes to the tradition. These additions refine, clarify, extend and perhaps also sometimes simply repeat the dilemmas of this mid-century formula.

In *Pacem in terris* Paul VI links the pursuit of the common good to the modern notion of rights and duties: 'it is agreed that in our time the common good is chiefly guaranteed when personal rights and duties are maintained'.[15] As we have noted, Luigi Taparelli was using the language of rights and duties in relation to the common good already in the 1840s, so this is not an innovation, although it is a strong emphasis. For some political theologians this marks a welcome watershed whereby the movement towards modern human rights is formally integrated with Catholic teaching on the common good and tied into the heritage of the earlier scholastic development of concepts of justice and law, used as the basis for the development of international law.[16] For others the formal connection between the common good and human rights norms has proved a controversial claim; such thinkers wish to pursue the connection between the common good and human dignity as a formal alternative to rights-based talk, not its inauguration.[17] This remains an actively contested area within current debate about CST.

John Paul II develops the analysis of the common good in two principal ways: he continues to address liberal scepticism about the usefulness of the idea and its exclusivist and communitarian leanings, and he continues the trajectory of post-war thinking adopted by his immediate papal

---

[15] *Pacem in terris*, §60.
[16] Amongst the two most impressive accounts of a constructive relation of human rights to CST, see Ethna Regan, *Theology and the Boundary Discourse of Human Rights* (Washington D.C.: Georgetown University Press, 2010) and Meghan Clark, *The Vision of Catholic Social Thought: The Virtue of Solidarity and the Praxis of Human Rights* (Minneapolis: Fortress Press, 2014).
[17] Catholic philosopher and virtue ethicist Alasdair MacIntyre, Anglo-Catholic theologian John Milbank and neo-Anabaptist theologian Stanley Hauerwas have all written on this theme.

predecessors, emphasizing personalism and the dignity and the rights of the person as the necessary moral focus. What is notably distinctive is the interest in phenomenological accounts of human action that John Paul II brings to his social teaching. Rather than deducing action from general principles he is concerned to explore the ways that the human person experiences social and political bonds. He places the self-conscious acting subject at the centre of his ethics. For John Paul II we become fully human by becoming freely choosing agents. This freedom to choose is not a liberal version of negative liberty but rather, shaped in response to the socialism that had so restricted his own life, he proposes a view of the person as an active, autonomous moral agent. This agent is capable of reflective, learning, repenting, forgiving, risk-taking moral agency. The action of each agent builds the social order. Communism had erroneously reduced the human person to little more than a set of social relationships – duties and dependencies. The indignity of this stultifies the moral agent and locks down the potential for a personalist moral agency that is necessary to create a dynamic free social order and thus the common good. This personalism is not individualist because it sees the moral subject as fulfilled only in and through a self-giving and receiving life in communion with others. But we must freely will and freely act to participate in and build that communion.

In contrast to liberal political thinkers who implied either a fundamental tension between the good of the individual and the good of the whole or a suspicion that classical notions of the common good could not handle pluralism, John Paul insisted that a Thomist personalist account of the common good implied no such foundational or irresolvable tension. Whereas previous papacies had emphasized that the good of the individual required pursuing the good of the whole, a papacy shaped by the rise and fall of state communism emphasized this in reverse: the good of the whole is only secured if the free moral agent is able to act in true freedom and to be responsible for that freedom. We learn in seeking a personal good which is tied to action with and for my neighbour how to protect the fragile good of the whole. In developing a new emphasis on the importance of solidarity as a virtue needed in a globalized age, John Paul II also attempts to delineate the ways in which solidarity connects to the basic social practices that foster the life of the common good. Solidarity implies personal, structural and sustained action to support the needs and goods of all. These goods are more than mere economic goods and include reciprocal practices of mercy, forgiveness and costly personal accompaniment. This is a Christ-shaped solidarity.

Benedict XVI's social teaching can be seen as both in continuity with the phenomenological personalism of John Paul II and marked by its own turn towards a distinct account of the Church in an age of relativism. Benedict turns his social teaching to a focus on the distinct vocation of the Church in the social realm. In this regard, his teaching does not directly mirror any of his post-1891 predecessors and has a real distinctiveness of its own. His account of the common good is shaped by a critique of the ideologies of late liberalism, most especially relativism, and a technocratic scientific and political paradigm which he believes distorts our views of freedom, nature and truth. He views a hyper and narrow materialism as a fundamental social error of the turn of the twenty-first century. We will not be saved by technical solutions or by a materialism that imagines human strife is solely economic in nature. We cannot manipulate nature or human nature in a self-creating fashion. Modernity continues to present with the diseases associated with an accelerating spiritual sclerosis.

It is unsurprising then that Benedict's core 'social' focus is upon the internal societal life of the Church itself and a call to a new intensity of Christian living. The common good will be renewed by a serious commitment to holiness, self-sacrifice and orthodoxy amongst the faithful. His vision is of a Church that may well be smaller for a generation but one that is willing to be counter-cultural, unafraid of confronting conflicting truth claims and a visible holy remnant illuminating the world. The bonds in this alternative community of love stand some small chance of influencing the path of justice in the world of politics. Formation in wisdom for virtue within the Church enables this process. Benedict therefore appears to draw a much clearer distinction between the distinct practices appropriate to the Church and those appropriate for the political community (the political community is viewed as external to, but related to, the Church as society). For the sake of the common good, the Church educates, forms, worships, accompanies through wise counsel and enacts loving service through face-to-face small communities. The political realm coordinates, legislates, distributes and negotiates in the light of true human goods. This it often falls short of. The Church emphasizes dignity, the common good, solidarity and subsidiarity as necessary principles for a good politics.

Subsidiarity in particular is necessary to the common good because it emphasizes communities of various scales, Benedict notes. He is at pains to point out that we are 'not merely the product of economic conditions, and it is not possible to redeem [humanity] purely from the outside by creating a favourable economic environment'.[18] What enables redeeming love, alongside justice, are communities small enough to mediate real relations of love. A range of scales of communities and associations 'leave space for individual responsibility, and initiative, but most importantly, they leave room for love'.[19] We need both large-scale political bodies to coordinate, distribute and organize, and these can be viewed in the widest sense as motivated *by* caritas or love for humanity and the world – but we also need associations and bodies that build on needs which exceed and precede this scale of operation, in which love is a *felt mutual social relation*. This happens in reciprocal forms of embodied human exchange, and that requires the hard graft of forming sustainable, place-based communities that meet needs which are material but not merely material. Subsidiarity enables a certain imitation of Christ in a way that large-scale structures do not. Interestingly, Benedict also notes that ecological movements give him some hope that a renewal of political society might come from paying attention to the nature of the material world itself, returning us to wider questions of nature, beauty and limit.

In *Deus caritas est* Benedict XVI attempts to differentiate between a formal ecclesial contribution to the common good – which he defines in threefold fashion as promoting rational argument on key questions of social life, generating the spiritual energy needed to sustain a commitment to justice in a fallen world and the work of church-based charitable organizations – and the role of individual lay Catholics in the world. This contrast with the Church as beacon the hill and leaven in the mass, to employ a scriptural motif, leads Benedict to argue, *pace* a contemporary reading of Augustine, that the truly political task belongs to individual Christians who have the vocation to enter politics, and enter it they must. Benedict also renews emphasis on the global dimension to the common good. He does this both through insisting that goods be thought through beyond the level of nation states and through his emphasis on the need for global institutions capable of fostering the social conditions necessary for the pursuit of global common goods.

Whilst such emphasis prompted debate and critique for a perceived withdrawal from a fuller vision of Christian life in the public square, Benedict offered a further and helpful clarification of his teaching in the

---

[18] *Spe Salvi*, §21.
[19] Benedict XVI, *A Reason Open to Love*, eds John Garvey and J. Steven Brown (Washington D.C.: Catholic University of America Press, 2013), p. 193.

subsequent encyclical *Caritas in veritate*. Here the broad thrust of Benedict's teaching on the common good is a lyrical and theologically rich restatement of the core of the tradition. He notes:

> Another important consideration is the common good. To love someone is to desire that person's good and to take effective steps to secure it. Besides the good of the individual, there is a good that is linked to living in society: the common good. It is the good of 'all of us', made up of individuals, families and intermediate groups who together constitute society. It is a good that is sought not for its own sake, but for the people who belong to the social community and who can only really and effectively pursue their good within it. To desire the common good and strive towards it is a requirement of justice and charity. To take a stand for the common good is on the one hand to be solicitous for, and on the other hand to avail oneself of, that complex of institutions that give structure to the life of society, juridically, civilly, politically and culturally, making it the pólis, or 'city'. The more we strive to secure a common good corresponding to the real needs of our neighbours, the more effectively we love them. Every Christian is called to practise this charity, in a manner corresponding to his vocation and according to the degree of influence he wields in the pólis. This is the institutional path – we might also call it the political path – of charity, no less excellent and effective than the kind of charity which encounters the neighbour directly, outside the institutional mediation of the pólis. When animated by charity, commitment to the common good has greater worth than a merely secular and political stand would have. Like all commitment to justice, it has a place within the testimony of divine charity that paves the way for eternity through temporal action. Man's earthly activity, when inspired and sustained by charity, contributes to the building of the universal city of God, which is the goal of the history of the human family. In an increasingly globalized society, the common good and the effort to obtain it cannot fail to assume the dimensions of the whole human family, that is to say, the community of peoples and nations, in such a way as to shape the earthly city in unity and peace, rendering it to some degree an anticipation and a prefiguration of the undivided city of God.[20]

---

[20] *Caritas in veritate*, §7.

Towards a Politics of Communion

Pope Francis has chosen to make the option for the poor and for the earth, and the motif of social dialogue the central focus of his large corpus of social teaching, proposing these as the pathway to reorientating our societies towards the common good. In his triptych of social teaching documents, *Evangelii gaudium*, *Laudato si'* and *Fratelli tutti*, Francis argues that patterns of socialization which he believes results in increased inequality and climactic harm indicate a need to place a pre-eminent emphasis on solidarity, or social friendship, and the preferential option for the poor as the key practices necessary to foster the common good in a world which he sees as on the brink. Following in the footsteps of his predecessors Francis offers his own summary of the core meaning of the common good. In effect there is no novelty in his definition, which repeats and simplifies each of the emphases found in *Caritas in veritate* (as quoted earlier). Francis writes:

> Underlying the principle of the common good is respect for the human person as such, endowed with basic and inalienable rights ordered to his or her integral development. It has also to do with the overall welfare of society and the development of a variety of intermediate groups, applying the principle of subsidiarity. Outstanding among those groups is the family, as the basic cell of society. Finally, the common good calls for social peace, the stability and security provided by a certain order which cannot be achieved without particular concern for distributive justice; whenever this is violated, violence always ensues. Society as a whole, and the state in particular, are obliged to defend and promote the common good.[21]

Francis' renewal of the common good tradition lies more in the strength of his threefold emphasis on the socio-cultural diagnosis of the challenges to the common good, in the renewed emphasis on the principles which might most guide us towards its achievement and in Francis' interpretation of the ways that the Church models and inspires a practice of the common good.

Using the metaphor of a virus, Francis diagnoses what he sees as the diseases afflicting the contemporary body politic. Where Benedict had emphasized relativism and the malleability of self-defined human nature, Francis diagnoses indifference to both the suffering of neighbours and of the planet, a consumerist throwaway culture, a tendency towards closed cultures

---

[21]*Laudato si'*, §156–7.

of hostility and binary opposition and a continued tendency to see some forms of human life as superfluous. A fundamental tendency towards social violence pervades our cultures, and in its ubiquity, it becomes somehow a banal form of normality. Proposing a Christian vision of the common good, rooted in doctrines of creation and redemption, seems especially difficult but even more necessary in this context. Francis is also attuned to the co-option of religion and religious ideas of the common good into the heart of these very forces.

Francis extends the theme opened up by John Paul II and Benedict XVI, proposing that we think again about the common good and its relation to the question of nature. He also explores the idea that the climate itself should be thought of as a common good, and in the light of both inequality and climate change, he suggests that we might foreground once again the intergenerational nature of the common good. The pursuit of human ends is impossible without an attention to the dependence on, duty towards and health of a wider ecological system. This system grounds the possibility of life and also provides a limit to human life. Any notion of a common good requires attention to our relationship to and within our common home.

One of Pope Francis' most controversial – and poorly understood – contributions to thinking about the common good is his thought on 'populism' and being 'a people'. In *Fratelli tutti* a lengthy exposition is given to this idea, and Francis further develops this in *Let Us Dream*. The idea is also present in his addresses and personal writings prior to, and during, his papacy. Francis argues that a healthy populism is key to cultural renewal. He counsels that we ought not to lose the value of the idea of being 'a people'. Describing the people as a 'mythic' rather than logical or mystical category, he argues that attention must be paid to the narrative, place-based, event-based character of societies, out of which real social relationships and meanings are fashioned. He rejects the notion that communities are formed only or primarily by rational agreement or that we are merely self-interested, choosing individuals. We are formed out of the embodied, time and place-based relationships that constitute our daily living. These are the contexts into which the Spirit moves, in which conscience is formed and enacted, and in which we become ourselves. These are simultaneously ecclesial, political, economic and cultural contexts. Several influences should be noted here. First, the Vatican II language of the Church as the 'people of God' is crucial. Francis' vision of synodality, a 'dynamic communion' of the baptized in communication with each other, discerning and sharing faith, is central to his full theological-ecclesial vision of being 'a people'. In *Let Us Dream* he suggests that this model of synodality is one the current world can learn from: how to do 'populism' well. Second, Francis' unfinished doctoral work on Romano Guardini bequeaths him the idea of the 'concrete universal': the time and place-based ways that embodied humans encounter the transhistorical truths that ground the whole. As he writes in *Evangelii gaudium*: 'grace supports culture'.[22] Third, the Argentine Theology of the People, led by figures including Lucio Gera and Juan Carlos Scannone, provided an alternative form of liberation theology which emphasized far less a Marxist–Hegelian dialectics and a sociological notion of the people and more a viscerally place-based and Incarnational understanding of the action of the Spirit in time and place. For this reason, the Church accompanies a process of the formation of a people, it is part of that mythos, but with its own memory of its origins and its destiny. To discern how a society views the common good requires an engagement with the mythos of a people and a willingness to be part of its (re)formation. In this way the narrative structure of a society is addressed, as is the expectation that the Church is capable of addressing the desiring, affective dimensions of a society evident in its 'loves' and its values, as much as society's wider material patterns of distribution and labour that emerge as its external signs.

It is not surprising then that Francis talks more of the need for new practices of social dialogue and social friendship for the sake of the common good rather than using the more abstract language of faith and reason favoured by his immediate predecessors. This appears to suggest the pursuit of a wider form of communicative ethics, one that does not preclude rational argument but which exceeds this practice. Francis does not fully define the ways in which he wishes us to understand such a commitment to dialogue but his own practice indicates the following: dialogue is about an engagement with difference and seeks to face and reconcile conflict and a perceived estrangement of interests; dialogue should be rooted pre-eminently in processes of Christian accompaniment and presence – dialogue is part of a logic of being *with* others, and this requires concrete local communities able to embody and mediate this work.

A frequent criticism made of common good thinking is that it fails to deal systematically with the challenges of stubborn and intractable conflict over goods, value pluralism and forms of politics which reject the language of the good entirely. However, in *Evangelii gaudium* Francis makes some progress in being willing to address the realities of forms of conflict as

---

[22]*Evangelii gaudium*, §115.

simultaneously a necessary feature and a source of opposition to the pursuit of the common good. Francis addresses the complex ways in which appeals to the sovereignty of states are both a legitimate concern and often a twisted and self-defeating manifestation of 'power politics' (an almost oligarchic form of politics, present within liberal democracies driven by global capital and narrow self-interest). He sees this as frustrating effective common good responses to financial reform, responses to climate change and the management of migration. Francis argues forcefully that narrow power politics is parasitic upon distorted ideologies of market autonomy, which succeeds in frustrating the exercise of political judgement for the common good by elected political bodies. Finally, Francis brings his own inflection to the developing theme of Christian political love found in the writings of John Paul II and Benedict XVI. Where John Paul II emphasized the indispensable personal and relational forms of welfare and charity that should characterize a Christian approach to welfare, Benedict emphasized a theology of gift and reciprocity in social relation, Francis argues in terms that seem to echo the Old Testament emphasis on the welfare of the city depending on the just man or woman, that seeking the common good calls Christians to suffuse the political order with small, personal acts of civic and political love. This focus on love as a political theme raises a number of questions. We will pick these questions up in later chapters.

Loose ends and areas for development

Despite the richness of the tradition we have encountered, the encyclicals arguably contain areas of unclarity about the meaning, content and implications of the concept of the common good. This unclarity has both practical and metaphysical components. The work of relating intrinsic Christian commitments to doctrines of creation and redemption with (what have been perceived as) more extrinsic material concerns for the social conditions that foster peace and justice remains incomplete. The patristic and scholastic traditions we encountered in the previous chapter offered an intrinsic account of the common good set within a single divine–human cosmology, in which, whilst separated by function and vocation, temporal government, the body politic and the Church are called to work in a differentiated but holistic way towards a realization of a truly common good. This is a good they do not themselves originate, do not determine alone and cannot control. Its logic is one of participation and communion.

And it is shaped by the distinctive Christian *mythos* which renders human relationality, the search for goodness and truth and a willingness to scandalize by identifying with weaknesses, need and vulnerable suffering the heart of the matter. These accounts do not, however, answer all the practical or metaphysical questions we might have about the common good, nor do they address the full range of questions posed by living in fast-moving complex late modern societies, composed of, paradoxically, increasingly homogeneous yet radically pluralistic communities.

In responding to such contexts, twentieth-century theories of the common good have tended to focus on extrinsic questions: differentiating public, individual, private and common goods that enable human flourishing (the ultimate horizon) and attempting to offer more detailed accounts of the conditions that foster such goods. The definition of the common good adopted by the Second Vatican Council and further developed in the *Catechism* and *Compendium* exemplify this shift. The British Catholic philosopher John Haldane offers a sophisticated and helpful exposition along these lines, distinguishing between five different kinds of goods. He notes that in ordinary conversation there is a tendency to use the term 'common good' as an umbrella term to cover what might actually be better understood as a series of quite different, although interrelated goods. By way of illustration, we often tend to think about the provision of public services, from existence of a national health service (in the UK) to ensuring clean public air, as matters of the common good. In a sense they are, but Haldane argues that in fact some of these kinds of goods are better conceived of as *public*: their possession or enjoyment by one group does not preclude similar benefits being enjoyed by others. By enjoying clean air, I don't use up a quota that prevents others from having access to the same good. Haldane also distinguishes private, individual and collective goods from common goods. *Private* goods are possessed by one party, such that another may not simultaneously possess it: an appointment with the hairdressers or the dentist, a specific allocation of food, a tutorial with a teacher. An *individual* good attaches to an individual independently of the well-being enjoyed by others: warmth, the absence of pain. A *collective* good denotes a set of individual goods: aggregate wealth. For Haldane, truly *common* goods are goods that relate to the life of collectives and can only be enjoyed through membership of groups. Haldane gives the example of the happy mood at a party.

> The state of happiness felt by those at a social gathering may be and typically is something other than the addition of the separate states

of happiness of each. It is something emergent that comes into being through social interaction and is enjoyed by each participant derivatively through membership of the group and not directly as an individual. By way of a chemical analogy, the resultant of interaction is not a 'linear combination' of additive sum of antecedent quantities. Common goods are neither individual goods nor mere collections of such goods; they are irreducibly communal. Notice, however, that the distinction between private and public goods is tangential to this, inasmuch as not every public good is possessed commonly and not every individual good is a private one.[23]

Such definitions are helpful because they make clear the irreducibly communal nature of the practices that sustain the common good. They emphasize its participatory nature and the kind of social action that creates a non-instrumental, but entirely material, form of social abundance. They identify a good which relates to a new or sustained reality, beyond the sum of its individual parts. Theologian David Hollenbach focuses on the solidaristic nature of a truly common good. He emphasizes common good practices as those that honour interdependence, maximize equal agency, engage reciprocal modes of social exchange and seek to manifest solidarity as an ethic in the face of social harm. He argues:

> One of the most important meanings of the concept of the common good, therefore, is that it is the good that comes into existence in a community of solidarity among active, equal agents. The common good, understood this way, is not extrinsic to the relationships that prevail amongst the members and sub-communities of a society. When these relationships form reciprocal ties among equals, the solidarity achieved is itself a good that cannot otherwise exist. Where such solidarity is absent, society falls short of the good it could attain and the lives of its members are correspondingly diminished. When a society not only falls short of the level of solidarity that it could reasonably aspire to but is shaped by institutions that exclude some members from agency altogether, the resulting interdependence becomes a genuine evil. . . . The kind of interdependence that exists

---

[23]John Haldane, *Faithful Reason: Essays Catholic and Philosophical* (London: Routledge, 2004), p. 142.

between US suburbs and core cities today provides a regrettable example of such shared harm.[24]

One area of unclarity within the modern encyclical tradition concerns the extent to which it is meaningful to claim that the common good can be thought of in universal and global terms. Benedict XVI and Francis have placed great emphasis on the need for global institutions and recognition of goods that must now be considered in a global context. What has not been worked through for the lay reader is how this can be done without the concept of the common good collapsing in on itself as either too abstract and generic to supply real moral meaning or simply morally overwhelming. Anglican theologian Oliver O'Donovan convincingly suggests that the common good must relate to specific kinds of communities (defined as contexts where communication is already meaningful, common interests can be discerned and their meaning reflected upon).[25] This implies that any notion of the global common good needs to be able to imagine contexts in which concrete communities of varying scales and purpose can meaningfully engage in real exchanges of goods and values. In other words, it doesn't really work to think of the global common good as analogizing or scaling up, or simply as a single community of universal moral agreement or reasoning.

All these contemporary accounts draw on the classical and medieval traditions, sit well with the mid-century encyclical definitions and are in tune with a broader natural law approach to universal moral reasoning. A question remains about the extent to which this contemporary tradition is so formed by a dialogue with, or perhaps better a construction of, its liberal and purportedly secular context (even when it sometimes claims that secular as its 'other'). In responding to this context, the contemporary tradition fails in two ways: to draw on the full richness of its own Christian narrative *and* to identify the ways that this tradition has its own internal weaknesses and failures. The answer therefore is not *just* to reach back into our past better; or to argue that we simply took the wrong fork in the

---

[24]David Hollebach, *The Common Good and Christian Ethics* (Cambridge: CUP, 2002), p. 189.
[25]Oliver O'Donovan, 'Communicating the Good: The Politics and Ethics of the Common Good', ABC Religion and Ethics blog, 6 December 2016, accessible at https://www.abc.net.au/religion/communicating-the-good-the-politics-and-ethics-of-the-common-goo/10096290 (accessed 6 February 2021).

theological road and must retrace our steps and start again from there. It is to say that, indeed, we might have suppressed or been forgetful of some of the power of our own Christian narrative – we might not yet have done full enough justice to the distinctive and demanding pathway to truth handed on between generations of Christians. It is also to say that the challenges of reflecting on the nature and task of the common good must always be revisable, open-ended and incomplete. They are so, partly because we have failed in the past and we fail to remember this properly, and partly because we face what is also new. In neither sense is history done with us. Many of the challenges we face now – ecological, political, familial – are at their heart questions of values and virtues, not merely of 'conditions'. The common good tradition needs to help us ask values and virtues questions of why, how, who and where. Christians ask these in the context of a form of remembering: a memory of origins and ends, and of the events of Incarnation, crucifixion and Resurrection. These questions, asked in the light of these events, make a real difference to how you determine the task of acting for the common good, and the answers stretch us beyond (but, of course, do include) a delineation of conditions.

Our current context seems to demand of us a fuller response, one that makes clear our theological reference points, shows a capacity to integrate our past in its giftedness and its failure, its gravity and its grace. It will do this not only from within its own wellsprings but will find itself when it can receive from, and give to, its other. The pluralist challenge is not one of simple mutual accommodation. The thrust of the common good tradition suggests that we are interdependent in the context of meeting every kind of human and creaturely need, moral and material: for food, shelter, meaningful labour, and for truth, beauty, goodness. This suggests that we do not reach the common good without honesty and humility in engaging with the epistemological and anthropological commitments of others. It also suggests that the common investment we have in a common life is tied to a desire that across a lifetime we come to experience goodness, love and justice, and not harm. The insight of the early church fathers and mothers was perhaps that we do not exist only to trade theories of the world but to meet each other's deepest bodily and spiritual needs, in order to honour our mutual humanity as a sign of a future already secured and to come.

What, then, of Benedict XVI's encouragement that we pay attention to the Church as called to embody the fullness of this ethic? We might say that the Church, as a distinct community, would see itself as pursuing the following approach to the common good: rooted in practices of love, seeking to proclaim life as gift and offer to the world a Trinitarian vision of a creation fashioned in love, redemption offered for all, and a Spirit who dwells in the world participating in the redemption of time. Rooted in justice, the Church seeks the equitable sharing of the material goods of the world, including its own share of those goods; the just sharing of burdens and benefits; and restitution for those afflicted by the failure of justice. Rooted in hope, such a community seeks to make tangible the often distant and impossibly scandalous seeming Christological claim that we are all members of one human family, mutually obligated and co-belonging. Our calling is to make this a concrete reality of human becoming through the formation of households, neighbourhoods, nations and regions that enact this fact through real communities of belonging and action. Seeking truth, such a community engages the reality of the world in dialogue, not in expectation of singular agreement or a homogeneous culture but as a path towards learning the reality of things as we can come to know them, which is through faith and reason and incompletely. This truth seeking and truth sharing is inseparable from learning the practices of mercy, justice and forgiveness. Resisting overbearing communitarian or state coercive accounts, such a community seeks to articulate a positive account of freedom in which the human person must claim and enact their creaturely role as co-creators of a humane social life, a claiming which requires a simultaneous capacity to confront failure and engage practices of repentance. Committed to the social contribution of all, this vision begins counter-intuitively not with 'doing' or activism but with a form of 'not-doing': a receptive awareness of a prior divine initiative that acts as the basis for human activism. This is a radically historical process of receptivity and action that requires a deep attention to the conditions of our own times.

If the modern social encyclical tradition and its revision of common good thinking was born out of a context of the sudden rise to dominance of the nation state, and the decline of the age of empire, in our age we are experiencing the resurgence of the idea of the nation but in the context of its practical fragmentation.[26] Our crises are political, ecological, economic and epistemological. Public debate manifests this brittle and oppositional logic, febrile and divided, gripped by a short-termism and a logic of friend

---

[26] I am indebted to Professor Jon Wilson, King's College London for conversation about his forthcoming book, *Out of Chaos*, for some of this formulation.

and enemy. For the popes, these crises are fundamentally manifestations of a broader spiritual crisis. It is unclear how our current tensions will settle. Migratory, economic and ecological trends mean that the most localized communities are increasingly 'global', and the most globalized realities become quickly local. The livelihoods of fishermen fishing from a Cornish boat are tied to a world of infinitely complex geopolitical relations they have little control over but much dependence on: new Cornish fish markets in China become suddenly volatile in the face of British government responses to protests in Hong Kong. A murder in Arizona is tied to the drug cartels in neighbouring Mexico and in turn to a global trade in human persons. The murder of a Black man by a police officer leads to global protests. And a pandemic simultaneously shrinks our world to a common space of vulnerability and resistance, and creates a new era of viral mobility and (temporary?) human immobility. A sense of passivity in the face of such interdependence is palpable; thus, an often nostalgic search emerges for a world simplified of such bewildering complexities, for a new freedom and control over our everyday lives. This mixes with powerful new movements, fluid and themselves complex, which cry out for a more humane and equitable future, one that is able to integrate its honourable and dishonourable past. This desire for participatory communities, for a hope beyond the passive interdependence, that erodes a sense of individual and communal selfhood is understandable. No effective political response appears yet to exist in the face of these multifarious complexities. It is perhaps unsurprising that it is the idea of the 'will' of the people that emerges resurgent. But this 'will' is often angry and grieving, and struggling to labour under the burden of its own hopes.

CHAPTER 8
THE BODY POLITIC
POLITICAL COMMUNITY IN THE SOCIAL ENCYCLICALS

The first principle of politics . . . is that politics is not the first principle.[1]

This council exhorts Christians, as citizens of two cities, to strive to discharge their earthly duties conscientiously and in response to the Gospel spirit. They are mistaken who, knowing that we have here no abiding city but seek one which is to come, think that they may therefore shirk their earthly responsibilities. For they are forgetting that by the faith itself they are more obligated than ever to measure up to these duties, each according to their proper vocation.[2]

Self-knowledge is only possible when we share in greater memory.[3]

In a slim pamphlet published by the Oxford Catholic Social Guild in 1955, the British Jesuit Cyril Clump reminded his readers of what distinguished a Catholic political philosophy from a secular, liberal one.[4] The pamphlet is composed of questions and answers on the topic of the purpose of human society, with the answers formed from a patchwork of papal quotations. Clump uses his extracts to emphasize to his reader the following: Catholics believe that, by nature, we are social and political animals, drawn to associate with each other that we might complete a social task we cannot achieve alone. As creatures made as an expression of order and form, we are drawn to order and form. We are made equal, but equality is only meaningful when it is an expression of the innate dignity of human beings, and this dignity attaches to their divine origins and divine ends.

---

[1] Alan Mittleman, *Hope in a Democratic Age* (Oxford: OUP, 2009), p. 255.
[2] *Gaudium et spes*, §43.
[3] *Lumen fidei*, §38.
[4] Cyril Clump SJ, *A Catholic's Guide to Social and Political Action* (Oxford: Oxford Catholic Social Guild, 1955).

Towards a Politics of Communion

Having set out his stall, Clump turns his attention to a Catholic critique of social and political liberalism. He reminds his readers that the papacy condemns liberal social contract theory as a 'false principle' for two reasons: first, because Rousseau (especially in the line of Clump's fire) insists that all men and women are created free and equal, but that this equality means an innate freedom from any kind of prior social link or bond. This is the opposite of a biblical account of creation, where equality is both given and is to be achieved relationally through the bonds we have with others. Second, Clump notes that for social contract thinkers our social bonds are not given but merely fabricated by choice, changeable at will. For the contract thinker politically liberal society is, as Hobbes' *Leviathan* taught, by nature an artificial creation of its free people, to preserve life and for self-interest. Clump marshals his papal extracts to fire shot after shot at this world view. For Catholics, hierarchy and equality are not contradictory, we are born with innate natural bonds of relatedness, but with a diversity of skills, talents and vocations, and we only achieve our human fulfilment by acting in obedience to these bonds. We can only honour the truth of these bonds through a life formed with others out of natural bonds. Political society therefore is no artificial creation of man; it is a divinely created and governed reality, which requires a language of createdness, dignity, hierarchy, order, obedience, liberty, rights, authority, law and so forth. The grammar of a Catholic social world view is thus absent from, or denied by, political and social liberalism. They cannot be bedfellows. And in turn, liberalism in effect takes the saw to the branch – freedom, equality, rights – it wishes to sit on.

Clump's pamphlet relies heavily on the teachings of Leo XIII and the two early twentieth-century Pian papacies that followed. It makes for fascinating reading, partly for its modern twist on the Thomistic form of question and answer, mainly because less than ten years after it was penned, this world view – itself fairly newly formed – would shift once again on its axis. Clump's pamphlet marks the end of an era. The world of the Second Vatican Council, led by Pope John XXIII, brought with it a new Catholic social vision and a new grammar of Catholic politics. By 1965 the Church had begun to teach its own vision of democracy, human rights, non-hierarchical dignity and personalism. It had not changed its view that the artificial construct of the social contract did not aid human bondedness or the common good, or that its fundamental philosophy of society, its account of equality and liberty, was off-key. Nonetheless, the Church had improvised from its own register on the theme of the political once more.

The Body Politic

Sidestepping any attempt to theologize the nation state (although other lay and ordained Catholics did), what emerged over the course of a century by 1965 was a wide vision of political society, newly defined by a set of democratic and pluralist practices, exchanges and institutions capable of forming a common world. In the post-war and conciliar era, the space of the 'political' – the body politic – emerges as a plural and differentiated but overlapping space of civic shared practice; of negotiated common projects and values; of regulated exchange, including labour and work; of law in all its forms, and in this sense, also of the relations of coercion and force to which we are subject and to which we consent or dissent; and of the space of common action and organization for communal forms of welfare. Although the papacy sets clearer demarcations and boundaries between the roles and functions of a juridical-institutional state, a market and a society, it simultaneously – and perhaps without ever quite fully joining all this up – retains its compellingly pluralist vision of a body politic that stretches far beyond the narrow confines of the infrastructures of the governing role of the state. This chapter attempts to chart something of this journey.

For the nineteenth- and twentieth-century papacies, the question of the body politic was never merely academic or speculative. An emerging vision – one that as we have just noted did not remain static – was forged in the crucible of intense change in the Church's own political position and standing. As Pope John XXIII noted in his remarks at the opening of the Second Vatican Council, Vatican II was the first council of the modern period at which the Church met without 'the undue interference of civil authorities'.[5] He reminded his audience that the past had not been a triumphant place of freedom for the Gospel to be preached or the Church to manage its own affairs, and that whilst the modern world presented many challenges, it was also a time and space in which the Church might claim her vocation with some freedom.

As John XXIII understood well, the very origins of the idea of a modern Catholic social teaching are umbilically tied to the de facto shifts in the nature, role and identity of the late nineteenth-century political community. It was out of the aftermath of the European revolutions of 1848, the brief exile of the papacy from Rome to Naples in the same year

---

[5] John XXIII, *Address on the Occasion of the Solemn Opening of the Most Holy Council*, 1962, §4. Latin text http://www.vatican.va/content/john-xxiii/la/speeches/1962/documents/hf_j-xxiii_s pe_19621011_opening-council.html (accessed 1 April 2021).

and the broader trajectory of a paradigm shift towards modern empires and eventually nation states that the papacy birthed its new social teaching. Over the course of one hundred years, and in the space between two Church councils, the coming into being of CST witnesses to a shift from a political theology of throne and altar to a notion of Christian action in a diasporic world. The Church would form consciences and communities rather than wield direct political power, and its social teaching was the means to this end. The question of the body politic and its shifting form was, therefore, part of the very coming of age of CST.

What the new tradition required was not merely an episodic commentary on external political events and forms, as viewed from the throne of St Peter, but a renewed theological conception of the social order as a whole. As Russell Hittinger notes, this was gradually to produce a single but differentiated view of modern social bodies, in which the Church was not *in* the state and the state was not *in* the Church, but both composed part of a single whole. As a new world view emerged, it was perhaps easier to formulate this relation as an antonym.[6] However, this was not to suppose a pejorative view of the relation but an interesting emerging ethical negativity in thought.

The early stages of a contestation of ideas about liberalism and modernity within the heart of modern European Catholicism had occurred within the crucible of post-Revolutionary France. The gradual emergence of ideas for the formulation of a Catholic liberalism – Felicité de Lamennais (1782–1855) and Alexis de Tocqueville (1805–59) exemplifying, in different ways this move – jostled for space with the counter-revolutionary conservative and ultramontane vision of Joseph de Maistre (1753–1821). Lamennais, through various more dramatic evolutions in his thought, and Tocqueville more steadily presented a possible productive relationship, a fruitful co-belonging, between Catholicism, liberalism and democracy. A Catholic anthropology could provide an ethical foundation and space of

---

[6] See Russell Hittinger, 'The Coherence of the Four Basic Principles of Catholic Social Teaching'. A paper for 'Pursuing the Common Good: How Solidarity and Subsidiarity Can Work Together', Pontifical Academy of Social Sciences, Acta 14, Vatican City, 2008, http://www.pass.va/content/dam/scienzesociali/pdf/acta14/acta14-hittinger.pdf (last accessed 1 March 2020); and Russell Hittinger, 'Social Pluralism and Subsidiarity in Catholic Social Doctrine', *Annales Theologici* 16 (2002), https://www.stthomas.edu/media/catholicstudies/center/ryan/curriculumdevelopment/vocationofthebusinessleader/Z0Hittinger-Subsidiarity02.pdf (accessed 1 March 2020).

renewal that liberalism itself could not provide. For anti-liberals this was impossible, for the very foundation of liberalism was based on a false and rival kind of theology. Both Catholic liberal and anti-liberal positions, forged in the fulcrum of revolution, remain living traditions now. Nowhere is this more evident perhaps than in the (also notably post-Revolutionary) Catholicisms of present-day North America. As Emile Perreau-Saussine argued in the conclusion to *Catholicism and Democracy*, the theatre of political Catholicism did not so much end in the mid-twentieth century but as the century ended, migrated from continental Europe across the North Atlantic.[7]

By the early twentieth century, the labours of Jesuit and Dominican moral theologians and the spiritual-political activism of leading priests and bishops had begun to feed into the papacy a new Catholic grammar for politics and society. The Italian priest and politician Luigi Sturzo (1871–1959) bequeathed to the newly emerging tradition the notion that the Church might think of itself as living according to a 'rhythm of social duality'.[8] Sturzo was a committed Christian democrat, later to play a leading role in the Italian post-war political party Partito Populare. Part of the challenge was to reflect on the de facto nature of the modern state and its juridical powers but to maintain a wider Catholic understanding of the political task and space: to refract the modern state through a Catholic lens required that reflection on political life *not* be reduced to reflection on the state alone. As Protestant theologian Dietrich Bonhoeffer noted in the 1930s, the state itself is not a biblical or theological category – the practice or exercise of government, and the formation of political community, is. This same emphasis, differently articulated, found its way into the writings of the French Catholic political philosopher Jacques Maritain (1882–1973). Maritain's formulation of the state as an organizational and administrative instrument whose purpose was to serve justice and the common good, but not to be elevated beyond this, gained traction, influencing the formulation of papal social teaching from the Pian papacies of the early and mid-century, through the Second Vatican Council papacies of John XXIII and Paul VI, to the political teachings of John Paul II.

What was required, Maritain argued, was a new scholastic theology of the wider body politic and a focused and limited understanding of the state

---

[7]Perreau-Saussine, *Catholicism and Democracy*.
[8]Luigi Sturzo, *Church and State* (New York: Longmans, Green, 1939), p. 563.

itself within this. For Maritain there was no love or grace in the state but there could and must be justice. For this reason, Christians are invested in the affairs of the state, and dependent on and responsible for the health of its life, but they owe no ultimate allegiance or absolute duty of obedience to it. The state serves the common good through the protection of natural rights and the upholding of dignity. Thus, rights could be theologized but not the state. Maritain formulated the relationship between natural law and natural rights thus: if – as natural law theory teaches – we can establish that we have a natural proclivity, need and desire to seek the truth, to preserve life, to raise families, to secure our material and moral well-being and so forth, then it follows that we have natural rights – human rights – to access and pursue the means to attain these ends. Protecting the natural rights that correlate to the natural law is the task of civil administration. This protects the condition of human freedom. It is not entirely surprising that formulated in this way, via a revisionist Thomism, the papacy found it easier to adopt into its canon the language of rights, including human rights, than it did liberal democracy. Whilst the language of natural rights predicated on natural law was already in circulation from the mid/late nineteenth century in neo-Thomist moral theology, Maritain significantly developed and brought this thread of thinking to a wider public and squarely into official social teaching.

What Maritain brought to the developing tradition was a grammar for thinking about the liberal-era political community as the temporal condition in which the Church must conduct its evangelizing task. The freedom of the Church in this new era lay in embracing its diasporic condition, in informing consciences, such that the common good – which includes the free pursuit of truth – might be pursued as a common task. The Church's distinctive vision of freedom or liberty – which renews the whole body politic – comes via an openness to love and grace. This lies beyond the temporal order but flows into it, making possible 'social resurrection' for the body politic.[9] Thus, a love born of the order of grace, that is extrinsic to the state, becomes the basis for the state's fullest pursuit of its own proper and limited task of realizing justice. The title of Maritain's 1951 mature work *Man and the State* is important to note – his intention was as much to communicate an anthropology, a theory of being human, as it was to

---

[9] Jacques Maritain, *Scholasticism and Politics*, ed. Mortimer J. Adler (London: Geoffrey Bles, 1940), p. 18.

produce a political philosophy; the one grounded the other.[10] The longevity of Maritain's influence – both his account of personalism, which strongly influenced the papacy's development of notions of human dignity, and his account of the state, rights and political community – is remarkable, although not unproblematic or uncontested, as we shall note shortly.

Whilst the papacy of Leo XIII had marked a watershed for new reflection on the body politic, *Rerum novarum* in fact had relatively little to say about the nation state, liberal democracy or political form. Nonetheless, in the forty years leading up to *Rerum novarum*'s publication, moral theologians had been exploring the question of social and political form in some detail. In exile in the Kingdom of Naples in 1850 the Jesuits had established a new publication, *Civiltà Cattolica*. Taking up the mantel of the sixteenth- and seventeenth-century neo-Thomists and jurists of the Salamanca School, *Civiltà*'s contributors conversed on the nature of law, authority, liberty and the common good. For its authors, what mattered was not which exact form of government – monarchy, aristocracy, democracy – might be squared with the Gospel but rather how one understood the underlying account of the nature of the social order. If liberalism insisted that plurality was the baseline human condition and unity needed to be drawn from, or imposed upon, that plurality through the formation of a social contract, then this left a fundamental theological-political problem for the moral theologians. They, like Fr Clump in his 1955 pamphlet, feared that the social contract tradition implied that unity is merely external or extrinsic, fragile, revisable and no more than artificial. Unity is rooted only in what can be agreed (social norms), what can be traded (the market) or what can be enforced (law). The latter, the idea that unity relies on authoritarian enforcement and is therefore tied intrinsically to the history of force, was especially worrying.

Theologically speaking, the Jesuit moralists of *Civiltà* wanted to start the other way around. Unity is the given, the ontologically prior fact. We do not ourselves establish this unity, it is created and gifted and therefore also renewed amongst us. God knows, we are not much good at achieving and maintaining this by ourselves. Unity, insofar as it is a meaningful social theme, relates to our origin, our mutual obligation and common bondedness (that we are given to each other in Christ), and our common destiny. This is what we are called to continually remember (recall and put back together

---

[10] J. Maritain, *Man and the State* (Chicago: University of Chicago, 1951).

again), as the basis for society. The way we work out this prior unity in a fallible, fragile, limited yet beautiful and good world is through expressions of plurality-in-dialogue. Some forms of plurality are, of course, tragic forms of brokenness and the result of the failure that human living risks. Other forms of plurality, those that work like musical harmony, are the outworking of the good, in created difference. We live with both, and both relate to the fact of, or memory of, a prior and eventual unity. The task of the body politic in this light is to create social forms that honour the fact of a given unity, can deal with the reality of failure and the tragic, and seek to give expression to healthy plurality. This vision finds its way into the pages of *Rerum novarum* and later Pius XI's *Quadragesimo anno* in its praise of multiple levels of community, workers guilds and unions, and the theory of subsidiarity (see Chapter 9). Both documents also note the differentiated, plural functions of different kinds of social bodies which aid both the unity and plurality of the whole: families, associations, civil authorities and so forth. Therefore, whilst *Rerum novarum* marks an important response to, and intervention in, debates about political community, the moment of real generative change in modern Catholic social and political ideas lies, probably, forty years later in the 1930s, then augmented again in a further shift in 1960s.

Whilst this new work was occurring gradually through the pages of journals like *Civiltà*, and through new Catholic movements and religious orders, it was the threat of totalitarianism and the upheavals of the 1930s that finally brought this thinking to visible light and into official teaching. American historian James Chappel brilliantly illustrates that this work gave way not to a singular Catholic social world view but to two new forms of modernist social Catholicism, traceable through movements and within papal teaching.[11] The first of these Chappel names *fraternal* modernism, the second *paternal* modernism. On the face of it these movements appear as rival expressions of social Catholicism. *Fraternal* modernism was unified in its opposition to nationalism, authoritarianism and fascism. Its adherents focused on rejecting nativism and racism, and tended to be egalitarian, paving the way for the post-war Catholic embrace of democracy, dignity and human rights. *Paternal* modernism, on the other hand, was unified primarily by its fear and rejection of communism and the Left. It focused on family, freedom, rights and remained hierarchical in its ethics. This was the basis for a strand of more socially conservative Christian democracy.

---

[11]Chappel, *Modern Catholic*.

Although Chappel does not use it as an illustration, Clump's pamphlet noted earlier is clearly an example of this second strand, and Leo XIII's social teaching remains largely within this paternal mode. Yet Chappel's skill as a historian is to show that these are not simply diametrically opposed views but sibling movements, born from the same historical forces, and equally bearing the mark of the forces from which they were birthed. Sibling rivals, they have been and remain, across nearly a century, sometimes cooperative, sometimes at war amongst themselves. The trace of both is to be found in the formulation of papal social teaching on the nature of democracy, rights and political community from the mid-century period until today.

To illustrate his typology, Chappel offers two compelling contrasting examples. The first is the Senagalese Catholic poet and politician Léopold Senghor. Writing in *Esprit* journal in the late 1940s, Senghor argues that Germany had been defeated, but Nazism had not. The fascist spirit lived on, and its threat would continue to be felt in appeals to a combination of high capitalism married to strident nationalist narratives of the nation state. A Catholic fraternal tradition must remain ever attentive to these realities, and root out and oppose every instance of the deathly fusion of capitalism and nationalism. By contrast, the German Catholic political figure Heinrich von Bretano, speaking to a stadium of 60,000 Christians during the same immediate post-war period, argued that the true threat to a Christian social spirit lay in communism. A necessary social resistance to the threat of communism lay in building strong national cultures married to strong military structures. As Chappel outlines, such radically opposed narratives were not the only story. In the post-war aftermath a coalition of paternal and fraternal Catholic actors shaped the development of Christian democratic political parties in continental Europe, producing a form of Christian politics shaped by a reformist vision of capitalism, a socially engaged state (with limits) and a focus on family and civic associationalism. These political parties tended to form in countries and contexts with strong anticlerical elements, as well as those marked deeply by the legacy of totalitarianism.

The influence of both movements is traceable within papal social documents. This is perhaps especially evident in Pius XII's wartime Christmas messages. Here a new Catholic language of rights, statism, democracy, anti-racism and pluralism is combined with a continued hierarchical and paternalist world view. Pius XII's wartime Christmas messages cover the following repeated social themes: peace, the order of states, human rights, dignity, security, liberty and the influence of technology. Delivered as radio addresses, they reached their audience as oral teaching never finding form in an official social encyclical. They offered a gradually emerging vision of a hoped-for world beyond the war. To the anger and bewilderment of critics, Pius dwelt relatively little on the content of the suffering of war itself and failed to strongly enough denounce or diagnose the specific suffering of the Jews. There is a notable failure to name the Final Solution, or to be clear about what the Church knew of the death camps. Instead, Pius focused his social teaching on what he believed to be a deep desire for a new social order following the war. The war seemed to make evident that there was a kind of common cause to be made between Catholics who had felt what Chappel calls a sense of temporal dislocation in the move into a modernist world and a more general moment of cultural, social and spiritual crisis in which all would feel that temporal dislocation. This was a space the papacy felt it could and should speak into.

The central theological focus of the messages, by dint of the medium chosen, becomes the child of Bethlehem and the relation between, to use Pius rather striking phrase, the wood of the cradle and the wood of the cross, and an evolving vision of peace, justice and human dignity that emerges within this meditative space. Pius speaks in 1939 of a 'supernatural peace', which is 'gained not with steel, but with the wood of the Cradle of this Infant Saviour and with the wood of His future Cross of Death, stained with His Blood – not the blood of hate or rancour, but that of love'. In this same 1939 address Pius speaks of the necessary conditions for a 'just peace': he names these as equality of rights, disarmament, reorganization of international life with new international institutions and the need for a new organization within states to protect minorities. There is some recognition of the difference between, even tension between 'nations' and 'peoples', and this becomes an interesting recurrent theme across the messages; we should not expect that there is a simple alignment between these two, and peoples with their inherent cultures must be respected. Finally, he insists on the need for recognition of a transcendent Divine Law that enables the pursuit of moral justice. In later messages, Pius adds three principles for their realization: collaboration, honesty and the eradication of the totalitarian state. In 1940 he builds on this vision arguing that a new world order must be based on a deep and true 'victory': this victory is characterized by victory over hatred that divides peoples and nations, victory over distrust which paralyses and prevents creative overcoming, victory over utility as the 'dismal principle' of society, victory over an economy of inequality and finally, victory over egoism and the will to power that drives politics. He denounces, in another striking phrase in his Christmas messages, the 'tournament of insincerity in public life'.

The Body Politic

Pius is clear that the dangers to the peaceful body politic come from all forms of totalitarian and nationalistic states; from a politics of mere coexistence rather than active collaboration and solidarity – and that this politics of mere coexistence can poison common life within nations as well as between states; from false economies (that place capital before labour) and from a politics of indifference, including the indifference of Christians to the social order. He talks of the necessity of an active Christian 'will' for peace. In his 1942 message Pius furthers his insistence on a deep relationship between the internal governance of states and respect for minorities, and integral harmony in economy and society and the possibilities for international good governance and peace. Integral peace takes account of the relation between these two forms of good governance. This distinctive emphasis on 'integral peace' within nations is a hallmark of his social teaching. In this context, Pius lays out two fundamental elements of the moral needs of human souls within political community: for good order and for tranquillity. These are things towards which the human soul tends naturally, deep desires – but desires open to distortion in their desire for recognition.

Pius' 1942 Christmas message is the most substantial of the five-year cycle of messages. In it he sets out a list of conditions for a new world order. He names these as tied thematically to recognition of the dignity of the person. The content of this dignity relates to an intrinsic set of rights to family life and marriage, to decent work, to worship and to carry out religious acts of charity, to work and to access to and use of material goods necessary to support a decent life. Pius repeats teaching on the dignity of labour from previous encyclicals, and given the wartime context, emphasizes the need for a restoration of juridical order and fair legal process. He concludes with a vision of a Christian government. This is not an appeal for a government in conformity to the Church, but rather the beginnings of a new pluralist vision infused with a Christian social imagination and a respect for the basic principles of the Church's social teaching, one that remains theological and resists relativism. Pius lays out a brief vision of Christian citizenship that requires of the Christian a form of social action that protects order, public kindness and just distribution, and seeks the good of the city. In doing so Pius prefigures the political theologies of Vatican II.

Key to, and distinctive to, Pius' social teaching is a repeated articulation of the conditions for social unity: again, we have a defence of the social whole, a resistance to the idea of an impersonal individualism that tends towards a mass culture of indifference and pulls away from social responsibility and from the dignified treatment of the person. A reoccurring theme in Pope Francis' own recent teaching is interestingly prefigured in Pius' Christmas messages: that inequity in the distribution of goods and the oppression of minorities causes an integral violence that threatens internal harmony. In one sense, Pius can be read as an organic and paternalist thinker in line with pre-Vatican II social teaching, but in another something distinctive and more interesting is emerging.

The second most substantial statement comes at Christmas 1944. Here Pius extends the tentative exploration of Christian citizenship and talks about a vision of post-war Christian democratic culture. He reminds his hearers, in broadly Thomist vein, that there is no opposition to democracy in Catholic teaching, nor any formal preference for any individual system of government; nonetheless, he wonders whether there is a collective cry from the peoples who have endured war, for limited forms of government, answerable to the people, which respect the idea that government should both be limited and uphold the dignity of the person. How, then, might the Church contribute to thinking about healthy forms of democracy?

The vision of healthy democracy that Pius lays out has two features worthy of comment. The first is the cautious Catholic working out of a vision of democracy that is less about autonomous individuals free from interference and brokering common interest or negotiated self-interest and more a vision of the person as part of a co-created, communicating social whole. This democratic vision is marked by a deepening consciousness of individual personality (via Maritain) and of freedom to achieve active goods, an active resistance to un-natural inequities (of respect, goods etc.), and a necessary limit that forces a state to hear the individual and their yearnings before compelling any obedience in the name of the whole. Pius talks about this as the life of 'a people' rather than 'a nation', defining a healthy democracy as an organic and organized unity of a people. This affirmation leads him to then name its contrast, a false democracy or a tyranny. Such a society is characterized by a mere mechanical bringing together of a shapeless mass of individuals (the 'masses', faceless and inert, to be more acted upon than acting). It is worth pausing to consider two extracts that note this contrast of healthy and unhealthy democracy from the 1944 message. The first reads as follows:

> The people lives and moves by its own life energy; the masses are inert of themselves and can only be moved from the outside. The people lives by the fullness of life and in the men that compose it,

each of whom – at his own proper place and in his own way – is a person conscious of his own responsibility and of his own views. The masses, on the contrary, wait for the impulse from the outside, an easy plaything in the hands of anyone who exploits their instincts and impressions; ready to follow in turn, today this way, tomorrow another.[12]

He continues:

> The elementary power of the masses, deftly managed and employed, the state can also utilize; in the ambitious hands of one or of several who have been artificially brought together for selfish aims, the state itself, with the support of the masses, reduced to the minimum status of mere machine, can impose its whims on the better part of a real people; the common interest remains seriously, and for a long time, injured by this process, and the injury is very often hard to heal . . . the masses . . . are the capital enemy of true democracy and its ideal of liberty and equality.[13]

This language of 'the people' is not addressed again in this way until the publication of *Fratelli tutti* in 2020.[14]

Pius' vision is clearly not yet the equitable, non-hierarchical, fraternal vision of *Gaudium et spes* and the Second Vatican Council, to which we shall come. Pius still holds to the view that there can be 'natural' forms of inequality and hierarchy (these relate to differences in giftedness and social function and standing), and the language remains in this sense conservative and paternalist. But it would be untrue to see this as entirely the language of his predecessors. The Church is learning and communicating something of the complexity of modern democratic politics, its virtues and vices.

---

[12]Pius XII, Christmas Message 1944, in *The Major Addresses of Pope Pius XII Vol 1-2*, ed. Vincent Arthur Yzermans (St Paul: The North Central Publishing Company, 1961), p. 81.
[13]Ibid.
[14]Interestingly, Austen Ivereigh, interviewer and editor of Pope Francis' book *Let Us Dream*, has noted in public talks on preparing the book that Francis shared with him that the vision of 'the people' as a participating body rather than a mere mass came to him during Masses he celebrated in a central square in Buenos Aires. It is perhaps coincidence, therefore, that the language matches so closely Pius' wartime messages.

Towards a Politics of Communion

It would be natural to move on in our account from the detail of Pius' Christmas messages into the post-war world that took up this vision: the world of emerging Christian democratic party politics, the international world of the formulation of human rights frameworks (reliant upon both Maritain's philosophy and the papal teaching on dignity) and the developments of Vatican II. However, instead of rushing onwards too quickly, we shall linger a little longer in the world of the mid and late 1940s, noting the resonance between Pius' themes and those of two other – less attended to – lay wartime thinkers: Simone Weil and Josef Pieper. Weil and Pieper (themselves very different writers) echo something important in Pius' writings and in this wartime moment in fascinating and important ways. These concern the call for a fundamental renegotiation of the social contract and the importance of reformulating the body politic according to a core set of particular moral and material needs: for rootedness, for relationship, for social communion and for relationships that resist the banality of utility.

The philosopher Simone Weil died at the age of thirty-four in Ashford, Kent, in August 1943. Weil, a French Jewish refugee and writer, teacher and activist, had fled occupied France and following the refugee trails of Europe reached the safety of the United States in 1942, travelling onwards to London. Here she had been determined to play a part in the French resistance effort. For over a decade she had been drawn to Christianity following a religious experience in Assisi, Italy, in the mid-1930s, and she combined her earlier training in Platonic philosophy with her increasing theological interests and her long commitment to activism. Weil had taken herself off to the Spanish Civil War, had placed herself on the floor of various factories to work as a labourer and frequently undertaken radical acts of personal solidarity with others who she judged to be suffering. Weil was a regular attender at Farm Street Jesuit Church in London during the last year of her life and was a frequent communicator with Catholic intellectuals and spiritual guides. She bid others receive baptism but did not herself enter the Church formally, remaining resistant to forms of collective life she worried she would be too drawn to and on the basis of a critique of the power of the Church. She remained outside the Church more out of a form of critical self-denial and in solidarity with others outside its membership than because of simple doubt.

Weil nonetheless kept abreast of intellectual developments in political theory and theology and became a stinging critic of the drift of 1930s personalism and rights discourse in Catholic circles. She penned a fierce and savagely comic philosophical essay in response to Jacques Maritain's 1942 publication *The Rights of Man and Natural Law*, in which she contested the idea of the *personne* that lay at the heart of Maritain's account.[15] She charged that that the idea was unnecessary, misleading and ultimately too small in focus to be properly theological. Whilst Maritain had been attempting to respond to the growing individualism and reductive materialism he saw as a growing threat to law and ethics in the early century, Weil saw this view as a wrong-headed reaction to modernity, more defined by its 'other' – modernity – than free from it. The *personne* for Maritain was an ensoulment, a unique unrepeatable personality, a mystery. A flat materialism or individualism failed to respect or honour these things. For Weil, the *personne* simply reproduced the modernism it claimed to amend.

Weil proceeds to argue that the idea of personality provides poor grounding for rights, dignity or citizenship for three main reasons. First, it is an opaque idea unsuited to public speech: it is a 'luminous' idea that cannot be perceived through 'the silent operation of thought'.[16] Personality is not really a public or rational category open to definition, negotiation and so forth. Weil felt that it was especially dangerous – a pathway to tyranny – to base public morals on an idea that is impossible to define. Second, she objects in principle to the idea that personality and its expansion is the ethical heart of the matter. What endures and has value about being human is not what is most personal and individual but what is most *impersonal* about the person. Weil offers a rebuttal through example. If I were to put out the eyes of a person I come across in the street, his 'personality' would still be intact: '[i]f the human personality were what is sacred for me, I could easily put out his eyes. Once he was blind, he would still have personality.'[17] And yet, this act would offend against all that is most sacred to the person. What is most sacred is 'not his person, which is not anything more than his personality. It is him, this man, wholly and simply'. She continues a paragraph later, '[i]t is him. Him as a whole. Arms, eyes, thoughts, everything.'[18] By contrast, the person is an unstable thing, a 'thing in distress', in search of warmth, comfort,

---

[15]'What Is Sacred in Every Human Being?' in *Simone Weil: Late Philosophical Writings*, ed. and introduced by Eric O. Springsted, translated by Eric O. Springsted and Lawrence E. Schmidt (Notre Dame: Notre Dame Press, 2015), pp. 103–30.
[16]Ibid., p. 104.
[17]Ibid.
[18]Ibid.

security.[19] It finds itself relieved of this anxiety only when it learns to move beyond itself, in attention, to the world and to God. This experience of being led beyond itself returns the soul to itself. Her third objection relates to this same problematic: because we experience ourselves as in need of comfort and warmth, *in our personalities* we are often drawn in the wrong direction towards the false promises of the collective, drawn to 'immolate' or 'drown' ourselves in mass identities and movements.[20] Weil sees the collective, in this regard, as often a false version of the sacred and an alternative path to embracing the necessary journey into the impersonal. The challenge is to provide the soul with its social warmth via a different route.

In place of a Christian personalism Weil suggests that a Catholic vision of political community takes as its basis the impersonal, expressed as the capacity of the unique person to belong to and be caught up in an order that is universal and enduring. Beauty, goodness and truth are of the order of the impersonal and yet are most truly human. Weil argues that 'the good is the only source of the sacred'. What is sacred about every person is not their individual characteristics and dispositions but a universal longing that every human person has, regardless of personality, that good and no harm will be done to them, a repeated aspiration even in the face of every atrocity. The reason that I should not put out your eye is because it offends against this universal aspiration to welfare, to know and receive the good. The event or fact of harm therefore lacerates the soul; it tears at the root of what is most human and most sacred in us. Viewing the human person as a situated or concrete universal, with corresponding and reasonable obligations and genuine needs, is a more stable basis for community than an appeal to rights and personalism. What is simultaneously sacred and social in Weil's view is the enacting of obligation. Obligation exists in relation to '[t]ruth, beauty, justice, compassion' which 'are always good, everywhere'.[21] We encounter the specific person in our path in the light of what is universal and particular about us both, and the givenness of our now present or already established relationship to each other (the ties that make our universal obligation concrete).

In beginning to embrace personalism and modern rights language, Weil worried that Catholic intellectuals and the Church were failing to spot the

---

[19]Ibid., p. 111.
[20]Ibid.
[21]Ibid., p. 118.

fundamentally problematic anthropology that undergirded both and to offer a truly compelling alternative vision to the artifice and individualism written into Liberal social contract politics and economics. Weil views in pejorative terms the linkage between modern rights language and the moral world of trade and exchange: '[rights language] has something commercial to it', she writes, being linked to the idea of 'sharing out, or exchange, of quantity'.[22] It is language that is inherently related to both force and contention: rights are to be contended and disputed and they rely upon some kind of enforcement or else they are simply 'ridiculous' claims. These ideas 'do not have their place in heaven, but are suspended in mid-air, and for this reason they cannot get any kind of bite on the ground'.[23] What Weil calls for is a properly 'heavenly' language that can penetrate the ground and root the good into social relations. Speaking of this necessary relation between the highest good and language that has the power to convince minds and convict human hearts, she writes '[o]nly the light that falls continually from the sky gives the tree the energy to push powerful roots into the earth. The tree is really rooted in the sky.'[24] Rights language alone, and the appeal to personalism, will not achieve this.

Weil's many essays explored the basis of ideas that came together most constructively in her only full book-length contribution, a manifesto commissioned by the Free French movement and dedicated to a vision for the rebuilding of France after the war. *The Need for Roots*, written during her exile and in the midst of the period of Pius' broadcasts, and published a year after Maritain's *The Rights of Man and Natural Law*, details Weil's proposition that post-war reconstruction needed to begin from a commitment to regenerating a social commitment to the basic universal human need for rootedness and relationship:

> To be rooted is perhaps the most important and least recognised need of the human soul. It is one of the hardest to define. A human being has roots by virtue of his real, active and natural participation in the life of a community which preserves in living shape certain particular expectations for the future. This participation is a natural one, in the sense that it is automatically brought about by place, conditions of birth, profession and social surroundings. Every human being needs

---

[22]Ibid., pp. 111–12.
[23]Ibid., p. 118.
[24]Ibid.

to have multiple roots. It is necessary for him to draw well nigh the whole of his moral, intellectual and spiritual life by way of the environment of which he forms a natural part.[25]

Weil is clear that reciprocal exchanges – the everyday relationships that fill the natural environs in which we live – are as important in shaping rootedness as any narrow physical sense of place. She is not advocating an ethno-nationalist agenda of 'roots' – her work has been drawn on inappropriately recently by revived ethno-nationalist movements in France and the United States. The problem, Weil thinks, is that most of our current modes of social organization pull away from formation and maintenance of a multifaceted form of rootedness. Our fundamental economic and political model uproots; the distribution of power uproots. For most, uprootedness is our universal modern experience. She writes:

Uprootedness is by far the most dangerous malady to which human societies are exposed, because it is a self-propagating one. For people who are really uprooted there remain only two possible sorts of behaviour: either to fall into a spiritual lethargy resembling death ... or to hurl themselves into some form of activity, necessarily designed to uproot, often by the most violent methods, those who are not yet uprooted or only partly so.[26]

Weil is talking here about a spiritual-political condition of *uprootedness* deep in the modern psyche, which exists in visible structural forms through work, governance, markets and the flow of capital. Weil believes that uprooted cultures are prone to spiritual crises and that uprootedness does not produce the conditions for thinking well in order to get us out of such crises: uprootedness deadens thought. Uprootedness also destroys the heart of politics, whose task Weil argues is to ensure a relationship of continuity between past and future. She does not mean an unchanging relationship but one in which memory, connectedness, a sense of intergenerational responsibility and judgement are meaningfully engaged.

Weil views the human being as the only truly eternal thing in the social order. Collectivities, therefore, serve the person like food does the body:

---

[25]Simone Weil, *The Need for Roots* (London: Routledge Classics, 2002), p. 43.
[26]Ibid., p. 47.

societies either poison or nourish human beings in their relations with each other and in the pursuit of their eternal destiny. She proposes, therefore, a theory of human *obligations* and human rootedness. She proposes that regardless of context or condition, we bear obligations towards the human person as such, and these obligations relate to concrete *needs*. She names these human needs as both *material* and *moral* – and, interestingly, she thinks we have a tendency to focus more on material needs to the detriment of moral needs. Responding well to both of these needs is part of what roots and re-roots us, and keeps uprootedness at bay. Her list of these needs is challenging. The obvious material needs for food, shelter and decent work make the list. But the moral needs she enumerates are less self-evident and no less important: the need for truth, to have access to it, to pursue it, to find our relation to it, which she sees as the most sacred need of the person (in common with Pius and Maritain); the need for order; the need for both risk and security; the need for responsibility; the need for liberty and equality; the need for private property and also for collective property; the need for healthy relations of obedience. A society that plays fast and loose with political truth, according to Weil, is an *uprooting* society. *The Need for Roots* is a dazzlingly distinctive text; it is a complex piece of work, and yet there is a remarkable affinity between Pius' Christmas messages and her vision. Weil is much more suspicious of institutions, of the organized Church, of the lure of false ideologies of solidarity than Pius, but nonetheless these works speak to each other and their moment in fascinating ways.

Several years after Weil had finished *The Need for Roots*, a young German academic named Josef Pieper was articulating his own Christian social vision. Writing in 1947, Pieper laid out the following claims for a vision of the common good fit for a post-war world, deeply resonant with Pius and Weil's claims.[27] Pieper lays out a vision of the common good in which he distinguishes between a liberal tendency to define the common good primarily in terms of what he calls 'the usable goods of production' and a Christian theological account of the good life, beyond mere utility. Pieper says that a theological account of the good forces us to look at both the material goods that are part of the life of necessity – the basic material needs of food, shelter, work, education and leisure that Weil and Pius are

---

[27] Josef Pieper, *Leisure: The Basis of Culture* (San Francisco: Ignatius Press, 2009).

also concerned to note. Yet, he says, we must also look at the goods that are neither usable nor marketable, but which are *entirely* real and indispensable to a good life together: the relations of care and love and contemplation and beauty that make our lives together valuable and sustain life. These goods represent the basis of a free life together beyond mere supply and demand – all the things that exist beyond what Pieper calls 'the total world of work'. It is vital to the common good that we protect the forms of social relation that cannot simply be 'put to use'. The valuing of this vision of a life beyond utility is properly a matter for the body politic.

Pieper also adds an interesting nuance to Pius' theme of the kind of political 'limit' necessary in a healthy society. He notes that whilst we can certainly list the basic material goods to which we all need fair access, and the problems that ensue when we don't have that access, what we cannot do so easily is define with any certainty or finality what the total common good should look like. In fact, Pieper goes further and argues that we should be very suspicious of any form of government that thinks it *can* define, beyond doubt, that total common good – the ultimate horizon of the good. Any form of political messianism that tells us there is a final vision, an end to the necessarily *open*-ended conversation of what the good might be, revisable at every turn, is to be suspected as the imposition of a total market or totalitarian view of society. There is a necessary *not-knowing* – a social apophasis – about the final form of the good for which we strive: that not knowing for sure is why the social conversation and the contexts within which it can happen must remain open, revisable and repentable. This is one dimension to thinking of the common good as a *via negativa*.

Weil and Pieper echo Pius in seeking to invite their readers into contemplation of the theme of moral unity. They speak of rootedness, of a necessary Christian account of non-utility as the basis of social relations and of a communicating good – a good material and moral – which ties dignified persons into the story of each other and the whole. Both Weil and Pieper were read by Popes John XXIII and Paul VI. Angelo Roncalli – then based in Paris and prior to his papacy – was so moved by Weil's work and her death that he wrote to her family in 1944. Paul VI named her as a critical influence. It is not clear in either case though that it was her social theology that made an impact rather than her wider spiritual writing and personal commitment. It is Maritain's emerging philosophy of natural rights and personalism that most visibly and powerfully makes its way into the main bloodstream of the papal and conciliar tradition of the 1960s and forms a critical part of its opening out to the modern world.

Democracy, rights and religious freedom

The foundations laid by Pius XII's radio messages were developed in significant ways by his two immediate successors. The first significant development occurred in response to the Cuban Missile Crisis of 1962. Although John XXIII had issued a previous social encyclical, *Mater et magistra*, his two most significant innovations in social teaching were initiated between his diagnosis with cancer in September 1962 and his death in June 1963. Both resulting documents would offer a new articulation of the relationship of the Catholic Church to the political community, one focused on human rights and duties, the other on religious freedom. The first, and by far the easier of the two to produce, was *Pacem in terris*. Its origins are said to lie in the public exhortation to peace John XXIII produced in October 1962 following private encouragement from Nikita Khrushchev.[28] *Pacem in terris* was drafted by the principal thinker who had also helped to draft *Mater et magistra*, Pietro Pavan, a priest and professor of social economy. Dealing with questions of war and peace and laying the foundations for a developing post-war Catholic theology of human rights, freedom and democracy, the document offered a new (although gradually evolved) Catholic vision of political community framed by a new natural law teaching. This new articulation was both drawn from deep Catholic sources but also unthinkable without the shaping influence of its post-Enlightenment Christian and secular context.

Pacem in terris laid out for the first time in official teaching an extensive and inclusive vision of human rights that integrated a Catholic insistence on natural law with a corresponding theory of the natural rights that could be extended from it. Rather than a break with tradition, *Pacem in terris* was able, following Maritain, building in turn also on a hundred years of development in moral theology via the Dominican and Jesuit moral manualists, and in tune with the drafter Pietro Pavan's own work, to articulate rights as a legitimate Catholic extension of a prior Scholastic reasoning. The natural law orientations of the human person towards truth, goodness and beauty corresponded to a primary right to religious freedom as the first right of the person (a new teaching first articulated in *Pacem in terris*). An orientation towards survival and material well-being implies

---

[28] See Peter Heblethwaite, *John XXIII* (London: Continuum, 1984), p. 232. This is taken from Pope John XIII's personal secretary.

accessible rights (often associated in secular terms with the Left and with worker's rights, but also here drawn from a Thomistic legacy in Catholic thought) to food, shelter, work, health and so forth. An orientation towards the order of society and preservation of peace implies not simply justice and charity but also freedom and personal self-determination, implying civic rights to free association, to emigrate and immigrate, to free economic initiative, for women as full members of society and to bodily integrity.

Despite the provocative headline run by a Milanese newspaper, 'Falcem in Terris' (the Sickle on Earth), John XXIII's list of rights cut across divisions between Left and Right, and it retained an independent Catholic anthropology as its basis. *Pacem in terris* consciously balanced an account of rights with an account of duties – one cannot exist within a Catholic social imagination without the other. It also regulated any appeal to rights with an account of the common good as an integrating principle of rights within the body of the social whole at the level of the local, national and international community. Rights talk cut adrift from such a wider envisioning of social relationships would not serve true justice, peace or freedom. The common good provides a moral framework for thinking about conditions under which I might choose to forego my right as an act of solidarity or sacrifice for another, but it remains an injustice if I am forcibly deprived of a natural right. It should be noted that the framing of the whole document is a theology of peace: rights and duties are the route to peace. As Drew Christiansen notes, the vision of the whole political order in *Pacem in terris* is that politics is, to use Augustinian language, part of the order of love.[29] Its task is peace and justice, but without acknowledging an animating human draw towards a communion with others and with God that politics serves as its source and its end, it lacks a lasting purpose and a telos beyond itself. Peacemaking, which occurs through respect for rights and the enactment of justice, is ultimately a 'requirement of love'. In all these regards *Pacem in terris* was undoubtedly novel, albeit with a discernible Catholic genealogy.[30]

Perhaps the clearest line of development from Pius' Christmas messages lay in the treatment *Pacem* gave to the question of political form: liberal

---

[29]Drew Christiansen, 'Commentary on *Pacem in terris*', in *Modern Catholic Social Teaching: Commentaries and Interpretations*, Second Edition, ed. Kenneth Himes (Washington D.C.: Georgetown Press, 2018), p. 235.
[30]Hebblethwaite, *John XXIII*, p. 253.

democracy. Previous teaching from the medieval period to the first social encyclicals had insisted that the Church did not have a solution to the question of a preferred governmental form. Aquinas had suggested that some combination of forms, an integrated model of aristocracy, democracy and monarchy, seemed likely to produce most virtuous and least dangerous rule, but the social encyclicals had not passed judgement. The antimodernists had still preferred some form of Catholic rule, a unity of government (throne and altar) or in its French Gallican form a 'lay' divine right of Catholic monarchs, and this remained a widespread view even until the eve of the Second Vatican Council and for some remains so. Building on Pius' messages, *Pacem in terris* for the first time expresses a positive appreciation of the value of liberal democracy, noting in particular the value of a separation of judicial, executive and legislative powers and the value of written constitutions, and the potential of democracy to contribute towards the participatory vision of the common good. Emile Perreau-Saussine, echoed in James Chappel's work, argues that it was bitter experience that in the end pushed the Church decisively to a public acknowledgement of the value of democracy. He argues that it had become clear to the papacy that it was no longer a question of Christian monarchy versus liberal democracy but authoritarianism and totalitarianism versus democracy.

The turn towards personalism in social teaching, which would intensify further with the promulgation of *Gaudium et spes* in 1965, enabled the development of a coherent Catholic account of rights, democracy and freedom that centred not on individualism, the social contract or moral autonomy but on the ontology of the dignified human person. Via this route the Church could find its own Catholic articulation of democratic values and rights language. But even as it did so, or precisely because it did so on its own terms, there remained a fundamental and lasting anthropological tension between the Church's account of freedom, rights and democracy and some strands of liberalism. The sticking points in Fr Clump's 1955 pamphlet had not been completely overcome. Catholic teaching continued to hold to the idea of a natural moral order and an objective tradition of truth. The opening words of *Pacem in terris* which frame its treatment of democracy and rights concerned the order of truth. Humanity is created in love and goodness, and in this image for the pursuit of truth in freedom. To honour the fullness of this creation requires a political community committed to protecting the dignified person who makes their way through freedom to, and in, the good. It is coherent in this context to think of natural human rights that protect this person, which place politics and economy in service of the person and not the other way around. It is consistent with this view to think of a separation and negotiation of power that maximizes participation and preserves order between cultures, nations and generations.

Nowhere is this distinction clearer than in the developing teaching on religious freedom. *Pacem in terris* noted for the first time in official CST that religious freedom constituted a fundamental right. Where the Church of the Syllabus of Errors (1864) had taught that error had no rights, the Church would now defend a freedom of religion. It did so not as a capitulation to relativism or founded on a new belief in the equality of plural world views but out of the same teaching on the (ontological) dignity of the human person as it had cast its approval of rights and democracy. Begun under John XXIII in 1963 but completed after his death, *Dignitatis humanae* was promulgated by the Second Vatican Council in 7 December 1965. Its terse prose and brevity belied the complex process of two years of drafting and revision. Whilst much commentary focused on a perceived dramatic reversal of Catholic teaching on religious freedom, *Dignitatis humanae* seeks to stress a narrative of continuity: the document does not repudiate previous Catholic teaching on truth and its claims upon conscience but does seek to offer a new articulation of a Catholic appreciation of the relationship between religious believers and political communities. The document parallels two major cultural developments in reflection on human dignity: the desire to protect a free expression of religion without state or religious coercion but also a limit to the constitutional role of government in the arena of belief. Both these desires are affirmed. The document reminds the Church of traditional Catholic teaching on the truth of the Catholic faith but notes that the social and rational nature of the human person drives persons to seek the truth. This search for the truth is a thoroughly social matter: it requires communities of inquiry, teaching, formation, worship and charity and is an open-ended search. Given that the pursuit of religion is always exercised *in society*, the appropriate context for discussion of religious freedom is therefore 'the inviolable rights of the human person' and 'the constitutional order of society'.

This reflection on religion *ad extra* is married to a treatment of the social dimensions and plural adherences of the person *ad intra*. As Russell Hittinger notes, 'DH [Dignitatis humanae] would have government mindful of the fact that persons are multi-dimensional: citizens, believers or non-believers, and members of societies other than the state. Where government emphasizes one so heavily that the others fade from view the person can be put at war with himself.'³¹ This is an important and often missed dimension of the Church's teaching on religious freedom: that it is part and parcel of a society's ability to deal with the multiplicity, incompleteness and changing shape of identity. For a Christian identity is already plural: we are simultaneously members of civic and ecclesial communities of belonging, pursuing the good of each. It is incumbent on liberal states to be liberal and to admit of the multidimensional nature of personhood. In the context of resistance to communism in Poland in the 1970s, Adam Michnik, Jewish and secular, recognized exactly this about the value of the Church's teaching on freedom as standing for more than a narrowly religious point: 'religious liberty is the most obvious sign that civil rights are healthy. The encroachment of power upon this liberty is always a sign of the totalitarianization of intellectual life. There is no exception to this rule, because it is only totalitarianism that is unable to accept the apostolic injunction "to obey God rather than man."'³²

Any teaching on religious freedom therefore draws from teaching about the social nature of the dignified human person and the communal and interconnected dimensions of religious belief in interaction with its social context. The document repeats familiar Catholic teaching on the role of conscience and its pre-eminence but also notes the necessarily public and social expression of the operations of conscience. The document addresses questions of the limitations of religious freedom. These are to be set by the state according to its own duties to safeguard public order and the common good. Where tensions arise in this context political prudence is needed to ensure a careful balancing of the needs of the 'common welfare' and the religious believer. The document does not discuss difficult cases but indicates that resolutions will be highly contextual matters rather than admitting of generic rules.

The teaching proposed by *Dignitatis humanae* is closely tied to the emerging wider political anthropology of Vatican II, which had begun to emphasize more heavily a separation of ecclesial and political spheres, and

---

[31] F. Russell Hittinger, 'Political Pluralism and Religious Liberty: The Teaching of Dignitatis Humanae', a paper for *Universal Rights in a World of Diversity. The Case of Religious Freedom*, Pontifical Academy of Social Sciences, Acta 17, 2012, p. 54. Accessible at http://www.pass.va/content/dam/scienzesociali/pdf/acta17/acta17-hittinger.pdf (Last accessed 1 March 2020).

[32] Adam Michnik, *L'Eglise et al gauche. Le dialogue Polonais* [1977], translated by A. Solonimski (Paris: Seuil, 1979), p. 170. Quoted in Emile Perreau-Saussine, *Catholicism and Democracy*, p. 132.

their dual duty to honour the dignified social person.[33] Hittinger notes, '[f]irst, and most importantly, *DH* presupposes that church, state, and society are distinct spheres. Society does not "belong" to either the state or the church. The individual who possesses the right of religious liberty has plural memberships which cannot be reduced to one another.' Hittinger notes three facets of legitimate and meaningful pluralism that underlies the teaching on religious freedom: a pluralism of social forms, a plurality of legitimate forms of government and a pluralism of belief and culture that flows from the social nature of the person.[34]

In attending to questions of religious freedom within the temporal realm the documents of the council make clear that the Church, under conditions of modernity, is not identified with or bound to any political system, that she might distance herself from the rights proclaimed by, and functions of, the state to preserve her true task and mission, and that she understands the separation of religion from politics in terms of a spatial differentiation of sphere and task. This is not in contradiction with its warmer embrace of liberal democracy but part and parcel of the same flow of thought. This language finds its most developed forms in *Gaudium et spes* and *Dignitatis humanae*. *Gaudium et spes* asserts: 'The Church, by reason of her role and competence, is not identified in any way with the political community nor bound to any political system. She is at once a sign and a safeguard of the transcendent character of the human person.' The Church 'does not place her trust in the privileges offered by civil authority. She will even give up the exercise of certain rights which have been legitimately acquired, if it becomes clear that their use will cast doubt on the sincerity of her witness or that new ways of life demand new methods'.[35] Building on the themes of *Mater et magistra*, *Gaudium et spes* also devotes space to the question of international bodies and agencies necessary for the promotion of international peacebuilding, humanitarian development and a global common good.[36] It is inconceivable that an age marked by what John XXIII had named 'socialization' (increased interdependence) would not

---

[33] It should be noted that John Courtney Murray, a chief architect of *Dignitatis humanae*, had previously been banned from writing on the theme of religious freedom, and his involvement in this process was itself a kind of act of resistance.
[34] Hittinger, 'Political Pluralism and Religious Liberty'.
[35] *Gaudium et spes*, §76.
[36] Ibid., §83–90.

bring with it greater duties to conceive of justice in global terms. The fact of socialization brings with it an obligation to act for justice in a sphere beyond the local and national.

Increasingly, the emphasis of the documents of the 1960s was less upon ecclesial power and recognition and more upon a twofold political theology. The Church would form consciences for action in the world based on a rational exploration of human obligations to form just communities that upheld dignity and the common good. Consideration of the conditions for human persons to fulfil their nature and to be able to participate fully in community was the basis of any proclamation of rights and duties. Collective discernment of the common good, ongoing, incomplete and informed by a process of reflection on moral order and purpose itself, becomes necessary to fulfil this process. This element of an emerging Catholic political theology focuses on the question of the human person per se and a reading of collective conditions. The second strand of the developing post-war Catholic political theology concerns the specific mandate the Church gives to the faithful: a new political theology of the laity. If the clergy of the Church are no longer the mediating context for a political theology, then it is the lay Catholic believer who becomes the mediating and integrating context, the embodied reality where political and ecclesial citizenship meet and are worked out. *Gaudium et spes* notes that the laity 'can show in practice how authority is to be harmonized with freedom, personal initiative with consideration for the bonds uniting the whole social body, and necessary unity with beneficial diversity'.[37] But this is no Catholic individualism, for *Gaudium et spes* reaffirms the need for plural social groups and intermediary bodies at every level of society. It communicates a vision of a plural state, composed of varying scales of participatory communities and where power exists centrally, an enabling rather than controlling state.[38]

In the social encyclicals that followed closely on the conclusion of the council, Paul VI moved to embrace questions of human development in its economic and political dimensions. In *Populorum progressio* he addressed – for the first time in more adequately global terms – the option for the poor and a right to development. Economic participation and attention to development in all its human dimensions was foregrounded. In *Octogesima*

---

[37] *Gaudium et spes*, §75.
[38] Ibid.

adveniens, an apostolic letter rather than an encyclical, Paul VI picked up this theme in its political dimensions. Developing further the emphasis on human dignity, the document calls for attention to the use of political power to serve the common good. It is impossible to think that such power could serve the good of all without its dispersal and more adequate mechanisms for participation, particularly by the most disenfranchised, in decision-making. These themes were echoed and developed by the meeting of the global Synod of Bishops in 1971, called to continue the implementation and development of the themes of the council. *Justitia in mundo* (Justice in the World) was released as a synodical letter on the theme of world justice. The letter argues for a Christian duty to work for the redemption and liberation of the human race. It mentions for the first time a commitment to the whole biosphere and not merely human beings. And it focuses on the political and economic failures of hunger, inequality, overconsumption, the arms race and the imbalance of power in decision-making within and between countries. It decries the threat to life in the context of refugee displacement, religious persecution and abortion.

Notably the letter did not focus in the way that *Pacem in terris* or *Gaudium et spes* had on the character of political community or the role of the state per se, but rather offered a compelling vision of a Christian and ecclesial duty to pursue justice and liberation. The letter offers a theological account of the freedom or liberty to which the Christian is called. The 'interior law of liberty' begins with the free, graced choice of the person to turn away from self-sufficiency and towards God and love of neighbour. This is the prior work of liberation that enables us to make a free gift of ourselves for the freedom of others. A Christian ethic of love implies an absolute demand for justice, and that justice implied protection of both the dignity and the rights of others. Although the document does not quite name it in these terms, what is implied is a second face of the common good as a *via negativa*: for the Christian, inspired by the example of Christ and moved by grace and the work of the Spirit in history, the task is to be present to those persons and in those situations where the common good is most clearly absent, debased and actively denied. The document calls Christians to a commitment to being present with the most marginalized as a voluntary act of Christian freedom in pursuit of justice. In this way, a Christian fosters the life of the body politic as a distinct Christian duty, situated within Christian community. In some ways it is strange that this document did not get picked up by those who wanted a more 'ecclesial' political theology in the last decade, for it has considerable potential to act as a point of integration between current ecclesial factions. It is perhaps the adoption of the language of liberation, as much as its focus on the struggle for justice as an integral task of the Church, and the later tensions between the papacy and Latin American theologians of liberation that eclipsed the insights of *Justitia in mundo*. Given its strong focus on a distinct ecclesial dimension to Christian action there are ironies to this later oversight that remain to be attended to.

In 1978 Karol Wojtyła became Pope John Paul II and almost immediately a figure of significance on the world political stage. Whilst his social teaching did not make major innovations in the way that the Church thought about political community, it did see the further development of the personalist themes augmented by the council. Much is made of the influence of a youth shaped by communism and the public role played by John Paul II in the final stages of Eastern European state communism. However, two further factors left their imprint on John Paul II's political teaching: first, his own philosophical training and background in phenomenology, and second, his perceptions of the political challenges that were emerging for the Catholic vision of rights, freedom and democracy set forth in *Gaudium et spes, Pacem in terris* and *Dignitatis humanae*.

John Paul II had inherited from the milieu of the Second Vatican Council a political-personalism that was now well developed. Both Maritain and John Courtney Murray had laid out a framework of natural law and human rights thinking that viewed society as serving the human person as its subject and end. The core of social teaching was therefore the dignified, acting person in their social context. Both state and society – to be seen as separated although related entities – served the needs of the human person seeking to reach their full stature. Only with the right legal and social conditions could the person achieve this end. The state was a limited entity composed primarily of juridical and administrative functions whose task, as Courtney Murray summarized in *We Hold These Truths*, was to contribute to the common good by ensuring justice, freedom, security, welfare, civil unity and peace. John Paul II continued to produce a vision of state and society in this vein. To the writings of Murray and Maritain he brought his own version of personalism, the foundations of which are to be found in his book *The Acting Person*, first published in 1969, nine years prior to his papal election.[39] Here he develops a vision of the human

---

[39] Karol Wojtyła, *The Acting Person*, translated by A. Potocki (London: D. Reidel Press, 1979) [Revised from the 1969 Polish edition].

person as an acting subject who shapes the world around them and is self-constituted through their actions. Personhood is bound up with every kind of action we undertake. In action we manifest ourselves, and each act expresses our being and our becoming. In important ways, we are what we do. John Paul II does not mean to imply a form of social determinism; we are in fact the very opposite of robotic programmed beings. Our capacity for self-reflection, for free conscience and therefore for judgement and responsibility, defines being human. This version of personalism enables John Paul II to develop his distinctive social teaching on human work and on solidarity (Chapter 10). The condition of work is a critical question for political community and the common good because we are so constituted as persons by what we do, by our acting, producing lives. Decent work, fairly paid and socially meaningful and productive, allowing for creativity and free enterprise, is a political matter. This is part of a concern for the general welfare. This was the vision of John Paul II's first social encyclical *Laborem exercens* and his final *Centisimus annus*.

It was this same vision of the freely acting person, however, that also led to tensions with the other main movement for the renewal of Catholic political theology during the 1970s and 1980s: Latin American Liberation Theology. Where the Church of the council had adopted a strong distinction between state and society, and focused its analysis of political community upon freedoms, rights and duties, the theologians of liberation and the statement by the Latin American regional bishops' conferences at Medellín and Puebla were concerned to expand the understanding of political community beyond the terms set by liberal democracy. The council was not wrong, but it had not said enough, and in doing so the Church failed the poorest people on the planet. On the one hand, liberation theologians had been involved in the establishment of small base ecclesial communities which combined prayer, liturgy and political action in an integrated way; on the other, they wanted to challenge the ideological power of neoliberal economics tied to notions of liberal statehood. The experience of poverty outside of Europe was tied to the dominant political and economic system, and its mutually reinforcing power structures. The Church could find no home here and must oppose such systems with prophetic power. A structural analysis of social sin was necessary and a personal-communal politics of resistance and liberation the only option. The political task of the Church was to cooperate in taking the crucified victims of history down from the Cross. The political theology of the Church could be no less than a permanent option for the poor and the formation of an ecclesial body politic that lived this as an ordinary reality. John Paul II's response to this vision is found in his second social encyclical *Sollicitudo rei socialis*.

One final comment might be made on the politics that shaped John Paul II's social teaching. John Paul II had been part of the discussions that led to the publication of the main social teaching texts of Vatican II. They represented a vision he believed in. Nonetheless, he came to think that the context in which that vision needed to find a home was becoming more problematic for the Church. Rights, freedom and democracy had always been tied within a Catholic anthropology to the idea of an objective moral order. Democracy would not be truly democratic unless it was hospitable to such a view of being human. John Paul II sensed a growing tension between liberal democracies and a key area of personal and sexual morality. The personal was political in ways that troubled the papacy, most especially on matters of the family, sex, gender, disability, reproduction and dying. It was on this increasingly embodied and anthropological grounds that the political theology of Vatican II would be tested. This belief shaped John Paul II's political reflection profoundly.

Given how central Joseph Ratzinger had been to the papacy of John Paul II, it was no surprise that when he was elected to the papacy Benedict XVI's social teaching carried forward many of the same themes and concerns. If there is a single overarching theme to his social teaching it is to reframe CST according to a systematic theology of love. His papacy did add, within this theological framework, to the canon of teaching on political community. Marked by a departure from the personalist themes of the post-war papacies and towards the revival of a more Augustinian and communitarian political theology, three notable contributions emerge from Benedict's teaching. First, Benedict XVI retrieves love as the central category of Christian social teaching and the unifying principle of human life in all its arenas of action. Second, he offers a vision of gift and gratuity as the basis of economic, political and ecclesial life. Third, he shifts the interpretation of what the Church's social teaching contributes to public life in a more reflective-intellectual direction.

Benedict frames his major social teaching documents with a theological reflection on love. He makes clear that Christianity is not a system of ethics or abstract teaching but the proclamation of an event, an encounter and a person. Its teaching is about the 'decisive direction' this event and encounter gives to human life, individually and communally. The logic of this encounter with love is one that changes everything and provides a new principle of unity. I may still dislike my neighbour, his personality and habits might annoy me intensely, but a mediating third figure enables me to will what is good for her or him and this too is my good. Communion is possible because I am now called to see another as God sees them. The same habits remain, I may not manage to like them, but I accept that they too are part of the economy of love achieved through the Incarnation, death and resurrection of Christ. Love thus becomes less a feeling or private sentiment brought in an unstable way into politics (what Arendt and others so disliked) and more a practice of a community, through graced willing. This is love purified and disciplined and fit for public life. This is how we enlarge public judgement and responsibility. This is also what motivates service to those who suffer and the meeting of material need. The earliest Christians saw the need for forms of material communion – in which goods were fairly and evenly distributed, turning mere fact of possession towards the holding in common and to meeting need. Benedict emphasizes that this love ethic is thus about the body as much as the soul and about the unity of the two.

This same logic is used as the basis for *Caritas in veritate*. This document, published two years after the 2007 financial crisis, proposes that a just and loving economy and politics be thought of in terms of the notion of gift exchange, instead of narrow self-interest. The public logic of love implies a model of economic and political action which maximizes participation and works on the basis of gratuity and gift exchange as the only way to a truly common good. Given the erosion of trust in politics and economics and the exploitation of the environment, a deep renewal of values and virtues at the heart of political economy is clearly needed. This cannot be achieved by the market, civil society or political authority alone – but by a renewal of each. Political authority serves this best by ensuring power is distributed and dispersed, the market provides a real service to the common good, and it is committed to genuine collaboration with civil and economic actors to bring renewal towards an economy of gift. In this way, *Caritas in veritate* presents the task of political community and its duties to justice and the common good in fuller terms than *Deus caritas est* did.[40] It also makes a call for global political coordination of questions that relate to a global common good, migration and the environment being obvious examples. A vision of reciprocal exchange in economic life is mirrored in the analysis

---

[40]There is a legitimate debate about the extent to which *Deus caritas est* can be viewed as a CST document. It is perhaps better to view it as a systematic theology text with profound implications for CST than as a social encyclical.

of human rights presented by the document. Reciprocal awareness of rights and duties is the framing for a consideration of the duties to the created order and the natural environment.

The third novelty in Benedict's social teaching on the theme of political community relates to his observations on the nature of CST itself. In *Deus caritas est*, and again in his Westminster Hall address, Benedict suggests that the role of the Church's social teaching is one of 'purification' of the reasoning that is used in public life. The task of the state is to enable justice. Achieving this is no mere instrumental task for it requires asking the question: What is justice? Benedict makes a sharp – arguably sharper than *Justitia in mundo* and the social documents of the Second Vatican Council – distinction between the role of the state and citizenry in pursuing this struggle for justice and the proper political role of the Church. The struggle for justice belongs to the state and its individual citizens, whilst it is the reflective space for shaping the speculative question of justice that is the meeting point of faith and politics. The shared ground is thus a space in which we ask together, in dialogue, the question 'what is justice?' Benedict envisions the Church's contribution to public life as thus threefold: through its social teaching it provides a reflective space to improve the quality of thinking that undergirds public action to achieve justice; through its charitable works it enacts its direct and unmediated responsibility to respond with love to individuals in suffering or material need (no state may prevent this because it is a divine duty to enact the works of mercy); through its laity it acts for the common good, because its laity take on the responsibility of citizens to join in work for justice through service in the organizations and institutions of public life – they do so as citizens but with well-formed consciences. The papacy and bishops enact the first, the Church through its organizations and through individual acts of Christian care enacts the second, the laity enact the third. *Caritas in veritate* nuanced this teaching, but fundamentally this intellectual-contemplative vision remains at the heart of Benedict's vision of CST.

The papacy of Francis has marked a further shift both in the understanding of the place of the Church's social teaching in public life and in the analysis of the political signs of the times. Transnational themes of migration, the environment, global inequalities and the crisis of democracy (all of which are interconnected crises for Francis) have dominated the agenda of his social teaching. Francis has given a high priority to the role of mass social movements as the 'social poets' who create mechanisms for participation for the politically marginalized and whose structures lead to a creativity of social solutions. Decent work as a key route to political and social participation has been a repeated theme. Dialogue emerges from the contexts in which we are meaningful stakeholders and actors. Land, housing and work has become a cornerstone papal mantra for political dignity. In this sense, Francis' teaching has not echoed the vision of social teaching Benedict offered in *Deus caritas est*. He places the struggle for justice – a collaborative struggle with social movements, other faith actors and those in authority who share a vision of the common good – as an integral part of the ecclesial task. In continuity with Benedict, however, he has continued to develop the themes of gift, communion and fraternity. *Laudato si'* (which we will discuss in more detail in the next chapter) develops the environmental opening created in *Caritas in veritate* and places the environment at the heart of the political agenda.

Both *Laudato si'* and *Fratelli tutti* appear to bear a kinship, twofold, with *Pacem in terris*. In the first instance, Francis seems gripped by a profound sense that his papacy occurs in a moment when the world is once again on the brink of catastrophe, as it had been when John XXIII had conceived of *Pacem in terris*. This time it is not the threat of nuclear war but of environmental devastation and a viral pandemic. As *Pacem in terris* was, so both *Laudato si'* and *Fratelli tutti* are framed by the themes of social violence and social peace. This social violence is seen in all pervasive and multifaceted terms, as part of a logic of domination and mastery that St Augustine would have seen as our sinful lust for domination: the hallmark of an anxious and chaotic self, turned inwards instead of towards God, creation and neighbour. In *Laudato si'* Francis offers a profound critique of a political, economic and cultural model that enacts domination as its primary mode of social operation. He names this as the technocratic paradigm. This paradigm which grips politics and economics tends towards undifferentiated and one-dimensional solutions and initiatives, and its techniques are possession and mastery as the route to transformation. In place of this paradigm, he calls for a root and branch reimagining of political and economic solutions according to the principles of solidarity and subsidiarity. He calls for diffused and shared power, creative localism, grassroots initiatives as well as national, regional and international ones committed to the common good. Francis names the greatest threats to the common good as lying in the degradation of both natural and human environments, with inequality and rights deprivations going hand in hand with the environmental threat. If these are the primary threats to the common good, then it makes sense that the route out is to begin with a politics of attention from below: hearing the cry of the earth and the cry of the poor. This is a political imperative for the sake of a common people in a common home.

Fratelli tutti echoes these themes and continues to develop a critique of political culture. One of the notable features of Francis' social analysis of politics is his refusal to see the state in terms of its instrumental and juridical character alone, and his development of cultural-political analysis. For some, this leads to accusations of imprecision and overblown rhetoric that clouds very precise theological teaching and analysis of political life. For others, what matters is the prophetic-imaginative and narrative tone to Francis' work, an approach able to get to the heart of naming the fundamental dynamics of political cultures gone astray. Francis is less interested in a careful demarcation of activities proper to state, market and society and more in tracing the wide human tendencies that are replicated across these arenas, mirroring and reinforcing each other across the supposed borders and boundaries in human life. In this vein, *Fratelli tutti* repeats the established themes of Francis pontificate: inequality is the primary social evil, and therefore the universal destination of goods (outlined in the next chapter) is its first constructive proper principle. A throwaway culture – of things and people – infects politics as much as it does the market and personal social relations. In politics this manifests in a lack of attention to the vulnerable, as well as tendencies of short-termism in policy and decision-making, and a refusal of intergenerational thinking (a core task of politics). It is connected to – a repeated theme across Francis' writings – the refusal, or loss of memory. In *Lumen fidei*, his first encyclical and one whose early drafting and conception he inherited from Benedict XVI, Francis talks about memory as the condition for self-knowledge and communal knowing. The conditions for knowledge and memory are themselves in turn relational. In *Fratelli tutti* Francis talks about a refusal of historical consciousness and a resulting devaluing of memory; this is part of the process that leads to the emptying out of meaning from core political concepts with deep theo-political roots: justice, freedom, democracy, rights. The capacity to remember – which for a Christian means not just to recall past history but also to remember what we are destined for and what is therefore happening all around us in any moment by way of creating potential – is critical for rights and duties, for positive and negative freedom, for the possibility of justice. This theme of memory is simultaneously historical and eschatological in Francis, and it is deeply politically important.

Finally, we should note Francis' distinctive – although not entirely novel – reflection on the theme of the people and his analysis of populism. As we noted earlier in this chapter Pius XII had adopted a positive theological usage of the political notion of being 'a people' during his wartime broadcasts. He contrasted a logic of the masses – impersonal, homogenizing, easily manipulated (as Simone Weil had also noted) – with the process of becoming a 'people', capable of differentiated, responsible thoughtful action towards common ends. This appeared to contain an implicit Augustinianism. Pope Francis' writing on the people echoes Pius' wartime treatment but draws also on the legacy of both the Second Vatican Council's *Lumen gentium* and the Argentine Liberationist Theology of the People.

The image of the Church as a people is core to the vision of Vatican II, and Francis sees this language as therefore essential to the Church, as much as to the political community. No one saves themselves and no one is saved alone; salvation is a thoroughly and integrally social reality, divine and human, albeit one in which we must willingly and meaningfully participate. Knowing faith, sharing it and acting upon it require the formation of a people. Equally the expression of rights, dignity, democracy and freedom are also socially mediated ideas and achievements. Some kind of notion of being 'a people' – of fundamental social *belonging* as well as *being* – is necessary for the historical practice of each. In this light, Francis refuses to pathologize the language of being 'a people' but differentiates between different kinds of 'populisms'. Closed populism imagines the 'people' in primarily ethnic and homogenous identity terms, refuses the gift of the stranger, sees itself as self-sufficient in its cultural resources. By contrast, an open populism embraces the need to form external cultural bonds, to accept and form new practices of social belonging, but practices these with an openness to those who do not yet belong – the new arrival, the next generation and so forth. Renewal comes in an antonymous way – from who or what is not yet present. This 'not yet present' can be intergenerational and intercultural. Cultures may (or may not!) be beautiful, wise and fruitful but they are importantly incomplete as expressions of full humanity or truth; and their possibility of human fullness lies beyond themselves, both in time and in relation to eternity. The specificity, value, yet incompleteness and fragility of cultures forms part of Francis' call for a politics of dialogue, hospitality and gift exchange, not merely of just distribution and human rights. This valuing of the culture of a people is also a strong emphasis in the Argentine Liberation Theology of the People.

Francis' Catholic populism – meaning a return to the notion of being a people – is not without its critics. For some, the notion of being a people is too closely tied to the language and politics of the Romantic tradition. For

The Body Politic

others, it narrows the theological resources we might wish to deploy. Yes, Christianity has used the language of the 'populus', but it is also noteworthy that St Augustine chooses as his overarching metaphor and analogy the 'civitas' or city. Francis' contribution is perhaps to return to our register one of a plurality of political analogies and metaphors that Christians adopted for their own use from the pre-Christian world. Arguably he does so, partly because of his own heritage and influences – Liberation Theology of the People and the language of the Church in *Lumen gentium* – and partly because it is again a resonant and powerful circulating idea within our cultural-political landscape. In a way entirely resonant with St Augustine's ambitions in *City of God*, Francis makes his own attempt to think about good and bad use of political language from a Christian point of view.

In doing so, Francis also returns us to the thread that was perhaps dropped at the end of the post-war period. Perhaps unintentionally, Francis has picked up the themes of rootedness and uprootedness, work and belonging, participation and non-utility, the politics of intergenerational responsibility and the questions of political value, character and obligation that marked Weil and Pieper's response to modernity. He has not repudiated the rights and duties, freedom and justice discourse that the tradition developed over the last half a century, but something of a trailing thread is seemingly rewoven into the fabric of reflection on the body politic.

CHAPTER 9
SUBSIDIARITY
A PRINCIPLE OF PARTICIPATION AND SOCIAL GOVERNANCE

Quadragesimo anno – the 1931 encyclical that introduced the idea of subsidiarity into the lexicon of Catholic social teaching (CST) – was addressed to a world in which confidence in both democracy and capitalism had been shaken. The dreadful events of the First World War, the financial crash of 1929, the Depression which followed and the rise of fascism and socialism in Europe had conversely increased the confidence of the Church in the relevance and urgency of her new body of social teaching. Pius XI had written a bold document, clarifying and reinforcing earlier teaching on living wages and the priority of workers' labour over capital and profit, repeating the right to private property used for the common good and pushing the frontiers of what he believed to be a reconciling social model that would bring together workers and owners, the state and the individual. Pius' vision of Catholic corporatism, as it is often referred to, was rich. However, it was also proved weak in its appreciation of the dangers of the fascist and nationalist draw to this same idea. Core to Pius' Catholic corporatist vision was the principle of subsidiarity, a principle that from its first annunciation in papal teaching, to our present moment, remains a principle both frequently misunderstood and the source of inspiration for a fascinatingly complex history of civil, social, political and economic action. The idea of subsidiarity shaped the history of mid-twentieth-century corporatism, including state corporatism, as well as anti-state distributism; it made its way into the wording of the German constitution and the Maastricht Treaty; it acted as an animating principle for the radical household hospitality and anarchist state resistance of Dorothy Day's Catholic Worker movement, and it has been a source of inspiration for Saul Alinsky, Cesar Chavez, Ed Chambers and Ernesto Cortes' broad-based civic community organizing movements. A principle which advocated pluralism in the civic body has fostered an extraordinary and controversial diversity of expressions.

Towards a Politics of Communion

Given Pius XI's own broad sympathies and interests, the movement with which *Quadragesimo anno* and subsidiarity was most immediately associated was corporatism. Corporatism had an obvious and strong counter-revolutionary Christian heritage, its advocates viewing social relationships as primarily organic and expressed through the dignity of diverse vocations and social roles, including work. It drew on the Pauline theology of the corporate body, each element playing its appointed part in harmony. Central to its assumptions was the belief that class conflict was not inevitable and should be avoided, that the state should not be seen as the ultimate organizing mechanism and that private property ownership, carefully stewarded, was a basic element of dignified human life. Small associations had been seen as bodies with legal and social personalities in the medieval Catholic context, and the move towards social contract theory was seen to diminish this, producing the idea that just as the state was itself a fictional creation of the people, so it in turn had the power to approve or not the role of any other intermediate body, whose existence, whilst potentially advantageous to the community, was also a kind of fiction. The social contract placed the state prior to its associations. Corporatists thus resisted capitalist, socialist and liberal narratives, and were strongly influenced beyond Catholic circles by two key thinkers: Lutheran thinker Otto von Gierke (1841–1921) and secular Jewish social theorist Emile Durkheim (1858–1917).[1] Corporatism proposed a model of society rooted in cooperative and collaborative relationship between economic interest groups and governing authorities. Based on the idea that society could avoid industrial unrest and class conflict whilst achieving higher levels of equality by organizing itself in an organic fashion around vocational groups, corporatists proposed linking together members of particular trades and industries (e.g. coal or health care) to form a

---

[1] Otto Von Gierke's work becomes a common source for Anglican social thinkers and Catholic social thinkers, with Pluralism developing in Anglican thought and subsidiarity in the papal social tradition. See Figgis' essays *Churches in the Modern State* for parallel earlier developments. The early writings of William Temple also carry some Pluralist influences and this remains traceable even in his later writings, including *Christianity and Social Order*. For a comparison of trends in Anglican and Catholic social thought, see my essay 'Fraternal Traditions: Anglican Social Thought and Catholic Social Teaching', in *Anglican Social Theology: Renewing the Vision Today*, eds Malcolm Brown, Jonathan Chaplin, John Hughes, Alan Suggate and Anna Rowlands (London: Church House Publishing, 2014).

single corporate group. This group, made up of employers, employees, managers and shareholders, should discuss fair wages, just prices, working conditions, welfare, quality of production and apprenticeships. Crucially, the establishment of such groups should be the initiative of workers and employers, not the state. Underlying such corporatist politics were communitarian and pluralist philosophies: the human person is social and interdependent by nature and expresses that nature most readily through the organizations of civil society, from trades groups and craft-based groups to churches. The state – whilst necessary – did not act as a natural first community for the human person; therefore, it should not be the first level of social organization. The social contract was not the foundation of society, rather labouring, productive (and reproductive) households were. Thus, a healthy range of associations acted as an irreplaceable context for participation, organization and conflict resolution, and thus were where most people learned practical political virtues. Whilst Pius' own draw towards Christian corporatism decried state control, it is easy to see how such organic and integralist thought became appealing to emerging fascist and nationalist movements, and the encyclical became quickly and problematically associated by taint with the spread of state corporatism in countries with large Catholic majorities, including Austria, Italy, Portugal and Spain.

However, corporatism (in its plural forms) was not the only movement that had taken inspiration from the vision of civic association and participation in *Rerum novarum*, now formalized in *Quadragesimo anno*. Emerging in the 1920s in response to the positive influence of CST and the perceived negative catalysts of state socialism and increasing economic materialism driven by capitalism, Christian distributists drew on both *Rerum novarum* and the developing principle of subsidiarity to propose a decentralized social order rooted in widely distributed property ownership, a return to craft, land and Christian religious tradition, and an emphasis on small scale, decentralized social organization for schools, agriculture, businesses and industry, crafts and town planning. The distributists believed that maximizing property ownership and minimizing concentrations of wealth, and political and bureaucratic power would be the best hope for establishing a just and charitable economic order. Thus, emphasis was placed upon redistributing the means of production rather than a direct redistribution of wealth. The best-known advocates of distributism were English Catholics Eric Gill (1882–1940), G. K. Chesterton (1874–1936),

Towards a Politics of Communion

Hilaire Belloc (1870–1953), Fr Vincent McNabb OP (1868–1943) and the Anglican writer Dorothy L. Sayers (1893–1957), with the best-known articulations of the project in Belloc's *The Servile State* (1912) and *An Essay on the Restoration of Property* (1936). Belloc proved a controversial advocate for social Catholicism because of his perceived partial support for Italian fascism and Spanish nationalism. Whilst distributism as a movement has no more politically innocent a history than the other movements we have encountered in this book, it has proved to have enduring appeal and relevance. Contemporary distributists emphasise the need to resist the power of big corporations and media, to live simpler lives dwelling fruitfully in local contexts, and to reduce the dependency of themselves and others on large-scale social systems. A smaller-scale, plural society – demilitarised, care-orientated, spiritually engaged, economically simpler and more equal and artistically creative – is central to this contemporary re-humanizing project.

One of the most enduring examples of distributist influence is found in the version of distributism that Peter Maurin took with him from France to North America and used alongside Dorothy Day as the foundation for the Catholic Worker Movement and its small-scale communities. This movement avoided the taint of nationalism and fascism that other forms of corporatism and distributism had fallen into, instead, adopting a blend of distributism, personalism and Christian anarchism. Dorothy Day placed the principle of subsidiarity at the heart of her work. The Worker movement privileged the works of mercy through face-to-face forms of hospitality and care for impoverished workers, those with mental and physical ill health and all those who needed temporary shelter. Day was clear that the Worker community houses were houses of prayer as well as hospitality, education, labour and advocacy. Day took CST seriously and gave a unique interpretation of subsidiarity (infused with a version of personalism) as simultaneously a political and a spiritual-devotional principle. She believed that subsidiarity implies that I am responsible for the person I encounter, and my responsibility is to meet their need and to pursue their good. A profound belief in self-determination and dignified work resulted in an equally profound commitment to community. True self-determination and meaningful autonomy required communities of belonging, co-creation and action. The meaningful context for Christian political action was therefore the local community and face-to-face relationship, through which both community and healthy autonomy of exchange and action for all could be pursued.

Returning to the core patristic common good text of Matthew 25, Day preached the works of mercy – feeding the hungry, clothing the naked, visiting the prisoner and so forth – as a matter of personal and civic obligation, the meeting point of the welfare of the soul and of the city and the defining politics of the Church. Performing the works of mercy did not limit the person to a purely charitable act; rather their performance indicated a wider care for the whole person connected to systems and structures that shaped more or less human outcomes. Work was key to a dignified life, and labour took priority over capital; welfare should have a person-to-person component to it and not be merely transactional; meeting real and immediate human needs meant also advocacy for the unemployed and a programme to offer skills and training. Catholic Worker farms provided an alternative model of living, with subsistence agriculture, prayer, hospitality and advocacy forming the pattern of community life.[2] Given the radical resistance to forms of militarism, civil disobedience became a hallmark of Day's communities. Day was involved in a range of forms of protest and civil disobedience, including the non-payment of federal taxes. Drawing on the principle of subsidiarity, Day paid local taxes but objected to federal taxes on the basis of their connection to the military-industrial complex into which Day believed the American state was bound. This model of community living remains active today in over 200 community projects across the globe and continues to draw on the principle of subsidiarity in its teaching.

Perhaps the best-known deployment of the principle of subsidiarity in practice is the post-war project of European social, political and economic integration. Through the influence of Catholic bureaucrats, philosophers and politicians Jean Monnet, Emmanuel Mounier and Jacques Delors, a plan for a new European political economy and an experiment in the fusion of CST and French social modernism was begun. The end goal of their project in social and political economy was the securing of new, pacifying forms of European social communion: a common good project with solidarity and subsidiarity at its heart. Whilst French social modernism bequeathed to the European project a progressive view of society as open

---

[2] As Kate Hennessy makes clear in her loving but also critical account of growing up in the Catholic Worker communities (Hennessy is the granddaughter of Day), the farms were also contexts in which abusive relationships did take place amongst some of the family groups who came to reside there. See *The World Will Be Saved by Beauty: An Intimate Portrait of My Grandmother* (New York: Simon & Schuster, 2017).

to transformation through effective social planning in the areas of industry, public services and welfare, CST offered a vision of power, social justice and social participation rooted in a fusion of Pius XI's principle of subsidiarity and versions of Thomistic personalism. The twin principles of solidarity and subsidiarity came to define the contribution of CST to a new post-national reality for Europe. Jean Monnet (1888–1979), Robert Shuman (1886–1963) and Jacques Delors (1925–) brought the texts and traditions of *Rerum novarum* and *Quadragesimo anno* and the differing personalisms and vision of Christian democracy of Emmanuel Mounier and Jacques Maritain to life as structures for political practice. In doing so they contributed to the development and understanding of the very principles they sought to incarnate.

As anthropologist Douglas Holmes argues, CST offered to the European project the conceptual apparatus to imagine structures that sustained both diversity and solidarity.[3] The founding fathers viewed the European project as a form of conflict resolution: where nation states imagined intractable differences the simultaneous reinvention of supranational and local forms of decision-making and power sharing would unlock forms of common interest.[4] As such, the marriage of CST and social modernism consciously played into the narrative of the decline of the nation state but did not do so cynically. Monnet reimagined the leadership of nations through their role in fostering a new generation of cooperation and reconciliation mediated through new institutional structures. Such political transformation was intended as a mechanism to foster increasing political responsiveness and accountability, and to foster post-conflict reconciliation and to help avoid potential future conflict.

---

[3] Douglas R. Holmes, *Integral Europe: Fast Capitalism, Multiculturalism and Neo-Fascism* (Princeton: Princeton University Press, 2000). See Holmes' discussion of the role that a Catholic political theory makes to the construal of autonomy and diversity, solidarity and subsidiarity in the European project, pp. 48–9. He argues that Maritain codifies this vision with clarity for a Catholic audience in his 1950 *Man and the State*.

[4] Holmes traces this narrative from the reports of Leo Tindemans (1922–2014) and Altiero Spinelli (1907–86) to the Maastrict Treaty and German constitution. Spinelli, a communist and Allies Group politician, developed the earlier work of Christian democrat Tindeman to produce the first report to employ the idea of subsidiarity as a practical mechanism for the distribution of powers. His *Reform of Treaties and Achievements of European Union* (1982) paved the way for the later *Draft Treaty Establishing European Union* (1984) and *Maastrict Treaty* (1992), which formalized subsidiarity as a working political principle for European Union.

However, Monnet and Shuman's project was, from the outset, passionately contested from within the Catholic community by European Catholic integralists. The integralists drew on the same Catholic social principles, including subsidiarity, but rejected all forms of economic and social modernism. Instead, they integrated Counter-Enlightenment, Romantic sources into their interpretation of society and in so doing reached very different social conclusions. They did not adopt the neo-Thomist personalism of the architects of the European Union. A range of integralist movements fought a European battle on two fronts: a political battle against the practical project of European Union, which the integralists believed denied national and local cultures their specificity, and an intellectual battle against what they saw as the alarming union of progressive and technocratic French social modernism and CST. Such movements drew from the Romantic and counter-Enlightenment traditions of Europe and focused on the importance of locality, land, craft and stability; they also offered a critique of global capitalism and its impact on these goods. Both conservative-right leaning and conservative-leftist versions of such movements existed. Such movements saw – and in their contemporary form still see – subsidiarity as a principle that helped foster the legitimacy of Counter-Enlightenment politics resistant to cultural, economic and political cosmopolitanism, hyper capitalism and global migration. In contrast, the structures of European Union were seen to foster not frustrate these globalist tendencies and therefore ought to be opposed as a co-option or false deployment of CST whose moral performance was in the end set against subsidiary structures. *Movimenti Friuli* in Italy, with strong lay and clerical involvement, typified such anti-modernist Catholic interpretation of subsidiarity.[5]

Whilst the Worker movement and distributist inspired groups continue to exist, and there has been a resurgence of both support for and opposition to the European Union project in recent years, much of this world of civic Catholicism influenced by *Quadragesimo anno* has now long passed. Arguably, the official papal social tradition focused much more heavily in the post-war years on developing, via a reading of Thomas Aquinas, a modern theory of rights, duties, justice and freedom and a dialogue with the liberal state and market. Nonetheless, it continued to own subsidiarity as a key Catholic social principle, continued to note the importance of

---

[5]See Holmes, *Integral Europe*, pp. 3–37.

civic associations, argued for direct Christian acts of charity and care as a primary 'law' above all human laws, and has noted the importance of a proper dispersal of power.

In his recent book *Field Hospital* – the title taken from Pope Francis' image of the Church called to move beyond itself to tend a wounded world – American political theologian William Cavanaugh argues that CST badly needs a return to the principle of subsidiarity and a vision of dispersed political authority.[6] Cavanaugh points to an era now marked by the penetration of the state by finance and corporations on a scale we could not have imagined even half a century ago. The nation state – dominant, in fact, in our lives only for a relatively recent and short period, as Jon Wilson argues, between the 1920s and 1970s – has seen its hegemony quickly eroded.[7] States remain powerful, of course, but power lies crucially with corporate giants, with family groupings who are able to sway national economies through concentration of ownership and with digital communication forces that are able to manipulate truth, opinion and mood for political and economic benefit in extraordinary ways. Equally, it is possible when looking at things from the peripheries, to use Pope Francis' language, to see the way that basic inequalities attached to income, geography, race, gender and so forth shape life choices in the most ordinary and profound of ways – shaping and limiting possibilities for public virtue and free action. Cavanaugh is not alone therefore in thinking that to talk of the body politic now is to confront a reality in which state and market are increasingly difficult to distinguish. Many of the state's most public functions are now privatized, including the increased privatization of the state's powers of force (prisons, immigration facilities, border controls). In turn, the state increasingly adopts a model of consumer and performance management in its relations with its own citizens. Within the market, especially the digital market place, concentrations of power that would be intolerable in a liberal political setting are now becoming a global norm.

Anticipating themes Pope Francis would later note in *Fratelli tutti*, Cavanaugh writes of the paradoxes with which we now live: 'people are simultaneously distrustful of government and fiercely loyal to the nation-

---

[6] William Cavanaugh, *Field Hospital: The Church's Engagement with a Wounded World* (Grand Rapids: Eerdmans Press, 2016).
[7] Jon Wilson, *Out of Chaos* (forthcoming OUP). I am grateful to Jon Wilson for advance sight of the draft manuscript proposal for this book.

state'.[8] The state has much to gain from advancing the narrative of being 'a people' but in fact, this is an idea that quickly slips through the fingers, serving a complexity of interests that do not seem to foster a true unity or honour a real plurality. A forensic focus on the empirical performance of the policies adopted by democratic nation states, Cavanaugh argues, reveals a preference less for the formation of communities and peoples and more for protecting and promoting individuals marked out by their preferences and choices. The attempt to reverse this piecemeal in the face of a highly 'social' viral pandemic has proved challenging.

Drawing on a range of voices Cavanaugh argues powerfully that in seeking to uphold individual rights in a consumerist mode, the state feeds into a process by which we become poor citizens. This is ultimately a self-harming civic process. Cavanaugh supposes that most people do not wish to spend large amounts of time thinking about or actively involved in formal politics, and this is no bad thing. When politics comes to dominate, something has gone badly wrong. And yet forming small-scale corporate bodies that give expression to our skills, desires and needs and provide for a face-to-face co-creative environment is a vital part of 'citizenship' and expressive, in theological terms, of our own nature. We do not all wish to be highly political, yet we do have a drive towards an engagement with the building of community and citizenship in its multiple forms: we volunteer, we play sports and train others for sport, we form food cooperatives, we organize our neighbourhoods and so forth. This is not necessarily how we become 'a people' with a unitary identity, and none of this is formally the business of the state, but it is how we form thriving resilient neighbourhoods, villages, towns and cities. It is the life of the *civitas*. The civitas is plural, admits of multiplicity, but forms a distinct pattern of living if it is to thrive and survive. It comes to live by its own 'laws' or practices, according to and revealing to others its abiding loves: where it places value. In a pandemic, this is the common life we have missed: the life of sociality, negotiation, jostling and plurality. The life of more than one household.

As noted in the previous chapter, St Augustine does not choose the language of the *populus* (people) or *imperium* (empire) but the *civitas* (city) as the central ethical motif in his *City of God*.[9] Cavanaugh draws on this

---

[8]Cavanaugh, *Field Hospital*, p. 144.
[9]I am grateful to Charles Matthewes for conversations on this matter.

same legacy in Augustine's thought.[10] He argues that the Body of Christ is the very definition of a 'corporation', a social personhood. For Cavanaugh the Eucharist is the enactment of the corporate body, at once multiple and local and yet simultaneously a performative union with a wider mystical whole. Yet the Eucharistic community is exactly the kind of ethical (in)corporation that is simply indigestible to the liberal state. It is a multiplicity and unity of form, a meaningful pluralism. Extending the kind of argument found in Gierke and in early twentieth-century Anglican Pluralism, Cavanaugh notes we have narrowed our sense of corporation to the body of the nation and the body of the business entity. For us to form multiple healthy civitates, and above all for Christians to live the life of the *civitas dei* (City of God), we need to pay wider attention to how corporate bodies can be formed and how power flows in our everyday interactions.

Whilst the emerging ideal-type model articulated gradually over the last century within CST – a differentiated but interconnected state, market, civil society – has some appeal, it is far from our daily experience of the blurred and hybrid reality we live with. The life of the city is, for most of us, an endlessly mixed-up affair. For this reason, Cavanaugh argues we need more than simply a better language of rights and dignity (as CST has tried to provide, and he remains sceptical of). What is needed is a powerful theological re-engagement with the Augustinian questions of values, loves and power. These affective questions have been insufficiently addressed in a systematic theo-political manner in the official CST tradition. This weakness applies to the Church, ironically, and not only to the secular liberal political realm. Nonetheless if Cavanaugh's call for a renewed Catholic social vision that takes its Augustinian legacy seriously finds a deep echo anywhere in the official CST tradition, it is in the twin principles of solidarity and subsidiarity. Cavanaugh makes this connection himself, devoting a chapter of *Field Hospital* to Benedict XVI's treatment of the principle of subsidiarity.

Though a critic of the encyclical tradition's focus on rights, duties and the state, Cavanaugh sees in *Caritas in veritate* an echo of the longer tradition of a genuinely pluralist social vision, present also in aspects of the Christian distributist, anarchist and pluralist traditions. Focusing on Pope Benedict's vision of an associational society, and a model of dispersed political authority, Cavanaugh argues intriguingly that the CST tradition

---

[10] It should be noted that Cavanaugh's use of Augustine for contemporary political theology differs from Matthewes in important ways.

is formed of two different, possibly rival, traditions of thinking about subsidiarity. The difference between the two accounts pivots on their more or less embracing view of the modern state.[11] The first account tends to offer a more procedural interpretation of subsidiarity, presenting it as primarily a matter of practical discernment about the appropriate level at which an activity might take place: higher or lower. According to this first account, power is assumed to reside legitimately in institutions of all scales, but there is an acceptance that the nature of contemporary social challenges and the organizing power of the state mean that the coordinating role of the state will be key. Thus, it is assumed that power is often being redistributed from the centre, the state, to smaller organs or else upwards from the state to a regional or global level. The de facto focus is upon the core agency of centralized power sending power helpfully elsewhere.

This view is contrasted with a second tradition, which is much more suspicious of the role of the state as power broker and distributor. This second account is resistant to seeing the state in primarily juridical functional terms: it views the state as an ideological and not just an organizing project, and one capable of being captured by other interests. In concrete moral terms, the modern state shows decided tendencies towards concentrations rather than dispersals of power and political authority. The role of other non-state, non-market groups may well be, as Cavanaugh expresses it, to 'outwit' the state and market. In this way Cavanaugh supposes a potentially agonistic relation between the organs of society. Drawing on examples of the state refusing the rights of intermediate groups in favour of individual rights to choose, Cavanaugh notes that the contexts in which small-scale religious communities operate remains far from neutral and the state far from a mere organizing mechanism.[12]

---

[11] Cavanaugh draws on two different secondary accounts of subsidiarity in CST to make the point in relief: he offers J. Byran Hehir's 'Religious Ideas and Social Policy: Subsidiarity and Catholic Style of Ministry', in *Who Will Provide? The Changing Role of Religion in American Social Welfare*, ed. Mary Jo Bane, Brent Coffin and Ronald Thiemann (Boulder: Westview Press, 2000), as an example of a more statist tradition of thought about subsidiarity in CST; and by contrast he notes Robert K. Vischer's 'Subsidiarity as Subversion: Local Power, Legal Norms, and the Liberal State', *Journal of Catholic Social Thought* 2:2 (Summer, 2005), as an example of the second resistance to state tradition. See Cavanaugh, *Field Hospital*, pp. 129–33.

[12] Interestingly, this distinction that Cavanaugh draws does not map straightforwardly onto the dual tradition of fraternal and paternal social Catholicism that Chappel offers (noted in the previous chapter). In fact, arguably both readings of subsidiarity can be found in the fraternal tradition, at the very least.

Towards a Politics of Communion

It is fascinating that Cavanaugh should re-enliven discussion of subsidiarity in CST by developing the more obviously agonistic and Augustinian line of argument in *Caritas in veritate* and suggesting an unresolved tension at the heart of the century-long modern CST tradition. Equally, his analysis of the contemporary challenges to any idealistic construction of state–market–civil society relations is helpful. Nonetheless, a nuanced reading of the encyclical tradition suggests that if two traditions do exist, they have emerged more from a necessarily double-sided account provided by the papacy than any simple opposition between Thomist and Augustinian tendencies or sources. It is to defending this account of a double movement in papal teaching on subsidiarity that we now turn.

In what follows I will explore a vision of subsidiarity defined theologically along the following lines. The Catholic social and political tradition might be said to be founded on the idea of a fruitful paradox – what Simone Weil might call a *meaningful* contradiction. CST teaches, as we have noted in the previous chapter, that political life is crucial to our earthly well-being and vital for fostering the social conditions that enable us to become human beings fully alive; and yet politics is not our final destiny and therefore not in itself of ultimate importance. This fact doesn't diminish political life, arguably it *intensifies* its proper meaning. It is a matter of the utmost seriousness that politics serve the common good, and it cannot serve that good without our active participation. It serves the common good by enabling a life that precedes and exceeds itself; it is of the essence of good politics, therefore, that it does not suffocate or dominate all else. Given the fallenness of all things, it will not achieve this alone, and the desire for domination St Augustine names will be a constant danger. Nonetheless, this does not render it inherently a grubby business. Politics gains its (limited) meaning as a participation in the wider, deeper, transcendent divine governing, creating principle at work within the world, a power that acts to renew all things. Through grace the human community participates in this constant creating action through all spheres of life, including the political. This constant creating action involves acts of resistance to power gone awry that the fullness of the human social vocation be given breath and life. Given that God's creating power is a present-tense activity, not merely a past event, the human person is both free to associate and has a duty to participate in a dynamic reality, as a co-conspirator in the constant renewal of creation. This can only be done in relationship with others. In the civic and political realm, we express this through our desire and need to deliberate and discuss the ordering of our lives, to make decisions about and organize the distribution of goods, to forge new beginnings towards repair and justice as a matter of hope. In this way, our civic and political instincts do not stem from sin alone but from our skills, vocations, relationships of exchange, from within the gravitational goodness of the created order. Engaging in the forms of social governance that constitute subsidiarity in action is simultaneously, therefore, a natural expression of an inherently social and political nature as well as a response to sin and finitude. Subsidiarity as a principle speaks to both the immense creative and cooperative capacity we have, and given the free-willing tendency we have to fall away from these goods, to the necessary capacity for resistance to the constant reality of systems that lose their way and become dominating rather than enabling mechanisms. These realities are mixed up in the political reality.

In more concrete terms, and evident from within the texts of the encyclicals, the principle of subsidiarity focuses on people and their relationship to – and participation in – social, political and economic groups and associations. Such groups might include everything from trade unions, local government, faith organizations, craft associations, football clubs, political parties, grassroots movements for social change to professional bodies of nurses or business entrepreneurs, women's institutes, social enterprises and charitable bodies. These intermediary associations, groups and institutions are referred to as the vital organs of 'social governance'. These are the bodies which lie betwixt and between the level of the family – the first social community – and the state and market; and they are the contexts in which we learn key social virtues and achieve social growth. The encyclicals describe such groups as 'the original expression of social life' and the realm in which the 'creative subjectivity of the citizen' is expressed. These are the face to face, dispersed groupings through which society is enabled to reach its common good. This language reveals that these groups, the organs of subsidiarity and of the social body, are not seen in merely functional terms but as part of a wider social anthropology. Often missed in this context is that such smaller groups are not argued to be a final good in themselves but relate in their own task and practice to a wider good. These groups fulfil a shared good and responsibility that exceeds them. For this reason, closed groups that become breeding grounds for abuse of every kind are in no sense a legitimate expression of subsidiarity.

With this proviso in mind, on the basis that these groups occupy such a central place in achieving the common good of a society, all 'higher' level organizations ought to adopt an attitude of 'subsidium', service or assistance with respect to the development, protection and promotion of such groups.

This is in the interests of virtue and value not merely of efficiency. The service the 'enabling' state might render to such groups might be economic, legal and institutional where necessary. That is to say, in an ideal scenario the state is envisaged as an engaged player, an active enabler of subsidiarity. Enabling power to flow in a dispersed way through plural smaller scale bodies fosters social creativity and human dignity in the life of organizations and groups. This constructive or 'positive' understanding of the principle of subsidiarity is balanced in the encyclicals by a more 'negative' emphasis on subsidiarity as a principle concerned with the limits of state and market powers.

The first encyclical to formally deploy the term 'subsidiarity' as a social principle was Pius XI's *Quadragesimo anno* (1931). Marking the fortieth anniversary of *Rerum novarum*, Pius XI's letter reinforced the basic themes of Leo XIII's document and offered further clarification of teaching on living wages and labour–capital relations. Whilst the constituent elements of the new principle had been apparent in the previous century, and implicitly in the pages of *Rerum novarum*, they had yet to be focused into a clear official teaching principle. *Rerum novarum* had noted that the human person not the state was the foundation of the social order, the cause and end of the body politic; it had also offered a positive limited justification of state intervention in matters of regulating the relation of rich and poor within a market society and had noted some reservations about the tendency of modern industrializing society to squeeze out the rich intermediate world of social guilds and local societies. A healthy society, Leo had noted, needs a proliferation of associations. Nonetheless, these thoughts were not tied together through a clear guiding norm. *Quadragesimo anno* proposes subsidiarity as this guiding norm.

Pius wrote out of what he considered a crisis in mid-twentieth-century modernity: that the liberal state and market capitalism showed themselves to have a tendency to squeeze out the traditional role of professional bodies, craft and trade associations, guilds and cooperatives. The decline of such bodies had not, Pius argued, resulted in an improved politics or a more efficient and humane economy but an increasingly bloated, inefficient state, a market that dehumanized its workers and generated worrying forms of social fragmentation and apathy. This is where we see the trace of Cavanaugh's second 'tradition' of subsidiarity. Pius XI writes:

> When we speak of the reform of institutions, the State comes chiefly to mind, not as if universal well-being were to be expected from its activity, but because things have come to such a pass through the

evil of what we have termed 'individualism' that, following upon the overthrow and near extinction of that rich social life which was once highly developed through associations of various kinds, there remain virtually only individuals and the State. This is to the great harm of the State itself; for, with a structure of social governance lost, and with the taking over of all the burdens which the wrecked associations once bore the State has been overwhelmed and crushed by almost infinite tasks and duties.[13]

He continues, with the paragraph most often quoted as the definition of subsidiarity in CST:

Just as it is gravely wrong to take from individuals what they can accomplish by their own initiative and industry and give it to the community, so also it is an injustice and at the same time a grave evil and disturbance of right order to assign to a greater and higher association what lesser and subordinate organizations can do. For every social activity ought of its very nature to furnish help to the members of the body social, and never destroy and absorb them.[14]

Pius' introduction of the ideal concept of subsidiarity was therefore preceded by a critique of state and market. That critique comes first. Making room for a more appropriate concept of social participation and governance required the Church to metaphorically elbow the newly bloated state and market out of territory it had wrongly colonized. It is not offering this vision into a neutral space. Therefore, whilst the primary 'positive' focus of the principle is concerned with the constructive task of fostering the life of the good through intermediary groups, of necessity the Church's social teaching must concern itself with the nature of the state and its limits as part of this account. The principle of subsidiarity thus functions 'negatively' to remind us of the need to restrain and limit power – and this has particularly sharp pertinence with regard to the modern state. Nonetheless, part of that positive account has included ways to suggest that limited power – rightly used – including that of the state, can foster participation and social creativity. This includes, in Benedict XVI's teaching especially, calls for forms of global

---

[13] *Quadragesimo anno*, §78.
[14] Ibid., §79.

governance, which coordinate state action at a regional and global level. Therefore, these are not necessarily inherently rivalrous interpretations but rather two faces of the principle: one a sober reading of the signs of the times, the other a Catholic anthropology of social participation. Both have been variously emphasized and developed in wider papal teaching and practice. In summary, subsidiarity is traceable in the encyclicals as *both* a theory of social participation *and* a doctrine of limits or a check on tyranny, focused on the flourishing of forms of social governance necessary for the common good.

Thus far we have placed particular emphasis on the *political* implications of subsidiarity. However, the teaching on social participation and limited power has implications for economic life too. This is clearest in teaching on the nature of work, the role of private property and the role of free enterprise. The encyclicals state that labour is basic to the human condition, a duty and a right, and thus exists as a free activity prior to the state. For this reason, only when questions of fair wages or just prices or the use of property in relation to the common good cannot be handled efficiently and justly should the state to intervene.[15] Circumstances warranting intervention by the state might include the implication of new technologies for employment or the 'rapidification' of change and its impact on inequality as another (*Laudato si'*). In *Mater et magistra* John XXIII argues that developments in technology and science suggest the need for greater state intervention in order to protect labour from capital. The goal of state intervention in light of the common good is to reduce economic imbalances and resolve tensions within nations and between nations and regions at the international level.[16]

During his pontificate John Paul II was particularly keen to emphasize the threat to the principle of subsidiarity posed by state communism and all forms of governance that failed to recognize private initiative and enterprise. He was equally critical of individuals, businesses or governments that fail to recognize the public function of private economic initiative:

> It should be noted that in today's world, among other rights, the right of economic initiative is often suppressed. Yet it is a right which is important not only for the individual but also for the common good. Experience shows us that the denial of this right, or its limitation in

---

[15] *Mater et magistra*, §44.
[16] Ibid., §54.

the name of an alleged 'equality' of everyone in society, diminishes, or in practice absolutely destroys the spirit of initiative, that is to say the creative subjectivity of the citizen. As a consequence, there arises, not so much a true equality as a 'leveling down.' In the place of creative initiative there appears passivity, dependence and submission to the bureaucratic apparatus which, as the only 'ordering' and 'decision-making' body – if not also the 'owner' – of the entire totality of goods and the means of production, puts everyone in a position of almost absolute dependence, which is similar to the traditional dependence of the worker-proletarian in capitalism. This provokes a sense of frustration or desperation and predisposes people to opt out of national life, impelling many to emigrate and also favoring a form of 'psychological' emigration.[17]

Nonetheless, the core themes of subsidiarity with which we opened this chapter are all repeated in John Paul II's social teaching: the market and state are both 'suffocating' human initiative, creating political, economic and cultural passivity. Such suffocating action stems from a refusal to accept limits and to commodify and objectify the human person. Both market and state thus seek dominium rather than service of the person. In contrast families and intermediate communities provide the ways that society becomes 'personalized' and thus give life to specific networks of solidarity.

The 2006 *Compendium* repeats this teaching on the suppression of economic initiative, the failure to recognize the public function of such initiative and the practice of monopoly as 'undermining the principle of subsidiarity'.[18] Ultimately private enterprise is valued not as a simple end in itself but in view of its social function, capacity to contribute towards just and equitable relations, and as such should be aided in a subsidiary fashion.

A crucial by-product of this principle is that enabling smaller communities to assume political, economic and social responsibilities, according to their capacity, enables the state to focus on the areas in which it is most competent. *Quadragesimo anno* argues that modern states have an in-built tendency to assume unto themselves a plethora of tasks which would be better done by others and which threaten to overwhelm the state

---

[17]*Sollicitudo rei socialis*, §15.
[18]*Compendium*, §187.

and 'dissipate its efforts'.[19] As a result the state becomes less competent in its exercise of power with regard to the things that truly it alone can accomplish. Thus, worryingly, the overwhelmed and ineffective state is more likely to become servant rather than master of economic forces. In failing to respect subsidiarity the modern state de-energizes political culture, reduces the spaces in which ordinary citizens learn to practice civic virtues and dispirits the populace, who lose confidence in the abilities of political leaders to lead. Trust in 'government' goes down, yet faith in the nation remains.

Whilst we can identify at each stage of this discussion the two sides of thought that Cavanaugh highlights, there remains some variation between papal authors in addressing the question of legitimate spheres of state action that goes beyond a mere dynamism in the face of changing circumstances. The pre-Vatican II papacies tended to focus a little more on the limited and primarily restraining role of the state. Popes John XIII and Paul VI adopt a more expansive emphasis on the facilitating role of the state with regard to welfare, expanding what could be seen as legitimate spheres of state action as an integral part of an understanding of subsidiarity. John XXIII explicitly introduces a new emphasis on the legitimate role of national and international structures of governance in facilitating the common good. However, reading the signs of the times in his own context John Paul II shifts this discourse again: whilst not repudiating the words of his predecessors he returns to a critique of the expansive involvement of the modern state in daily life and a concern to uphold a doctrine of limits. Arguably, John Paul II renews the theme of subsidiarity as resistance: resistance to bureaucratic and economic forms of tyranny.

John Paul II's reflections are caught up with two important tendencies in his writing – a theological turn in his reading of the social tradition and his contextual reflections on the experiences of communism in Eastern Europe. Both economic and bureaucratic changes have brought new kinds of privations or lack – forms of political poverty – into the life of nations. Thus, he seeks to remind his readers of the role of the state in exercising a form subsidium: the state has a duty to create conditions that will ensure job opportunities, and the state ought to intervene when monopolies create obstacles to development. The state may also intervene when social sectors or business systems are too weak or are just getting under way: '[s]uch supplementary interventions, which are justified by urgent reasons touching the common good, must be as brief as possible, so as to avoid removing

---

[19] *Quadragesimo anno*, §80.

permanently from society and business systems the functions which are properly theirs, and so as to avoid enlarging excessively the sphere of State intervention to the detriment of both economic and civil freedom.'[20]

However, John Paul's social teaching on subsidiarity was also marked by a particularly sharp critique of the growth of welfare states. In his third social encyclical *Centisimus annus* he suggests that there is some tension between the principles of subsidiarity and solidarity and what he calls the 'Social Assistance State':

> By intervening directly and depriving society of its responsibility, the Social Assistance State leads to a loss of human energies and an inordinate increase of public agencies, which are dominated more by bureaucratic ways of thinking than by concern for serving their clients, and which are accompanied by an enormous increase in spending. In fact, it would appear that needs are best understood and satisfied by people who are closest to them and who act as neighbours to those in need.[21]

This critique is not simply based on the idea that needs are best understood at a lower level, but that certain kinds of welfare needs lie beyond the level of material provision. The pope writes, 'One thinks of the condition of refugees, immigrants, the elderly, the sick, and all those in circumstances which call for assistance, such as drug abusers: all these people can be helped effectively only by those who offer them genuine fraternal support, in addition to the necessary care.'[22] There are kinds of relational solidarity, accompaniment and modes of being with others which the state can help facilitate but cannot really deliver. These are the face to face, relational forms of welfare that rely on subsidiary organizations and entities.

Benedict XVI repeats this concern that subsidiarity be seen as a principle rooted in reciprocal forms of human giving rather than in a merely contractual and redistributist logic of justice:

> Subsidiarity is first and foremost a form of assistance to the human person via the autonomy of intermediate bodies. Such assistance

---

[20] *Centisimus annus*, §48.
[21] Ibid.
[22] Ibid.

is offered when individuals or groups are unable to accomplish something on their own, and it is always designed to achieve their emancipation, because it fosters freedom and participation through assumption of responsibility. Subsidiarity respects personal dignity by recognizing in the person a subject who is always capable of giving something to others. By considering reciprocity as the heart of what it is to be a human being, subsidiarity is the most effective antidote against any form of all-encompassing welfare state.[23]

Intense change in social relations driven by and producing globalization has proved a catalyst for a gradually emerging papal focus on the question of international organizations and the principle of subsidiarity. It is unclear in Cavanaugh's analysis whether he views the focus in CST on subsidiarity and global governance as a feature of a more pro-statist logic or whether this could also be part of a resistance associationalism, especially given it is a central feature of *Caritas in veritate*'s political theology. In theory, one could imagine it being read either way. In any case, a decisive move to embrace the possibilities of international-level organizations emerges as a key theme from *Pacem in terris* and *Mater et magistra* onwards. *Pacem in terris* made the first thoroughgoing application of the principle of subsidiarity to international-level organizations and relations, and generates a theme developed by each of John XIII's successors: recognition of the increasing weakness of nation states in dealing with processes of globalization and a consequent appeal for international public bodies to be established to deal with the pressing transnational political, economic and ecological problems of the age. Paul VI and John Paul II focused on the need for subsidiary governance at an international level to foster a constructive international development agenda; Benedict XVI and Francis have developed the same idea variously in relation to global financial systems, the environment and climate change, and the management of migrant and refugee flows.

Francis' teaching on subsidiarity has been marked by two features: first, an emphasis on the concerning diminishment of politics in the face of economic power and the need to assert new forms of political governance in economic affairs, guided by a focus on reducing inequalities, environmental destruction and promoting the common good; second, a greater integration of ecclesial and social reflection on subsidiarity. Francis

---

[23]*Caritas in veritate*, §57.

has been as concerned to initiate the process of ecclesial subsidiarity as political-social. On the first theme, Francis connects the failure of politics in the realm of the economic with a profound failure in relation to the poor, the environment and non-human creaturely relations:

> The mindset which leaves no room for sincere concern for the environment is the same mindset which lacks concern for the inclusion of the most vulnerable members of society. For the current model, with its emphasis on success and self-reliance, does not appear to favour an investment in efforts to help the slow, the weak or the less talented to find opportunities in life.[24]

On the second theme, it is also notable that *Evangelii gaudium* and *Laudato si'* make much greater use of the insights of regional bishops' conferences, and Francis consistently places a greater emphasis on local and regional rather than central Vatican initiative in the area of social teaching. He has renewed the emphasis on subsidiarity as a principle for the governance of the Church and on synodality. Francis has also repeatedly emphasized the 'messiness' of subsidiary processes and the necessity of understanding the role of conflict.

Perhaps Francis' most interesting and thought-provoking intervention on subsidiarity occurs in his General Audience Covid-19 catechesis. On 23 September 2020 he devoted an address to the theme of subsidiarity as a principle of hope. He deals directly with the frequent misunderstanding that subsidiarity implies a simple localism or is a principally technocratic matter of levelling decisions. Francis describes subsidiarity as a principle with a double movement, from 'top to bottom and bottom to top'. It is the maximization of participation and the fostering of responsibility at every level for the common good that marks a good process of subsidiarity. In this sense it is a principle of participation and unity, Francis notes. He challenges his audience to ask: Who is listened to? Who is seen as an expert on poverty, migration, climate change and so forth? Any action that sees itself as promoting subsidiarity must be simultaneously an option for the poor – both privileging a listening process to the most marginalized communities and enabling the initiative and contribution of all. In this sense, Francis argues there is no solidarity without subsidiarity. Where

---

[24]*Laudato si'*, §196.

Towards a Politics of Communion

there is a deficit of contribution, with respect to autonomy and capacity, there remains a negative subsidiarity measure. The opportunity for the local and global to be in communication and for everyone to 'have the possibility of assuming their own responsibility in the healing process of the society in which they are a part' is part of how hope is reborn. The virtue that most clearly correlates with subsidiarity is, therefore, hope.

Conclusion

Papal teaching on subsidiarity has been taken up, and transformed in understanding, by a variety of Catholic and civic social, political and economic movements. Some of these movements have themselves been subject to critique, but many have also been held up as inspiring forms of politics and have drawn attention back to the tradition that animated them. Nonetheless, significant internal debate about the consistency and meaning of the principle is ongoing. William Cavanaugh's questioning of the papal tradition is not a lone intervention. In his work on the twin concepts of solidarity and subsidiarity, Johan Verstraeten has questioned the extent to which the 'positive' and 'negative' elements of subsidiarity are fully integrated in papal teaching. Other commentators have suggested that the issue is less one of a lack of clarity in papal teaching about the meaning of the terms, than it is an issue of idealization of associational life. A mere plurality or multiplicity of groups, even with dispersed authority, still relies on the hope that the internal life of groups is generally sufficient to achieve good outcomes. What keeps these groups healthy? How is the relation between associational groups to be mediated as a matter of the common good? These questions develop a greater urgency in a moment like our own when the rise of a plurality of identity and interest groups with what appear to be opposing agendas and increasingly entrenched lines of opposition produces, or makes more visible, significant fissures in public life. The agonism rather than the harmony implied in subsidiarity is a very present reality.

Equally, the Church's own internal crises prompt as many questions about the development of its teaching on subsidiarity as a principle of participation and social governance as its external social realities do. The Church's sexual abuse crisis makes this challenge and failure most apparent. For others, the failure to integrate women fully into decision-making and governance roles in the Church also raises questions about the maturity of this teaching as a principle of participation. A level of structural violence has been present in church, social and associational contexts, and this history has yet to be robustly reflected on theologically or politically. This includes the legacy of the very groups held up as examples of Christian subsidiarity in action. Each of the groups we have examined in the early stages of this chapter has faced challenges connected with the abuse of power: distributist movements, Catholic Worker communities and most recently L'Arche communities have proved contexts in which abuse was still able to occur without sufficient challenge – and crucially where theological ideas themselves were part of the structure of what proved to be abusive.[25] This has also been a reality for more conservative ecclesial small groups and communities, including notably the Legionaries of Christ and Opus Dei.[26] It is also the case that the tendency to view groups and associations as entitled to their own ethics, and as prior communities to the state, was a philosophy (and theology) that has been exposed as deeply problematic in cases such as religious involvement in the child migrant schemes, which saw Catholic orders and other Christian groups involved in practices that led to the physical, mental and sexual abuse of children. Questions remain about the operation of Church bodies with investigations into this abuse and the very establishment of the schemes themselves.[27] Oswald von Nell Bruening, as a key architect of papal social teaching, claimed that CST should be 'a permanent process of learning'. If it is to be so, then we have barely begun attending to this process with regard to the principle of subsidiarity. None of this is to suggest that subsidiarity is rendered anachronistic by such challenges and changes. Rather that the relation of the twin principles of solidarity and subsidiarity needs to be thought with some acute attention to how the idea has to be used in practice. How did it come to be deployed as part of a theological justification for racial inequalities, fascism and nationalism as much as for radical hospitality and resistance to a military-industrial complex?

---

[25]https://www.larche.org.uk/news/inquiry-statement
[26]https://www.americamagazine.org/faith/2019/12/23/legionaries-christ-report-chain-abuse-victims-went-abuse-others (last accessed 6 February 2021); https://thetablet.org/case-of-opus-dei-priest-raises-fresh-questions-about-clerical-abuse-crisis/ (accessed 6 February 2021).
[27]See Gordon Lynch, 'Catholic Child Migration Schemes from the United Kingdom to Australia: Systemic Failures and Religious Legitimation', *Journal of Religious History* 44:3 (2020), pp. 273–94. Stephen Constantine, Majory Harper, and Gordon Lynch, *Child Abuse and Scottish Children Sent Overseas Through Child Migration Schemes: Report for the Scottish Child Abuse Inquiry* (Edinburgh: Scottish Child Abuse Inquiry, 2021).

CHAPTER 10
SOLIDARITY
A DEVELOPING THEORY

'Teacher, which commandment in the law is the greatest?' He said to him, '"You shall love the Lord your God with all your heart, with all your soul, and with all your mind." This is the greatest and first commandment. And the second is like it: "You shall love your neighbour as yourself." On these two commandments hang all the law and the prophets.' (Matthew 22: 37–40)

[T]here does not exist an orthopraxis which is simply just, detached from a knowledge of what is good.[1]

CST and solidarity: Something old, something borrowed, something new?

On 9 March 2021 *The Guardian* newspaper carried a photograph of a forty-five-year-old Burmese religious sister Sr Ann Rose Nu Tawng kneeling in front of a line of armed police, arms held out cruciform by her side. Taking part in organized peaceful protests in Myanmar against a military coup, *The Guardian* reported that Sr Ann had walked slowly towards the riot police and fallen to her knees to plead that they cease shooting into the crowd, which contained groups of children as well as adults. This was the second time she had pleaded with riot police to stop shooting, having made the same gesture ten days previously. She told the interviewing journalist, 'I have thought myself dead already since 28 February. . . . I can't stand and watch without doing anything.' To talk about solidarity movements of the past century is to encounter a case study in the porous boundaries between the religious and the political. From the role of nineteenth-century Nonconformists in leading the call for full voting franchise, the significance of Methodism and Catholicism in the formation of the British

---

[1]Benedict XVI, https://www.vatican.va/roman_curia/congregations/cfaith/documents/rc_con_cfaith_doc_20020602_ratzinger-eucharistic-congress_en.html (accessed 6 February 2021).

Towards a Politics of Communion

Labour movement, the role of Catholics in the Polish Solidarity movement, the significance of the Black churches in twentieth-century civil rights and twenty-first century Black Lives Matter movements to a religious sister kneeling before police in Myanmar, religion has proved a vital component of solidarity movements.

However, the picture is more complicated and interesting than mounting a set of claims that religion has been vital to the freedom and rights movements of the last two centuries. The very language of solidarity, used to inspire such movements, is itself a migration and secularization of a previously Christian set of ideas. Solidarity enters the modern lexicon on the slipstream of the revolutions of the eighteenth and nineteenth centuries, expressing what had been thought of over centuries in Christian usage as fraternity and friendship. This new idiom of solidarity took these older ideas and wove them through with an emerging Enlightenment language – itself the offspring of Reformation world views – of freedom and equality. In so doing what emerged into popular usage was an importantly new formulation of earlier ideas, now integrated with a modern individualism and emerging rights-based formulation of freedom and equality. Liberty, equality, fraternity (solidarity).

Over the last two centuries solidarity, now largely (but not entirely) secularized, has become deeply associated in our popular imagination with movements for civil, racial and gender rights, and more recently ecological politics. The story of the arrival of the language of solidarity into twentieth-century CST complexifies this migration and integration of ideas a step further. It was from its new, modern secular formation that it was re-received and returned to its theological origins, in a renewed form. Solidarity first appeared in CST briefly in Pius XII's 1939 encyclical and more extensively in John XXIII's *Mater et magistra*; it emerged as an organizing virtue for the governing of states in *Pacem in terris* and as a Christological social emphasis in the Second Vatican Council's *Gaudium et spes*.[2] In the late mid-century documents, solidarity is both a way of thinking about the responsibility of states in a more interdependent world and the normative motif of salvation history. Christ's birth, death and resurrection, is the ultimate model of solidarity for the Christian.

If the principle and virtue of solidarity is identified with a single papacy, it is surely that of John Paul II; and its accompanying image was the blood-red

---

[2] For an excellent overview of the use of solidarity in CST, see Clark, *The Vision of Catholic Social Thought*, especially pp. 18–33, 110–24.

lettering – Solidarność – painted on a white canvas banner, adorning a public stage or carried through the streets by processions of Polish workers. John Paul II chose to foreground this language in parallel with the development of the iconic Polish Solidarity movement and in the wake of the civil rights and anti-colonial struggles of the previous thirty years. Yet, as Meghan Clark argues, solidarity in its papal social guise is not merely a borrowing of language, nor simply a convenient descriptor for a globalizing age. In the teaching of John Paul II, building on the documents of the 1960s, it is clear that solidarity develops as a 'theoretical way to understand many different aspects of the human person and the human reality'.[3]

That the idea of solidarity is used in dialogue with, but not merely on the back of, the social movements of the twentieth century is of further significance given American novelist Marilynne Robinson's argument, made forty years after John Paul II's writings, that many of the movements of the last hundred years so clearly inspired by the idea of solidarity can be seen now either to have achieved their core goals or to have lost their edge and faded over time.[4] Even Pope Francis writes of the idea in *Evangelii gaudium* as potentially a little worn round the edges and poorly understood in its fuller implications.[5] Robinson notes that the risk for even the most radical solidarity movements is that they fade from impressive flowering into trivialities. Yet, for neither Robinson nor Pope Francis ought this to lead to cynicism and despair, as one awakening of solidarity fades another is often born or sometimes reborn. We live in the midst of a moment when both insights – the fading and rebirth of solidarity movements – seem especially true.

One of the paradoxes of the political history of solidarity movements is that despite the role played by religious ideas and faith communities in the solidarity movements of the twentieth century, the very foundation of solidarity as a modern political concept happened not only as an easy secularization of religious language but at times in conscious contradistinction to Christianity. The early socialism of the nineteenth century presented its doctrine of solidarity as the effective theoretical and practical antidote to an ineffectual and class-complicit ethic of Christian charitable love. Where Christian love was perceived to have failed to

---

[3]Ibid., p. 20.
[4]Marilynne Robinson, 'Christianity: Ethos not Identity', Theos lecture, 2013.
[5]*Evangelii gaudium*, §188.

address, even driven and legitimated, inequality in wealth, ownership and education, a socialist ethic would foster a rational solidarity that could build new structures. In this sense, the notion of solidarity was always a structural and communitarian notion – by its very definition it reached towards the idea of a community of action beyond individual acts of assistance.

In an address given before he became pope, Joseph Ratzinger draws on this history, singling out the figure of Pierre Leroux, an early socialist, and noting his hostility to a Christian foundation for social change, in favour of a radical solidaristic socialism.[6] Refusing an account of transcendence as the true foundation or heart of solidarity was, Ratzinger notes, Leroux's mistake. The contemporary Catholic must situate the Eucharist as the heart of any lasting and true movement of solidarity. Yet Ratzinger does not note, as he might have done, the interesting humanitarian mystical leanings and interests of Leroux. Leroux's work argues not only for a structural response to poverty and workers' conditions but for a humanitarian mysticism and, with echoes of Ratzinger's own language, speaks of the moral 'communion' of all peoples. His continued appeal to such ideas caused much criticism from fellow socialists. Theological roots do not, it seems, die so easily, even if they do migrate into new ideas of core communities of practice. A continued immanent-mystical humanitarianism has arguably been the hinterland for much of the secular solidaristic thought of the last two hundred years, and if carefully engaged provides a basis for mutual dialogue. Perhaps somewhat in this vein, Ratzinger does go on to note in his 2002 address that the handling of the concept of solidarity in the Catholic social tradition is best viewed as an adoptionist one, a creative work of theological re-reception.

We can say, therefore, that the theologized social principle of solidarity represents the weaving together in the Catholic tradition of something as ancient as the Church itself, something inherently its own; and something borrowed. In so doing, CST produces something new – beyond its own roots alone, but also beyond a simple borrowing from the coda of the

---

[6]Joseph Ratzinger, 'Eucharist, Communion and Solidarity', Address given to the Bishops' Conference of the Region of Campania in Benevento, Italy, https://www.vatican.va/roman _curia/congregations/cfaith/documents/rc_con_cfaith_doc_20020602_ratzinger-eucharistic-congress_en.html (last accessed 1 April 2021). It is a further irony, in this light, that Charles Curran comments on the replacement of the language of love with solidarity language by John XXIII in *Pacem in terris*. See Charles Curran, *Catholic Social Teaching 1891-Present: A Historical, Theological and Ethical Analysis* (Washington D.C.: Georgetown University Press, 2002), p. 74.

modern Left. It exists in a relationship of critical affinity with a range of contemporary movements.

First, something old: Catholic teaching on solidarity explains that it is rooted in the insights of the Catholic biblical, doctrinal and philosophical views of human and divine nature, the nature of society and of political virtue. The authors of *Gaudium et spes*, John Paul II and Benedict XVI all make clear that any Catholic appeal to the idea of solidarity is rooted in the person of Jesus Christ. It is the fact of a prior transformative personal relationship that transforms all other personal relationships. Ratzinger makes an explicitly and exclusively Eucharistic argument for solidarity's foundations in his June 2002 address.[7] He argues, based on two scriptural texts – one Pauline, one Johannine – that a vertical communion with Christ in the Eucharist becomes simultaneously a horizontal communion with all others. The Eucharist is the communication of Christ himself to us, such that the communication of goods and of love and justice between humanity might flow. This communication is tangible and embodied but also to be pursued by the Christian as a good to be achieved in structural-relational terms between nations, regions and peoples. Ratzinger notes that the nature of the Church is not merely deliberative – the Church must deliberate – but primarily it communicates through an intimate companionship of worship and divine reception, which flows outwards as transformation into the world. An action which is Christ's action of gift, self-giving in the flow of body and blood, enacts a transformation in the receiving Christian, which opens the heart to a wider radical action of receptivity to the neighbour. We do not transform our neighbour – the act of Christ is the truly active principle. Our own action is one of ever wider receptivity to the reality of the world, but this receptivity becomes reciprocally transformative on the horizontal plane. This register is deployed but shifted again in the direction of a theology of creation, as we shall see, by the interfaith focus of Pope Francis.[8]

As Ratzinger indicates, however, solidarity is undeniably an idea also borrowed. As we have noted, talk of 'solidarity' as a duty and a virtue enters gradually into the canon of Catholic social teaching (CST), emerging in

---

[7]Ratzinger, 'Eucharist, Communion and Solidarity'.
[8]Meghan Clark argues for a deep connection between a theology of creation and the principle of subsidiarity from John XXIII onwards. See Clark, *The Vision of Catholic Social Thought*, pp. 20–21. We might argue that it is this connection, already woven into the documents of the 1960s, that Francis picks up and re-threads.

its Catholic form in close interaction with new forms of nineteenth- and twentieth-century social theory and social movements. Such social theory used the language of solidarity to denote the common interests that united a group of people, from workers forming trade unions to a nation seeking to find and express a common life. It would be a mistake, however, to view Catholicism or theological notions as simply external to these secular movements. Rather the migration of ideas between church and social movements, whose membership often overlapped, indicates a fluidity in the exchange of ideas and practices that we often fail to grasp. This is true even when that migration happens *in reaction to*, rather than simply as an adoption of, theological ideas. The relationship remains in some meaningful sense dialogical. It would also be a mistake to view the Church's adoption of solidarity language as an inappropriate or weak 'secularizing' of the Church: the first appearance of the word 'solidarity' in the canon of CST, via the pen of Pius XII on the eve of war in 1939, is as a descriptor of the sociality of the Church itself. It is language that enriches the Church's ability to talk about its own social life.

This mutual critical dialogue between theological anthropology and social theory that began to crystalize in the social teaching documents of the 1930s, bearing fruits in the 1940s and 1960s, was exemplified in the work of German Jesuit economist Fr Heinrich Pesch (1854–1926) and German Jesuit theologian-sociologist Fr Oswald von Nell Breuning (1890–1990). Their work provided a vital context for the development of insights crucial to the emergence of a Catholic theory of solidarity. They drew their use of the phrase 'solidarity' from a reading of the Scriptures, natural law theory and nineteenth- and twentieth-century French and German language of *fraternité* and *solidarnus*, rooted as much in the readings of Roman law as in the sociology of Auguste Comte and Emile Durkheim. At stake in this dialogue are competing accounts of the essence and purpose of human social life. Heinrich Pesch was driven by a belief that the emerging twentieth-century theories of individualism and socialism, gaining in power and influence, represented false and impractical abstractions from the ways in which human beings sought to operate in concrete contexts. What had been in one sense sound insights about the co-belonging and mutual responsibility of human beings risked being theorized into a form of odd abstraction. There was something anthropologically misguided about these movements, Marxism and corporatist and nationalist fascism especially, and theology had both the responsibility and capacity to address this problem. Pesch argued that our true nature, expressed in observable deep human practices of social cooperation, is betrayed by narrow appeals to competitive individualism or overarching collectivism. To correct this profound empirical and theoretical error he laboured to produce an economic theory of solidarity that took into account a cooperative understanding of human nature and the common good that could be drawn on by social movements as well as the Church. Pesch's *Lehrbuch der Nationalökonomie* was widely credited as a significant influence upon Pope Pius XI's social encyclical *Quadragesimo anno*.

If the principle of human dignity is impelled in its development by the horrors of war, then also the principle of solidarity can be said to be given impetus by the mid and late twentieth-century experiences of war, revolution and resistance – from Western Europe to North and Latin America and Central and Eastern Europe. Whilst the pre-war years provide a fertile context for dialogue between social movements adopting solidarity as a central social principle, it is with the papacy of John Paul II that the idea comes into its own. In John Paul II's writings, Bruening and Pesch's earlier commitment to dialogue with 'secular' political and intellectual movements and the council's desire for a more overtly theological direction to the Church's social teaching become more clearly integrated. Influenced by his engagement with the Solidarność movement in Poland and his struggle to engage in a constructive response to the theories of solidarity emerging amongst liberation theologians in Latin America, John Paul II offers to CST a version of solidarity as a form of virtue theory that sits within its own evolving theory of society.

Developing reflection on solidarity in the encyclicals: 1891 onwards

Rerum novarum did not explicitly use the term 'solidarity'. However, the ideas later expressed as a theory of solidarity can be meaningfully correlated with Leo XIII's discussion of friendship, charity and justice, and his critique of liberalism and communism. They are also nascent in his articulation of the role of new social groups and the state. *Rerum novarum* might be said to offer four foundational elements integral to the later Catholic solidarity argument: first, the transcendent and covenantal basis to human solidarity and the consequent role for religion in motivating and sustaining solidarity; second, the threat to solidarity posed by all forms of social inequality and division and therefore the need to understand and respond to social division with ever new practices of social cooperation and mediation; third, the role of the state as a necessary, positive but profoundly limited organizing expression of solidarity; and fourth, a repeatedly stated belief that sustainable social results happen where causes learn how to overcome their estrangement and cooperate through the formation of civic friendship. This fourfold vision integrates theological norms with empirical practices, but for theological reasons it resists the idea that being practical means being narrowly prescriptive.

One of the defining features of the way that solidarity is understood in the first fifty years of the social encyclical tradition (1891–1961) is its heavy focus on the context of industrial work and the changing European social order. The key agents of solidarity are (male) workers and owners, struggling to live virtuous lives in a context where social division appears to be intensifying. In this context, *Rerum novarum* argues that religion itself is the most fundamentally solidaristic mechanism for drawing together rich and poor. The Church provides a context where human interests are identical, not opposed; where a common dignity is shared as gift; where a common Spirit is available to guide and heal; and where duties towards each other are rooted in a common duty to justice and charity. Social unity begins with a discussion of common origins, a common nature and a common destiny: of covenant and only then social contract.

Pope Leo contrasts this with the factors that mitigate against this same drawing together of interests in wider society: wage depression, usury, practices of monopoly, narrowed concepts of social contract rooted in a focus on economic life. However, *Rerum novarum* is clear that all human means must conspire to alleviate poverty and facilitate human capability and well-being, 'results don't happen save where all the causes cooperate'.[9] In a section on the explicit part that the state should play in fostering cooperation, *Rerum novarum* outlines the following duties. The first duty of the state is to make sure that the laws and institutions, 'the general character and administration of the commonwealth, shall be such as to produce of themselves public wellbeing and private prosperity. This is the proper office of wise statesmanship and the work of the heads of state'.[10] The state is understood to prosper by morality, flourishing family life, respect for religion and justice, moderation, equal distribution of public burdens, progress in arts and trade and abundant yield of the land. Solidarity enacted

---

[9]*Rerum novarum*, §31.
[10]Ibid., §32.

by institutions continues the focus on character, not simply on pragmatic and technical function: the *character* of public administration matters if it is to be an agent for the good.

Leo XIII also asserts that a commitment to solidarity requires critical attention to the role of markets. In this context, it is the threat to universal friendship, justice and charity posed by the development of nineteenth-century free market capitalism that meets with most sustained comment in *Rerum novarum*. More concretely, Leo XIII expresses concern about the isolation and relative powerlessness of workingmen in the face of unrestrained market competition, new forms of usury, practices of monopoly and the use of contracts to regulate labour practices. Leo sees this multifaceted power imbalance as 'a yoke little better than slavery itself'.[11] *Rerum novarum* warns against the 'false' social remedies to these problems represented first by the communist desire to eradicate private property and grow a collectivist and centralized state, and second, the (economically) liberal desire for a market largely free from intervention. He is also strongly critical of workers or owners who ferment social or economic division. He praises by contrast those who foster mediation, relationship and new forms of social cooperation.

Leo XIII suggests that in addition to just economic practice, necessary acts of personal charity and the work of guilds and associations, there must be a cautious use of the state as a form of structural solidarity to aid the family or household in need. The state should not penetrate and pervade the family, but if the family finds itself in great difficulty and 'utterly friendless' it is right that extreme necessity be met by public aid, 'for each family is part of a commonwealth'.[12] Strong words are used to warn against absorbing the individual or family into the state, or increasing the fundamental dependence of the person upon the state. The role of the state is rather to anxiously safeguard the potential for lives of virtue within the community. However, much of the logic of non-interference in family life is framed in strongly paternal(ist) language: the family is 'a continuation of the father's personality', and children are property of the father.[13] Later encyclicals frame an understanding of the family in more theological language and less overtly paternalistic terms, although a debate about the representation and agency of women in CST continues to the present.

---

[11] Ibid., §3.
[12] Ibid., §14.
[13] Ibid., §14.

Rerum novarum also offers a moral basis for structural solidarity with the poorest. The solidaristic function of the state requires those who govern to benefit every order of the state, to promote to the highest degree within its citizens the interests of the poorest and consult widely amongst the commonwealth on the terms of the common good. The more the needs and interests of the working population are served by the general laws of the land, the less there will be need for particular means of poor relief. The state should be conscious that its poorer citizens are its majority, the wealthy its minority. To violate this balance of interest is an offence against distributive justice: that each person should receive his or her due, guided by the principle of the universal destination of goods. The state's chief practical duty is to act with strict distributive justice, in relation to persons and classes. Whilst all citizens are duty bound to participate according to gifts and capacities for the sake of the common good, the state must recognize that not all can contribute in the same way or to the same extent. Any contributory principle needs to be understood in a pluralistic, proportionate and capacity-oriented manner. Engaging the contributory principle in the light of this teaching on solidarity implies, first, maximizing conditions for capability and participation, and, second, a personal duty to find ways to contribute to the common good appropriate to each person and institution. Here we see clearly that the common good that the state needs to safeguard and maximize the conditions for is much less about seeking a formal consensus of ideas, a common mind, and much more about the expression of a plurality of forms of life seeking to be, to create and to participate in the life of the common good, in the light of the search for truth.

There are, however, things the state simply *cannot* do with regard to solidarity. These limitations relate primarily to the formation of personal, reciprocal and transformative just and charitable friendships, which are necessary forms of social relationships for individuals to be able to recognize the life of the common good. These forms of life are reserved for person-to-person relationships that can be fostered between individual persons and within smaller scale associations. First, *Rerum novarum* emphasizes the role of new associations, trade unions and guilds, saving particular praise for those who have arranged for new ways to organize seemingly opposed interests into new partnerships – Leo names in particular associations of working men, workers and employers together into groups, founding insurance societies and new forms of philanthropy.[14] He praises solidarity

---

[14]*Rerum novarum*, §41.

expressed through creative associationalism in its many forms. He is at pains to communicate the message that unionization is a good because it is a form of human organizing that seeks to unify workers in pursuit of a positive just goal and to counter the Marxist narrative of class enemies and conflict. Second, Leo XIII repeatedly reinforces a message present in every subsequent social encyclical: personal charity (caritas) will always be a social necessity and a vital form of friendship. It is a religious duty with transcendent dimensions that connect us to our divine origins and a permanent social necessity. The interpenetration of justice and charity as the basis and expression of solidarity is a key theme here.

We have spent some time on this encyclical because its major 'solidaristic' themes – covenant and cooperation, mediation and civic friendship across seemingly estranged groups, associationalism and a limited assistance state, just distribution of goods and the necessary interrelation of justice and charity – set the foundations for subsequent letters which interpret, develop and improvise on these themes.

Forty years later, and set against the context of rising fascism and nationalism, *Quadrogesimo anno* develops a more explicit Christian theory of solidarity. Pope Pius XI reinforces the idea that society should be understood as ontological oriented towards cooperation and builds on the language of friendship and shared interest. A new urgency is evident in Pius XI's talk about the universal basis for human friendship and cooperation. Contra fascism, Pius stressed *universal* human kinship set against attempts to place priority on solidarity *within* ethnic, national groups and consequent claims to racial superiority. Yet a focus on solidarity amongst workers and between industrial labour and capital continues to be a particular hallmark: owners, managers and workers bear mutually cooperative responsibilities. Solidarity continues to emerge as concrete and universal, personal and structural. Pius repeats and develops reflection on the torn halves of charity and justice: charity is more than justice, requires us to go beyond giving each their due into personal relationships of care, accompaniment, repentance, forgiveness and trust. However, charity alone does not express the fullness of care required in the social order and justice itself is a form of caritas:

> Charity cannot take the place of justice unfairly withheld, but, even though a state of things be pictured in which every man receives at last all that is his due, a wide field will nevertheless remain open for charity. For, justice alone, even though most faithfully observed, can remove indeed the cause of social strife, but can never bring about a

union of hearts and minds. Yet this union, binding all men together, is the main principle of stability in all institutions, no matter how perfect they may seem, which aim at establishing social peace and promoting mutual aid. In its absence, as repeated experience proves, the wisest regulations come to nothing.[15]

Pius XI reinforces Leo's teaching on the solidaristic responsibility of the state for the common welfare – in particular the duty to foster harmony between classes and groups. This requires functional intermediary groups and forms of organized citizens and workers. The health of the state depends not simply on what the state does but on its relationship to a wide range of in-between groups. Therefore, the state (in its own interest) should foster the conditions necessary for such groups to flourish. *Quadragesimo anno* reminds its readers that private personal or business conduct should also be oriented towards solidarity and the common good. Pius praises the use of jurisprudence to develop new ways of thinking about the provision of protection against poverty and suffering, health and housing; praises the foundation of new unions and criticizes those following solely laissez-faire economic approaches. The concept of the living wage is developed in greater detail as a necessary condition for cooperation and social harmony.

The first formal uses of the term 'solidarity' in magisterial texts occur on the eve of the Second World War and in its aftermath. In Pius XII's 1939 encyclical *Summi pontificatus* ('On the Unity of Human Society') and his 1950 Christmas message, solidarity emerges as an expression of natural and divine law: a 'law' that relates to our common human origins and destiny, our equality in light of both the pervasive reality of sin and the promise of salvation. Nonetheless, the first use of this language is applied to the experience of the Church in a time of crisis and as a response of suffering, rather than as a social ethic, as it is often later perceived. Insofar as it emerges as a social principle it is presented as a necessary precondition for wider social collaboration and as a practice that supports the basic units of the associational order; solidarity is also presented as a practice necessary for peacebuilding at both the interpersonal and international level.

It is with the publication of John XXIII's first social encyclical in 1961 that the Catholic theory of solidarity begins to be given a more expansive theological base and to be articulated as a more systematic

---

[15]*Quadragesimo anno*, §137.

guide for social and political action. John XXIII moves away from solidarity conceived primarily as reflection on the relationship between labour and capital, industrialist and worker. He shifts CST towards greater engagement with the realities of being a global church in the context of radically unequal relations between global north and south. Thus, *Mater et magistra* focuses on the challenges and need for solidarity *between*, as well as *within*, nation states. John sees this as necessary given the fact that social processes of industrialization and globalization are increasing the de facto interdependence between states, and that a Catholic vision of the international order has long been oriented towards cooperation.

However, shifting practices of post-war solidarity in Europe are also important. John XXIII sees the development of post-war welfare states as a key 'sign of the times'. *Mater et magistra* praises social insurance and social security as forms of distributive justice, addressing inequity between groups and classes. However, John XXIII is careful to return to the developing theme that solidarity and subsidiarity should be balanced throughout the body politic, and that the state must not give in to the idea of a perfect bureaucratic form of justice. John XXIII exhorts politicians to foster balance through freedom of groups to act autonomously whilst also encouraging cooperation within a wider regulated system. John argues that if – and only if – this balance is respected then the extension of state welfare will not inevitably be overly burdensome nor dependency oriented. Mirroring his own rural background, he chooses an agricultural rather than industrial example to illustrate his point: mutual aid societies and professional associations help to protect prices, offer ways to learn about best practices and new technologies, provide for fellowship amongst agricultural workers and enable effective advocacy. All of these are subsidiary forms of welfare and promote human freedom and agency. But he warns: you need to be organized into groups to be heard. Once again, a vision of solidarity emerges rooted in both dire need and a natural human capacity for mutual assistance.

Pacem in terris focuses on solidarity in the context of questions of peace, war and human rights, attending to the global dimensions of solidarity: the importance of solidarity *within* each political community and *between* political communities. This letter introduces formally into CST the notion that each political community has a meaningful common good of its own, and that solidarity is the engine for driving towards the common good. One theme that links the national, regional and global politics of solidarity is evidence of rising politics of fear and distrust. John XXIII expresses concern about a vicious political cycle taking hold in which public opinion and public policy reinforce one another in a negative cycle of the defensive and destructive. He argued provocatively that rather than acting to overcome fear and distrust, public policy under democratic conditions seems at times to feed it. Democracy is not in itself a guarantee against cycles of fear and distrust. He notes the tie between the democratic and authoritarian politics of 1960s and increased militarization. Why do public policy decisions seem to prioritize armament over food and pursue militarization as a private interest, dressed up in a false language of public interest? He argued with passion that such public policy displaces basic social and economic development needs, forgetting to invest in the needs and capabilities of people as the basis of development: the basic characteristic of human relations and the purpose of social institutions is solidarity. *Mater et magistra* posited that this cycle actively thwarts the conditions necessary for the growth of a politics of collaboration and solidarity. Fostering cooperation and basic human capability is the necessary basis of a different – more theological – cycle of response to fear and distrust.

The contribution of the Second Vatican Council to the developing understanding of solidarity took a slightly different turn again. The council was marked by a desire to reconnect Catholic theology with its biblical and patristic roots. As such *Gaudium et spes*, the main social teaching document produced by the council, is marked by the halting beginnings of a more doctrinal take on solidarity. Drawing on themes of Incarnation and soteriology the document emphasizes that we are saved and made holy not merely as individuals without bonds but by being made into a people, a communal character consummated in the work of Jesus Christ, Word made Flesh. God willed to share in our nature and as a unique act of solidarity Jesus Christ takes on the form of our solidarities. We share in kinship with Christ who becomes the firstborn of many brethren. Through the gift of the Holy Spirit, we are united into His Body, the Church. The long revolution of faith requires a constant increase in, and ever-renewed practices of, solidarity – which we receive and enact as practices of communion – until the day it is brought to perfection in God's kingdom. This is therefore a thoroughly communitarian and ecclesial ethic: the community of Jesus is to be a community of solidarity, and we are saved as members of a community of faith, but the wider doctrinal and natural law emphasis of the document means that this is never *solely* envisioned a practice of the visible Church alone.

Gaudium et spes also continues to develop the new mode of reflection on solidarity set within the global context of greater wealth but more inequality, greater interaction but more alienation, greater socialization but less personalization. The document offers further development of universal kinship themes; it maintains and further develops the parallel theme of worker solidarity. It reinforces the Catholic view of globalization as an essentially neutral process – open, if engaged with through the virtues, to opportunities for greater socialization whilst also containing new possibilities for inequality and oppression. Globalization, for example, means that we see more plainly and concretely beyond our national and particular groups to the universal kinship of humanity. Ideas of universal kinship can sound very theoretical and abstract, but become something we can reach out and touch through travel, new forms of social communication, cultural exchange and economic cooperation. However, structures of sin take on global dimensions too and threaten the fragile solidarity that globalization invites.

The pre-conciliar encyclicals had tended to talk about 'the law of human solidarity', rooting the call to solidarity in a natural law account of the human person. Through the years of the council a parallel biblical and doctrinal interpretation developed which did not repudiate the earlier natural law emphasis but which supplemented a more Christological and ecclesiological account. Representing this shift in his first post-conciliar social encyclical, Paul VI moves to talking about the Christological 'duty' of human solidarity. As Mark Potter argues, Paul VI also introduces a greater sense of teleology to Catholic discussions about solidarity.[16] Paul VI does this through his introduction of the term 'integral' or 'authentic' human development in *Populorum progressio*. Whilst this term remains ambiguous in meaning, acting in more heuristic than precise terms (as with much in the social encyclical tradition), it functions to remind readers of the social encyclicals that the social order must operate according to a goal, consideration of how we reach this goal necessarily takes us by way of reflection on the need for and nature of human solidarity. As Potter notes, this solidarity is both the necessary way to reach the goal and also intrinsically part of the goal itself.[17] Interestingly, he also sees a serious challenge to the Church, considering itself to be a global community, in

---

[16]Mark W. Potter, 'Solidarity as a Spiritual Exercise: A Contribution to the Development of Solidarity in the Catholic Social Tradition', Boston College, 2009, unpublished PhD. I am grateful to the author for sharing a copy of this thesis.
[17]Ibid.

living solidarity within her own life: How can the Church relate across differences of culture and extreme differences of wealth and poverty, race, class and gender politics, without addressing these real social divisions and overcoming them in the life of the Church? If the task of the Church is to facilitate the conversion of the world, then the capacity for the Church to be a visible sign of the solidarity it wishes the world to desire needs to lead to careful attentiveness, dialogue and communal reflection.

International development and the possibilities of solidarity-as-communion through a trinity of charity, trade and aid dominate Paul VI's 1967 *Populorum progressio*. For the first time this social encyclical also raises the question of cultural difference and the need for attention to intercultural dynamics in conceiving of global relations of solidarity. He sees threats to solidarity in the forms of unregulated economy that widens inequality; social conflict driven by imbalances of possessions and power; and breakdown of traditional forms of social ties through increased industrialization. The spirit of solidarity, expressed as authentic human development, is the framework for exploring aid, trade, charity and conflict resolution. As Meghan Clark notes, for Paul VI the capacity to act in and for solidarity is seen as itself the fullness of human development. Development is not merely the instrumental end point, but the practised virtue of solidarity *is itself* a form of fullness of being human.[18] We can talk therefore about a 'development in solidarity', as well as solidarity as the basis for economic and political development. The text appeals for practical ways to promote communion between nations through solidarity (aid), social justice (trade) and charity (mutuality and participation). In his subsequent apostolic exhortation *Octogesima adveniens* Paul VI begins to make tentative connections between human freedom and solidarity: the deepest character of freedom is found in building up active and lived solidarity.

In *Justitia in mundo*, the 1971 Synod of Bishops deploys the developing language of solidarity to talk about the pursuit of justice. Solidarity is necessary to secure human dignity, the common good and a true humanity. A right relation to God is unimaginable without taking in the dimensions of solidaristic human relations. This is not imagined as 'law', duty or penance – a taxation due on divine benefits. Rather, an economy of intersecting relations, a constant flow of interconnected human–human, human–divine

---

[18]Clark, *The Vision of Catholic Social Thought*, p. 21. Clark notes equity and mutuality as the hallmarks of the vision of solidarity and development in *Populorum progressio*.

relations is presented, in which solidarity is both a divine and human action, and in which learning the virtue of solidarity opens up fullness of life as a communion of creatures and with the Creator.

Thus, whilst earlier papacies begin a tentative social theological use of the language of solidarity, John Paul II's papacy contributes to its theological-political development in three key ways: first, he formalizes solidarity as a permanent principle of CST, second, he adds further theological depth to the notion of solidarity and third, he brings a new emphasis focusing on the concrete, practical nature of solidarity. In so doing he articulates a more overtly personalist and structural account of solidarity as a Catholic social principle.

John Paul II was the only pontiff to write part of the modern canon of CST who had come to the papacy already having produced his own body of work on the philosophical and theological basis of the idea of solidarity. Karol Wojtyła had laboured as a young philosopher priest in Poland to produce a new synthesis of the Thomism he had been taught in the seminary and the phenomenology he encountered amongst his colleagues involved in Christian–Marxist dialogue. His book *The Acting Person* was the result. Wojtyła was convinced that theologians needed to renew their thought by working from an understanding of how the person experiences the world: to experience ourselves in action. He believed that reflecting on the acting person would bring us – via a different path – to the same metaphysical truths Aquinas' system proposes, but it would correct the tendency in Thomism to underplay the dynamic nature of the human person.

These ideas of the free, self-governing and yet radically interdependent person were developed in dialogue with the work of German philosopher Max Scheler and Polish priest-philosopher Józef Tischner. If Scheler helped Karol Wojtyła to develop his personalist theory of moral personality, Tischner helped him to develop his theory of solidarity as the praxis of community. Tischner's *The Ethics of Solidarity* focuses on the role of conscience and work as providing deep structures for renewing solidarity. Arguing that the deeper problem of economic and social crisis was an issue of enacting conscience, Tischner offers a compelling account of the need for the Church in building a solidarity of consciences. Tischner's work, whilst centred on conscience as a moral category, should not be read as an individualistic or personalist account lacking in structural or communal engagement. For Tischner – who also acted as the first chaplain to solidarity movement in Poland – dialogue and work become key categories, for consciences need to operate in the context of dialogue about value, and a crucial everyday context for such dialogue is work. Work becomes a form of solidarity in the sense that labour is a co-creative process and a mechanism through which we participate in an intergenerational – past, present, future – conversation about labour and value. The first social encyclical produced by John Paul II, *Laborem exercens*, mirrors many of Tischner's concerns.

One of the distinctive hallmarks of *Laborem exercens* is the attempt to set out a narrative and background history within which to situate the developing Catholic conversation about solidarity. John Paul II begins by placing talk of solidarity firmly in the context of reflection on work. He observes that the practical movements of solidarity as historical forces have been a reaction against the degradation of man as the subject of work and exploitation in wages, conditions and social security. Solidarity of workers has produced new forms of cooperation, yet as new forms of solidarity are created – workers sharing in the running of companies, social legislation on pay and conditions, including living wages – so, simultaneously, new forms of injustice emerge and new challenges (increased automation, and as the pandemic has made clear gaps between knowledge industry and manual and caring work). These observations shouldn't lead to pessimism and passivity. Solidarity is never a fruitless struggle, but it is an arduous struggle that needs to be understood in the dimensions of time as well as space. Just as work itself is a sort of solidarity – sharing in the activity of the Creator and expressing of a common nature and purpose – so acts of solidarity are expressions of work: an arduous good, representing incomplete but compelling forms of practical love. In response we need to work and study for the development of ever new movements of solidarity of and with workers, attentive to *both* the endlessly inventive nature of degradation, exploitation, poverty and hunger *and* the possibility for human cooperation and communion. The reality of work is caught up in both these cycles.

Catholic reflection on solidarity is driven by a set of simultaneously ontological and historical claims. Solidarity can be viewed in empirical terms as something observable in the way that human beings operate: as an inherent, traceable way of being that can be affirmed by secular as well as theological reasoning. Nonetheless, the theological account is argued to exceed the secular in so far as it offers a 'thicker' ontology to ground the call to solidarity: solidarity is first and foremost a divine act before it is something that we do, a divine gift to humanity through creation, renewed, deepened and extended in the Incarnation and through redemption. Read through the lens of divine law, solidarity becomes both gift and duty, an act corresponding to the calling latent within our nature and an act grounded in that which we first receive – and which in a fallen world we memorialize and re-receive in sacramental and liturgical form. In this sense solidarity is both a fact and a call to action.

John Paul II's social encyclicals present a pluralist, associationalist vision of solidarity as a virtue or duty to be enacted by individual persons, amongst the professions, by classes, by small-scale communities and by nations. This vision influences John Paul II's critique of the 'suffocation' of the person between market and state. He notes the many levels of relationship needed to 'personalize' and 'socialize' and enable human relations to 'breathe': family, associations and groups that cross labour–capital, class, ethnic, national boundaries. The oxygenation of social life – and of work as one vital facet of this reality – requires not only the commitment of the individual and of the institution or organization to the pursuit of genuine individual, public and common goods but also the flourishing of an associational and public life that is external to the workplace. A Catholic theology of work whilst placing very significant emphasis on work as a context for the generation of value does not reify work within a self-enclosed world, nor imagine that institutions or organizations will pursue genuine goods without some level of external challenge or inspiration.

His vision is also grounded in an unsurprisingly realist appeal to truth as the grounds of 'integral' or 'authentic' human development. What sets John Paul II's account of globalization apart from contemporary secular accounts is his emphasis on the search for and free submission of the self to truth. Real and sustained relationships of solidarity need to recognize the fundamental drive of the human person for the search for truth and its pre-eminent human importance. Through this process we learn how to choose the common good, a good that is our own good and the good of the whole. Only recognition of these empirical realities can enable us to move from a sociological observation of the *fact* of complex social interdependence to a *moral and spiritual apprehension* of interdependence as a call for a new understanding of human dignity and an invitation to forms of life in communion. Thus, in *Sollicitudo rei socialis* interdependence is presented as a globalized system determining relationships (economic, political, cultural and religious) and as a moral category. Solidarity within society means mutual recognition of personhood, cooperation whereby the stronger aid the weaker and reciprocal cooperative action whereby the weaker or poorer resist the trap of passivity or narrow rights-claiming approaches to seek means of participation. International relations, solidarity between nations, is rooted in the principle that the goods of creation are meant for all. The products of human work, shaped from common raw materials, are destined to serve equally the needs and the good of all. John Paul calls for solidarity to be practising above all as a way of *seeing*: seeing persons, peoples and nations as sharers, helpers and neighbours in the banquet of life, to which all are equally called. Hence, ultimately, solidarity is rooted in and requires a religious re-awakening of both persons and peoples.

John Paul II's work on solidarity offers two theological innovations of particular note for the development of CST: he suggests we need more focus on both sin and love as themes to be applied to the complex social and political realities that threaten peace. These themes of love and sin can be seen as a logic follow on from his concern to address questions of truth and to understand the social conditions that seem to block or frustrate access or apprehension of this truth. John Paul II's theological development of reflection on solidarity drew also on the growing influence of Latin American liberation theologians' reflections on inequality, love and sin as social themes. To talk about social sin is not just to harp on in a dreary fashion about moral conduct but opens to us a series of practical actions and categories not typically present in political analysis: forgiveness, mercy, repentance and conversion. These remain categories of justice which are not contained within the realm of the political alone and require theological language, exposition and practice. This language of sin relates to persons and to structures: the capacity of nations and blocs to manifest 'sin' and the negative significance of such structures in working against the development of 'a true awareness of the universal common good'.[19] Solidarity emerges as the way that we resist structures of sin and keeps open a space for the apprehension of the common good as a necessary social pursuit. John Paul grounds his personalist virtue of solidarity in the universal destination of goods – the principle that the goods of the earth are intended for the benefit of all. In doing so he insists on the connections between solidarity and justice, and an attention to inequality as an integral part of Christian solidarity.

John Paul II extends earlier treatment of these themes in CST and addresses directly the social and political dimensions of sin, forgiveness, mercy, repentance and conversion. He insists that there is no route towards dealing with world problems of peace and development without engaging

---

[19] *Sollicitudo rei socialis*, §36.

the fallen and redeeming realities of interdependence as a moral reality. There is also no process of politics without some form of dispossession – reflecting on the fact that politics involves being willing to give things up. He challenges us by asking: What are we required to give up to engage in a more adequately moral form of social exchange? His answer highlights the politics of blocs, all forms of economic, political and military imperialism, forms of mutual fear and distrust in favour of practical collaboration focused on shared needs. These forms of dispossession are not 'losses' but acts 'proper to solidarity'.[20] Peace as the fruit of justice becomes peace as the fruit of solidarity. Here he draws on biblical roots in Isaiah 32.17 and James 3.18. This pushes the idea of justice beyond solely each being given their due into a prior consideration of the virtues that foster togetherness and increase the chance of each being given their due.

Equally significant from a theological point of view is John Paul II's desire to relate the Christian concept of solidarity back to its roots in charity and holiness. Solidarity is called to go beyond itself, to take on the specifically Christian dimension of total gratuity, forgiveness and reconciliation. This orientation requires us to acknowledge that our neighbour is not just a competing rights-bearer but an image of the living God, shares a common paternity and kinship through God, and is made to be part of the sacrament of communion. The disposition appropriate to solidarity is therefore caritas. Here John Paul II draws attention to the saints as models of solidarity, particularly the sixteenth-century Jesuit patron saint of slaves Peter Claver and the twentieth-century Franciscan saint who took the place of a stranger in Auschwitz Maximillian Kolbe. He also draws into CST reflection on pneumatology, a generally underdeveloped theme in Catholic social thought: it is through the Spirit that we are able to move beyond ordinary solidarity into this space of gratuity.

Benedict XVI takes further this task of re-theologizing the relationship between charity and justice. He places a greater emphasis on making explicit the transcendent basis of true solidarity and authentic human development: rooted in an acceptance of the divine image present in our neighbour. An implicit move within Benedict's writings is the move away from use of the word 'solidarity' and towards the language of fraternity. Benedict continues to use the language of solidarity in order to refer to forms of civic coexistence, as a virtue that secular societies can aim for and

---

[20]Ibid., §39.

should embody as a minimum condition. In his writings, solidarity is a principle and practice necessary within markets and within each individual transaction. Solidarity builds trust and without prior forms of solidarity trust will diminish. Trust is the basic category necessary for both political and market relations, so it is ironic and problematic that both tend towards self-harm by working against the very conditions they require to function.

Whilst the term 'solidarity' does not disappear in his writings, Benedict XVI makes much fuller theological use of the term 'fraternity', drawing out its connections to ideas of reciprocity, gift and gratuity. It is possible that Benedict's turn towards the language of fraternity is an attempt (as some have argued) to move away from any perceived individualism or secularity that might be perceived to cling to the language of solidarity and to return the idea of solidarity to its pre-Enlightenment roots. In drawing on the language of fraternity Benedict is judged to have emphasized the communal and reciprocal character of Christian social relations and their rootedness in Christian liturgical life and community. At very least, Benedict appears to present a preference for fraternity as a form of social language that captures the fact that Christian social life – and therefore all social theology – originates in a receptive movement in which we are first loved and therefore given to each other in and for love.

Benedict offers this logic of fraternity as the basis for a critique and reconstruction of liberal economic and social transactions – he believes that contract logic, emphasizing exchange and duty, has dominated our thinking and gift logic has been left behind, often dismissed. He argued that a logic of gift and communion in political and economic thinking takes us beyond an ethics of mere duty, obligation or right – the other person as 'law' and limit – and towards an ethics of encounter, exchange and relational abundance. Such thinking does not diminish notions of obligation or rights, but it frames the social imagination in a very different way, and this mattered deeply for Benedict. Solidarity is never mere duty or indebtedness, rather it expands outwards from an initial experience of gift and reciprocity, in a circle of exchange without limit, in search of both justice and love, impelled by a prior experience of both. In *Caritas in veritate*, drawing partly on the work of Catholic 'civil economy' thinkers Stefano Zamagni and Luigino Bruni, Benedict argued the case for a new, post-financial crash model of economy as gift.[21]

---

[21]Fraternity brings with it the rich association of a religious society or guild built on relationships of reciprocal friendship and the common use of goods. However, given the

Solidarity

It is interesting, then, that the papacy of Francis has sought to re-emphasize the principle of solidarity in categorical terms but has also continued to develop the language of fraternity foregrounded in *Caritas in veritate*. In doing so, Francis has both repeated the solidaristic themes of John XXIII, John Paul II and Benedict, and produced an integrated social teaching of his own. Francis emphasizes the primary importance of a Christian doctrine of creation and redemption for shaping a distinctive understanding of human interdependence and solidarity; the practical evidence of a solidaristic mindset in a willingness to think and act in terms of community, including in its intergenerational dimensions, and as a wider biospheric ethic; and the structural dimension to solidarity which requires an institutional and personal commitment to ensuring a priority of human life over capital, profit and the 'appropriation of goods by the few'. Francis has placed a concrete emphasis on the communal pursuit of land, housing and decent work as the work of solidarity.

Francis' apostolic exhortation *Evangelii gaudium* contains an urgent emphasis on solidarity as a crucial virtue and principle, most particularly as it relates to the preferential option for the poor. Francis states: 'The word "solidarity" is a little worn and at times poorly understood, but it refers to something more than a few sporadic acts of generosity. It presumes the creation of a new mindset which thinks in terms of community and the priority of the life of all over the appropriation of goods by a few.'[22] He continues:

> Solidarity is a spontaneous reaction by those who recognize that the social function of property and the universal destination of goods are realities which come before private property. The private ownership of goods is justified by the need to protect and increase them, so that they can better serve the common good; for this reason, solidarity must be lived as the decision to restore to the poor what belongs to them. These convictions and habits of solidarity, when they are put into practice, open the way to other structural transformations and

---

obviously gendered roots of the word – which passes without comment in the official teaching texts – there has been significant comment from those uncomfortable with a non-inclusive use of this phrase, especially in an era when CST is trying to reflect on some of its more paternalist tendencies. This debate emerged following the publication of *Caritas in veritate* but intensified in the wake of *Fratelli tutti*.

[22] *Evangelii gaudium*, §188.

make them possible. Changing structures without generating new convictions and attitudes will only ensure that those same structures will become, sooner or later, corrupt, oppressive and ineffectual.[23]

In *Laudato si'* Francis expands his use of solidarity to encompass a commitment to sustainable development. He argues that sustainable development is only possible if we are inspired by a vision of *intergenerational* solidarity – politics as the present connection between past and future, as he later argues in *Fratelli tutti*. In *Laudato si'* he notes:

> We can no longer speak of sustainable development apart from intergenerational solidarity. Once we start to think about the kind of world we are leaving to future generations, we look at things differently; we realize that the world is a gift which we have freely received and must share with others. . . . Intergenerational solidarity is not optional, but rather a basic question of justice, since the world we have received also belongs to those who will follow us.[24]

Francis uses *Laudato si'* to reimagine solidarity not merely in intergenerational terms but in more expansively intragenerational, creaturely and biospheric terms.[25] He presents a narrative of human beings as creaturely beings, embedded in a wider natural world, in which each part of that world is reaching towards its future. A biospheric teleology marks the basis of this account of solidarity, an interdependent, dynamic process of becoming marks the whole earth. Francis writes sharply: 'the ultimate purpose of other creatures is not to be found in us'.[26] The horizon for ultimate purpose is transcendent, not immanent, and marked by a capacity to relate to difference. Solidarity is marked by a respect for this fact.

Two other key addresses develop Francis' teaching on solidarity. In two addresses to popular movements Francis talks about solidarity as increasingly a 'dirty word', seen as naïve and worn. He reiterates the older CST themes we have noted earlier, that solidarity means thinking in terms

---

[23]Ibid., §189.
[24]*Laudato si'*, §159.
[25]This is not a new connection in CST – John Paul II makes such connections to the virtue of solidarity and also to structures of social sin in *Evangelium vitae* §10 and *Sollicitudo rei socialis* §26.
[26]*Laudato si'*, §83.

of communities of mutual belonging, of a structural priority of human persons above both capital and concentrations or appropriations of wealth or goods and a willingness to actively struggle against the structural causes of poverty and inequality. He suggests a need for Christian social action both to address the conditions of lack or privation of the basic goods of human life and to actively secure those goods, which he names in material terms as decent work, land and housing. Without these three the conditions for solidarity as well as human dignity are threatened.

In his Covid-19 public audiences during the summer of 2020, Francis explored each principle of the Church's social teaching in an accessible manner and with reflection on the pandemic.[27] He paired each principle with a theological virtue – in this instance, solidarity with faith. He offers one distinctive emphasis in this address and highlights a striking metaphor. In his theological treatment of solidarity, Francis explains that without honouring the transcendent basis to our human interdependence – which he summarizes neatly as recognition of a common origin, a common home, a common life and a common destination – we are at great risk of forgetfulness about the mutuality that anchors our common life, turning interdependence into dependence. There is only proper recognition of interdependence or toxic cycles of dependence. Where interdependence is not noted and honoured, unhealthy forms of dependence become the norm. He had already named these in his 2014 address to the popular movements as evidenced in extreme inequality, violence, dislocation, trafficking and forced emigration. He uses the biblical story of Babel and the event of Pentecost as his hermeneutic frame of reference. Babel involves building higher to reach the heavens but without a mindset of communal communication and mutual belonging. Pentecost, by contrast, infused by the Spirit, honours participation and the contribution of each. It is at this point that Francis draws a striking metaphor for understanding solidarity through a CST lens is drawn from the pandemic itself. Francis argues that as a Pentecostal community God inspires faith as a virtue in God's people, making the impossible a reality – a unity in diversity and solidarity. It is this faith that provides the '"antibodies" that ensure that the singularity of each person – which is a gift, unique and unrepeatable – does not become

---

[27] Pope Francis, *To Heal the World: Catechesis on the Pandemic*, Preface by Cardinal Peter Kodwo Turkson (Vatican City: Libreria Editrice Vaticana, 2020), pp. 51–8.

sick with individualism, with selfishness'.[28] Francis goes on to suggest that a social body that can honour 'diversity in solidarity' possesses antibodies that help heal social structures that have 'degenerated into systems of injustice'.[29]

In *Fratelli tutti* Francis arguably adopts solidarity as the framework for the entire encyclical, although he chooses the language of fraternity to express this ethic. As with Francis' other writings on solidarity, *Fratelli tutti* returns solidarity to a doctrine of creation: a common fatherhood and a common siblinghood, or fraternity in Christ. Francis' handling of the theme of solidarity is marked by a notably mystical emphasis: to perceive the common fatherhood we share and to view others as sisters and brothers is first to apprehend the reality that makes this so. This is a contemplative activity, and it is this contemplation that marks the basis for a properly expansive and sustainable practice of solidarity: the view that we are all related to all, and responsible for all, and together saved. The Church is the doxological, liturgical and diaconal reality that binds this community of Christ in and for the world, with and for others. In the conclusion to this book, I explore the particular use of the Good Samaritan passage as a theological heart to Francis' biblical account of solidarity. In addition, Francis repeats both the earlier themes we have already noted in the twentieth-century CST tradition. He adds a particular note of emphasis to the family and educators as the first contexts for formation in solidarity and of acts of service and care as the concrete manifestations of solidarity. This theme of solidarity as service, through the works of mercy, has the usual Francis embodied rallying call – solidarity as service looks into the face of the other, touches flesh and 'suffers closeness' to the suffering of others. Two further reflections emerge in *Fratelli tutti*, which echo comments made during in a range of addresses. First, the importance of recognizing in non-patronizing terms that the poorest communities are often most expert in the need for and practice of solidarity as a means of survival and resistance, and from these communities grow the possible seeds of movements that might bring new history. They are not merely the beneficiaries of solidarity done *to* or *for* them. Second, that forms of 'closed' populism, as Francis names them, which appeal to the solidarity of the group but are closed to those beyond the identified group, are not truly solidaristic but in fact risk being forms of narcissistic localism. He repeats Benedict's theme

---

[28]Ibid., p. 55.
[29]Ibid.

Solidarity

that without solidarity and mutual trust as an internal practice of market systems, economies will fail to provide solid and ethical growth.

The development of solidarity as a Catholic social principle

The 1993 *Catechism* of the Catholic Church describes the principle of solidarity as follows:

> The principle of solidarity, also articulated in terms of 'friendship' or 'social charity', is a direct demand of human and Christian brotherhood. An error, 'today abundantly widespread, is disregard for the law of human solidarity and charity, dictated and imposed both by our common origin and by the equality in rational nature of all men, whatever nation they belong to. This law is sealed by the sacrifice of redemption offered by Jesus Christ on the altar of the Cross to his heavenly Father, on behalf of sinful humanity.' Solidarity is manifested in the first place by the distribution of goods and remuneration for work. It also presupposes the effort for a more just social order where tensions are better able to be reduced and conflicts more readily settled by negotiation. Socio-economic problems can be resolved only with the help of all the forms of solidarity: solidarity of the poor among themselves, between rich and poor, of workers among themselves, between employers and employees in a business, solidarity among nations and peoples. International solidarity is a requirement of the moral order; world peace depends in part upon this. The virtue of solidarity goes beyond material goods. In spreading the spiritual goods of the faith, the Church has promoted, and often opened new paths for, the development of temporal goods as well.[30]

This statement presents the threefold account of solidarity we have seen emerging through our discussion of the encyclicals: as an anthropological fact and theological reality; as an ethical principle or moral outlook; and finally, as a structural and institutional imperative. These three elements help us to see the difference between solidarity as a 'load bearing' and

---

[30] *Catechism of the Catholic Church* (1993 Edition), §1939–42.

distinctive concept in CST and more general ideas about compassion and neighbourliness.

First, it begins with an explicit ontology. Anthropologically speaking, the principle of solidarity is rooted in an account of the human person as essentially relational, social and interdependent, having a common origin and possessing a common and equal rationality. Theologically speaking, this is an account of created nature, universal kinship and a common redemption offered through Jesus Christ. CST's anthropology of solidarity stands in contrast to a social order understood as inherently and ultimately conflictive and competitive. The essential and abiding core of the human personality is seen to be relational, cooperative and oriented towards reciprocity, communication and gift exchange. We create social structures and processes that enable this nature to be secured, protected and expressed as much as to restrain our conflictive, violent and destructive human tendencies. The idea of solidarity is not intended as a denial of conflict, violence, brokenness and loss; rather, what CST has to say about solidarity is unthinkable without an acknowledgement of these darker realities. Our social nature is a prior gift that enables us to live with, through and over-against conflict and loss. And yet we need to be equally clear to avoid implying that CST is proposing a false dualism or weak dialectic at the root of our social relations: our cultures, institutions and structures express the constant intermingling of these realities, which will only be separated, as the wheat and tares, at the end of time. In the context of this intermingled reality cooperation – and the stronger 'theological' possibility of communion – stands at the basis of the social order prior to conflict and competition. It is also at the end of the social order: our destiny as human persons is to be caught up in the *communion* life of the divine. For CST, therefore, conversion towards a life which seeks communion, cooperation and gift exchange as practices of resistance and as a participation in what already is and shall be stands at the heart of all social, political and economic life. We can say, then, that CST begins its reflection on solidarity by presenting an anthropological view of solidarity as *ontological* and *teleological*.

If we are willing to contemplate our interdependent nature from a moral point of view, then we are led to reflect not simply on the consequences of our nature but also to reflect on solidarity as an active virtue and a dynamic moral reality. Solidarity as a moral perspective brought to bear upon our social, rational and interdependent nature leads us towards one of the most complex human struggles: to recognize that our human interdependence is profound enough to mean that we are called to something more than, as John Paul says, 'vague compassion or shallow distress', rather to 'a firm and persevering determination to commit oneself to the common good; that is to say, to the good of all and of each individual because we are all really responsible for all'.³¹ Far from being a loose and saccharine concept of human connection, the principle of solidarity requires a practical, moral engagement with ideas of universal human kinship and the universal destination of material goods that challenges the dominant political, economic and social arrangements of the world of nation states and late capitalist economies.

All of this teaching is steeped in a world view that refuses to see human relationships as primarily pragmatic, instrumental or contractual. An ethics of friendship, charity and justice is the *intrinsic* basis of institutional as well as personal life: rightly this takes different form in different contexts and involves much plurality. It represents a strong critique of a world view that has been repeatedly in danger of settling for a version of common interest politics that could talk only, at best, about extrinsic duties and goods. So, to come full circle back to where we began this chapter, with the language of solidarity viewed as something old, some borrowed and something new. Matthew Lamb argues that this understanding of solidarity, whilst borrowing from the language of Enlightenment politics, stands in contrast to modern notions of solidarity as extrinsic and voluntarist: for CST 'the ontology of solidarity is the fact of the human species'.³² This positive theological appraisal of solidarity is not a dualist denial of the reality of social conflict but views solidarity as ontologically prior to violence and therefore as a practical, concrete reality to be enacted for transformation in the midst of violence and conflict.

---

³¹See *Sollicitudo rei socialis*, §38.
³²Matthew Lamb, 'Solidarity', in *The New Dictionary of Catholic Social Thought*, ed. Judith Dwyer (Collegeville: Liturgical Press, 1994), p. 911.

CHAPTER 11
THE UNIVERSAL DESTINATION OF GOODS
TOWARDS AN INTEGRAL ECOLOGY

God has written a precious book, 'whose letters are the multitude of created things present in the universe'.[1]

We consume not only food and drink, but also the things we use, symbolic and cultural values, and even one another. For this reason, the right ordering of our labour and trade depends upon the right ordering of our consumption or desire.[2]

The challenge for a world in the grip of a climate emergency is to grasp that the only way to confront it with hope is through conversion to a vision of an integrated or integral ecology. Ultimately, this is a question not only of rational thought about the state of the world we inhabit; it is a matter of the desires that orientate that thought and their ordering. The idea of an integral ecology is Pope Francis' favoured language for attempting to persuade a generation driven by practices of high consumption, rapid growth, economic inequalities and indifference towards both other humans and other creatures and living forms that there might be something seriously amiss with the structure of our desires. What is amiss relates not only to our relationship with 'nature' but to a wider web of relationships to work, to trade, to land, to other creatures and life forms, and to bodies. This chapter might, therefore, read to some as an unlikely combination of exegesis, covering as it does not only the ecological content of recent encyclicals but also the long body of teaching on the universal destination of goods and work. Nonetheless, its ambition is precisely to stay with the connections to which Pope Francis point, to draw together

---

[1] *Laudato si'* §85.
[2] John Hughes, *The End of Work* (Oxford: Blackwell Press, 2007), p. 229.

what so often we attempt misguidedly to hold apart and to find the sinews of their co-belonging already threaded through the body of Catholic social teaching (CST), even if some of those threads might prove in need of some unpicking and reweaving. It is to explore the terrain of Pope Francis' claim in *Laudato si'* that an integral ecology is inseparable from a notion of the common good.

The gradually developing body of CST on ecological issues – in their widest sense – has been gathering momentum since the papacy of John Paul II and finds its most developed articulation to date in *Laudato si'*. Francis' encyclical teaches that an integral ecology is rooted first and foremost in a receptive awareness of the interconnectedness of all created things. Woven *a priori* through creation, this interconnectedness is divinely intended and a social reality that must be actively forged by co-creative human action. The vision of interconnection and integral development Francis speaks of in *Laudato si'* is not merely an attractive mystical seeing of the co-belonging of all creatures and life forms, a generic and slightly sentimental sense of all things belonging together. Rather, he proposes both a mystical account of the common origin, purpose and destiny of living forms – an intimacy of all life – and an analytical account of the de facto interconnectedness (for better and worse) that is evident in our ways of thinking about being creatures inhabiting a common world. He attempts to reveal the soft underbelly of our thinking that we are rarely willing to subject to integrated scrutiny: the crises that connect our politics and economics are rooted in a poverty of social relationship, which manifests and reproduces itself in structural form, as well as having accrued historical structural causes. For these reasons, it is not a Christian evasion of the hard issues to say that social renewal requires a process of deep conversion as integral to an account of liberation. Quite the opposite. The theological narrative that aims to move us towards such a conversion begins, in the encyclical tradition, with the fundamental logic of gift, gratuity and communion that underlies all of creation and forms the condition for the very possibility of hopeful thought itself. This process of thinking about the interconnectedness of all things – biological, historical and metaphysical – may require, as part of a hopeful process of renewal, an openness to lament and mourning. It is a mourning – an *inaugurated* mourning, as the philosopher Gillian Rose would say – through which we hope to become ourselves, more graciously and more fully, in relation to a world out of which we are bodily composed and in which we are given to

The Universal Destination of Goods

each other as a sign of communion.[3] A givenness which nonetheless, we are free to choose or to reject.

The proposal that the same basic architecture of ideas connects the way that we view our bodies, the land, trade, work, leisure and the built and natural environments puts us in familiar territory in CST. The documents of the tradition have long insisted that we do not have fundamentally separate ethics for these things, even when we think we do. The encyclicals present the paradox that life is so clearly structured by interconnected experiences and ways of seeing, and yet something pulls us back from sensing and thinking this moral interconnectedness at the heart of our lives. The very way we live as moderns means that the interconnectedness of things is simultaneously an intense reality and yet often shielded from thought. Little in late modernity encourages us to perceive and evaluate these connections in their fullness. Part of this experience of disconnection in a yet interconnected world is existential. Our work lives can feel disconnected to our politics or personal values, our personal relationships can feel ethically separated from our work life, what we own and how we consume does not necessarily feel immediately connected to our views of race and so forth. What the encyclicals propose is that even if we do not routinely think much about these connections, the way we trade, eat, house and clothe ourselves, love, the way we take our leisure, what and how we own, how we travel are all interconnected by both sets of cultural ideas as well as by political and economic structures.[4] And for most of us in the Northern Hemisphere and Western societies, these ideas even when they appear to be largely secular often have identifiably Christian roots.

The tradition of CST is therefore not merely a guide to the territory, a source to help us think about what we are doing and why, and what we might do better but also a tradition implicated in the critical historical questions of our age. To begin with the first claim – that CST is a helpful guide to

---

[3]Gillian Rose uses the motif of mourning, drawn both from classical philosophy and from Freud, to propose a necessary process of mourning which befits a public life, and a form of law, which must confront the reality of its situation. It is the politics of imperfection, capable of being troubled by its past but with responsibility moving towards a future which risks again in the name of love and justice. In this way, public life does not remain trapped in aberrated mourning, a mourning that does not cease, but moves through to the morning that grief can give way to, fruitfully. See Gillian Rose, *Mourning Becomes the Law: Philosophy and Representation* (Cambridge: CUP, 1996).
[4]*Laudato si'* §6.

thinking about the interconnectedness of ecological, economic, bodily and political questions – CST has become perhaps the most developed body of formal ecclesial thinking, alongside the Orthodox tradition, on the question of an integrated environmental response. In many ways, it has made but a beginning in addressing these themes, but it is a significant beginning nonetheless. The idea that these realities form part of a single question can be traced back to *Rerum novarum* and finds expression in some form in each formal CST document since. The notion that to examine any of the complex social questions we face requires us to see the interconnection of the social, bodily, economic and political, and the ecological – both how they have been connected in the past and how we would like them to be connected – has sometimes been a source of bewilderment and controversy for readers of the tradition who would prefer to select, for example, elements of its economic teaching but jettison its focus on migration or interpersonal relationships, or adopt its stance for the family but doubt its core view of the created world and the economy and so forth. It is a defining and unavoidable feature of the social encyclicals that these be viewed as a whole, and where development is needed within the tradition it has ramifications for the wider ecology of the whole social tradition itself. The tradition is as interconnected as the reality it seeks to name. Pope Francis noted that *Laudato si'* was not to be understood as simply 'an encyclical on the environment'. He was unhappy with this reductive shorthand, even though the environmental crisis clearly lay at the heart of the document. *Laudato si'* proposed instead an integral ecology rooted in a Catholic social theology of creation.

In *Laudato si'* Francis offers, in pursuit of this integrating task, what theologian Vincent Miller describes as a threefold vision of integral ecology.[5] Miller argues that integral ecology is, variously, a way of seeing, a mode of analysis or understanding and finally a moral principle or imperative.

Francis presents integral ecology first as a way of seeing: a mystical perception gained by gazing at the world in its createdness and perceiving it through grace as a communicating sign of its Creator. The diversity of creation in its multiplicity of relationships speaks of the goodness of the Creator and His desire to draw all life into a logic of communion. To develop Miller's case, we might also see this same emphasis in Thomas

---

[5]Vincent J. Miller, 'Integral Ecology: Francis's Spiritual and Moral Vision of Interconnectedness', in *The Theological and Ecological Vision of Laudato Si': Everything Is Connected*, ed. Vincent J. Miller (London: Bloomsbury, 2017), pp. 11–28.

The Universal Destination of Goods

Aquinas' *de potentia*: being produces, or is the cause of, multitude as an expression of the goodness of being. This multitude – both plurality and multiplicity in creation – is not a scattering of the Creator's creation into divided form like the shattering of a glass once whole into fragments and shards, but each thing is in itself already a unity as well as forming a part of a greater whole, and all together are one by a unity of order they do not themselves achieve but instead compose and strain towards.[6] This is a vision of a communicating multiplicity held within a single order of being.[7] Reflection on that multiplicity draws us into a contemplation of the originating divine cause, the condition of being itself. Francis uses this logic to note that starting to think through the lens of creation, rather than merely nature, is to begin with a world view that sees that all is gift, nothing is superfluous and creation in all its elements is purposeful, even if sometimes mysteriously so! Creation emerges not from chaos or accident but from divine intellect, decision and intentionality. Australian theologian Denis Edwards argues that *Laudato si'* lays greater emphasis on the notion that all living creatures are an expression of a divine presence than previous formal social teaching.[8] The appropriate mode of action that is fitting in response to this basic Christian claim is attention, seeing and receiving. This in turn leads to a doxological response: praised be you (laudato si'), the very title of the document. Francis writes:

> The universe unfolds in God, who fills it completely. Hence, there is a mystical meaning to be found in a leaf, in a mountain trail, in a dewdrop, in a poor person's face. The ideal is not only to pass from the exterior to the interior to discover the action of God in the soul, but also to discover God in all things.

This mystical and doxological response is also a properly political response for Francis: in responding to creation in this receptive manner as gift of a Creator we take a step towards become placed and rooted in creation,

---

[6] See Thomas Aquinas, *Quaestiones Disputatae De Potentia Dei [On the Power of God]*, translated by the English Dominican Fathers (Westminster: Newman Press, 1952), reprint of 1932. Question III, Article XVI, Reply to Third Objection.
[7] As noted in previous chapters, this is not to deny the kind of plurality that results from brokenness in creation, a shattered or break that stems from action and event.
[8] Denis Edwards, "'Sublime Communion": The Theology of the Natural World in *Laudato Si'*", *Theological Studies* 77 (2016), p. 383.

rather than displaced and uprooted as Francis thinks the humans of modernity tend to be in their relationship to other creatures and the earth. In this sense, from its inception an integral ecological perspective is already a mystical-political practice.

In *Laudato si'* Francis deliberately challenges the idea of a nature–culture binary. Viewed from the vantage point of a theology of creation there can be no idea of a separated realm of the natural and no claim to a form of culture completely removed from nature. Francis argues that in the Jewish and Christian traditions creation has a broader meaning than nature. It implies the idea of a Creator, a loving plan and a value and significance to each facet of creation. He notes: '[n]ature is usually seen as a system which can be studied, understood and controlled, whereas creation can only be understood as a gift from the outstretched hand of the Father of all, and as a reality illuminated by the love which calls us together into universal communion.' Building on and developing Pope Benedict's focus on a theology of love and gift in *Caritas in veritate*, *Laudato si'* proposes that an integral ecology ought to be grounded in an approach to the environment as created gift, expressive of the loving work of a Creator who invites us into a communicative engagement with each part and the whole, and through the whole created order brings us home to Himself. Gift, encounter and dialogue are the hallmarks of each of Francis' social teaching documents.

The notion that each part of the created order addresses itself in some act of being and communication to the other parts of the whole is an important part of Francis' vision. This is no mute kinship but a process of being mysteriously addressed by creaturely otherness, which bespeaks a further otherness which is an absolute difference-in-relationship: Creator to creature. Within this order of communication freedom is construed as an original gift and intention; each creature and living form is free to seek its own excellence, its own purposive ends. A telos is therefore in mind; each living form seeks to express its being and is oriented towards some kind of fulfilment and towards a final drawing of all things towards communion. We noted in the previous chapters that this notion of communion in time is not a sentimental vision of easy harmony but a struggle towards communion – at once a receptive and co-operative movement but a labour in the conditions of time. There are 'new ills, new causes of suffering and real setbacks' which our intelligence and capacity for love must confront.[9]

---

[9]*Laudato si'*, §79.

The Universal Destination of Goods

We have noted in our earlier consideration of the common good the importance of the Christian doctrine proposed by the early Church that God – Father, Son and Spirit – creates *ex nihilo*, from nothing. As Anglican theologian Simon Oliver notes, drawing in turn on John Milbank: this doctrine implies a logic of gift in which there can be no separation between the sustaining gift of divine life and nature or creature. Oliver argues:

> Creation is, as John Milbank puts it, 'a gift of a gift to a gift'. There is no 'pure nature' to which God subsequently donates the gifts of his love. Put another way, there is a paradox at the heart of the gift of creation: creation is autonomous because it is not God, but that is no autonomy at all because creation's 'otherness' is always to be received from God in his act of creation ex nihilo. God 'holds back' creation from himself in order that creation can be itself.

At the core of creation there is thus only a circulating – although asymmetrical – logic of gift. God's own giving in creation is sheer gratuity. We cannot give anything back in return that is an equivalent gift to the gift given. We can only exchange gifts within the already sustaining gift which is existence, breath, order and form itself. Every gift given is sustained within gift. Thus, we can imitate something of God's gratuity but in imperfect creaturely form: hence Francis' careful use of both the idea of gratuity and reciprocal gift exchange as two connected but distinguishable notions in his teaching on migrant welcome.[10] A gratuitous act is one which is a total and free giving, without condition or expectation of reciprocation. It is a complete act in itself. The care of a parent for a child is perhaps the closest experience to truly gratuitous giving and receiving we enact. Gift exchange suggests a reciprocal, although often asymmetrical, giving. A newly arrived migrant gives of their gifts and skills to a new culture both as part of their own self-expression and as a contribution to participating in a social world; in return membership rights are given offering security and participation. Each gives from what is appropriate to the excellence and purpose of, in this case, the person and political community. The parent–child giving is an example of a giving simply because it is an act of love to do so (more on that in the conclusion to this book), the other is a mutual exchange of diverse gifts for the enrichment, renewal and flourishing of the whole. Both kinds

---

[10] See *Fratelli tutti*, chapters 3 and 4, and also Chapter 3 of this book.

of giving sustain the common good, and both participate within a wider divine reality of gift.

Second, as Miller notes, the idea of integral ecology implies a mode of analysis and understanding in which we try to think about the way that our various human and ecological crises might be interconnected. As part of this second move Francis suggests we try to make sense of the interconnection between the way we treat the most marginalized humans (through the manufacture of marginalization) and the way we treat the earth. This enables us to give voice to the mistreatment of life 'in all its forms'.[11] This second analytical mode relates, in turn, to a third: integral ecology as a moral principle or imperative used to help us judge how to act in the present and future moment to foster mutual purposeful flourishing. The option for the poor and the option for the earth are necessarily connected dispositions and practices. This analytical-moral mode correlates to a broad see, judge, act approach – although this final point is not drawn out by Miller.

Benedict XVI and Francis are consistent in their basic diagnosis of the mistreatment of life. Both note the dangers of a technocratic paradigm in politics and economics, and its connection to the environmental crisis. The 'technocratic paradigm' is a phrase used to denote the tendency to consider nature as a thing or an object to be manipulated, cultivated and extracted from. This paradigm tends to foster an instrumentalist gaze upon the world: identifiable in world views, policies and practices that view nature as valuable insofar as it renders utility or matter for consumption. A technocratic outlook tends to see creation-as-nature as an inert form of life, to be acted upon, rather than as a communicating life form with a value beyond mere instrumental use. Technocratic paradigms see culture as the dynamic entity which shapes nature to its own ends. The logic of this nature–culture binary tends towards practices of human mastery and control. Francis writes of this paradigm as treating nature as 'something formless, open to manipulation' and 'where everything is simply our property': its philosophy does not admit of the idea of limit as an ethical norm; it tends to be driven by the idea of unlimited growth; and its by-product, quite literally, is a throwaway culture. *Laudato si'* presents this paradigm as constituting more than a mere method or means to an end.[12]

---

[11] *Laudato si'*, §230.
[12] In *Laudato si'*, as part of his establishment of a papal tradition of commentary against instrumentalization and a technocratic paradigm, Francis references John Paul II's 1979

The Universal Destination of Goods

Rather, the technocratic paradigm tends to morph into an epistemology of its own, coming to imply a normative way of being and a given status quo in culture, economy and politics. Francis writes at some length:

> [t]his paradigm exalts the concept of a subject who, using logical and rational procedures, progressively approaches and gains control over an external object. This subject makes every effort to establish the scientific and experimental method, which in itself is already a technique of possession, mastery and transformation. It is as if the subject were to find itself in the presence of something formless, completely open to manipulation. Men and women have constantly intervened in nature, but for a long time this meant being in tune with and respecting the possibilities offered by the things themselves. It was a matter of receiving what nature itself allowed, as if from its own hand. Now, by contrast, we are the ones to lay our hands on things, attempting to extract everything possible from them while frequently ignoring or forgetting the reality in front of us. . . . This has made it easy to accept the idea of infinite or unlimited growth. . . . It is based on the lie that there is an infinite supply of the earth's goods, and this leads to the planet being squeezed dry beyond every limit. It is the false notion that 'an infinite quantity of energy and resources are available, that it is possible to renew them quickly, and that the negative effects of the exploitation of the natural order can be easily absorbed'.[13]

Francis returns to this theme in *Fratelli tutti*, but this time focusing on the grip this paradigm has on current politics and governance. Its political hallmarks are a homogeneity without real unity, a monotony of form that in fact leaves a trail of fracture and division, over centralization of initiative, a tendency towards short-termism, a politics that trails the economy and a cultural way of living that loses its historical consciousness.[14] For some critics, this is Francis given to overblown and imprecise rhetoric, producing sweeping cultural analysis that fails to land anywhere concrete. For others, it is a prophetic far-seeing that aims to promote an awakening to a crisis

---

Redemptor hominis, §287, as well as *Caritas in veritate*.
[13]*Laudato si'*, §106.
[14]*Fratelli tutti*, see the whole of the analysis presented in Chapter 1.

that is fundamental and all-encompassing, and in the end spiritual and theological.

In both *Laudato si'* and *Fratelli tutti* Francis writes in this mode to name a deep malaise or moral hopelessness and growing despair about our way of life, a faltering in real hopefulness about the human and ecological future. Francis writes: 'We fail to see the deepest roots of our present failures, which have to do with the direction, goals, meaning and social implications of technological and economic growth.'[15] The only root out of social hopelessness is to grasp these deep and pervasive roots and imagine an alternative, an alternative that begins in receptivity and service of the other. Here he echoes and develops the constant theme of the encyclicals from 1891 onwards: at the heart of our social malaise is a spiritual crisis that manifests itself in visible form in our everyday experience of work, love, trade and governance, and our wider relationships with the material world.

Laudato si' also warns against the dangers of responding to the current crisis by introducing or reinforcing a pseudo-spirituality of nature. This can be seen in the trend to respond to the mastery of nature narrative by proposing the idea of a natural world which should be reified as other, often ringfenced and protected from 'culture'. This does little, in fact, to address a dualism of nature–culture. It does not instate an integrated vision of the world as creation, nor does it integrate a social analysis that connects the option for the poorest with the option for the earth and can become part of same system of inequalities and exclusion that operates more widely within our social world. This is a point *Laudato si'* makes sharply in comments on 'green' projects that protect wild or green spaces but in ways that reinforce human inequalities and enable de facto privileged access. Francis lambasts eco projects which create a mere artifice of tranquillity and which reinforces the zoning of wealth and poverty, leaving 'disposable' human beings to reside and move in different spaces.[16]

Francis draws from Orthodox Patriarch Bartholomew to argue for a fundamental shift in world view, away from mere technical solutions and towards the 'ethical and spiritual roots of environmental problems, which require that we look for solutions not only in technology but in a change of humanity'.[17] Francis repeats Bartholomew's turn against a logic of scarcity

---

[15]Ibid., §109.
[16]*Laudato si'*, §45 and 49.
[17]Ibid., §9.

and austerity as the answer to the crisis and counter-proposal of a logic of love. This alternative ethic pivots the technocratic paradigm on its axis replacing 'consumption with sacrifice, greed with generosity, wastefulness with a spirit of sharing' and 'an asceticism which "entails learning to give, and not simply to give up"'. This is 'a way of loving, of moving gradually away from what I want to what God's world needs. It is liberation from fear, greed and compulsion'.[18] Such a mindset, Bartholomew argues, stems from a willingness to accept 'the world as a sacrament of communion, as a way of sharing with God and our neighbours on a global scale. It is our humble conviction that the divine and the human meet in the slightest detail in the seamless garment of God's creation, in the last speck of dust of our planet'.[19] *Laudato si'* proposes this vision of social communion be used to orientate Christian ecological thinking, providing its grounding and its telos. The notion of creation as a sacrament of communion is explored in *Laudato si'* and proposed as a constant dynamic process of communication and participation.

This understanding of social covenant and communion – about which Benedict XVI had written at length in *Caritas in veritate* – is to be interpreted in the context of a wider theological account of the good. In turn, this analysis produces, in *Caritas in veritate* and *Laudato si'*, a threefold theological-ecological vision of the communication of goods. In the first instance, the goodness of the Creator is communicated gratuitously through the whole of creation, instantiated in the originating act of *creation ex nihilo*. Creation is ontologically distinct from the Creator; is not itself divine, although it communicates as a sacrament or sign of the Creator. Second, the encyclicals emphasize the goodness of each thing in itself in relation to a purposeful reality. This remains a communicating, participating reality, each thing called to its purpose and perfection. Third, the encyclicals emphasize the divine intention that the created goods of the earth are given to meet the material and moral needs of all and should be communicated – circulated easily – through a community in order that these needs be adequately met. The events of the Incarnation, death and resurrection of Christ and the teachings of the New Testament are witness to the renewal and perfection of the original goodness of the divine intention. The Spirit is sent that this new proclamation of creation in the Kingdom in Christ be the

---

[18] Ibid
[19] Ibid.

fruitful work of love of every generation. Taken together, these principles of the communication of goods/goodness enable us to walk 'towards the fullness of freedom' to which God calls us.

We have encountered previously in our discussion of the common good the importance of an emphasis on the goodness (but not the divinity) of creation and the purposeful part living forms play within creation, straining towards its telos. The third teaching on the social communication of created goods within community is the basis for the CST principles of 'the universal destination of created goods' and 'the option for the poor'. Any talk of either social covenant or an ecological ethic without attention to these principles and practices is likely to fall away into vacuity and reinforce established ecological, including human ecological, inequities.

Without the underpinning theology of creation, the principle of the universal destination of goods can be difficult to place or make sense of. It is not a principle with an obvious liberal corollary. It is a principle which disrupts the liberal idea that societies begin simply with a conscious decision to form self-interested units or contracts, without a prior mutual obligation or inherent tie. The universal destination of goods is rooted in the idea of a social world brought into being by a transcendent Creator who bears a formal intention for humanity and the desire for humanity to form community and contract based on a prior divine–human covenant. Society is never merely a decision; it is the expression of a prior activity and intent. This means asking a question of purpose as part of the question of ownership and use of material goods. The teaching on the universal destination of goods begins, therefore, with otherness, with a non-human intentionality, form and order, to be discerned and worked with, renewed and struggled for, in time and place. This teaching may come to share certain characteristics with a range of liberal-era philosophies, but it remains distinguishable (and contestable, of course) in this important and defining regard.

It does not help that many summaries of this principle fail to begin with a theology of creation and begin instead by addressing the question of a defence of private property rights and then move on to establish some wider universal social duties having established a prior limited right to private ownership. The phantom in the room is fear of collectivist ideologies and a wish to distinguish CST from them. The danger is that this phantom comes to skew the properly theological basis of this teaching and limits our perceptions of the breadth of its implications. Certainly, this principle includes discussion of the question of property, but this is not its central or sole concern or application nor its foundation. The principle of the universal destination of goods is the grounds for thinking about human rights and obligations, an ecological ethic, and might have much to offer to addressing rising questions of adequate post-colonial responses.

The 2004 *Compendium* begins, as we have done here, by rooting the universal destination of goods in a theology of creation. It deploys Aquinas' teaching that in goodness, and from nothing, God creates the material world to communicate the truth of the divine nature, and as part of this same logic, to meet the needs for sustenance and growth in perfection of all creatures and living forms. The material goods of the world have a 'needs meeting character'.[20] To frustrate access to the material (and in the case of humans, also, moral) goods required for development and flourishing is therefore to deny the divine intention in the act of creation – which is, as we have noted, always a present-tense activity – for fullness of being or existence for creaturely life. It notes, '[g]oods, even when legitimately owned, have a universal destination' and continues 'any type of improper accumulation is immoral, because it openly contradicts the universal destination assigned to all goods by the Creator. Christian salvation is an integral liberation . . . which means being freed not only from need but also in respect to possessions'.[21] The text draws on patristic teachings on the necessary 'flow' of goods like a river or a renewing fountain circulating through the community. The greater the frequency with which water is drawn and used, the fresher the fountain for all. In this way, the *Compendium* stresses that all forms of exchange, ownership and economic activity are intrinsically moral matters. The goods of the earth, once a divine intention in creation is understood, are already imbued with a moral meaning; we do not write upon the goods we own, trade, exchange as if on a moral tabula rasa.

In *Laudato si'* Pope Francis connects the universal destination of goods explicitly to his vision of an integral ecology, which embraces the economy and environment in a single ethic. He reiterates that the earth is a shared inheritance, its fruits are meant to benefit all; and that in a world where this is manifestly not the case, a commitment to moving *towards* the universal destination of goods, as a destination to reach not merely a point of origin but of restitution, must begin with the option for the poor. It is significant

---

[20]Daniel Finn, *Christian Economic Ethics: History and Implications* (Minneapolis: Fortress Press, 2013), p. 193.
[21]*Compendium*, §328, p. 167.

that the universal destination of goods is both a divine intention and a reality that in a fallen and unjust world we are required to work towards. This implies an ethic of present and future action that draws history into itself and carries history responsibly into its future.

In his social encyclicals Francis returns to the century-long CST concern with the right to, and limits to the right to, private property. He repeats the themes of Leo XIII, noting that private property is a subordinate right and that all ownership of private property carries a social mortgage. Private property, whilst conceivably a form of just ownership, establishes the terms of its justice in relation to a wider social reality. It is not just on the terms of mere possession. Whilst the right to private property was a central theme in *Rerum novarum*, asserted in the context of a rebuttal of socialism, discussion has continued as to the exact theological formulation of this defence. *Rerum novarum* had taught that property could be privately owned, enabling personal development (the expression of personality), stability of life and a stewardship for the common good. As scholars of CST have long noted, this teaching appears to be a fusion of Thomism and the liberal theory of property rights articulated by John Locke in his *Two Treatises of Government*. This fusion, likely to have been the work of the nineteenth-century Jesuit and moral theologian Luigi Taparelli, brings together Locke's defence of personal rights against government and the Thomist tradition of a limited right to property. As Thomas Shannon points out, Aquinas' defence of property was largely a defence of property as an expedient social convention but not an unassailable natural right. It is a matter of human law, to be reasoned and agreed by each generation, according to the common good and the meeting of the needs of each. It is a natural right, however, that each person has access to the goods necessary for their own survival. This is divine providence made material in the abundant goods of the earth. Where Locke's influence can be felt is in *Rerum novarum*'s proposal that the human person in some way owns what they have worked for or what they have cultivated. Locke had taught that the first possession of the person was themselves: we own ourselves. This is the basis of both freedom and possession. It is curious that a papacy committed to reinventing Thomism and defending against the anthropology of liberalism should adopt, even indirectly, elements of a philosophy of self-possession as the basis of a new teaching on private property. This remains, arguably, a thread in the CST tradition that requires some attention and possible development through a retrieval of a more thoroughly Catholic anthropology. The slight distance that *Laudato si'* and

Fratelli tutti establish from this tradition, without any direct repudiation of it, is notable in this regard.

In a similar vein, and returning to a more thorough Thomist account of collective goods and the life of the commons, *Laudato si'* teaches that the natural environment is to be recognized as a collective good, intended for the benefit of all. It is the patrimony of all and also the responsibility of everyone. Finally, Francis concludes his section on the universal destination of goods in *Laudato si'* by noting that unbalanced overconsumption is not mere greed but the denial of existence to others, present and future.

It is in this context that questions of work, distributive justice and private property have been considered by the long CST tradition. Each is treated as part of this vision of the communication or flow of goods, the purposeful nature of human activity and the implications of both for our participation in a wider common good. What is proposed is a holistic vision in which, as Anglican theologian John Hughes noted, we are called to order production, exchange and consumption towards nothing less than holiness.[22]

An integral ecology of work

In *Laudato si'* Francis is clear that his vision of an integral ecology includes the questions of labour and work.[23] He draws on the tradition of reflection, most especially *Rerum novarum* and John Paul II's *Laborem exercens*. The central focus of *Rerum novarum* was the condition of work in an increasingly industrial age. Leo XIII taught that we are created with a vocation to work. Work, even when based on fair wages, is never a mere transactional arrangement; it is a context for becoming moral selves. It is a reciprocal exchange, through which we both become ourselves and learn to encounter what is not ourselves. This is why the monastic tradition insisted on physical labour as important to the contemplative life. The monastic orders taught that personal growth, as Francis notes, came from 'the interplay of recollection and work'. Work, *Laudato si'* notes, is a context for 'creativity, planning for the future, developing our talents, living out our values, relating to others and giving glory to God'.[24]

---

[22]Hughes, *The End of Work*, p. 229.
[23]*Laudato si'*, §124–9.
[24]Ibid., §127.

Laborem exercens, John Paul II's great tribute to *Rerum novarum*, extended rather than simply repeated Leo XIII's themes. John Paul delved more deeply into the ideas present in *Rerum novarum*: that work is made for the human person and not the human person for work, and that labour always has a value and priority over capital. As John Hughes notes, John Paul II suggests that labour has a threefold purpose: that we are able to be self-sustaining, that labour enables social transformation through new forms of production and that labour enables the transforming of self and society through cultural production. John Paul II is interested in both the 'objective conditions' of work – the changing conditions, technologies and patterns of work that shape production and the 'subjective dimension' to work: what work comes to mean to us, how it shapes our sense of being human in the world.

John Paul II laid greater emphasis than Leo XIII had done on the cultural value of work and the subjective meaning of work – what we might call the 'worlding' qualities of work. The subjective dimension to work – our experience of work as human beings – matters more than any consideration of mere utility. Humans are never, in the context of work, mere instruments or simply utile. In this sense, it is also true that work itself – because it always contains this subjective dimension – is never mere utility. It is always the shaping of people, for good or for ill, and it is the shaping of a cultural world. The question is simply *how* it is doing this and the extent to which we wish to reproduce or renew, or even resist and overthrow, this production. This writing has some affinity with Joseph Pieper's post-war writing on leisure as the goal of work and his call for a resistance to both a culture of mere utility in work and its corollary, a culture of total work which he saw as increasingly the logic of late modern capitalism. John Paul II continues to walk the fine line of seeking to uphold a high view of the value and meaning of human work whilst also wishing to resist any instrumentalization of the worker or any total work culture.

John Paul II viewed work as 'the essential key, to the whole social question'.[25] Francis has developed this theme in his work on social dialogue: work is the key to how we become involved in a meaningful social dialogue. The absence of work is therefore not merely an affront to dignity and self-determination as well as creativity but also frustrates real social dialogue and exchange. It is through work that solidarity becomes a

---

[25]*Laborem exercens*, §3.

meaningful reality for us, and it forms a (not the only) basis for new social movements which bring renewal to the wider social body. John Paul II clearly has in mind at this point the example of Polish workers and the Solidarność movement.

John Paul II is careful to note that participation and co-creation is the correct Catholic theological framework for thinking about work.[26] Nonetheless, this should not be understood as implying either a divinization of human activity or a claim that God is the original Creator but that we somehow pick up the tools and complete the task, subduing and cultivating the earth by divine fiat as we go. Our labours are not held within a progressivist history of gradual human mastery and cultivation of the earth.[27] They are labour held within the architecture of the action of God, whose creating action is different in kind from our own human creative activity. God's activity remains a permanent sustaining activity, making possible every present and future temporal moment. In work, we seek to achieve ourselves, in material and moral terms, and to form worlds with others. In labouring at these goods, we work in participatory way within the flow of a constant divine creating action. Francis returns to these themes in *Laudato si'*, exploring the value of labour insofar as it develops the world as a form of care and a participation in bringing about the potential of the world, inscribed in it through its creation (Sir 38:34). The underlying question of work is framed as a question of the relationship of humans to things other than themselves, as well as being about the development of the self. It is what ties these two things together in a relation.

Lest this begin to sound too rosy a presentation of work compared to many of our daily experiences, John Paul reminds us that in Genesis work is both a true good, part of the original intention of God for humanity in Eden, and a curse when it becomes not merely blessing but necessity following the Fall of Adam. Work is both a blessed labour and a necessary toil. The struggle for work to be creative, productive and generative is what leads to the more 'negative' teaching of the encyclicals: the necessary elements that enable us to resist work gone awry. Workers need social

---

[26]Ibid., §24–5.
[27]Reading *Laborem exercens* with the benefit of forty years of passing time, the text does appear jarringly heavy on the language of work as mastery and domination, and with the benefit of the insights drawn from ecological theologies, this might be significantly revised in a new encyclical on work.

movements and cooperatives. Good societies need good unions, as Francis notes summarizing Leo XIII. Work cultures also need to support enterprise and initiative. The availability of decent, purposeful work and the fair remuneration of that work through living wages are constant CST document themes, as we noted at the outset of this book. Gifts and goods of different kinds, material and moral, are what is exchanged at every level in the human experience of work. Remaining attentive to this logic of the exchange of gift and value humanizes work.

Caritas in veritate discusses in some detail a wider theory of economic exchange that might emerge from a theology of gift and communion. Drawing on the work of the civil economy thinkers Stefano Zamagni and Luigino Bruni, *Caritas in veritate* seeks to reject the framing architecture of neoclassical economics, seeking instead to ground all economic exchange in the logic of the gift and the threefold understanding of justice as commutative, distributive and social or contributive. *Caritas in veritate* challenges the basic view of the human person that it believes lies at the heart of neoclassical economics. The portrayal of *homo economicus* is insufficiently relational, vulnerable and solidaristic to be true to human experience, insufficiently attentive to what I have noted earlier as the 'worlding' qualities of work, labour and economic exchange. Benedict writes:

> The Church's social doctrine holds that authentically human social relationships of friendship, solidarity and reciprocity can also be conducted within economic activity, and not only outside it or 'after' it. The economic sphere is neither ethically neutral, nor inherently inhuman and opposed to society. It is part and parcel of human activity and precisely because it is human, it must be structured and governed in an ethical manner.[28]

In truth we cannot *but* take our vulnerable, relational, moral selves to work (even if there are appropriate boundaries set for healthy workplace practices), and it takes practice to actively separate these facets of ourselves and maintain an alternative conception of economic selfhood in the context of our interpersonal sense of ourselves. The myth that *homo economicus* seeks autonomous self-realization merely through trade in forms of self-

---

[28]*Caritas in veritate*, §36.

interest is structured into the meta-account of an autonomous economic system. Such an understanding of the market or the economic individual tends, in a self-harming fashion, to erode the very basis of all economic exchanges: trust. Benedict notes: '[w]ithout internal forms of solidarity and mutual trust, the market cannot completely fulfil its proper economic function.'[29]

Rejecting the commodification of life, narrow understandings of value in economic exchanges and profit as a singular end in itself (profit is not bad, but it is not a single end in itself aside from wider questions of labour and value), Benedict XVI proposes instead an 'economy of communion'. Such an economy sees just exchanges at every stage of market and non-market transactions as both possible and necessary. Civil economy thinkers suggest that we broaden our understanding of the 'goods' of the market beyond a narrow view of public and private goods, to include the relational goods that tend to be the goods that attach most closely to personal and social well-being, and yet are least theorized as part of economic exchange. Although *Caritas in veritate* does not make this connection formally, the conclusion one might draw from its discussion of neglected relational goods is that our economic models might learn to take better account of fostering the development of the moral goods upon which its activity, and the wider human good, is predicated. Drawing on Zamagni and Bruni's work, Benedict writes:

> The Church's social doctrine has always maintained that *justice must be applied to every phase of economic activity*, because this is always concerned with man and his needs. Locating resources, financing, production, consumption and all the other phases in the economic cycle inevitably have moral implications. *Thus every economic decision has a moral consequence.* The social sciences and the direction taken by the contemporary economy point to the same conclusion. Perhaps at one time it was conceivable that first the creation of wealth could be entrusted to the economy, and then the task of distributing it could be assigned to politics. Today that would be more difficult, given that economic activity is no longer circumscribed within territorial limits, while the authority of governments continues to be principally local. Hence the canons of

---

[29]Ibid., §35 (italics are retained from the original text).

justice must be respected from the outset, as the economic process unfolds, and not just afterwards or incidentally.[30]

However, Benedict is at pains to stress that the social teaching of the Church is not merely concerned with hard-wiring the threefold Thomistic understanding of justice into every stage of economic exchange but wishes to change the fundamental imaginative moorings that hold such exchanges in place.[31] It is the social imagination that must first shift if a sustainable approach to a more just economy is to emerge. Once again, this is a crisis of desire not just of dialogue and achievement. A Christian theology of economy begins with a vision of gift and gratuity. The first transaction that makes all other transactions possible is a relational and intimate one of covenant, not contract; all sustainable contracts sit within a prior logic of covenant: life itself is a super-abundant act of self-giving from the Father to creation, a donation of being. This super-abundance of life itself is always a giving beyond what is merely due, for God owed us nothing. Thus, caritas is the first logic, the first exchange, that begins the chain of all other exchange, and its trace should remain. It is this that sustains the giving and receiving of what is due: justice.

One of the criticisms levelled at *Caritas in veritate* is that it remained too individualistic in its theology, despite its core vision of relationality and communion. Somehow, it fails in some key aspects to follow through on its own heartfelt vision. Leonardo Boff, a leading first-generation liberation theologian, lamented the lack of attention to the structural dynamics of the market, to overconsumption and to the basic models of ownership and production. Interestingly, this became a major focus for *Laudato si'*, which addressed precisely these dynamics whilst also incorporating the economy of communion model from Benedict's earlier document.

---

[30] Ibid., §37.

[31] As an aside, along the same lines, but in his own inimical parabolic style, Pope Francis is reported to have addressed a gathering of economists, financiers and bankers in Rome using the following informal words: 'Our meal will be accompanied by wine. Now, wine is many things. It has a bouquet, colour and richness of taste that all complement the food. It has alcohol that can enliven the mind. Wine enriches all our senses. At the end of our feast, we will have grappa. Grappa is one thing: alcohol. Grappa is wine distilled. [He continued] Humanity is many things – passionate, curious, rational, altruistic, creative, self-interested. But the market is one thing: self-interest. The market is humanity distilled. . . . Your job is to turn the grappa back into wine, to turn the market back into humanity.' This is taken from Mark Carney, former Governor of the Bank of England's report of the conversation in *The Guardian* newspaper in March 2021.

A postscript on integral ecology: Race, place and the desire for communion?

Vincent Miller argues that integral ecology is, for Francis, the ultimate expression and development of the virtue and principle of solidarity.[32] If this is so, there remains a further dimension to the vision of integral ecology that has yet to be explored more fully within the official CST tradition. This concerns the experience and history of race. There is good – and troubling – reason to think that there are deep connections between the history of racism and the ways that we have thought about land, creation and community. The vision of integral ecology offered in *Laudato si'* and *Fratelli tutti* seems to beg, but not to offer, a fuller account of racial solidarity, justice and the call to a truly universal communion. It is not difficult to imagine how this might be developed in line with the foundations already laid: a covenantal understanding of the common good and our common life, a non-possessive model of social exchange and a commitment to (intergenerational) justice in its threefold form.

In work that fascinatingly parallels the logic of covenant and communion that the social encyclicals advocate, the North American Baptist biblical theologian Willie James Jennings connects the ways we have thought about land and place to the ways we have thought about race.[33] He sees a common Christian architecture of thought that has shaped Western and Northern Hemisphere thinking about bodies and land. This architecture is found in the interconnected ways that we have thought about freedom, possession, value, use and worth. Just as we began to think about land as utility, inert matter for cultivation, possession and mastery, so we extended this same logic of ownership and cultivation to the bodies that occupied those colonialized lands. Of particular concern for advocates of CST should be Jennings' analysis of the interconnected histories of thinking about race, land and private property. He is notably critical of the adoption of Lockean assumptions into Christian social theologies, whether Protestant, Reformed or Catholic. He notes that Locke's theory of private property privileges a logic of ownership which begins with the idea that the first

---

[32]Miller, 'Integral Ecology', pp. 11–28.
[33]This work is part of a draft monograph as yet unpublished, but an online presentation of these ideas can be found at https://www.youtube.com/watch?v=SGMXeE6p-tQ (accessed 1 April 2021).

property we possess is ourselves. This is a logic in which freedom is defined in terms of self-possession, 'to claim oneself, was to possess oneself'. This logic of possession is extended outwards to all that can be cultivated. In this tradition, possession of land, of other people and ourselves, has been deeply connected. These connections have formed the ways we have thought about productivity, use, value, voice and worth. Locke is not alone in being responsible for such a logic, of course, but Jennings' notes how powerful the idea has been that we shape freedom inside ideas of possession. He also notes that Christian biblical interpretation has often been used to justify such practice.

This legacy has had a long and pernicious history inside and outside of Christian theology, and ought to be addressed as part of any genuinely integral ecological ethic. As Pope Francis argues, so Jennings notes: everything is connected, and an integral ecology relates always to the question of the common good. We have lived with a legacy of the racialized body which has been the burden of Black and brown communities and has been toxic for those who 'benefitted' from it. Jennings suggests that an understanding of being a covenantal community of the commons offers a way forward. By contrast, Jennings' notes, a logic of covenant speaks of possession framed inside the freedom for relationship. A covenantal modality imagines already a world of reciprocal exchanges and speech acts, exactly as *Caritas in veritate* and *Laudato si'* had spelled out. However, neither encyclical makes the connections with questions of race, in either critical or constructive mode. Jennings' work is suggestive not only of the ways that CST might address the historical usage of its own ideas in a way that is able to think race and ecology together, as part of a search now for a truly integral ecology, but it also suggests a necessary reconsideration and rearticulation of much CST discussion of private property. The task of CST thinking about private property in the context of the universal destination of goods is not merely to indicate limits to, or rights to, property, its procurement and use but is suggestive that we need to think again about the basic theological foundations to the very notions of possession and freedom that structure such thought.

Jennings argues that rejecting a logic of possession as the first form of freedom begins with a revised theology of creation. It begins with naming nature as creation and accepting that our relationship with land and other living forms is morally charged, it has a claim on us. This is, as the CST tradition makes clear and in Jennings' words, a communicating reality: 'It speaks of the possibility that the world speaks to you . . . it reimagines the commons as a space of reciprocity with animals, plants and seasons.'³⁴ Our patterns of ownership and possession are never separate from this question of the created world, they are integral questions both in point of historical fact and in the way we might now imagine a world fit for co-habitation. Jennings is clear: this covenantal option is sustained by God, ever renewed as a possibility we might adopt as our social vision, and it is the work of the Spirit in history to draw all things towards awareness of this interconnectedness and towards communion. The work that Jennings points to is, by and large, work that remains to be done by advocates of CST. An integral ecology that includes a proper Catholic theological handling of race as part of its account is a task that lies in front of us.

---

[34] Ibid. See link in previous footnote to view Jennings' presentation.

CONCLUSION
TOWARDS A POLITICS OF COMMUNION
BETWEEN TIME AND ETERNITY

Communion has to integrate persons in their true identities, as bodily beings who establish their identities in their histories, in which contingency has a place. In this way, the central concept which makes sense of the whole is communion, or love, defining both the nature of God, and our relation to him.[1]

In his interpretation of the Good Samaritan, Catholic priest and radical writer Ivan Illich challenges what he believes to be a problematic trope in modern interpretation of Luke's parable.[2] He argues that, following the trajectory of modernity, modern interpretation has tended to flatten the passage, rendering it somewhere close to an abstract moral lesson in the general duties we bear to a generalized mass of fellow human beings: the passage is rendered as a lesson in moral and social cosmopolitanism or universal humanitarianism. To be clear, in what follows Illich is not against the idea that we should treat all humans as our neighbours and accept responsibility for a wounded other; nor is he anti-cosmopolitan. However, he describes many readings of Luke's story as tending to see the world in terms of space rather than time and therefore missing an unsettling but life-giving dimension of this story. Illich argues that the core problem of spatial 'everyman' readings of the Good Samaritan is that they, like modern ethics more generally, pull us in the direction of anonymizing and abstracting our ethics from the interrupting 'thisness' and contingency of our real lives. In the draw to construct general rules such interpretation underplays how God tends to work in our lives. Our capacity to be stopped in our tracks, to

---

[1] Charles Taylor, *A Secular Age* (Cambridge: Harvard University Press, 2007), p. 279.
[2] Ivan Illich, *The Rivers North of the Future: The Testament of Ivan Illich as Told to David Cayley*, ed. David Cayley (Toronto: Anansi Press, 2005). For David Cayley's further brilliant exposition of Illich's work, see https://www.davidcayley.com/blog/2015/10/22/christ-and-anti-christ-in-the-thought-of-ivan-illich. For Charles Taylor's extended discussion, see *A Secular Age*, pp. 737–44.

change direction, to be confronted with grace which comes in unexpectedly interrupting, and often embodied, forms to us is an utterly temporal and particular experience. These are the ways that the kingdom becomes woven into our own lives and we part of its unfolding history.

Illich proposes a Christian reading of the Good Samaritan that takes account of what Jesus is telling us about the interrupting specificity of the encounter between *these* particular people, on *this* particular dangerous road (this 'bloody road' as St Jerome says), and why this becomes an *event* of neighbourliness not merely a lesson either in Christ saving us, generally speaking, or in needing to be a neighbour to all. The man lying wounded by the roadside is a 'tiß' (tis) person – a certain person of uncertain identity. The doctrine which makes sense of this ultimately mysterious encounter between this certain–uncertain man and this certain Samaritan is, for Illich, the Incarnation. The fact that Word become flesh is the rupture which changes the conditions under which love is possible. It explodes our moral horizon, challenging us to live lives of the flesh in a radically different, more truly temporal and embodied fashion. Charles Taylor summarizes Illich's take on the Good Samaritan brilliantly thus:

> For Illich this story represents the possibility of mutual belonging between two strangers. Jesus points to a new kind of fittingness, belonging together, between the Samaritan and the wounded man. They are fitted together in a proportionality which comes from God, which is that of agape, and which became possible because God became flesh. The enfleshment of God extends outward, through such new links as the Samaritan makes with the Jew, into a network we call the Church.[3]

To be fitted together in a proportionality which comes from God is, aside from anything else, a rather lovely theological turn of phrase and image. Illich interprets the story as a dynamic action of event that flows into event: it is the prior action of the Father in Christ and in the Spirit, the sending forth into the world that is the basis of the new scandalous fittingness between a despised man and a wounded man stripped of all identity, a man who does not speak at all, even to ask for help or to express thanks. The

---

[3]Charles Taylor, 'Foreword', in *The Rivers North of the Future: The Testament of Ivan Illich*, ed. David Cayley (Toronto: Anansi Press, 2005), xi.

Conclusion

action of Christ in taking flesh, dying as his flesh is tortured and wounded and rising in the flesh for all who shall be born and die takes on new flesh in the intimate exchange that takes place between the wounded man and the Samaritan. Flesh calls to flesh, because of the dignity it holds in an economy of love and mercy.

What makes this exchange possible, what moves the Samaritan to interrupt his journey and turn his attention to the man, is not reason or nature alone. It did not seem reasonable to the two who passed by first. Luke says that it is compassion or mercy (*splagchnizomai*), stirring in the very guts of the Samaritan, that stops him in his tracks and changes his plans. The specific word used to describe the compassionate process that occurs in the Good Samaritan is one that is used only a handful of times in the Synoptic Gospels and is usually reserved for the way in which Jesus himself is moved before performing a miracle. It is also used of the father as he faces the sight of the returning prodigal son and opens his arms to him, setting a feast. Interestingly, it is a word written in the middle voice – somewhere between a passive and active voice, for which we do not have a direct English equivalent.

In drawing attention to the Incarnation as the framing event which gives meaning to the encounter between the two men, Illich's reading can be seen in the long tradition of combined allegorical and moral readings of this passage. Allegorical readings of the Good Samaritan, notably those offered by Irenaeus, Origen, Clement of Alexandria, Augustine and Aquinas, tend to focus on uncovering the hidden Christ disclosed at the heart of the story. According to the allegorical tradition – and its plural interpretations – Jerusalem is the heavenly condition, Jericho the worldly sinful condition; the wounded man lying naked by the side of the road, humanity; the Good Samaritan, Christ; the inn, the Church; the innkeeper, St Paul or the Holy Spirit; the two coins, the old and new covenants or the Father and the Son, and so forth. Nonetheless, these allegorical readings – Augustine in particular – did often tend towards the same moral universalism as we find in more contemporary interpretations. This turn is not, as perhaps Illich seems to imagine at points, a modern invention. Karl Barth chastises for precisely this.[4]

The allegorical-moral reading offered by Illich stresses that in Christ we belong together and are capable of being moved by recognition of this co-belonging and mutual responsibility, by that prior act of grace and

---

[4] See Karl Barth, *Church Dogmatics 1/2* III (London: Bloomsbury, 2010), §18 pp. 418–19.

self-giving, through Christ in the Spirit, as an active principle enfleshed in the world. This prior self-giving at work in the relation of the wounded man to the Samaritan is, we have to assume, a giving present already in both men. This implies, incidentally, that something other than mere suffering victimhood might be the basis of what is evoked in the unspoken exchange between the wounded man and the Samaritan; that this is not an ethics of the heroic Christian (Samaritan) doer and the (Jewish) done-to. If Christ is seen to be at work as the saving principle in the whole story then the framing question – who is my neighbour? – might lead to a response that sees *both* the Samaritan *and* the wounded man, already held within an economy of grace, and neighbour to each other. It is a divine creating in which they cooperate, a divine creating in the present tense. In this sense, the neighbourliness in the passage is not necessarily singular: Christ is neighbour to us in drawing close to us in cradle, cross and resurrection; he is neighbour to the Samaritan in the graced movement of compassion born in that moment in him, the wounded man is the event and occasion of the evocation of a new possible recognition and belonging between the two men, the Samaritan is neighbour to the wounded man in the aid he is able to bring. These are perhaps the dimensions of proportionality that Illich refers to between the actors in the parable: the reciprocal dimensions of a non-symmetrical economy of neighbourliness.

As Karl Barth notes in his critique of some ethical readings of Luke's parable, there is an ever-present danger that Christians use this passage to turn the neighbour into the law: seeing in the wounded man a dualism of need and obligation. This leaves the 'thingness' that the naked man is reduced to intact, despite assistance. Barth is adamant that is not good theology; it evades the Gospel and the grace mediated by the Christic event. The neighbour is a sacrament of grace. Barth sees the neighbour as always particular and as my benefactor. In this sense, the embodied encounter with the person who becomes neighbour is both an entirely temporal event and an eternal one. It is a temporal and eternal mercy which passes as rupturing event between the two men. The Samaritan is able to act in a timely way, to be within time, accepting the fullness of timely responsibility and blessing, because of the eternal reality that grounds him. Eternity enables an openness to time and to person. In this sense my neighbour is difficult blessing and me to him, and not, despite my intended kindness, task or law. In openness to this event, the neighbour is recognized as, and becomes in reality, sister or brother; a fellowship which was always possible and called out for, but not guaranteed or inevitable, takes flesh and form. In this sense, Illich's interpretation is suggestive of a simultaneity in allegorical and moral readings.

Illich's account is further marked by the relationship he supposes between acts of solidarity and care and the formation of the body of the Church. Illich implies that Christian living is above all else an extension of enfleshment in Christ that forms a new pattern of mutual belonging. In its concrete form, this community of extended belonging is the Church and is therefore a visible, tangible entity with borders and a physical and limited existence. It is, however, a bordered community without fixed parameters and with uncertain membership: its borders are open to an embodied extension without limit in history, and its members are to be found in unexpected places. Unlike the nation state, or the business corporation, the Church's proportionality, as Illich says, is not determined by its own members, and its politics of membership echo this truth. Barth echoes this in his own reading of the Good Samaritan. Christ is present to the Church through the neighbour. As Eric Gregory, commenting on Barth's writing notes, the neighbour is summoned with us to fellowship with God. This interpretation only makes sense, as Gregory notes, if you take seriously the idea of divine mercy, love and compassion. The Eucharist is the core enactment of this in time, but the wider work of the Spirit in time gathers and draws towards this fellowship. Communion is a multi-layered process of the formation of, and sharing in, the body of Christ.

Illich's wider work is rooted in a Christian critique of modernity. The age we live in – modernity – is for Illich neither a natural partner for Christianity nor its antithesis. Rather it is best seen as a viral mutation of Christianity. Modernity takes the core of a Christian world view but renders it without true transcendence. It removes its mystical core. In doing so, it removes its source of mediation, otherness, accountability and true co-belonging. Without this transcendence we risk simultaneously collapsing inwards into nothing more than our fragile and shifting sense of our own identities and abstracting our ethics into rules and codes, such that we vacate the very bodies and timely existences that mark the true possibilities, the gravity and grace, of our fragile, mortal lives. Nonetheless, to take time seriously is to take our identities, relationships and the very contingency of our lives seriously as the place of unstable encounter with the eternal stability of God.

If Illich and Barth are guilty of a limitation in their own interpretations of the Good Samaritan passage, it is perhaps that they are insufficiently Trinitarian in their exploration: Christ is rendered the rupturing but stable presence, yet the pneumatological instability of all our lives is underplayed. The Father and Son in the Spirit enable what seems impossible, dangerous and irrational to become real. It is a pneumatological encounter with the Spirit that holds the instability of the event in its temporal and eternal relation. In this way Illich is right: what Christianity renders is not a new general code, or a better set of rules, but rather the revelation of an action in time that we are called to become a living part of. Against a logic of doing *to* or *for* others, of technique, mastery or self-possession, even communal self-possession, we are offered a different language of freedom: a communion established through receptivity, participation and reciprocal exchange. It is a recognition of our embeddedness, not indebtedness, that is the logic of such freedom. In such a way, the bare fact of life becomes a fraternal relation, held within a community of extended fellowship. The Church is the Church when it is a witness to, and a means of bringing about, this life of freedom, this saving unity. It is the enfleshed continuation of the action of Christ in the world, but it is not necessarily the only context in which that continuation is at work.

There is no particular reason to think that Pope Francis has read Ivan Illich. Nonetheless, he too picks up similar themes of temporality and enfleshment in his social teaching. In *Evangelii gaudium* Francis notes, drawing from Michel de Certeau, that for the Christian time is greater than space. Modernity tends to pull us towards spatial rather than temporal ways of thinking – occupying, filling, colonizing space. He is not proposing a binary logic of space bad, time good. Rather, Francis uses this claim to re-root the human beings of modernity – products of our own times as we inevitably are – in slow patient processes of engagement: contingent, risky, unstable, without guarantee. Dialogue, gift exchange, attentive listening, a disposition of humility and a belief in the grace of the Spirit to underpin all these are our only guarantees. This is how a dual process of conservation and transformation happens. And its core is both mystical and political. Francis too uses the Good Samaritan passage as the core of his reflection on human fraternity and communion in *Fratelli tutti*. He concludes his exegesis of co-belonging with a call to recognize that what Jesus does in the telling of the Good Samaritan story is to reframe the question from a rules or codes question – who is (and is not?) my neighbour? – to a dynamic one of everyday temporal becoming. Without fixed parameters the Christian is called to a properly temporal process of becoming a neighbour more fully and more truly through the development of a radical attention to the world, to what and who *is* in the world. This process of becoming is possible only by a practice of embodied attention to the person encountered and to the fostering of the networks of care and belonging that sustain such action.

Francis notes that his interpretation owes a debt to Martin Luther King Jr. In a series of sermons on the Good Samaritan, King too focuses on the radical call to interruption and to a logic of co-belonging. That co-belonging relates to the timely question: What will happen if I do not stop? This is love's question. However, King also reflects on the dynamics of justice that build towards communion: the logic of possession, freedom and ownership implied in the passage. He notes that the logic of the robbers is: what is yours is mine. It is an age-old logic of domination and mastery and acquisition. The logic of the world, embodied in those who pass by is: what is mine is mine, what is yours is yours: freedom as non-interference. The logic of hope, love, faith and justice is that of the Good Samaritan: what is mine is yours, for the good of us both and for the world. This is the free act that fosters communion. For King, freedom is shaped by a capacity to imagine the universal destination of goods as part of the life of caritas.

Illich, Pope Francis, Barth and King's exegeses find an interesting echo in Simone Weil's interpretation of this same passage.[5] Weil shares with our prior interpreters a supernatural reading of the 'ethics' of the Good Samaritan. Drawing on the wider themes of her work – attention, affliction, decreation – Weil argues that the parable is a 'temporal event of affirmation'. Any true event of human affirmation is supernatural in nature – it is akin to a moment of genius, or the miraculous. By our own nature we find turning deep attention to another person extremely difficult and demanding. We may think we are good at this, but in fact if we are honest, it is extremely difficult to achieve and sustain. It is also equally difficult for the person who is afflicted to believe and trust in the quality of attention offered by the stranger or neighbour. Each has reason to recoil from the other, and each feels their own shame as they do so. For each to overcome this difficulty requires something supernatural. This supernatural event is God in us. She writes: 'It is God in us who loves when we are afflicted, it is God in us who

---

[5]Simone Weil, 'How to Love Your Neighbour: A Reflection on the Good Samaritan on the Jericho Road', an extract from *Love in the Void: Where God Finds Us*, ed. Laurie Gagne (New York: Plough, 2008). Extract available online https://www.plough.com/en/topics/community/service/how-to-love-your-neighbor (accessed 1 July 2020).

loves those who wish us well.'[6] She is excoriating, however, of those who she thinks pervert this logic to say that in loving my neighbour I am merely loving God. The miracle is that through God loving in me, and in my neighbour, I am able to truly love this person. It is much harder to do that than to love God. This is the real miracle: that the Samaritan is moved with compassion *for this man* and that *this man may receive this act*, whether with gratitude or not. We do not in fact know that the wounded man is grateful or expresses gratitude.

This is Weil's take on the fitting together in Christ that Illich speaks of, the new proportionality. What Weil offers is an account of the sheer difficulty and beauty of this. Pope Francis seems to echo this sentiment when – more evident in the Spanish translation of *Fratelli tutti* – he speaks of the *struggle* for communion. Weil suggests, finally, that the helpful way to think about the grounds of the supernatural act of neighbour love is to return to the doctrine of *creation ex nihilo*: it is only God who can think that which did or does not exist and by thought bring it into being. This is the sustaining moment-by-moment continual creation of the world, in the present tense, that holds all that is in being, including the potential of a future I cannot yet see and yet might yearn for. My openness to participation in this is crucial. Weil is unsparingly severe in her view of the challenge of this process and suggests: turning my attention to the person that has been rendered a thing, or to a future that seems impossible, requires a creative attention that does not extend my own power but seeks to give existence to something outside of myself. It is a creative act of renunciation of the promise of power or mastery. And yet it gives expression to the height of freedom: '[w]hatever a man may want, in cases of crime as in those of the highest virtue, in the minutest preoccupations as in the greatest designs, the essence of his desire always consists in this, that he wants above all things to be able to exercise his will freely.'[7] This freedom of willing is grounded in a divine giving that is renewed temporally and eternally.

The rupturing gift of Christian faith to the world is rooted in this vision of communion. It becomes possible only with communities that sustain this vision as a constant, timely practice. It cannot be reduced to

---

[6]Ibid. (extract without page numbers), https://www.plough.com/en/topics/community/service/how-to-love-your-neighbor (accessed 1 July 2020).
[7]Ibid. Online extract (without page numbers), https://www.plough.com/en/topics/community/service/how-to-love-your-neighbor (accessed 1 July 2020).

Conclusion

principles, rendered as abstracted general rules for living or turned into blueprint solutions. It would be much easier if it could, but it cannot. And it is reliant upon a transcendent account of mercy and compassion. Its path is demanding and risky, but also potentially beautiful. It is from contingency, limit and the desire for the life of communion that CST itself is born in the modern era. It was born out of the suppression of the religious in modernity and comes to define itself in some ways against a constantly unstable 'other', although this 'other' is partly also of its own construction. But in this contingency, and with all its limitations, CST seeks to a fullness of life that it does not believe is adequately contained in any of the other philosophies or political theories of our age.

In our own context, this tradition of teaching offers to us, in a relatively impoverished intellectual landscape, a vision of the good life, a vision of the unity and plurality of humankind, a call for a new relationship to the natural world and an acceptance of the limits of growth. It roots this vision not in austerity of imagination but in a plenitude found only in what might happen – and is already being renewed – between us, in the possibilities of creativity in time. Nothing is arbitrary, and when we feel that it is, it is because we are wounded. In an age of cynicism and post-truth the Church's social teaching calls us to venture again into the space of imagining that some things are true, and we are wired to seek out that truth and to share it. If we choose to vacate the fullness of that social ambition – the restless search for what might be true and the ambition to secure it as our good – then others with intentions we cannot guarantee will fill that space. This dignified struggle is the basis of a politics of communion worth its name.

> Only the light that falls continually from the sky gives the tree the energy to push powerful roots into the earth. The tree is really rooted in the sky.[8]

---

[8] Simone Weil, *Gravity and Grace*.

APPENDIX 1

Social Encyclicals and Apostolic Exhortations

Pope Leo XIII, *Rerum novarum* (15 May 1891), available at: http://www.vatican.va/content/leo-xiii/en/encyclicals/documents/hf_l-xiii_enc_15051891_rerum-novarum.html

Pope Pius XI, *Quadragesimo anno* (15 May 1931), available at: http://www.vatican.va/content/pius-xi/en/encyclicals/documents/hf_p-xi_enc_19310515_quadragesimo-anno.html

Pope John XXIII, *Mater et magistra* (15 May 1961), available at: http://www.vatican.va/content/john-xxiii/en/encyclicals/documents/hf_j-xxiii_enc_15051961_mater.html

Pope John XXIII, *Pacem in terris* (11 April 1963), available at: http://www.vatican.va/content/john-xxiii/en/encyclicals/documents/hf_j-xxiii_enc_11041963_pacem.html

Pope Paul VI, *Populorum progressio* (26 March 1967), available at: http://www.vatican.va/content/paul-vi/en/encyclicals/documents/hf_p-vi_enc_26031967_populorum.html

Pope Paul VI, *Octogesima adveniens* (14 May 1971), available at: http://www.vatican.va/content/paul-vi/en/apost_letters/documents/hf_p-vi_apl_19710514_octogesima-adveniens.html

Pope John Paul II, *Laborem exercens* (14 September 1981), available at: http://www.vatican.va/content/john-paul-ii/en/encyclicals/documents/hf_jp-ii_enc_14091981_laborem-exercens.html

Pope John Paul II, *Sollicitudo rei socialis* (30 December 1987), available at: http://www.vatican.va/content/john-paul-ii/en/encyclicals/documents/hf_jp-ii_enc_30121987_sollicitudo-rei-socialis.html

Pope John Paul II, *Centesimus annus* (1 May 1991), available at: http://www.vatican.va/content/john-paul-ii/en/encyclicals/documents/hf_jp-ii_enc_01051991_centesimus-annus.html

Towards a Politics of Communion

Pope Benedict XVI, *Caritas in veritate* (29 June 2009), available at: http://www.vatican.va/content/benedict-xvi/en/encyclicals/documents/hf_ben-xvi_enc_20090629_caritas-in-veritate.html

Pope Francis, *Evangelii gaudium* (24 November 2013), available at: http://www.vatican.va/content/francesco/en/apost_exhortations/documents/papa-francesco_esortazione-ap_20131124_evangelii-gaudium.html

Pope Francis, *Laudato si'* (24 May 2015), available at: http://www.vatican.va/content/francesco/en/encyclicals/documents/papa-francesco_20150524_enciclica-laudato-si.html

Pope Francis, *Fratelli tutti* (3 October 2020), available at: http://www.vatican.va/content/francesco/en/encyclicals/documents/papa-francesco_20201003_enciclica-fratelli-tutti.html

Documents of Vatican II:

Second Vatican Council, *Dignitatis humanae* (7 December 1965), available at: https://www.vatican.va/archive/hist_councils/ii_vatican_council/documents/vat-ii_decl_19651207_dignitatis-humanae_en.html

Second Vatican Council, *Gaudium et spes* (7 December 1965), available at: https://www.vatican.va/archive/hist_councils/ii_vatican_council/documents/vat-ii_const_19651207_gaudium-et-spes_en.html

Further official publications cited extensively in this text, see

Pope Pius XII, *The Major Addresses of Pope Pius XII, Volume 1: Selected Addresses and Christmas Messages*, edited by Vincent Arthur Yzermans (St Paul, Minnesota: The North Central Publishing Company, 1961).

Pope Pius XII, *Exsul Familia* (1 August 1952), available at: http://www.vatican.va/content/pius-xii/la/apost_constitutions/documents/hf_p-xii_apc_19520801_exsul-familia.html, an unofficial English translation is available https://www.papalencyclicals.net/Pius12/p12exsul.htm (accessed December 2020).

Synod of Bishops, *Justitia in Mundo* (30 November 1971), in Catholic Social Thought: The Documentary Heritage, edited by David J. O'Brien and Thomas A. Shannon (Maryknoll, NY: Orbis Books, 2010), pp. 304–18.

Appendix 1

Pope John Paul II, *Evangelium Vitae* (25 March 1995), available at: http://www.vatican.va/content/john-paul-ii/en/encyclicals/documents/hf_jp-ii_enc_25031995_evangelium-vitae.html

Pope John Paul II, *Erga Migrantes Caritas Christi* (14 May 2004), available at: http://www.vatican.va/roman_curia/pontifical_councils/migrants/documents/rc_pc_migrants_doc_20040514_erga-migrantes-caritas-christi_en.html

Pope Benedict XVI, *Deus caritas est* (25 December 2005), available at: http://www.vatican.va/content/benedict-xvi/en/encyclicals/documents/hf_ben-xvi_enc_20051225_deus-caritas-est.html

Compendium of the Social Doctrine of the Church (26 May 2006), available at: https://www.vatican.va/roman_curia/pontifical_councils/justpeace/documents/rc_pc_justpeace_doc_20060526_compendio-dott-soc_en.html

Pope Benedict XVI, Westminster Hall Address (17 September, 2010) http://www.vatican.va/content/benedict-xvi/en/speeches/2010/september/documents/hf_ben-xvi_spe_20100917_societa-civile.html

INDEX

References to information provided in footnotes is given in the form xxnxx.

Action Française   28, 29 n.12
agonistic thinking   112 n.2
almsgiving   143–4
Althaus Reid, Marcella   74
Ambrose, Saint   39
antagonistic thinking   112 n.2
Aquinas, Thomas   40, 51, 143–4
   common good   123, 135–8, 144
   de potentia   273
   De Regno   136, 136 n.11
   law and justice   30–2, 139–42
   material goods   78–9, 145–6, 281–2
   politics   137–8, 199
   Summa Contra Gentiles   123, 135
   Summa Theologiae   40, 135
Arendt, Hannah   3–4, 8–11, 115
   Augustine   131–2
   The Human Condition   8
   Men in Dark Times   1–2
   transcendence   4, 26
Argentina
   Theology of the People   168, 212
Aristotle   125–6, 132
Atkins, Margaret   38–9
Augustine, Saint   38–9, 52, 125, 128–33
   caritas (as central ethic)   38, 42
   Christian citizenship   131–3
   City of God   39, 125, 127–9, 223–4
authoritarian politics   252

Barth, Karl   296–8
Bartholomew   278–9
Basil the Great, Saint   133
beatitude   137, 155
Belloc, Hilaire
   An Essay on the Restoration of Property   218
   The Servile State   218

Benedict XVI (pope)   62–3, 81, 163–5, 209, 234, 259–60, 276, 279. *See also* Ratzinger, Joseph
   Caritas in veritate   165, 208, 209, 260–1, 279, 286, 288
   Deus caritas est   164, 209
   economic exchange   286–8
   social structures   101–2
   social teaching   163, 207
   solidarity   259–60
   subsidiarity   233–4
   Westminster Hall address (2010)   6–7, 32
Biden, Joe   125
body politic. *See* politics
Boethius   54
Boff, Leonardo   288
Bolshevism   15–17
Bonhoeffer, Dietrich   181
borders
   geographical *vs.* human self   86
   and migration   82, 91
von Bretano, Heinrich   185
Bruni, Luigino   260, 286
burials (dignity in)   56

Cahill, Lisa Sowle   41–2
capitalism   185, 247
   reform of institutions (Pius XI)   228–9
   in *Rerum novarum* (Leo XIII)   247
   and work (human labour)   21, 24–5
caritas (charity)   249–50
   Augustine   38, 42
   and solidarity   259
Catholic Action   29 n.12
Catholic social teaching (CST)   13, 54, 209, 259. *See also* Catholic social thought; *Compendium of the Social Doctrine of the Church*

Index

(Pontifical Council for Justice and Peace); encyclicals; papal social teaching
Augustinian legacy 224, 226
body politic (influence of) 179–80
developing tradition of ix, 2–7, 27–9, 46, 94, 95, 258–9
key principles of viii–ix
  dignity 21–2, 47–50, 57, 64
  natural law 30–1, 33–6, 43–5
  politics 17–19, 42
  race 104–5
  role of 209, 220, 271–2
  social and structural sin 104–9
  solidarity 90, 240–4, 255, 258–9, 266
  subsidiarity 224–6, 225 n.13
  war and peace 37–8, 41–4
Catholic social thought 24, 35, 68
Catholic Worker (CW) Movement 218, 219 n.3, 221, 237
Cavanaugh, William 109, 222–6, 225 n.13, 234
Chappel, James 15–16 n.3, 184–5
charity (caritas). *See* caritas (charity)
Chomsky, Noam 113
Christian citizenship 16, 131–3, 188
Christian governance 187
Christian living (call to) 163
Christiansen, Drew 198
Christian Socialism 16 n.3
Christology 53, 253
Church
  as community 212, 297
  contribution to public life 209
  key social principles of viii–ix
  limitations to solidarity 253–4
  perceived power of 96
  political freedom of 179–82, 202–3
  relationship with state 17–19, 163, 180
  and social unity 246
Church of the Syllabus of Errors 200
Cicero 51, 126
citizenship
  Christian 16, 131–3, 188
  civitas 223–4
City of God (Augustine). *See* Augustine, Saint
civil disobedience 219

civil economy 29
Civiltà Cattolica (Jesuit publication) 183
civitas 223–4
Clark, Meghan 241, 243 n.8, 254
Claver, Peter 259
climate 167, 269
Clump, Cyril 177–9
coercion (in law) 139
collective struggle 113
collectivities (mass identities) 192, 194–5
common good 117, 126, 132, 135–6, 146, 154, 156–7, 161, 164, 167–8, 208, 210
  Aquinas 134–7
  Caritas in veritate (Benedict XVI) 165, 208
  City of God (Augustine) 128–9
  vs. common need (Pieper) 119–21, 124
  communal nature of 111–13, 126, 130, 136–8, 146, 152, 157, 162, 166, 172–4
    being a 'people' 134, 145, 167
    socialization (John XXIII) 159
    solidarity 171–2, 251
    subsidiarity (Benedict XVI) 163–4
  critique of 8, 120–1, 168–9
  definition/forms of 115, 117–19, 126, 132–4, 137, 153, 170
    in *Mater et magistra* (John XXIII) 153, 155, 159
    theological metaphysics 121–2
  'end' (goal of) 136–7, 153, 155–6, 158
  Mater et magistra (John XXIII) 153
  modern encyclicals 152–3, 169–70
  Pacem in terris (Paul VI) 161
  in politics 112–13, 116–18, 125, 159, 167, 196, 204
  private goods 144–6
  public, individual and collective goods 170
  pursuit of 112, 128, 134, 165, 226
  state (role of) 163, 248
  suffering for 131, 141, 147–8
  theological grounding 121–3, 127, 130, 133–4, 160–1
    Christian philosophy 131–3, 144, 149–50
  work (importance of) 206

307

Index

communion   60, 87, 100 n.17, 254, 293, 300–1
   as destiny   266, 274
   economy of   29, 287
   language of   9–10
   parable of the Good Samaritan   297–300
   politics of   10–11
   social covenant   6, 279
communism   162, 205
   Church's view on   16 n.3
   as threat   185, 230–1
   and work (human labour)   21
communitarian action   97, 217
communities   39, 224, 234, 237, 251
   civitas   223–4
   need for   226–7
   social governance   227–31
   solidarity   248–9, 251
   subsidiarity   163–4, 166, 227–31, 234
Compendium of the Social Doctrine of the Church (Pontifical Council for Justice and Peace)   13–14, 35–6, 62, 100, 154, 281
Conference of Latin American bishops (CELAM)   93–8, 95 n.4, 101
conflict. *See* war theory
Congregation for the Doctrine of the Faith   98, 105–6
Constitution on the Church in the World (*Gaudium et spes*). *See Gaudium et spes* (Constitution on the Church in the World)
contemplation   5, 87
contraditions (*Widersprüche*)
   vs. contrapositions (*Gegensätze*)   87–8
contributory principle   248
corporations, power of   222, 224
corporatism   216–17
Courtney Murray, John   202 n.33
covenant (*vs.* contract)   5, 79, 279, 290–1
Covid-19 pandemic   viii, 113, 263–4
creation. *See also* work (human labour)
   ex nihilo   129, 130, 275, 279, 300
   goodness of   279–80
   theology of   273–5, 281

CST (Catholic social teaching). *See* Catholic social teaching (CST)
Cuban Missile Crisis (1962)   197
culture (in Catholic social thought)   97, 254
cummutative justice. *See* justice

Daly, Daniel   101
Daughters of Charity (*The Echo*)   75–6
Day, Dorothy   29, 45, 218–19
death penalty   46
Declaration on Religious Freedom (*Dignitatis humanae*)   6, 61
de Lamennais, Felicité   180
de la Tour du Pin, René   24
Delors, Jacques   219, 220
Delos, Joseph-Thomas OP   156
de Lubac, Henri   94
de Maistre, Joseph   180
democracy   188–9
   and authoritarian politics   252
   liberal   20 n.5, 199, 207
deterrence   42
de Tocqueville, Alexis   180
dignity   48–50, 56–7, 59, 66, 71, 85, 157. *See also* personhood
   Benedict XVI   62–3
   Compendium of the Social Doctrine of the Church   62–3
   Declaration on Religious Freedom (*Dignitatis humanae*)   61
   Dignitas humanae (John XXIII)   200–3
   encyclicals   57–66
   foundations of   48–51, 54–8, 60, 65–6, 70
   Gaudium et spes   60–1
   insults to   60–1, 63
   language of   49–50, 62, 65
   Laudato si' (Francis)   63
   of office   59, 64
   Pacem in terris (John XXIII)   58–9
   Pius XII   47–9, 187
   Populurum progressio (Paul VI)   62
   Quadragesimo anno (Pius XI)   57–8
   Rerum novarum (Leo)   57–8
   secular use of   50, 66, 68
   social and structural sin   93–6
   Sollicitudo rei socialis (John Paul II)   62

Index

displacement. *See* migration
'dispossessed' 96
distributism 217, 221, 237
di Vitoria, Francisco 32, 40-1
Dollfus regime (Austria) 27
Douglas, Benedict 67
Durkheim, Emile 216
duties (*vs.* rights) 198

ecology (integral) 269-76, 281-2, 289-91
economic exchange 286-7
economic initiative (suppression of) 231
economics 222, 286-8
economy of communion 29, 287
Edwards, Denis 273
encyclicals 28, 152-3, 169-70. *See also* Leo XIII (pope); Pius XI (pope)
'end' (goal of common good) 136-7, 153
Enlightenment 65
entrustment 55
environment 210-11, 235, 278-9
    as collective good 283
    integral ecology 266, 269-76, 281-2, 289
    sustainable development 262
    technocratic paradigm 276-9
equality 177-8
Errejón, Íñigo 111-14
ethno-nationalism 116-17, 194
Eucharist 224, 242, 243
Europe 219-21
European Court of Human Rights 67
European Union 221
evil (*malum*) 130
excellence, human 54
exile. *See* migration
Exodus 79

faith 79
Falangist regime (Spain) 27
family (and state intervention) 247
fascism 27
Fiddian-Qasmiyeh, Elena 56
Figgis, John Neville 23
Finnis, John 32 n.13, 116, 140-1
flourishing (human) 39, 82, 136, 138, 146-9, 153-4
force, history of 107-8
forgiveness 60

Foucault, Michael 115
France 155-6, 193, 221
Francis (pope) 19, 46, 63, 85, 87-8, 90, 141, 168-9, 211, 222, 276, 288 n.31, 298
    Catholic social teaching (CST) 209-13
    common good 166, 168-9, 210
    Covid-19 viii, 30, 235, 263-4
    environmental concerns 278-9
        integral ecology 269-76, 281-2, 289
        technocratic paradigm 210, 276-9
    Evangelii gaudium 166, 168, 241, 261-2, 298
    Fratelli tutti 10, 20, 43-4, 63, 84, 86, 88-90, 103-5, 144, 166-7, 210-11, 264, 277-8
    fraternity 87, 260, 298
    interconnection (of life) 271-2, 274, 276
    interdependence 263-4
    Laudato si' 63, 86, 102, 210, 262, 270-4, 276-8, 281-3, 288
    Let Us Dream 87, 103, 167-8
    Lumen fidei 211
    migration 84-91
    the 'people' 189 n.14, 212
    populism 167, 212-13
    right to private property 282-3
    on social and structural sin 102-3
    social contemplation 87
    solidarity 261-4, 262 n.29
    subsidiarity 234-5
    synodality 103, 167
    universal destination of goods 281-3
    war and peace 43-4
    work (human labour) 283-4
Fratelli tutti (Pope Francis). *See* Francis (pope)
fraternity 90, 260-1 n.21, 264, 298
    Benedict XVI 260
    Francis 264, 298
    as response to migration 90
freedom 107, 151, 182
    as foundation of dignity 60
    human 35-6, 63, 254
    natural law 36-7, 182
    political 179-82, 202
    religious 61, 197, 200-3

Index

Gaudium et spes (Constitution on the Church in the World) 60–1, 99, 154, 160–1, 202–3, 252–3
Gearty, Conor 71
Genesis 129
Gera, Lucio 168
Germany 15, 50
von Gierke, Otto 216, 216 n.1
gift exchange 208, 275, 286–7
globalization 86, 97–8, 234, 254, 257
    Catholic social teaching (CST) 209–10
    common good 164, 208
    growth of 174–5, 234
    solidarity 251–3
God 79, 123
goods
    types of 144–6, 170–1
    unequal distribution of 188
    universal destination of (*see* universal destination of goods)
Good Samaritan, parable of 293–300
governance 33, 229–30, 234
grace 106, 130
Gregory, Eric 297
Groody, Fr Daniel 56
groups. *See* communities
Guardini, Romano 87

Haldane, John 170–1
Hamao, Cardinal 77
Hanvey, James 55, 70
Harmel, Léon 24
Harrison, Carol 129–30
Hawksley, Theodora 37, 42
Heyer, Kristin 84
Hitler, Adolf 15, 16
Hittinger, Russell 180, 200–2
Hollenbach, David 171–2
Holman, Susan 133–4
Holmes, Douglas 220, 220 n.5, 220 n.6
Holy Spirit 160
homo economicus 286–7
Hughes, John 283–4
humanitarianism 44, 85, 89, 91, 242. *See also* fraternity
human nature. *See* person, human
human rights. *See* rights
Hungary 116

Illich, Ivan 293–8
Incarnation 79, 294–5
indifference 86, 141, 187
indignity 63. *See also* dignity
individualism 20, 48, 116, 223, 229, 244–5
inequality 34, 189, 211, 222, 254, 278
injustice 141–2. *See also* justice
integralism 221
interconnection (of life) 271–2, 274, 276
interdependence 263–4, 266–7
international cooperation 41–3
Irish Constitution (1937) 50
Italy 29
    Movimenti Friuli 221
    Social Weeks 155–6

Jennings, William James 289–91
Jesuits 183
John Paul II (pope) 80–1, 80 n.7, 98–101, 108, 161–2, 205, 230–3, 257–8
    The Acting Person 205
    on Catholic social teaching (CST) 35–6, 258–9
    Centisimus annus 206
    Evangelium vitae 46, 99–100, 100 n.17
    Laborem exercens 206, 256, 284–5, 285 n.27
    Reconciliatio et paenitentia (1984) 99
    solidarity 240–1, 245, 255, 257–9
    Sollicitudo rei socialis 62, 80 n.7, 100–1, 109, 207, 257
    on state intervention 232, 234
    work (human labour) 284–5
John XIII (pope) 232
John XXIII (pope) 34, 41–2, 153, 158–9, 232, 234. *See also* Second Vatican Council
    Dignitas humanae 200–2
    Mater et magistra (1961) 153, 155, 159, 250–2
    Pacem in terris (1963) 34, 41–2, 58–9, 197–200, 210, 251
    political freedom of Church 179–80
jus gentium (law of nations). *See* law of nations (*jus gentium*)
justice 143, 157, 204–5, 209, 259–60
    in economics 287–8
    social 27, 83, 156–7
    and solidarity 254–5, 258
    Thomistic 139–42

Index

Justice in the World (Synod of Bishops (1971)). *See* Synod of Bishops (1971)
just war theory   37–8, 40–1, 43–5

Kant, Immanuel   51
Kateb, George   70
Ketteler, Bishop Wilhelm von   24–5, 26
King, Martin Luther, Jr   299
Kirchhoffer, David   64, 68–9
Kirk, Russell   115
Kolbe, Maximilian   259

labour. *See* work (human labour)
laity   203, 209
Lamb, Matthew   267
Lampedusa (Italy) address (Francis)   85
L'Arche communities   237
Latin America   93–7
Latin American Liberation Theology   206–7, 258
law   67, 68, 138–40. *See also* natural law
law of nations (*jus gentium*)   32, 40–1
Lebech, Mette   51–2, 55, 70
Leo XIII (pope)   20–1, 25, 30–1, 33
    Rerum novarum   20–1, 24–8, 57–8, 183, 184, 217, 228, 245–9, 282
    work (human labour)   26–7, 283–4
Leroux, Pierre   242
Levi, Primo   71
Lewis, V. Bradley   155–6
liberal democracy   199–200, 207
liberalism   20 n.5, 69, 116, 178, 180–1, 183, 199
liberationism   94, 98, 107–8, 206–7
Liberatore, Matteo   26
liberty. *See* freedom
Locke, John   282, 289–90
love   viii, 3, 7, 164, 169, 241–2, 258, 275
    and gift exchange   208, 275
    neighbour love   40, 144–5
    as principle of human life (Benedict XVI)   207–8
    tensive   10
Luke
    Good Samaritan   293–300

Manning, Cardinal   24–5
Mansbridge, Jane   117–19, 127
Marchetto, Archbishop   77

Maritain, Jacques   27, 29, 50, 181–3, 191, 196, 220
market (economic)   222, 247
Marx, Karl   113
Marxism   113
Massingdale, Bryan   104
Mater et magistra (Pope John XXIII). *See* John XXIII (pope)
material goods   78–9, 158, 281–2
materialism   191
Matthew   25, 133
Maurin, Peter   218
Maurras, Charles   29 n.12
mercy   143, 219, 295. *See also* almsgiving
Mexico   16, 28–9
Michnik, Adam   201
migration   73–92. *See also* refugees
Milbank, John   69
militarization   252
Miller, Vincent   272, 276, 289
minorities, oppression of   187–8
mistreatment (of life)   276
modernism   184–5, 221
modernity   24, 26, 191, 297–8. *See also* Leo XIII (pope); 'social question'
Monnet, Jean   219, 220
morality   207
Morsink, Johannes   50–1
Mouffe, Chantal   112 n.2, 113–14
Mounier, Emmanuel   27, 29, 68, 94–5, 219, 220
Moyn, Samuel   50–1, 68, 157
multiplicity (*vs.* unity)   53, 54
Murray, Courtney   205
Myanmar   239
mythos   168, 170

nationalism   185
nation state
    dominance of   174, 222
    vs. people   186, 188–9
natural law   30–7, 45, 81–3, 90, 253. *See also* law
    and Catholic social teaching (CST)   30–1, 33–6, 43–4
    in *Gaudium et spes*   60
    in *Pacem in terris*   197
nature (and the common good)   167. *See also* environment

Index

Nazism (National Socialism)   15–17
neighbour love   144–5, 296–9
von Nell Bruening, Fr Oswald   237, 244
Nietzsche, Friedrich   113
nouvelle théologie   94, 107

obligations   34, 192, 195
O'Donovan, Oliver   172
Oliver, Simon   275
Orbán, President Viktor [Hungary]   116
Ormerod, Neil   96, 105
Oxford Catholic Social Guild   177–9

Pacem in terris (1963). *See* John XXIII (pope)
pacifism   41, 43–5
pantheism   20 n.5
papal social teaching   24, 156, 185, 237
paternalism   26, 28
Paul VI (pope)   34, 41–2
   Octogesima adveniens   35, 203–4, 254
   Pacem in terris   161
   Populorum progressio   35, 62, 203, 253–4
   on state intervention   232, 234
Pavan, Pietro   197
peace   38–9, 41–3, 186–8, 258. *See also* pacifism
Péguy, Charles   29
Pentecost   80, 263
people
   being 'a people'   145, 160, 167, 188, 189 n.14, 211
   vs. nation   186, 188–9
'people of God' (Vatican II)   167
perfection (of human person)   31, 153, 155–6, 158
Perreau-Saussine, Emile   124, 181, 199
person, human   54, 136–7, 159, 162, 205, 266. *See also* personhood
   as acting subject   206, 255
   nature of   144, 201, 203, 206
   perfection of   32, 153, 155–6, 158
personalism   27, 95, 107, 157–8, 192–3, 205
   and the dignified human person   199–200
   as response to communism   162, 205
personality (*vs.* person)   191–2

personhood   52–3, 67, 69, 90. *See also* Christology; dignity
   as basis for Catholic social teaching (CST)   54, 62
   in *Gaudium et spes*   60–1
Pesch, Fr Heinrich   244–5
Pieper, Josef   284
   common good   119–21, 124, 195–6
   on nature of human person   144
   and the social contract   190–1
Pinckaers, Servais   137
Pius XI (pope)   24, 33, 156, 215–17
   Divini redemptoris   15, 49, 157
   letters   15–17, 28–9, 49
   Quadragesimo anno   57–8, 152, 156, 184, 215–17, 228–9, 231–2, 249–50
   reform of institutions   228–9
Pius XII (pope)   33, 47–9, 58, 158, 186, 188
   being 'a people'   188–9, 212
   Christmas messages   47–8, 64, 185–7, 250
   Exsul familia   75–7
   on social order   48–9, 95, 186–7
   Summi Pontificates 'On the Unity of Human Society'   158, 250
pluralism   80, 114, 183, 202–3, 217, 223. *See also* communities
   vs. unity   48–9, 183–4
plurality   273 n.7
'pluriculturality'   98
pneumatology   259
polis. *See* state
Polish Solidarity movement   241, 285
political authority   137–8, 208
political community   156, 159, 160
political order   39, 42
politics. *See also* state
   body politic   166, 179–81, 184, 187, 204–5
   in Catholic social teaching (CST)   29–30
   Catholic *vs.* secular   177
   fear and distrust of   251–2, 259
   ideologies   15–21
   political authority   222, 224–5
   political failure   235
   political Left   112–13
   political love   169, 208

Index

political power   169, 204
pursuit of the common good   165, 226
Pontifical Council for Justice and Peace
  Compendium of the Social Doctrine of the Church   13–14, 35–6, 62, 100, 154, 281
Pontifical Council for the Pastoral Care of Migrants and Itinerant Peoples   77
poor. *See* poverty
populism   167, 212–13, 264. *See also* 'people' (being a)
Populorum progressio (Pope Paul VI). *See* Paul VI (pope)
Porter, Jean   138–9
Potter, Mark   253–4
poverty   203, 235, 246, 248, 264, 280
  Latin American Liberation Theology   206
power   222, 237
  dispersal of (subsidiarity)   228, 231–2
  limiting (subsidiarity)   229
privatization   222
property, private   25, 282–3, 289–90. *See also* material goods
public realm (in Catholic social teaching)   1, 3

Quadragesimo anno (Pope Pius XI). *See* Pius XI (pope)
Qasmiyeh, Yousif M.   56

race   103–5, 289–91
Rahner, Karl   61, 71, 107
Ratzinger, Joseph (later Pope Benedict XVI)   10, 52–3, 207, 242, 243
reason   7, 51, 54, 58–9
reconstruction (of Europe)   48–9
refugees   56, 73–4 n.1
religious orders   39, 75
Reno, R. R.   116
Rerum novarum (Leo XII). *See* Leo XII (pope)
responsibility (personal)   108
Revelation, book of   73–4
rights
  vs. duties   34, 198
  during the Enlightenment   65
  human   161, 161 n.16, 199–200

language   34, 65, 192–3
  reciprocal awareness of   208–9
rights movements. *See* solidarity
right to development   203
Right to Protect   44
'right to remain'   81–2
right-wing politics   116. *See also* ethno-nationalism
Robinson, Marilynne   241
Roncalli, Angelo Giuseppe (later Pope John XXIII)   2, 196. *See also* John XXIII (pope)
roots (as human need)   193–6
Rose, Gillian   271 n.3
Rosen, Michael   70

saints   259
Salamanca, School of   40–1
Salazar regime (Portugal)   27
salvation   55, 94
Sandel, Michael   111, 113, 142
Scalabrinians [religious order]   75
Scannone, Juan Carlos   168
Scheler, Max   255
Schmitt, Carl   115
Schuck, Michael   24
Schuman, Robert   220
Schwalm, Marie-Benoît OP   156
Scriptures   74–5, 133–4, 143
Scruton, Roger   115
Second Vatican Council   42. *See also* John XXIII (pope)
  Constitution on the Church in the World (*Gaudium et spes*)   60–1, 95
  Declaration on Religious Freedom (*Dignitatis humanae*)   6, 61
  Lumen gentium   95, 212
  on social and political order   34, 36, 178–80
  on solidarity   252
Second World War   20 n.5, 64, 76–7. *See also* Pius XII (pope)
secularism   51–2
self-determination   15, 16
Senghor, Léopold   185
sexual abuse (within Catholic church)   109, 236–7
Shadle, Matthew   42–3
Shannon, Thomas   282

313

Index

sin   107–8, 145, 258
   in Catholic social teaching
      (CST)   104–9
   social and structural   6, 93–6, 98,
      103–5, 108, 258
Sluga, Hans   114–15, 122
social action   5, 263
social and structural sin. *See* sin
social contract theory   65, 160, 178,
      190–1, 216
social governance   227–31
social 'herding'   48
socialism   16 n.3, 241–2, 244–5
socialization (complex
      interdependence)   158, 166,
      202–3, 252
social justice   27, 83, 156–7
social lives   160
social order   23, 26, 34, 132, 183, 187
   Pope Pius XII   48–9, 95, 186–7
   in *Rerum novarum* (Pope Leo
      XIII)   25–6
   and solidarity   253, 266
'social question'   21–4, 29–30
social roles   57–8
social structures   101–2
social teaching. *See* Catholic social teaching
      (CST)
social unity   246
social visions   103
Social Weeks   155–6
solidarity   241, 245–8, 253–4, 257–9, 262,
      264–6
   agents of   246, 264
   and caritas (charity)   249–50, 259–60
   in *Catechism* (1993)   265–6
   in Catholic social teaching (CST)   90,
      240–4, 255, 266
   and the Church   240, 241, 246, 297
      Catholic theory of   244
      Eucharist   242, 243
      limitations of   253–4
   common good   171–2, 251
   communion   254, 266
   communities   248–9, 251
   as duty or virtue   243–4, 257, 260
   Francis   261–4, 262 n.29
   in *Fratelli tutti* (Francis)   264
   in *Gaudium et spes* (Constitution on the
      Church in the World)   252–3

   global nature of   251–4, 257–8
   John Paul II   240–1
   John XXIII   251
   Joseph Ratzinger (later Pope Benedict
      XVI)   242, 243
   in *Laborem exercens* (John
      Paul II)   256
   language   240, 244, 250
   Lehrbuch der Nationalökonomie
      (Pesch)   245
   in *Mater et magistra* (John
      XXIII)   250–2
   movements   239–41, 245, 285
   in *Pacem in terris* (John XXIII)   251
   in *Populorum progressio* (Paul
      VI)   253–4
   in *Quadragesimo anno* (Pius XI)
      249–50
   in *Rerum novarum* (Leo XIII)   245–9
   as response to migration   81, 90
   roots of   243, 252, 253
   and Second Vatican Council   252
   secular *vs.* theological   245, 256–7
   and social order   253, 266
   state   248, 250–2
   and subsidiarity   220, 224, 235–7,
      251
   work (human labour)   249, 255–7
Solidarnosc movement (Poland)   245
sovereignty (migration)   82
Spain   111
state   34, 46, 159, 181, 187, 222–3, 248. *See*
      also nation; politics
   definition of (Aristotle)   125–6
   fear and distrust of   251–2, 259
   intervention   230–2, 247
   as 'a people'   223
   relationship with church   17–19, 23,
      163, 180
   role of   181–2, 246–8
   solidarity   246–8, 250
   welfare state   233–4, 248, 251
Stump, Eleanore   147
Sturzo, Luigi   181
subsidiarity   164, 166, 215, 221–2, 227,
      229
   Benedict XVI   233–4
   in Catholic social teaching
      (CST)   225–6
   communism as threat   230–1

communities (groups)   163–4, 166, 218, 227–31, 234
corporatism (Pius XI)   215–16
distributism   217, 221, 237
Francis   234–5
John Paul II   230–3
John XXIII   251
post-war European integration 219–20
in *Quadragesimo anno* (Pius XI) 215–16, 228–9, 231–2
questions on   236–7
and solidarity   220, 224, 235–7, 251
suffering   71, 131, 141, 147–8
Summa Theologiae (Aquinas). *See* Aquinas, Thomas
Summi pontificatus (Pius XII). *See* Pius XII (pope)
synodality   103, 167
Synod of Bishops   254
   Justitia in mundo (Justice in the World) (1971)   99, 204–5

Taparelli, Luigi   155–6, 161, 282
Taylor, Charles   118, 151–2, 294
technocratic paradigm   210, 276–7 n.12, 276–9
Theology of the People (Argentina)   168
Tischner, Józef
   The Ethics of Solidarity   255
totalitarianism
   and religious freedom   201
   threat of   184–5, 187
transcendence   4, 26, 102, 122, 242, 297
transformation (of 'cultures of peoples')   97
truth (and solidarity)   257–8
tyranny   139, 188–9

UN Charter (1945)   50
unionization   249
United States   30, 104
United States Conference of Catholic Bishops   104
unity   48–9, 183–4, 187, 196
   vs. multiplicity (Ratzinger)   53, 54
Universal Declaration of Human Rights (1948)   50–1, 58

universal destination of goods   77–9, 82, 211, 248, 258, 280–3
   and integral ecology   281–2
   and private property   290–1
uprootedness   193–5

Vatican II. *See* Second Vatican Council
Verstraeten, Johan   236
violence. *See also* war theory
   social   210
   states *vs.* acts of   94–5
   as violation of charity   43
virtue   138–9, 146

Walsh, David   57
war theory   37–8, 41–5. *See also* just war theory; peace
wealth, distribution of   156
Weil, Simone   29, 107–8, 190–3, 195
   on communion   300–1
   life of   190–1
   The Need for Roots   193–5
   parable of the Good Samaritan 299–300
   personalism   29, 157–8, 192–3
welfare state   248
   growth of   233–4
   post-war   251
whistle-blowers   147–8
White, C. Vanessa   103–4
Whitmore, Todd   45
Williams, Rowan   132
Wojtyla, Karol (later Pope John Paul II)   205, 255. *See also* John Paul II (pope)
Wollstencraft, Mary   51
women, role of   26
work (human labour)
   as act of solidarity   255–7
   dignity of   21–2
   importance of   206, 218, 230, 283–5
   in *Laborem exercens*   284–5, 285 n.27
   in *Rerum novarum* (Pope Leo XIII)   26–7, 283–4
   state intervention   230–2
World War II. *See* Second World War

Zamagni, Stefano   260, 286

www.ingramcontent.com/pod-product-compliance
Lightning Source LLC
Chambersburg PA
CBHW050135240426

43673CB00043B/1673